MODEL(ING) JUSTICE

The International Criminal Tribunal for the former Yugoslavia (ICTY) was the first and most celebrated of a wave of international criminal tribunals (ICTs) built in the 1990s and designed to advance liberalism through international criminal law. *Model(ing) Justice* examines the practice and case law of the ICTY to make a novel theoretical analysis of the structural flaws inherent in ICTs as institutions that inhibit their contribution to social peace and prosperity. Kerstin Bree Carlson proposes a seminal analysis of the structural challenges to ICTs as socially constitutive institutions, setting the agenda for future considerations of how international organizations can perform and disseminate the goals articulated by political liberalism.

Kerstin Bree Carlson is an associate professor at the University of Southern Denmark and is affiliated with The American University of Paris and iCourts at the University of Copenhagen. Kerstin's research theorizes structural challenges inherent to international criminal law as a means of considering the potential social impact of international criminal justice. She is the recipient of two Fulbright awards (the first to Croatia and the second to UNESCO in Paris), and several teaching awards.

Model(ing) Justice

PERFECTING THE PROMISE OF INTERNATIONAL CRIMINAL LAW

KERSTIN BREE CARLSON
University of Southern Denmark; The American University of Paris

CAMBRIDGE
UNIVERSITY PRESS

CAMBRIDGE
UNIVERSITY PRESS

University Printing House, Cambridge CB2 8BS, United Kingdom

One Liberty Plaza, 20th Floor, New York, NY 10006, USA

477 Williamstown Road, Port Melbourne, VIC 3207, Australia

314–321, 3rd Floor, Plot 3, Splendor Forum, Jasola District Centre, New Delhi – 110025, India

79 Anson Road, #06–04/06, Singapore 079906

Cambridge University Press is part of the University of Cambridge.

It furthers the University's mission by disseminating knowledge in the pursuit of education, learning, and research at the highest international levels of excellence.

www.cambridge.org
Information on this title: www.cambridge.org/9781108417693
DOI: 10.1017/9781108278157

First published 2018

Printed in the United States of America by Sheridan Books, Inc.

A catalogue record for this publication is available from the British Library.

Library of Congress Cataloging-in-Publication Data
NAMES: Carlson, Kerstin Bree, 1972–, author.
TITLE: Model(ing) justice : perfecting the promise of international criminal law / Kerstin Bree Carlson, University of Southern Denmark; American University Paris.
DESCRIPTION: New York : Cambridge University Press, 2018. | Includes bibliographical references and index.
IDENTIFIERS: LCCN 2018016471 | ISBN 9781108417693 (alk. paper)
SUBJECTS: LCSH: International Tribunal for the Prosecution of Persons Responsible for Serious Violations of International Humanitarian Law Committed in the Territory of the Former Yugoslavia since 1991. | International criminal courts. | Criminal procedure (International law). | Yugoslav War Crime Trials, Hague, Netherlands, 1994–
CLASSIFICATION: LCC KZ1203.A12 C36 2018 | DDC 345/.01–dc23
LC record available at https://lccn.loc.gov/2018016471

ISBN 978-1-108-41769-3 Hardback

Contents

Preface and Acknowledgments

This project began nearly twenty years ago, when I traveled to Bosnia as a researcher for the University of California Berkeley International Human Rights Law Clinic. We were three US law students paired with three Bosnian law students, and we spent the summer interviewing local judges and prosecutors from each of the three constituent ethnicities in Bosnia about their impressions of the work of the ICTY.[1] The book you are holding in your hands is in many ways the product of that formative experience, which was in equal parts moving, surprising, and galvanizing. For two months, based in Banja Luka and with weekly trips to Sarajevo to debrief with the rest of the team, the indomitable Tamara Todorović and I drove all over Republika Srpska to interview judges and prosecutors. The war had ended a few years before and its ravages were still fresh: checkpoints between the entities; temporary, rickety metal bridges over ravines; whole towns of skeletal, abandoned houses; lands emptied of people, like the eerie, uneasy quiet of our afternoon in Zvornik, 20 km away from Srebrenica. Yet Bosnia is beautiful, it was summer, and we were two young women (oftentimes three, with our interpreter, Borja) on the road trying to rebuild the world, all of which made the contrasts between the staggering horror of war, the stubborn persistence of destructive nationalist rhetoric and politics, and the warmth, humor, and humanity of the people we met more striking. I wanted to *do* something for those people and that place. And I saw, in the course of that summer, that the assumptions implanted in me as a US law student about the capacity of law and its institutions to direct social change were culturally and contextually specific, and required studied consideration, analysis, and challenge. This, then, is what I did, and this book is the result.

Over twenty years of work, the debts accrued are extensive. The list must begin with the University of California Berkeley International Human Rights Law Clinic,

1 Our study was published as "Justice, Accountability and Social Reconstruction: An Interview Study of Bosnian Judges and Prosecutors," 18 (1) *Berkeley Journal of International Law*, 2000, referenced in the Bibliography under Carlson *et al.* (2000).

and extend to professors Steven Bundy and the late David Caron at Boalt Hall, who loaned me books (Damaška's *The Faces of Justice and State Authority*; Shapiro's *Courts*) and opened my mind to the possibilities, ideologies, empowerment, and subjugation that accompany legal processes. Malcolm Feeley guided me to law and society studies, and stuck with me through my long gestation; even today I see how the questions he asked a second-year law student remain the questions at the core of all my inquiries, and shape the guidance I offer my own students. Enormous thanks to my committee, as well: Martin Shapiro, who helped me challenge accepted status quos; Kristin Luker, who taught me to work smarter, not harder; and Ronelle Alexander, for teaching the language once known as Serbo-Croatian "the adult way" and proofing my PhD manuscript with the kind of gimlet eye that changes how you write in the first place.

In the early years, Paul Frymer, Chris Kendall, Francis Mathew, and Gabriella Zim Kremer all pounded out ideas late at night, around dining room tables, fueled by coffee and cookie dough. Judge David Folsom and Carly Anderson Slack taught me how to think like a lawyer (in a good way!). As I worked to submit the PhD while practicing law, then teaching full-time, and rearing two toddlers, Susan Perry and Kim Murphy made themselves available to read, debate, or kvetch, all of which was simply indispensable. As a post-doc at iCourts, surrounded by like-curious researchers in a singularly exciting, supportive research center, Director Mikael Rask Madsen's intellectual challenges were (irritatingly!) reliably and immensely helpful. Jakob von Holtermann, Mikkel Jarle Christiansen, Solomon Ebobrah, and Marina Aksenova all advanced my considerations of the capacity of international criminal law. My students and colleagues at The American University of Paris kept driving me towards the important questions: Waddick Doyle, Brian Schiff, Charles Talcott, Lissa Lincoln, Michelle Kuo, students in my Transitional Justice and First Bridge classes, thank you. Colleagues in both the law and international politics departments at the University of Southern Denmark redefined how warm a Danish welcome could be, including with cake, and students in our Masters of International Security and Law (MOISL) program have helped me fit specifics into the big picture. Brad Roth invited me to present my research early, and repeatedly, in Dubrovnik, and remains my aspirational intellectual model. Likewise, David Kennedy and the Institute for Global Law and Policy at Harvard Law School offered intellectual growth spaces, as does the Law and Society Association, Berkeley's Jurisprudence and Social Policy Department, the International Studies Association, and the University of Southern Denmark. I received financial support from Columbia, Fulbright, the Foreign Languages and Area Studies fellowships program, UC Berkeley, The American University of Paris, iCourts,[2] and Syddansk Universitet. David Klein at the *Journal of Law and Courts* helped me clarify my arguments, and

[2] Funded by the Danish National Research Foundation grant DNRF105 and conducted under the auspices of iCourts, the Danish National Research Foundation's Centre of Excellence for International Courts.

John Berger and two anonymous reviewers at Cambridge tightened the manuscript. Thanks to *Denver Journal of International Law and Policy*, *Italian Law Review* and the *Journal of Law and Courts* for permission to reuse some previously published material.

My family and friends on both sides of the Atlantic have offered massive support. From chocolate sent to Sarajevo to long weekends babysitting, they have put the kettle on and turned up the duvet at a moment's notice, and called again even when it's my turn to call back. For hospitality and friendship all over the world I thank Adam, Bojana and Jozo, Brad, the VT Carlsons, Cary, the Cornells, the Delais, Heidi, Helen, the Kremers, Nicolas, Nina, the Levys, J3, Jamie, the Lailliers, the MacIntyres, Maeve, the Martins, Peter, the Portland group, the Ragones of NJ and NY, Shivani, Stefan, Tammy, the Todorovićs, and the Torts. On the ground in Copenhagen, I have had tremendous logistical (read: babysitting!) and emotional support from Amalia, Brooke, Clara, Greta and John, Jasna and Raul, Bea, Anna and Lars, Lars and Shira, Mor and Far, Jens and Saane, Jan and Lisbeth, Tom, Juanan, Pola, Jed, Jakob, Shai, Henrik, Zuzanna, Amelia, Carolina, Lene, Ayo, Amy and Bjørn, Martin and Alana, Emma and Steven, Anja and Mads, Jenna and Jin: you are my village, thank you. Even while geographically distant, Brennan, Laura, Kim, Ray-Ray, Carly, Mel, Lisbeth, Gabi, Tamći, Serena, and Jackie always have an ear and a word for the ridiculous, the tragic, or the combination. Finally thanks, plain and simple, to Mom and Dad, for everything; to Brennan, for everything plus; to Claudio, who checks all the equations; and to Sam, Alice, Lolo, and Niamh, who never fail to make it fun or, barring that, memorable.

Table of Authorities

UN RESOLUTIONS, STATUTES, AND REPORTS

Convention for the Amelioration of the Condition of the Wounded and the Sick in Armed Forces in the Field (Geneva Convention No. I), August 12, 1949, *6 UST* 3114, 75 UNTS 31

Convention for the Amelioration of the Condition of Wounded, Sick, and Shipwrecked Members of Armed Forces at Sea (Geneva Convention No. II), August 12, 1949, *6 UST* 3217, 75 UNTS 85

Convention Relative to the Treatment of Prisoners of War (Geneva Convention No. III), August 12, 1949, *6 UST* 3316, 75 UNTS 135

Convention Relative to the Protection of Civilian Persons in Times of War (Geneva Convention No. IV), August 12, 1949, *6 UST* 3516, 75 UNTS 28

Report of the Secretary-General Pursuant to Paragraph 2 of Security Council Resolution 808 (1993) S/25704, May 3, 1993 ("Secretary General Report")

Dayton Peace Agreement, signed in Paris December 14, 1995, UN Doc. S/1995/999, 35 *ILM* 75 (1996)

"Report of the Expert Group to Conduct a Review of the Effective Operation and Functioning of the International Tribunal for the Former Yugoslavia and the International Criminal Tribunal for Rwanda" A/54/634, November 22, 1999 ("UN Expert Report [1999]")

"Comments on the report of the Expert Group to Conduct a Review of the Effective Operation and Functioning of the International Tribunal for the Former Yugoslavia and the International Criminal Tribunal for Rwanda" A/54/850, April 27, 2000

Judge Kevin Parker, Vice President, "Report to the President: Death of Milan Babić," June 8, 2006, The Hague

"Updated Statute of the International Criminal Tribunal for the Former Yugoslavia" (as amended September 2009) ("ICTY Statute")

"Rules of Procedure and Evidence" T/32/Rev. 48, November 19, 2012 ("ICTY Rules of Procedure")

UN General Assembly, *Rome Statute of the International Criminal Court (last amended 2010)*, July 17, 1998, ISBN No. 92–9227-227–6, available at www.refworld.org/docid/3ae6b3a84.html (accessed July 2, 2013)

Security Council Resolution 827, May 25, 1994

Security Council Resolution 1329, December 5, 2000

Security Council Resolution 1503, August 28, 2003

Security Council Resolution 1534, March 26, 2004

INTERNATIONAL CRIMINAL TRIBUNAL FOR THE FORMER YUGOSLAVIA (ICTY)

Aleksovski

Prosecutor v. *Zlatko Aleksovski, Trial Chamber Judgment*, Case No. IT-95–14/ (June 25, 1999) ("*Aleksovski* Trial Chamber")

Babić

Prosecutor v. *Milan Babić, Sentencing Judgment*, Case No. IT-03–72 (June 29, 2004) ("*Babić* Sentencing Judgment")

Prosecutor v. *Milan Babić, Appeal Judgment*, Case No. IT-03–72 (July 18, 2005) ("*Babić* Appeal Judgment")

Blagojević and Jokić

Prosecutor v. *Vidoje Blagojević and Dragan Jokić*, Case No. IT-02–60 (January 17, 2005)

Blaškić

Prosecutor v. *Tihomir Blaškić*, Case No. IT-95–14 (March 3, 2000) ("*Blaškić* Trial Chamber")

Prosecutor v. *Tihomir Blaškić*, Case No. IT-95–14 (July 29, 2004) ("*Blaškić* Appeals Chamber")

Branin

Prosecutor v. *Radoslav Branin*, Case No. IT-99–36 (September 1, 2004) ("*Branin* Trial Chamber")

Prosecutor v. *Radoslav Branin*, Case No. IT-99–36 (April 3, 2007) ("*Branin* Appeals Chamber")

Delalić et al.

Prosecutor v. *Zejnil Delalić, Hazim Delić, Zdravko Mucić, and Esad Landžo*, Case No. IT-96–21 (November 16, 1998) ("*Delalić* Trial Chamber")

Prosecutor v. *Zejnil Delalić, Hazim Delić, Zdravko Mucić, and Esad Landžo*, IT-96–21 (February 20, 2001) ("*Delalić* Appeals Chamber")

Deronjić

Prosecutor v. *Miroslav Deronjić*, Case No. IT-02–61 (March 30, 2004) ("*Deronjić* Sentencing Judgment")

Erdemović

Prosecutor v. *Dražen Erdemović*, *Sentencing Judgment*, Case No. IT-96–22 (November 29, 1996) ("*Erdemović* Sentencing Judgment")

Prosecutor v. *Dražen Erdemović*, *Appeals Judgment*, Case No. IT-96–22 (October 7, 1997) ("*Erdemović* Appeals Judgment")

Prosecutor v. *Dražen Erdemović*, *Sentencing Judgment*, Case No. IT-96–22 (March 5, 1998) ("*Erdemović* Sentencing Judgment II")

Furundžija

Prosecutor v. *Anto Furundžija*, *Trial Chamber Judgment*, Case No. IT-95–17/1 (December 10, 1998)

Galić

Prosecutor v. *Stanislav Galić*, *Trial Chamber Judgment*, Case No. IT-98–29 (December 2, 2003)

Prosecutor v. *Stanislav Galić*, *Appeals Chamber Judgment*, Case No. IT-98–29 (November 30, 2006)

Gotovina et al.

Prosecutor v. *Gotovina*, *Čermak*, *and Markač*, *Decision on Several Motions Challenging Jurisdiction*, Case No. IT-06–90-PT (March 19, 2007) ("Gotovina *et al.* Decision on Motions Challenging Jurisdiction")

Prosecutor v. *Ante Gotovina*, *Ivan Čermak*, *and Mladen Markač*, *Amended Joinder Indictment*, Case No. IT-06–90-PT (March 12, 2008) ("*Gotovina* Joinder Indictment")

Prosecutor v. *Ante Gotovina*, *Ivan Čermak and Mladen Markač*, Case No. IT-06–90-PT (April 15, 2011) ("*Gotovina* Trial Chamber")

Prosecutor v. *Ante Gotovina and Mladen Markač*, *Appeals Chamber Judgment*, IT-06–90 (November 16, 2002) ("*Gotovina* Appeals Chamber")

Jelisić

Prosecutor v. *Goran Jelisić*, *Appeals Judgment*, Case No. IT-95–10 (July 5, 2001) ("*Jelisić* Appeal Judgment")

Karadžić

Prosecutor v. *Radovan Karadžić*, Case No. IT-95–18 (March 24, 2016)

Kordić et al.

Prosecutor v. *Dario Kordić and Mario Čerkez*, *Appeals Chamber Judgment*, Case No. IT-95–14/2-Y (September 18, 2000)

Stakić

Prosecutor v. *Milomir Stakic,"Order Summoning Dr. Biljana Plavšić Propio Motu to Appear as a Witness of the Trial Chamber Pursuant to Rule* 98," Case No. IT-97–24-T (January 9, 2003)

Prosecutor v. *Milomir Stakić*, Case No. IT-97–24 (July 31, 2003) ("*Stakić* Trial Chamber")

Prosecutor v. *Milomir Stakić*, Case No. IT-97–24 (March 22, 2006) ("*Stakić* Appeals Chamber")

Stanišić and Simatović

Prosecutor v. *Jovica Stanišić and Franko Simatović*, Case No. IT-03–69 (May 29, 2013)

Prosecutor v. *Jovica Stanišić and Franko Simatović*, Case No. IT-03–69 (December 15, 2015) ("*Stanišić and Simatović* Appeals Chamber")

Prosecutor v. *Jovica Stanišić and Franko Simatović*, Case No. IT-03–69, on retrial before the Mechanism for International Criminal Tribunals

Šešelj

Prosecutor v. *Vojislav Šešelj*, Case No. IT-03–67 (Int'l Crim. Trib. for the former Yugoslavia March 31, 2016)

Prosecutor v. *Vojislav Šešelj*, Case No. MICT-16-99 (Int'l Residual Mechanism for Crim. Trib. April 11, 2018)

Sikirica et al.

Prosecutor v. *Duško Sikirica, Damir Došen, and Dragan Kolundžija, Sentencing Judgment*, Case No. IT-95–8 (November 13, 2001) ("*Sikirica* Sentencing Judgment")

Tadić

Prosecutor v. *Duško Tadić, Jurisdictional Decision*, Case No. IT-94–1-T (February 10, 1995)

Prosecutor v. *Duško Tadić*, Case No. IT-94–1-T, Trial Chamber II (May 7, 1997) (Tadić Trial Chamber)

Prosecutor v. *Duško Tadić*, Case No. IT-94–1-A, Appeals Chamber (July 15, 1999) (Tadić Appeals Chamber)

Tolimir

Prosecutor v. *Zdravko Tolimir, Sentencing Judgment*, Case No. IT-05–88/2 (December 12, 2012)

Todorović

Prosecutor v. *Stevan Todorović, Sentencing Judgment*, Case No. IT-95–9/1 (July 31, 2001) ("*Todorović* Sentencing Judgment")

Vasiljević

Prosecutor v. *Mitar Vasiljević, Appeals Judgment*, Case No. IT-98–32 (February 15, 2004)

INTERNATIONAL CRIMINAL TRIBUNAL FOR RWANDA (ICTR)

Prosecutor v. *Jean-Paul Akayesu (Trial Judgment)*, Case No. ICTR-96–4-T, (September 2, 1998)

INTERNATIONAL CRIMINAL COURT (ICC)

Prosecutor v. *Omar Hassan Ahmad Al Bashir,* Case No. ICC-02/05–01/09 (pre-trial) (hibernated)

Prosecutor v. *Thomas Lubanga Dyilo (Verdict)*, Case No. ICC-01/04–01/06 (March 14, 2012)

Prosecutor v. *Callixte Mbarushimana,* Case No. ICC-01/04–01/10 (pre-trial) (December 16, 2011)

Prosecutor v. *William Samoei Ruto and Joshua Arap Sang,* Case No. ICC-01/09–01/11 (April 5, 2016)

Prosecutor v. *Uhuru Muigai Kenyatta,* Case No. ICC-01/09–02/11, charges withdrawn

INTERNATIONAL COURT OF JUSTICE (ICJ)

Bosnia and Herzegovina v. *Serbia and Montenegro* (February 26, 2007)

EUROPEAN COURT OF HUMAN RIGHTS (ECHR)

Case of Sejdić and Finci v. *Bosnia and Herzegovina* (Applications nos. 27996/06 and 34836/06) (December 22, 2009)

WORLD WAR II-ERA CASES

Trial of the Major War Criminals before the International Military Tribunal, Nuremberg, 1947

Trial of Josef Kramer and 44 others, British Military Court, Luneberg, September 17–November 17, 1945, UNWCC, Volume II

Velpke Children's Home: Case No. 42, Trial of Heinrich Gerike and Seven Others (The Velpke Children's Home Case) British Military Court, Brunswick, VII Law Reports of Trials of War Criminals 76 (1948)

Mauthausen U.S. Military Tribunal, Volume XI *Law Reports* 15.

Krnojelac

Prosecutor v. *Milorad Krnojelac, Trial Chamber Judgment*, Case No. IT-97–25 (March 15, 2002)

Prosecutor v. *Milorad Krnojelac, Appeals Chamber Judgment*, Case No. IT-97–25 (September 17, 2003) ("*Krnojelac* Appeals Chamber")

Krstić

Prosecutor v. *Radislav Krstić*, Case No. IT-98–33 (August 2, 2001) ("*Krstić* Trial Chamber")

Prosecutor v. *Radislav Krstić*, Case No. IT-98–33 (April 19, 2004) ("*Krstić* Appeals Chamber")

Kunarac et al.

Prosecutor v. *Dragoljub Kunarac, Radomir Kovač, and Zoran Vuković*, Case No. IT-96–23 and 23/1 (February 22, 2001) ("*Kunarac* Trial Chamber")

Prosecutor v. *Dragoljub Kunarac, Radomir Kovač, and Zoran Vuković*, Case No. IT-96–23 and 23/1 (June 12, 2002) ("*Kunarac* Appeals Chamber")

Kupreskić et al.

Prosecutor v. *Drago Josipović, Vladimir Šantić, Zoran Kupreskić, Mirjan Kupreskić, Vlatko Kupreskić, and Dragan Papić*, Case No. IT-95–16-T (January 14, 2000) ("*Kupreskić* Trial Chamber")

Prosecutor v. *Drago Josipović, Vladimir Šantić, Zoran Kupreskić, Mirjan Kupreskić, Vlatko Kupreskić, and Dragan Papić*, Case No. IT-95–16-A (October 23, 2001) ("*Kupreskić* Appeals Chamber")

Kvočka et al.

Prosecutor v. *Miroslav Kvočka, Mlao Radić, Zoran Žigić, and Dragoljub Prcać*, Case No. IT-98–30/1-T (November 2, 2001) ("*Kvočka* Trial Chamber")

Prosecutor v. *Miroslav Kvočka, Mlao Radić, Zoran Žigić, and Dragoljub Prcać*, Case No. IT-98–30/1-A (February 28, 2005) ("Kvočka Appeals Chamber")

Milošević (Dragomir)

Prosecutor v. *Dragomir Milošević*, Case No. IT-98–29/1 (December 12, 2007)

Milošević (Slobodan)

Prosecutor v. *Slobodan Milošević*, Case No. IT-02–54 (case uncompleted)

Mladić

Prosecutor v. *Ratko Mladić*, Case No. IT-09–92 TC (November 22, 2017)

Mrđa

Prosecutor v. *Darko Mrđa, Sentencing Judgment*, Case No. IT- 02–59 (March 31, 2004)

Nikolić (Dragan)

Prosecutor v. *Dragan Nikolić, Decision on Defense Motion Challenging the Exercise of Jurisdiction*, Case No. IT-94–2-PT (October 9, 2002)

Nikolić (Momir)

Prosecutor v. *Momir Nikolić, Sentencing Judgment*, Case No. IT-02–60/1-S (December 2, 2003) ("*Nikolić* Sentencing Judgment")

Obrenović

Prosecutor v. *Dragan Obrenović, Sentencing Judgment*, Case No. IT-02–60/2 (December 10, 2003)

Ojdanić et al.

Prosecutor v. *Milan Milutinović, Nikola Šainović, Dragoljub Ojdanić, Nebojša Pavković, Vladimir Lazarević, and Sreten Lukić, Motion Challenging Jurisdiction*, IT-05–87-PT (May 21, 2003) ("*Ojdani* Motion Challenging Jurisdiction")

Orić

Prosecutor v. *Naser Orić, Judgment*, Case No. IT-03–68-T (June 30, 2006)

Perišić

Prosecutor v. *Momčilo Perišić, Decision on Admissibility of Expert Report of Patrick Treanor, Separate Opinion of Judge Moloto*, Case No. IT-04–81 (November 27, 2008)

Prosecutor v. *Momčilo Perišić, Judgment*, Case No. IT-04–81 (September 6, 2011)

Plavšić

Prosecutor v. *Biljana Plavšić*, Case No. IT-00–39 and 40/1-S (February 27, 2003) ("*Plavšić* Sentencing Judgment")

Decision of the President on the Application for Pardon or Commutation of Sentence of Mrs. Biljana Plavšić, Case No. IT-OO-39 and 40/l-ES (September 14, 2009) ("*Plavšić* Early Release Decision")

Popović et al.

Prosecutor v. *Vujadin Popović, Ljubiša Beara, Drago Nikolić, Ljubomir Borovčanin, and Radivoje Miletić, Sentencing Judgment*, Case No. IT-05–88-T (June 10, 2010)

Simić

Prosecutor v. *Blagoje Simić, Miroslav Tadić, and Simo Zarić, Trial Chamber Judgment*, Case No. IT-95–9 (October 17, 2003)

Prosecutor v. *Blagoje Simić, Miroslav Tadić, and Simo Zarić, Appeals Chamber Judgment*, Case No. IT-95–9 (November 28, 2006)

Introduction

Using Courts to Heal Countries – Transitional Justice and International Criminal Law

I THE PROBLEM: CONTEMPORARY CHALLENGES TO INTERNATIONAL CRIMINAL LAW

In August of 1992, images of starving men held in Bosnian Serb detention camps raised the specter of genocide in Europe for the first time since World War II. The following year, the United Nations Security Council passed resolution 827, setting up the International Criminal Tribunal for the former Yugoslavia (ICTY), the first of several ad hoc tribunals inaugurated in the 1990s[1] carrying the threat of criminal sanctions for perpetrators of war crimes, and the promise of justice (as well as international recognition) for victims. The International Criminal Tribunal for Rwanda (ICTR) quickly followed, and the permanent International Criminal Court (ICC) came into being less than a decade later.

The fervor for international criminal justice was animated, at least in some measure, by the promise of law to advance political liberalism (Slaughter 2000) and, therein, peace. In the twentieth century, rule-of-law liberalism[2] underwrote prosperous, democratic, and human-rights-respecting nations (which came to include Germany and Japan, against whom the first international criminal tribunals were constructed) and eventually claimed victory in the Cold War (Fukuyama 1992). It was therefore but a short ideological step to seek to apply law, as operationalized by international courts, to resolve internecine conflict, an experiment that reached its pinnacle with the creation of the ICC in 2002.

[1] A list of such international criminal tribunals from the 1990s and beyond would include the ad hoc tribunals of the ICTY (1993), the International Criminal Tribunal for Rwanda (1994), the Ad Hoc Tribunal for East Timor, Indonesia (2001), the Special Court for Sierra Leone (2002), the Extraordinary Chambers in the Courts of Cambodia (2003), the Special Tribunal for Lebanon (2007), and the permanent International Criminal Court (2002).

[2] Rule-of-law liberalism refers to political liberalism regulated by legalism. In short, it is a commitment to transparent government processes equally applied to all actors in society. The genesis and political work accomplished by these ideas is explored in depth in Chapters 1 and 2.

More than a decade after its creation, the optimism and enthusiasm that accompanied the ICC's creation is now significantly muted even in the most committed quarters, however. At the time of writing, three African countries have declared their intent to exit the statutory regime constructing the ICC.[3] This follows a recent dismissal by the ICC of an indictment against Kenyan Prime Minister Ruto,[4] citing the same reasons that accompanied its dismissal of an indictment against Kenya's President Kenyatta in 2014:[5] whole-scale witness tampering, including untimely deaths[6] and the recanted testimonies of several prosecution witnesses, which destroyed the prosecution's case. Together with the ICC's "hibernation" of its case against Sudan's Al-Bashir[7] due to repeated failures of member states to turn him over to the court, these abandoned prosecutions against leaders charged with violations of humanitarian law challenge the ICC's capacity to make good on its mandate to "end impunity." The situation at the ICTY, as its practice draws to a close, is arguably no less challenging; on March 31, 2016, the ICTY's ten-year prosecution of Serbian far-right politician and paramilitary leader Vojislav Šešelj ended in acquittal,[8] joining several other failed prosecutions against those alleged to be most responsible for the war.[9] Even the ICTY's "successful" prosecutions generate complaint, such as the mixed reception to the Karadžić (2016) and Mladić (2017) verdicts. Both of these defendants were found guilty for crimes including genocide at Srebrenica, but acquitted of genocide across

3 South Africa; Burundi; The Gambia.

4 *The Prosecutor* v. *William Samoei Ruto and Joshua Arap Sang*, Case No. ICC-01/09–01/11 (Int'l Crim. Ct. April 5, 2016).

5 *The Prosecutor* v. *Uhuru Muigai Kenyatta*, Case No. ICC-01/09–02/11, charges withdrawn (Int'l Crim. Ct.).

6 See, for example, "Discovery of witness's mutilated body feeds accusations of state killings" *The Guardian* January 6, 2015, www.theguardian.com/world/2015/jan/06/witness-mutilated-body-kenya-government-killing-meshack-yebei-william-ruto.

7 Cite to Al-Bashir "ICC chief prosecutor shelves Darfur war crimes probe" *The Guardian* December 20, 2014, www.theguardian.com/world/2014/dec/14/icc-darfur-war-crimes-fatou-bensouda-sudan.

8 *Prosecutor* v. *Vojislav Šešelj*, Case No. IT-03–67 (Int'l Crim. Trib. for the former Yugoslavia March 31, 2016). The Office of the Prosecutor appealed, and in April 2018 the appeals chamber sentenced Šešelj to ten years' prison for events related to a 1992 speech; this sentence is the equivalent of time served. *Prosecutor* v. *Vojislav Šešelj*, Case No. MICT-16-99 (Int'l Residual Mechanism for Yugoslav Crim. Trib. April 11, 2018). Šešelj represented himself and beleaguered the institution with motions and demands; his is a stunning example, more stark even than that of Slobodan Milošević, the president of Yugoslavia who famously used the ICTY as a foghorn, of the efficacy of a *defense de rupture* at international criminal law. *Defense de rupture* is discussed further in Chapter 2.

9 See, e.g., *Prosecutor* v. *Ante Gotovina, Ivan Čermak, and Mladen Markač*, Case No. IT-06–90-PT (Int'l Crim. Trib. for the former Yugoslavia November 16, 2012); *Prosecutor* v. *Perišić*, Case No. IT-03–69 (Int'l Crim. Trib. for the former Yugoslavia February 28, 2013); *Prosecutor* v. *Jovica Stanišić and Franko Simatović*, Case No. IT-03–69 (Int'l Crim. Trib. for the former Yugoslavia May 30, 2013); *Prosecutor* v. *Vojislav Šešelj*, Case No. IT-03–67 (Int'l Crim. Trib. for the former Yugoslavia March 31, 2016) and *Prosecutor* v. *Slobodan Milošević*, Case No. IT-02–54 (case uncompleted due to Milošević's death) (the evolving pattern of convicting low-level perpetrators and acquitting leaders is discussed further in Chapter 4).

Bosnia.[10] Writing about the Karadžić verdict in the Guardian,[11] Ed Vulliamy, one of the journalists whose reporting in August 1992 brought the horrors of the war to international attention, spoke of the empty "triumphalism" of a tribunal unable to find Karadžić liable for genocide in rural areas of Bosnia, where official policies of ethnic cleansing disappeared whole villages whose inhabitants are still mostly unaccounted for, likely buried in mass graves still undiscovered.[12]

The political and workaday problems faced by international criminal tribunals (ICTs) such as the ICTY and the ICC serve to illustrate a deeper challenge to their practice. International criminal tribunals have built an impressive institutional legacy: they have produced reams of jurisprudence and hundreds of judgments, and have spawned an industry. Yet as regards the tall order of respect for the rule of law, recognition of "core" rights,[13] and value of transparent governance (i.e., the liberal aims that underwrote the international criminal law project), ICTs' records are, at best, mixed. Although war has not resumed in Bosnia, Rwanda, Sierra Leone, and Lebanon, none of these countries has experienced a concurrent embrace of rule-of-law liberalism. In each of those places, international humanitarian norms are generally celebrated when used against one's enemies, and rejected as means to organize oneself or one's friends. In other words, the experience of post-conflict countries subjected to international criminal justice to date suggests that international criminal law remains a political tool, not an ideological framework, in the regions where it has been applied. Moreover, and perhaps more significantly, as the bold doctrinal pronouncements of early ICT decisions are muted by later jurisprudence, and as ad hoc tribunals close without replacement, it appears that the powers bankrolling the international criminal law experiment may be becoming as unconvinced as the local populations subject to it. This is of course in stark contrast to the

10 *Prosecutor* v. *Radovan Karadžić*, Case No. IT-95–5/8 TC (Int'l Crim. Trib. for the former Yugoslavia March 26, 2016); *Prosecutor v. Ratko Mladić*, Case No. IT-09–92 TC (Int'l Crim. Trib. for the former Yugoslavia November 22, 2017).

11 Ed Vulliamy, "I saw Karadžić's camps. I cannot celebrate while many of his victims are denied justice" *The Guardian* March 27, 2016, www.theguardian.com/commentisfree/2016/mar/27/i-saw-radovan-karadizic-camps-cannot-celebrate-verdict-ed-vulliamy.

12 See, for example, continuing grisly discoveries of mass graves in the Prijedor region: "Bosnia Finds 600 Body Parts in Mass Grave" *Balkan Insight* October 29, 2015, available at www.balkaninsight.com/en/article/six-hundred-mortal-remains-found-in-bosnia-grave-10–29-2015. Ed Vuillaimy, "Bringing up the Bodies in Bosnia" *The Guardian* December 6, 2016, available at www.theguardian.com/world/2016/dec/06/bringing-up-the-bodies-bosnia.

13 "Core" rights are protected by international humanitarian law, and are those rights that "may never be suspended at any time or in any circumstances." They include prohibition of slavery, torture, and cruel, inhumane, or degrading treatment. See the International Red Cross Commentary on the Geneva Conventions and their related protocols, at: www.icrc.org/en/war-and-law/treaties-customary-law/geneva-conventions. International humanitarian law (the law of war) is operationalized by international criminal law, which recognizes four core crimes: war crimes, crimes against humanity, genocide, and aggression. This is further discussed in Chapters 1 and 2. On the overlaps and distinctions between international humanitarian law and human rights law, see Provost 2003; Teitel 2012, and discussion in Chapters 1 and 2.

central ideological and institutional role that rule-of-law liberalism occupies in these donor nations.

If recognition of core rights is a central achievement of the twentieth century, pushing a global "justice cascade," (Sikkink 2011) and international criminal law is the embodiment of this revolution at a global level, then the question is, what happened? How have ICTs failed to convince their audiences, both local and international? This is the problem animating *Model(ing) Justice*. The book takes as its subject a case study of history's most productive and respected ICT, the ICTY. No ad hoc tribunal has worked longer or produced more jurisprudence than the ICTY, and this makes the ICTY the best test case students of modern international criminal justice have for assessing the field's development. Drawing from emblematic examples of ICTY practice and its evolution, *Model(ing) Justice* demonstrates that the practice of international criminal law does not reflect the ideology of political liberalism driving it.

Model(ing) Justice makes this argument through the development of two theories that describe the paradoxes of illiberal practice in pursuit of rule-of-law liberalism: (1) the international criminal justice template and (2) the problem of non-derogable legal doctrine. Together, these two theories detail the limitations inherent in focusing on liberal outcomes in place of liberal processes, and demonstrate how ICT practice has often consciously and unapologetically departed from liberalism's constraints, a situation the book labels "post-rule of law". Part I of the book constructs and applies the two theories, tracing their emergence from the seminal International Military Tribunal (IMT) at Nuremberg through to the construction of modern ICTs. Part II examines the paradox of "progressive" international criminal law through two detailed case studies, the ICTY's development of procedural law (Chapter 3) and the central substantive legal doctrine developed in ICTY jurisprudence, the "joint criminal enterprise" (JCE) theory of liability (Chapter 4). Part III considers the soft-law elements of ICTY jurisprudence, examining the ICTY's impact in the former Yugoslavia (Chapter 5) and conflicting socio-legal constructions of "reconciliation" between two significant ICTY cases (Chapter 6). In its final chapter, the book argues that a return to process is necessary in order to retain rule-of-law ideas at the center of peace and development in this century.

II THEORIZING LAW AS A TRANSITIONAL JUSTICE MECHANISM

In the more than two decades since the ICTY's creation, a rich field has developed considering the ICTY from a transitional justice perspective (Meernik 2005; McMahon & Forsythe 2008; Orentlicher 2008, 2010, 2013; Subotić 2009; Hodžić 2010; Nettelfield 2010; Hagan & Ivković 2011; Kostić 2012; Nalepa 2012; Clark 2014; Gow, Kerr & Pajić 2014). Transitional justice is a normative and theoretical discourse rooted in law and political science (Israël & Mouralis 2014) that highlights the necessity of acknowledging past events in order to build a secure future (Huyse

1995; Teitel 2000; Elster 2004; Hazan 2004; Kritz 2009; Quinn 2009; Olsen *et al.* 2010b; Rowen 2017). First theorized and identified in the 1980s in relation to the process of identifying and remembering illiberal state practices in South America, transitional justice exploded in the wake of the Cold War.

In most transitional justice-based assessments of the ICTY's impact in the former Yugoslavia, the scholarly debate generally ranges between those who insist that the ICTY should or will contribute meaningfully to the construction of history, progressive legal norms, and reconciliation/social reconstruction, and those who agree with this construct, but who regardless find that the data show that ICTY-generated narratives are not taking root among local populations. These empirical considerations, however, overlook the larger theoretical discussion of whether, or how, the policy and legal-consciousness-building capacities attributed to domestic courts (Scheingold [1964] 2004) might function at a transnational level. International criminal tribunals are structurally distinct from domestic courts in myriad ways, from their often-international staff, location, and procedure, to their discretionary choice of cases and lack of enforcement powers. Yet despite these important differences, proponents of using ICTs to perform transitional justice functions often look past the question of whether ICTs enjoy the same constitutive social capacity that domestic courts arguably do to assert ICTs' potential social impact. Transitional justice itself has developed into a broad and amorphous field.

Recent transitional justice literature has begun charting this boundlessness (Israël & Mouralis 2014; Vinjamuri & Snyder 2015; Ainley 2017; Daly 2017; Gissel 2016; Sharp 2018). *Model(ing) Justice* joins this literature, addressing transitional justice's theoretical indeterminacy through its introduction of (1) the international criminal justice template and its discussion of (2) the problem of non-derogable legal doctrine.

A *The International Criminal Justice Template*

Model(ing) Justice's first theoretical contribution is a tripartite prototype of international criminal justice enumerating ICTs' received benefits, *the international criminal justice template.* This is an ideal type designed to demonstrate the illiberal construct of international criminal law institutions to date. The template identifies the prototype that underlies assumptions about ICT capacity as transitional justice or governance mechanisms. This ideal type holds that ICTs (i) bring progressive international criminal law to bear on individual actors, (ii) establish the facts of crimes committed in the chaos of war or secret chambers of government and (iii) assist in social reconstruction and reconciliation through both the content and the process of their practice.

The book argues that this template emerged from the first ICT prototype, the IMT at Nuremberg; this is the subject of Chapter 1. The prototype's three elements can be divided into *first-order* functions regarding legal doctrine (the articulation of progressive international criminal law jurisprudence) and *second-order* functions regarding social impact (the capacity to articulate history and the ability to shape discourse and narrative). The first- and second-order functions are related, because it is the received legitimacy of the first that impacts the capacity of the second.

The first element of the international criminal justice template, the development of progressive international criminal law, is the element most directly related to ICTs' institutional design as tribunals tasked with finding the guilt or innocence of individuals through judicial processes. International criminal tribunals require international criminal legal content in order to adjudicate cases, and ICTs must necessarily make interpretations of international criminal law, which is predominantly treaty and customary international law, in order to bring it within ICT ambit. Central to the international criminal justice template's categorization is that such articulation will be "progressive." The injunction that ICTs produce progressive international criminal law is central to the legitimizing narrative for ICTs, the book shows, because ICTs often breach strict legality rules by retroactively articulating law. The principle of legality is the constraint that turns the rules associated with law into "justice" rather than the raw application of force. Retroactive articulations of law breach "the principle of legality." Yet under international criminal law, such retroactive legal pronouncements are legitimized as means of advancing rights, combatting impunity, and achieving social progress. "Progress" is therefore central to international criminal law's legitimacy, and the international criminal justice template teases out the articulation of progress as a response to legality challenges in individual adjudications beginning at the IMT, and continuing through to ICTs today.

The second and third functions of the international criminal justice template – ICTs as (ii) historians (iii) capable of pronouncing an "objective" "official version" of events that may assist a population in reconciliation – are not directly related to ICTs' primary case adjudication mandate but rather are argued to flow from it (Wilson 2011; Rauxloh 2010). These second and third "indirect" functions are the capacities imagined for ICTs that have made them central as transitional justice mechanisms. They are also the amorphous functions that are simultaneously claimed by ICTs in defense of the value of their work and rejected by ICTs as bars against which to assess their accomplishments. This leaves a conflicting situation where the ICTY justifies its value in terms of reconciliation in some circumstances[14] while steadfastly rejecting such a measurement in others.[15]

[14] The ICTY's discussion of its outreach program reads as follows:

> The establishment of Outreach in 1999, six years into the ICTY's existence, was a milestone in the Tribunal's progression to maturity. It was a sign that the court had become deeply aware that its work would resonate far beyond the judicial mandate of deciding the guilt or innocence of individual accused. With the establishment of Outreach, the Tribunal recognized that it had a role to play in the process of dealing with the past in the former Yugoslavia, one of the key challenges for societies emerging from conflict.
>
> www.icty.org/en/outreach/outreach-programme (accessed January 20, 2017).

[15] "Where did you hear that, that the ICTY does reconciliation? Where, on what website? I'd like to see it, we'll find it right now! There is only one website [that matters] and there is no mandate for reconciliation. Look in the Security Council documents, the court documents, it's not there. This

Model(ing) Justice shows that the structure of international criminal law to date works directly to undermine ICT capacity in the spheres of value defined by the international criminal justice template. Drawing from criminal law theory and criminology studies, the book argues that ICTs as currently constructed cannot produce progressive law – the very task that animates and legitimizes them – due to their illiberal structure and function. This illiberal function, in turn, impacts ICTs' potential as socially constitutive organs, either in terms of producing official histories/narratives or in advancing reconciliation.

The international criminal justice template defines an ideal-type, notional value of ICT capacity to further transitional justice ideals. Few observers would argue that ICTs are certain to produce these outcomes; even the most idealistic, early proponents of ICTs as transitional justice mechanisms spoke of ICT *potential* to produce progressive international criminal law, establish historical fact, and effect social reconstruction (Akhavan 1998). Rather, as with Weber's ideal types (Weber 1904/1949; Swedberg 2017), or Shapiro's (1986) prototype of courts, the template's value lies in identifying the imagined, aspirational capacities surrounding ICTs as transitional justice mechanisms. *Model(ing) Justice* argues that these ideological elements of ICT capacity continue to define our expectations of ICTs, in spite of the empirical, theoretical, and historical evidence challenging ICT capacity in these areas. We know that ICTs often fail to produce progressive law, write official histories, or reconcile bitter foes. Yet these tasks, in the aggregate, continue to describe the entirety of ICTs' purpose, providing the terms and ideals against which even the most sophisticated recent assessments of international criminal law institutions measure ICTs (Subotić 2009; Nettelfield 2010; Wilson 2011; Clark 2014).

B The Problem of Non-Derogable Legal Doctrine

The book's second theoretical contribution lies in showing how the elements of the international criminal justice template, though routinely articulated or assumed as legitimizing arguments for international criminal law, are in fact structurally unachievable for ICTs. This is due to the paradoxical standard at the center of international criminal law: the *problem of non-derogation*. The scope and power of international humanitarian law lies in its protection of rights presented as "non-derogable": such rights, emerging from natural-law constructions (Sohn 1982) are immutable, inalienable, universal, and absolute, admitting no contingency or context. The absolute and universal status of core rights secures the legitimacy of those institutions of international criminal law that would try violations of these rights

idea of reconciliation has been projected on to the ICTY by diplomats. But it's ridiculous to charge the court with reconciliation ... It is true that senior ICTY officials sometimes mention reconciliation. Goldstone, Cassese, etc. But just because some senior officials say it doesn't make it our mandate." Interview, Senior ICTY official, The Hague, May 5, 2005, notes on file with author.

through processes approximating domestic criminal law trials, trumping positive law particulars that might prevent protection of non-derogable rights through law.

It is the use of individual criminal trials at international criminal law that triggers the problem of non-derogation. Domestic criminal law is rife with mitigating circumstances and affirmative defenses, many of which can completely protect an individual from punishment (beyond the punishment incurred by being subjected to the intrusion of the state [Feeley 1979]). Almost any definition of crime is subject to forms of derogation, alienation, and/or challenges to universality at domestic criminal law: only those crimes that fall under "absolute" or "strict" liability escape such derogation. Domestic criminal processes resist absolute liability: justice and fairness concerns advocate on behalf of the importance of context and/or intent in the adjudication of criminal culpability (Hart 1968). Absolute liability at criminal law makes for unpopular domestic policy for precisely this reason (de Than & Heaton 2013: 432–433).

International criminal law practice is challenged by the confrontation between the non-derogable norms accompanying violations of core rights with the justice and fairness demands present in criminal law. This is because natural-law-based rights face predictable structural obstacles when operationalized as sovereign-based criminal justice. At international criminal law, violations of international humanitarian law are always criminal, regardless of context. Moreover, this doctrinal insistence is central to the "progress" imagined for international criminal law, and a key element legitimizing international criminal law practice, *Model(ing) Justice* shows. In contrast to human rights legal practice, which recognizes a "margin of appreciation" that imagines the possibility of different standards for different acts in different contexts, international criminal law explicitly forbids such recognition. The catch is that, in order to legitimize itself, international criminal law forbids such recognition in the name of universally recognized human rights. In this way, human rights (though not its doctrinal tradition, specifically its recognition of context) are put in service to international criminal law. The problem of non-derogation describes the phenomenon of international criminal law that renders it closer to "strict" or "absolute" liability than to the communicative purpose (Ashworth 2009; Duff 2009) animating liberal domestic criminal legal orders.

Finally, the problem of non-derogation is made possible by the conflict of interest faced by ICTs in terms of their own accountability. International criminal tribunals generally answer to the UN or donor nations, while often serving a population distinct from the UN and donor nations, resulting in what Jan Klabbers (2015) has identified as a generalized problem of accountability characteristic of international organizations. For ICTs, accountability issues assume particular significance because the perceptions of third-party observers (the tribunals' audiences) are central to institutional legitimacy. Thus while all international organizations suffer accountability challenges, these are particularly acute for ICTs because they implicate their legitimacy and thus their efficiency.

III STRUCTURE AND CONTENT OF THE BOOK

The book is divided into three parts of two chapters each. The book's first two chapters articulate and explore its two theoretical contributions, the structural impossibility of the prototype that governs aspirational, imagined capacity for ICTs, the international criminal justice template and the conflict between international criminal law's universalist, natural-law foundations and its application as criminal law, the problem of non-derogation. Its final four chapters apply those ideas to examples culled from ICTY practice and impact, using the work and reception of the ICTY as a paradigmatic argument for the challenges facing ICTs and international criminal law more generally. While much of *Model(ing) Justice* is rooted in the particulars of ICTY practice, procedure, and experience, its arguments are not case or circumstance specific, but rather generalizable across ICTs.

Part I, consisting of Chapters 1 and 2, develops the book's two central theories. Chapter 1 shows how the IMT at Nuremberg, the progenitor of ICTs and the immediate ancestor of the ICTY, defined an ideal type of what ICTs might accomplish, setting up the future development of transitional justice; Chapter 2 discusses theoretical, structural challenges to international criminal law's practice. Part II maps those central theories onto ICTY practice, considering ICTY procedure (Chapter 3) and the ICTY's most notorious contribution to substantive law (Chapter 4). Part III examines the second-order functions of the ICTY identified by the international criminal justice template, as historian and reconciler, to connect the theoretical shortcomings evidenced by the international criminal justice template and the problem of non-derogation to the ICTY's social "legacy" project. Each part is preceded by a short introduction to situate the reader, and readers most interested in, for example, legal constructions of reconciliation in the former Yugoslavia can skip directly to Part III, aided by the short introduction summarizing the theoretical work of Chapters 1 and 2. The comprehensive Appendix A, summarizing all ICTY decisions at the time of writing (a nearly complete record of the institution's work) is available to assist the reader in making sense of ICTY jurisprudence.

Chapter 1 demonstrates how the international criminal justice template emerges from the legacy of the IMT at Nuremberg, history's seminal ICT. The legacy of the IMT at Nuremberg credits it with several achievements beyond the adjudication of the individual cases that came before it, including recognition of the Holocaust and the construction of democratic Germany. Modern ICTs operate in its shadow. The bulk of the chapter demonstrates the emergence of an IMT legacy, where "Nuremberg" has become synonymous with social reconstruction along democratic and human rights-recognizing axes, as the basis for the international criminal justice template. The mixed reception and tangled legacy of the International Military Tribunal for the Far East at Tokyo is briefly considered, as a counter-demonstration of the dominant international criminal law narrative emerging from the legacy of the IMT. Finally, the chapter traces the lineage between the IMT and the ICTY.

Chapter 2 considers the ideals underwriting the ICTY against the practice of the institution, over its twenty years. The chapter argues that the transitional justice aims assigned to ICTs (which include acting as historians and models of institutional governance) derive from the social control associated with domestic criminal justice. At the end of World War II, the Allied powers formed ICTs and tasked them with public identification and punishment of those individuals "most responsible for the war." The Allied trials at Nuremberg – and, as discussed in Chapter 1, to a lesser degree at Tokyo – heralded a new era both in international law and in the Kantian (1991), political liberal project of "cosmopolitan law." When international law was retooled, via a Kantian search for total justice, from the law between states to a law capable of directly impacting individuals, the field of international criminal law was born.

The second and third parts of the book apply the theories developed in Chapters 1 and 2 to the practice and impact of the ICTY. Chapter 3 demonstrates that the ICTY's hybrid procedure sacrifices defendants' rights to procedural efficiency and institutional demand. In so doing, it fails to articulate a progressive international criminal law standard. Relying on legal positivism – the fact that each element of procedure adopted by the tribunal has roots in a balanced and just criminal procedure – the tribunal has looked past the *purpose* of the domestic criminal systems from which it has borrowed procedure. Such purpose, domestically, is always to balance the power of the state against the rights of the individual; without effective balance, the state's legitimacy – and with it, law's legitimacy and capacity as a social agent – is threatened. While the debate between the letter of the law and the purpose of the law is a classic one within legal studies (Hart & Fuller 2010), the ICTY articulates a jurisprudence the book labels "post-rule of law" because it rejects an interest in legal purpose altogether.

Chapter 4 considers the paradox of legitimizing the work of ICTs through their articulation of progressive law by examining the legal substance of the ICTY's controversial articulation of JCE, a theory of liability that stretches "commission" along a common law conspiracy scale to reach, at its farthest point, crimes that are "foreseeable consequences" of individuals' projects and actions. Following the troubled, and troubling, development of the ICTY's JCE jurisprudence, this chapter demonstrates the difficulty of articulating the content of illegality for international criminal institutions, where institutions such as the ICTY are required to translate non-derogable human rights norms into criminal law specifics that can be applied to individuals.

Part III considers the second-order functions of the international criminal justice template, the social impact of ICTs, by looking at the ICTY's work as a historian and reconciler. Chapter 5 considers the distinction between the history uncovered by the ICTY's case law and the narratives of the war that obtain across the former

Yugoslavia. Chapter 6 contrasts the divergent treatment of two "remorseful" defendants before the ICTY to consider problems in the tribunal's practice.

IV JUSTICE MODELS AND MODEL JUSTICE

Published as the ICTY closes down, reflecting on ICTY practice and looking to the future, *Model(ing) Justice* has several goals. Centrally, as demonstrated by the title, it seeks to consider the distinction between that justice which rule-of-law liberalism aspires to construct and which follows from a Lockean social-contract-legitimizing government (which might be considered a "model" justice, communicating shared norms transparently, predictably, and with equanimity) against the illiberal justice practiced by ICTs at present, i.e., the institutional practice they are in fact "modeling."

International criminal law draws on the Kantian project of "cosmopolitan justice," seeking a universal human rights standard (Rawls 1999, 2001; Kymlicka 1992). In the 1960s and 1970s, lawyers and activists "rediscovered" law's humanitarian capacity. In works like A *Theory of Justice* (Rawls 1971) and in the creation of organizations like Amnesty International and Helsinki Watch, law was set at the center of the discourse of fairness and political legitimacy. These supporters of law as insurer of human rights placed stock in law vesting at the level of the individual (Dworkin 1986) whereas realists, rationalists, and liberals had always viewed international law and actions as a purview of the state. Günther Teubner (2015: 10) calls these former constructions "sociological natural law" because they "use[s] societal constitutions to reconstruct the rationalities of diverse subsystems within the legal system and transform them into binding principles." In this projection, international law is universal based on its underlying morality. Such morality may be based on fairness (Franck 1995) or universality (Koh 1997). These "universal" fairness principles are the substitutes for consent, i.e., that which relays legitimacy, in public international law.[16] International criminal law presents a series of moral claims drawn from a natural-law base regarding the universal nature of the rights that it recognizes, and thus does not require the "consent" of individuals because its universality constitutes its legitimacy.

Rule-of-law liberalism argues for the didactic value in modeling justice for states perfecting their own governance structures. International criminal tribunals such as the IMT at Nuremberg and the ICTY have been fêted as such model institutions, where part of their value lies in their capacity to teach a target populace. In calling attention to the illiberal practice of the model (be it the IMT at Nuremberg, the ICTY, or other ICTs), the book challenges the capacity for ICTs as model mechanisms. As such, and informed by the critical legal studies movement (which has

[16] Public international law as used here includes international human rights law, international criminal law, and international humanitarian law.

generally sought to reveal how law's "objectivity" serves particular political and power interests), *Model(ing) Justice* might be read as a critique of liberal legalism.

Yet although the story told within these pages styles itself as an alternate reading of the practice and structure animating ICTs, the book's central purpose remains the *perfection* of international criminal law, not its elimination. In calling attention to the ways that ICTs, as self-styled representatives of a universal, global rule-of-law liberalism, have used their position as a "global conscience" to justify an illiberal development of international criminal law and its related legal phenomena, the book seeks to modify such practice. Thus, to the degree that the international criminal justice template assists in defining expectations of ICTs, the critique is positioned within liberal legalism. *Model(ing) Justice* would address the "mainstream," practitioners and students of international criminal law, transitional justice, or peace studies, those students and professionals working towards the heady utopian goals of increasing rights awareness and reducing violations of international humanitarian law. The failure of ICTs has so far been a failure of recognition of the structural features inherent in their practice that render such practice illiberal. While the challenges ICTs currently face are significant, they are not insurmountable.

In the 2003 *Nikolić* sentencing judgment[17] the ICTY trial chamber articulated the potential, and the impact, of the tribunal as follows:

> [At the time the Srebrenica massacre took place in July 1995] [t]he Tribunal was seen by many – including persons in the former Yugoslavia – as more of an academic or diplomatic response to the armed conflict and the violations being committed therein rather than as an operational institution where one might face criminal proceedings ... International humanitarian law and international criminal law were not seen as enforceable law, but rather aspirational, if not academic, ideas. Thus, expectations of impunity for ones [*sic*] crimes, no matter how egregious, were the norm. A stark example of this expectation of impunity and total disregard for the law in 1995 was provided by [the defendant] Momir Nikolić ... when he was asked during his cross-examination in the Blagojevic trial whether he was required to abide by the Geneva Conventions in carrying out his duties in and around Srebrenica in July 1995. Momir Nikolić replied with a mix of incredulity and exasperation:
>
> "Do you really think that in an operation where 7000 people were set aside, captured, and killed that somebody was adhering to the Geneva Conventions? Do you really believe that somebody adhered to the law, rules and regulations in an operation where so many were killed? First of all, they were captured, killed, and then buried, exhumed once again, buried again. Can you conceive of that, that somebody in an operation of that kind adhered to the Geneva Conventions? Nobody ... adhered to the Geneva Conventions or the rules and regulations.

[17] *Prosecutor* v. *Momir Nikolić, Sentencing Judgment,* Case No. IT-02-60/1-S (December 2, 2003) ("*Nikolić* Sentencing Judgment"); see Appendix A for a full list of all ICTY cases.

> Because had they, then the consequences of that particular operation would not have been a total of 7000 people dead."
>
> During the past ten years, as international criminal law has moved from "law in theory" to "law in practice," the principles of international humanitarian law have taken hold to the extent that in the face of such widespread and massive crimes a person being called to participate in the criminal enterprise might consider the Geneva Conventions and the consequences of disregarding the principles contained therein.

For the *Nikolić* sentencing chamber, the ICTY's impact can be measured in a heightened awareness of the international humanitarian norms enshrined in the Geneva Conventions.

International criminal law is built on the theory that *awareness* of international humanitarian law might direct, and ultimately deter, those individuals who would otherwise violate international humanitarian norms. Surely most would agree that this worthy goal animating international criminal law practice merits our efforts and excuses some growing pains. *Model(ing) Justice* is written in the shadow of this aim, the "more just world" to which the ICC aspires.

In the following pages, *Model(ing) Justice* illustrates the structural obstacles that inhibit international criminal law from embodying its rights mandate in order to make the case for a vigorous application of liberalism's processes, rather than liberalism's borrowed outcomes, in the expansion of the recognition and protection of core rights in the twenty-first century. The book argues that the focus on liberalism's ideal outcomes rather than its processes explains the gap between the justice ICTs are designed to model and the work they in fact perform. In response to the structural challenges the book identifies in ICTY practice, it invites reforms designed to address the structural inadequacies that render ICTs illiberal, so that international criminal justice might come closer to realizing its potential as a progenitor of peace, rule of law, and respect for human rights.

PART I

Theorizing International Criminal Justice

The first part of the book develops the book's two central theoretical arguments. Chapter 1 develops the international criminal justice template, the ideal type that describes what international criminal tribunals (ICTs) are arguably designed to deliver. The international criminal justice template is the legacy of the International Military Tribunal (IMT) at Nuremberg made manifest. The template distills areas in which ICTs are argued to be socially constitutive into three categories. These are (1) the articulation of progressive international criminal law, (2) the production of historical archives and accepted facts, and (3) the generation of reconciling narratives capable of defining a shared future from a fractured past. The chapter traces the development of these categories from their emergence in the discourse surrounding the IMT at Nuremberg, to the challenge posed to these categories by the IMT's sister tribunal, the International Military Tribunal for the Far East at Tokyo, and finally to the IMT's direct descendant, the International Criminal Tribunal for the former Yugoslavia (ICTY).

The international criminal justice template is a valuable theoretical device because it offers both a definitive exploration of the transitional justice capacities imagined for ICTs and an examination of the structural impossibility for ICTs to deliver on these promised capacities. Chapter 1 showcases ICTs as transitional justice ideal types and suggests how these functions cannot be delivered; later chapters demonstrate these structural inadequacies through examples of ICTY practice.

Chapter 2 develops the central problem of the international criminal justice template, which is its reliance on articulating "progressive" law to legitimize its legal formulations. Chapter 2 labels the particular problem at work in this operationalization of violations of core rights the "problem of non-derogation." International criminal legal practice, Chapter 2 shows, relies on the rationales underwriting domestic criminal law without echoing the logic or safeguards practiced in domestic criminal law. This results in legal formulations that fail the communicative function of criminal law, challenging the larger normative social purpose underwriting international criminal law.

1

Nuremberg Defines Our Time

The Promise of International Criminal Law

The International Military Tribunal (IMT) at Nuremberg is a cornerstone in the Western narrative of World War II, "one of the most significant tributes that Power has ever paid to Reason."[1] In that narrative, the victorious nations "stayed the hand of vengeance"[2] through the imposition of the rule of law. The narrative maintains that in place of purely political resolutions by the victorious powers, enemy actors were subjected "with complete and judicial objectivity" to a public hearing before an "impartial" judicial body, the decisions of which were subsequently followed by the leadership of the victorious power and "grounded in the rule of law."[3] The central legacy of the IMT is thus the capacity of substituting legal process for political violence. In this telling, law is not itself illiberal or political but rather righteous and just.

Yet the IMT was a deeply flawed court. It applied *ex-post facto* laws that it engineered in order to include only selected acts and enemies.[4] In other words, the IMT violated central, basic rule-of-law norms. Contemporary international criminal law practitioners have all but forgotten the respected legal theorists who joined German defendants in challenging the IMT's brand of justice as hollow,

1 Opening statement of US Prosecutor Justice Jackson, November 21, 1945. Nuremberg Trial Proceedings Volume 3, December 4, 1945, available at http://avalon.law.yale.edu/imt/12-04-45.asp.

2 *Ibid.*

3 Opening statement of Sir Hartley Shawcross, Britain's Attorney General, November 20, 1945. Nuremberg Trial Proceedings Volume 3, December 4, 1945, available at http://avalon.law.yale.edu/imt/12-04-45.asp. The full quote reads: "And so we believe that this Tribunal, acting, as we know it will act notwithstanding its appointment by the victorious powers, with complete and judicial objectivity, will provide a contemporary touchstone and an authoritative and impartial record to which future historians may turn for truth, and future politicians for warning. From this record shall future generations know not only what our generation suffered, but also that our suffering was the result of crimes, crimes against the laws of peoples which the peoples of the world upheld and will continue in the future to uphold – to uphold by international co-operation, not based merely on military alliances, but grounded, and firmly grounded, in the rule of law."

4 Writing contemporaneously, renowned legal theorist Hans Kelsen (1947) noted, "What really impairs the authority of the judgment is that the principle of individual criminal responsibility for the violation of rules of international law prohibiting war has not been established as a general principle of law, but as a rule applicable only to vanquished States by the victors." Reprinted in Mettraux 2009b.

vengeful, and antithetical to rule-of-law processes, however. Today international criminal tribunals (ICTs) use the IMT, and the contemporary jurisprudence it begat, as a foundation and justification for their own work.

The IMT legacy thus comprises a paradox: it asserts that it represents the power of the rule of law, but its own operation challenged basic rule-of-law tenets. Although this paradox is sometimes acknowledged, its implications are underexplored. Modern democratic nation states promise to advance rights, equality, and prosperity through rule of law (Müller 2011). The rule-of-law paradoxes inherent in the IMT are thus typically considered operational or circumstantial instead of ideological or structural. This chapter challenges this interpretation. It shows that the IMT's rule-of-law defects were foundational. More significantly, it shows that these defects have remained intact in modern international criminal law practice, and represent the central ideological and structural obstacles international criminal law faces in achieving the social and political goals that underwrite its practice.

To examine the IMT's lasting legacy, this chapter distills it into three categories that comprise the received wisdom of the functions the IMT performed. This is the *international criminal justice template*, and it describes the prototype of the value of ICTs as institutions. The international criminal justice template asserts that ICTs (1) articulate progressive international criminal law (this is their *first-order function*, the central rationale for their work); (2) act as historians or historical archives; and (3) generate narratives capable of producing official versions, which make reconciliation possible (these latter roles are *second-order functions*, the purported social consequences of ICTs). The first part of the chapter considers the IMT's creation and operation in these terms.

Sections II and III consider the International Military Tribunal for the Far East (IMTFE) at Tokyo and the International Criminal Tribunal for the former Yugoslavia (ICTY) through the lens of the international criminal justice template. Section II considers the IMTFE because although both the IMT and the IMTFE were simultaneous, nascent constructors of international criminal law, the Tokyo legacy is far less sanguine that that of Nuremberg. In Section III, the ICTY is introduced as the IMT's direct descendant – the remainder of the book examines the ICTY through the international criminal justice template. Taken together, these sections show how the IMT at Nuremberg birthed a prototype for what international criminal institutions can and should do, while simultaneously defining the paradoxes and impossibilities present in the prototype.

I THE IMT AND THE ESTABLISHMENT OF INTERNATIONAL CRIMINAL LAW

The IMT at Nuremberg marked the emergence of the use of law to redress totalitarian violence (Shklar 1964/1986; Primus 1996). As World War II drew to a close, the Allied powers faced a two-tier challenge as they sought to use law to define the coming peace. First, the crimes the IMT addressed were largely novel, and thereby violated the legality principle, which prohibits after-the-fact articulations of law. Second, the crimes that the Allies sought to prosecute emerged not from Nazi law*less*ness but rather from a strict and terrible law*ful*ness: the positive law, i.e., written, textual law of the Nazi regime, had made many of the atrocities perpetrated before and during the war legal in Germany.

To circumvent these challenges, the IMT drew on natural-law arguments regarding a universally recognizable "human good" to legitimize its practice (Citron 2006). In its judgment, the IMT argued that in "circumstances [where the defendant] must know that he is doing wrong, ... so far from it being unjust to punish him, it would be unjust if his wrong were allowed to go unpunished."[5] Facing a significant positive-law challenge, the IMT nominally legitimized itself by reaching back to what it articulated was established law. In practice, however, the IMT largely looked forward to what the law "should be." This normative task provided the IMT with legitimacy as it invented legal doctrines and applied them retroactively to individuals. In this way, the task of pronouncing "progressive" law became central to the IMT's operation.

A *Establishing the IMT*

The Allied powers began discussing what to do with their vanquished foes well before the end of World War II. As early as 1942, the Soviets had raised the need to try "the Hitlerite invaders and their accomplices for the crimes committed by them in the occupied countries of Europe."[6] The possibility of trying Nazi leaders as war criminals enjoyed a sort of precedent: the Treaty of Versailles that concluded World War I had condemned Germany for waging aggressive war and made provisions for Allied war crimes trials (Bass 2000). The alternative, of course, was execution; Stalin reputedly estimated that executions of between ten thousand and fifty thousand Germans were in order. Though Churchill was said to be horrified by the scale of Stalin's suggestion, the British also favored executing Nazi leaders, whose guilt was seen as "simply too obvious" for a trial (Bloxham 2001: 9). Execution did not rule out a trial apparatus, of course: when the Russians, Americans, and British met at Yalta in 1944 to discuss the coming peace, Stalin reputedly told Churchill, "In the Soviet Union, we never execute anyone without a trial," to which Churchill is said to have replied, "Of course, of course. We should give them a trial first."[7] Even after agreeing to the trials suggested by the United States, the Russians wished such trials to exist as an exceptional law against the defeated. It was the United States that championed

5 *Judgment*, in 1 Trial of the Major War Criminals Before the International Military Tribunal, Nuremberg, November 14, 1945–October 1, 1946.

6 Stalin's foreign minister, Molotov, published in a cable October 1941 (quoted in Roberts 2006: 141).

7 See http://law2.umkc.edu/faculty/projects/ftrials/nuremberg/nurembergaccount.html

"an episode that would leave an enduring judicial monument, to mark a giant step in the growth of international law" (Taylor 1970: 80).

During the summer of 1945, a team of Allied jurists, led by US Supreme Court Justice Jackson, drafted the charter for the IMT, the document that defined how the institution would work, what charges it could make, and what defenses individuals might raise. Problematically, this process was undertaken by individuals who later went on to serve at the IMT (Jackson, who served as prosecutor for the US; Nikitchenko, the Soviet judge), which arguably violated the separation of powers doctrine as well as prejudicing participants (Burchard 2006).[8]

The IMT charter defined international criminality through four charges: waging an aggressive war, crimes against humanity, war crimes, and conspiracy to commit the preceding three crimes.[9] Of these, only "war crimes" existed in any defined manner prior to the Nuremberg trials; the other three were all without precedent in international law. Moreover, under established principles of international law, which places state sovereignty at its center, states' treatment of their own citizens was not a topic for international law to address. The central innovation of the IMT was to challenge this formulation and make individuals criminally liable for acts performed in service to their state: both in its focus on *individuals* as well as its pronouncements regarding *criminality*, the IMT charted novel ground. In response to concerns that retroactive application of newly minted laws contravened rule-of-law maxims, Jackson assured US President Truman that the tribunal would "punish acts which have been regarded as criminal since the time of Cain and have been so written in every civilized code."[10]

B Putting Defeated Nazis on Trial

As an ad hoc tribunal, limited in time and scope, the IMT was distinguishable from domestic criminal courts in a number of ways. The IMT was not tasked with punishing *all crime* or *all crime of a particular character* within a geographic or temporal period, but rather with locating some – sometimes the worst, sometimes not – perpetrators and establishing their guilt. At the IMT, the question of who would be indicted, whether (and which) politicians, military leaders, prominent businesspeople, cultural figures, and from which countries such defendants should be drawn, was debated for months. The final list of entirely German indictees represented a series of political compromises between the British, American,

8 In fact, the defense filed a joint motion during the trial itself protesting the "all in one" nature of the IMT, where "the creator of the Statute of the Tribunal and the rules of law" also served as "prosecutor and judges." *Judgment*, in 1 Trial of the Major War Criminals Before the International Military Tribunal, Nuremberg, November 14, 1945–October 1, 1946, pages 169–170.

9 Article 6, Charter of the International Military Tribunal, available at http://avalon.law.yale.edu/imt/imtconst.asp.

10 Robert H. Jackson, Report to the President on Atrocities and War Crimes, June 7, 1945, available at http://avalon.law.yale.edu/imt/imt_jack01.asp.

French, and Soviet powers. It was devised as representative of German aggression and the evils of the Nazi regime, with a nod to political practicality (namely who the Allied powers had captured).[11] In addition to the twenty-four individuals indicted by the IMT, six Nazi *organizations* were arraigned as well.[12] This action, novel in the extreme, opened the possibility for finding participants in "guilty associations" guilty by association and was developed in order to facilitate later prosecutions. This charge was rejected in the eventual tribunal judgment.[13] Ultimately, of the twenty-two defendants who eventually stood trial, twelve were sentenced to death, seven were sentenced to prison terms, and three were acquitted.[14]

Modern attempts to harmonize and codify agreement on how to wage war are typically said to begin with the Hague Conventions of 1899 and 1907, which sought to define the laws of combat. Known as "the Law of The Hague," these conventions prohibited attacks on undefended towns, as well as the use of poisonous weapons, and claimed special protections for hospitals and religious and cultural sites (Ratner et al. 2009). This is the genesis of what are today identified as "war crimes" and prohibited through the Geneva Conventions of 1949 and their related Protocols.[15] Today, the rules that obtain in war or other forms of organized, systemic violence are organized under the heading "international humanitarian law" or "the law of war."

The staple core crimes that define international humanitarian law – war crimes, crimes against humanity, and genocide – today circulate in mainstream discourse and are recognized and employed far beyond a specialized cadre of international criminal law jurists. It is therefore sometimes forgotten that the central charge at the IMT was not war crimes, crimes against humanity, or genocide (a term that was only coined following the IMT), but rather "aggression," the criminalization of Nazi Germany's acts towards "waging aggressive war." The US representatives to the

[11] For example, Admiral Erich Rader (sentenced to life in prison by the IMT, released after nine years) and one of Goebbels's propaganda officials, Hans Fritsche (acquitted by the IMT), were included in the indictment because they were in Soviet custody.

[12] Die Reichsregierung (Reich Cabinet); Das Korps der Politischen Leiter der Nationalsozialistischen Deutschen Arbeiterpartei (Leadership Corps of the Nazi Party); Die Schutzstaffeln der Nationalsozialistischen Deutschen Arbeiterpartei (commonly known as the "SS") and including Der Sicherheitsdienst (commonly known as the "SD"); Die Geheime Staatspolizei (Secret State Police, commonly known as the "Gestapo"); Die Sturmabteilungen der NSDAP (commonly known as the "SA"); and the General Staff and High Command of the German Armed Forces. Minutes of the Opening Session of the Tribunal, at Berlin, October 18, 1945. The question as regards these organizations was whether they were criminal.

[13] *Judgment*, in 1 Trial of the Major War Criminals Before the International Military Tribunal, Nuremberg, November 14, 1945–October 1, 1946. This nonetheless requires our attention, because the desire to find a "shortcut" to criminal liability for bad actors, while rejected by the IMT, continues to animate ICT jurisprudence, and has arguably found form in early articulations of the ICTY's joint criminal enterprise doctrine. This is discussed further in Chapter 4.

[14] See US Holocaust Memorial Museum, available at www.ushmm.org/outreach/en/article.php?ModuleId=10007722

[15] Available at www.icrc.org/eng/war-and-law/treaties-customary-law/geneva-conventions/overview-geneva-conventions.htm

prosecution argued that "waging aggressive war" had become illegal following the Kellogg–Briand Pact of 1928, which renounced "war as an instrument of national policy."[16]

Even at the time of the IMT, the argument that "waging aggressive war" had become illegal in 1928 was resisted as unreasonably legalistic. Some participants to the drafting of the charter rejected the novel charge; the French participant, for example, called the aggressive war charge "a creation of four people who are just four people" (Douglas 2005: 52). Moreover, beyond the retroactivity problem, the charge of aggression suffered from definitional blurriness. Where other criminal categories like war crimes and crimes against humanity enjoy the possibility of objective determination, the crime of aggression suffers heavily from the challenge of perspective, where one party's "aggression" is another's "self-defense".[17] The eventual defeat of the charge of aggression before the IMT was so total that the charge was largely abandoned following the IMT (and related American trials). Only now, after two decades of practice before the International Criminal Court (ICC), is the crime of aggression being provisionally considered.[18]

After aggression, the second argument developed by the US prosecution at the IMT, "conspiracy," was particularly contentious. The conspiracy charge was developed as a means of bringing the German treatment of German Jews within the scrutiny of the IMT (Bloxham 2001; Douglas 2005). Conspiracy is not generally recognized in the civil law tradition, however;[19] the French and Soviet representatives vigorously resisted its inclusion during the drafting of the charter (Meltzer 2004). According to one participant in the proceedings, the IMT judges "took a conservative view" on the conspiracy charges (King 2009); ultimately, they acquitted fourteen of the twenty-two defendants charged with conspiracy.

"Crimes against humanity" was in many respects the boldest invention of the IMT. The phrase originated during World War I, when the Allied powers issued a statement decrying the Armenian genocide as a "crime against humanity" (Schabas 2011). At the end of World War I, the US rejected proposed trials of "violations of the laws of humanity" as legally imprecise, however (Cryer 2014). At the IMT, the charge was meant to encompass the violence visited by states on their own nationals: such violence fell outside the legal category of "war crimes," and was understood even at the time as an important part of the story of Nazi atrocity. Moreover, the particular horrors that are described by the "catch-all" category of crimes against humanity emerged juridically from the IMT's process. So although the prosecution's case at

16 Judgment, page 220, available at http://avalon.law.yale.edu/imt/12-04-45.asp. See also Clark 2007.

17 Self-defense is of course permissible under international law; this is recognized, for example, in the UN Charter under Article 51.

18 ICC-ASP/16/Res.5 December 14, 2017 "Activation of the jurisdiction of the Court over the crime of aggression." See also ICC ASP Working Group on the Crime of Aggression September 5, 2006, ICC-ASP/5/SWGCA/INF.1, available at https://crimeofaggression.info/documents/6/2006_Princeton.pdf (discussing content of the charge).

19 See further discussion in Chapter 3.

the IMT centered on the waging of aggressive war, the sentences imposed by the IMT reflected an acknowledgment of the larger horrors attending World War II. Defendants found guilty of conspiracy and crimes against peace but not war crimes or crimes against humanity were sentenced to prison terms; those found guilty of crimes against humanity were sentenced to death (Douglas 2005).

In addition to setting out the charges that the IMT could hear, the charter circumscribed possible defenses. Defendants were not permitted to challenge "the Tribunal, its members . . . or their alternates";[20] defendants did not enjoy immunity based on their official position;[21] and following orders was not a complete defense (though it might be considered in mitigation of punishment).[22] In its judgment, the tribunal also rejected attempts at using obedience to national law and *tu quoque* ("you too," which uses examples of similar crimes committed by the other side to defend the legitimacy of a defendant's actions) by defendants.[23]

Thus while the charter governing the IMT and the IMT's judgment might be said to have "wove[n] together all the different and separate strands of the nascent international human rights and humanitarian law" (Martin 2006: 5), crimes against peace (or the waging of aggressive war), crimes against humanity, and conspiracy were all crimes for which there was little precedent. Their articulation at the IMT represented a novel construction of legal categories. Moreover, the application of these categories against individuals constituted a novel application of international law, heretofore applied to sovereign states and not individual actors.[24]

C The IMT's Legal Legacy

One of the organs of the newly minted postwar United Nations was the International Law Commission (ILC).[25] The ILC was tasked with "codifying" international law, a long-imagined project. In 1950, the ILC set out the "Nuremberg Principles," a codification of the crimes and norms recognized by the IMT.[26] This document was developed from the IMT charter and judgment, and did not draw on the example or jurisprudence of the IMTFE at Tokyo (Bassiouni 2011: 171).

20 Article 3, Charter of the International Military Tribunal, available at http://avalon.law.yale.edu/imt/imtconst.asp

21 Article 7, Charter of the International Military Tribunal, available at http://avalon.law.yale.edu/imt/imtconst.asp

22 Article 8, Charter of the International Military Tribunal, available at http://avalon.law.yale.edu/imt/imtconst.asp

23 *Judgment,* in 1 Trial of the Major War Criminals Before the International Military Tribunal, Nuremberg, November 14, 1945–October 1, 1946.

24 There is one exception to this statement, which is that prior to the IMT, international law had governed the treatment of pirates as individuals operating outside sovereign borders and control.

25 UN resolution 174 II 21 November 1947, available at http://legal.un.org/docs/?symbol=A/RES/174(II)

26 *Yearbook of the International Law Commission*, 1950, vol. II, para. 97, available at http://legal.un.org/ilc/texts/instruments/english/draft_articles/7_1_1950.pdf

Leila Sadat (2015: 5) has paraphrased the Nuremberg Principles as "eschew[ing] collective responsibility in favour of individual criminal responsibility; provid[ing] that no human being (even a head of state or other responsible government official) is above the law with respect to the most serious crimes of concern to humanity as a whole." While the Nuremberg Principles are frequently referenced today, the declaratory document itself is mostly a treatise frozen in time. For example, it cannot be said that the Nuremberg Principles present a "codification" of crimes when the crimes therein recognized were laid out by the IMT charter and rejected in the IMT judgment, such as conspiracy and aggression.[27] Seventy years later, several of the Nuremberg Principles remain poorly or only partially operationalized in international criminal law, and some of those crimes that were not contentious for the IMT (such as sovereign immunity) are facing growing contemporary pushback.[28]

The more powerful legal legacy of the IMT is the use of a legal instrument to address social violence, and the individualization of state-sponsored crime. This broadening of the reach of international law, no longer recognizing the boundaries of sovereignty and empowered to try individuals, combined with the suggestion that the rule of law was a possible and preferable response to social upheaval, constitutes the revolution occasioned by the IMT. The "true spirit" of this revolution was "to find a legal response for man's inhumanity to man by following the due process of law and ascribing individual liability" (Burchard 2006: 801). And this legacy, unlike the particularities of the IMT's legal categorizations, has taken firm hold. Following the IMT at Nuremberg, it became possible to sentence individuals for crimes committed in service to their state.

More centrally, and more problematically, the IMT bequeathed a legal legacy suggesting that the importance of core crimes, or their recognition by a tribunal, could trump established processes attendant to law. These processes are central to the construction of law as "justice" and not merely "power" or punishment.[29] Yet the importance of the IMT's work in punishing individuals for acts argued to be universally understood as criminal was seen as an adequate pardon for its overtly politicized processes, and its violation of principles of legality. From this perspective, the IMT emerges as the institution that made it possible to know about Nazi atrocity, and to recognize such atrocity as criminal. In this way, the IMT's legal legacy is inextricably linked to its social and historical legacy.

[27] See further discussion of "aggression" and the Nuremberg Principles as applied in modern ICL in Tomuschat 2006.

[28] This can be seen, for example, in difficulties the ICC has experienced in asserting jurisdiction over sovereigns, and the African Union's formulation of Amendments to the Malabo Protocol recommending an African court in response to this dispute.

[29] This argument is explored in greater detail in Chapter 2 when considering the non-derogability of international criminal law.

D The IMT as Historian

The IMT and its related processes are popularly understood as laying the foundation for modern Germany. At one level, this story has become true through its own mythology: the IMT narrative consists of Allied powers asserting rule-of-law solutions over a vanquished Germany and modern Germany tells this same story. Yet data points along a historical axis beginning with the end of the war indicate a much more varied narrative among Germans about Germany, the war, the occupation, and German guilt. In other words, the Western narrative – wherein the Allies/West were committed to the rule of law above vengeance or retribution – has stayed constant and the German narrative regarding Germany's place in the West has altered so as to become incorporated with this Western narrative.

There are two claims made regarding the capacity of the IMT as a historian that factor prominently in the argument that ICTs are valuable as historians, a second-order function for ICTs identified in the international criminal justice template. First, it is asserted that the IMT's work in gathering and preserving Nazi documents has made these materials available to future generations: without the IMT, the argument goes, these documents might well have been lost, or at the very least, less well known. The second argument is that the trials themselves established credible historical records. The evidence from the actual experience of the IMT, however, challenges both of these suppositions.

More than 100,000 German documents were reviewed in preparation for the Nuremberg Trial, of which approximately 4,000 were entered as exhibits. Millions of feet of film were examined, together with 28,000 photographs, and 1,800 were used as trial exhibits (Douglas 2005). The organized, bureaucratic nature of the Third Reich, combined with the necessity of showing connections between orders and acts in order to support the conspiracy charge, made this rich documentation central to the Nuremberg proceedings. This documentary trove, assembled for the purposes of prosecution, has become part of the narrative of the value of the Nuremberg Tribunals. By this reckoning, the prosecution organized documents that might otherwise have been lost or destroyed, therefore making our knowledge of the Nazi war machine possible. These valuable documents form the foundation of our understanding of the Nazi regime and Nazi criminality, and without the Nuremberg process, it follows, they would not have been preserved and would not be available for study today.

The Nazis were particularly organized and thorough as regards the historical record of their crimes. We cannot know what might have happened to this historical record had there been no tribunal, and indeed it is possible, though it seems hardly probable, that the records might have been lost. There is another side to this observation, however: the threat of a tribunal, or retribution based on documentary evidence, can result in the concerted destruction of documents. In the case of Japan, for example, two weeks elapsed between Japanese surrender and Allied occupation, and Japan's skies were reportedly black with smoke from the mass documentary burnings.[30]

More subtle, more problematic, and more contested is the question of what *kinds* of history are produced by ICTs. In *Eichmann in Jerusalem*, Hannah Arendt critiqued the use of the defendant Eichmann to construct the Israeli state. Arendt (1963/2010: 251) famously iterated:

> The purpose of the trial is to render justice, and nothing else; even the noblest ulterior purposes – "the making of a record of the Hitler regime … " can only detract from the law's main business: to weigh the charges brought against the accused, to render judgment and to mete out due punishment.

This rendering of "justice" is constrained by the charges brought. The charges are in turn constrained by the parties' capacities to match extant law to demonstrable fact. At the IMT, this played out in a prosecution strategy designed to prove that Germany engaged in crimes against peace by waging an aggressive war. Although the extent and particular focus of Nazi criminality against European Jewry was known at the war's end, the legal and political possibilities of making a case along these lines appeared less certain (less winnable) to the prosecution. In other words, the novel charge of waging aggressive war, doctrinally situated in a violation of the 1928 Kellogg–Briand treaty, was arguably the least risky option from a juridical point of view (Douglas 2005). Crimes against humanity, for example, represented a real stretch for international law, comprising a finding of *individual criminal liability* for a category of crimes that had been specifically rejected as too vague by the United States following World War I. The inherently conservative, backwards-looking nature of legal practice argued against such "progressive," novel categorizations.

Bringing a case at law means trying to tell the *easiest* or *most winnable* story (as conscribed by existing law), not necessarily the most central or significant story; this is perhaps the most central manner in which courts differ from historians. While it is true that courts can function as "epistemic engines" (Holtermann 2017: 207), how such content measures up as "history" remains debated, and debatable. First, there are important distinctions in how historians and courts seek, clarify, and utilize knowledge. These epistemological distinctions build a distance between historians, who theorize "in the broader frame of probabilities" (Evans 2002: 330), and courts seeking proof beyond a reasonable doubt. Second, there is the problem of objectivity; courts, particularly courts operating in common-law jurisdictions, are presented with information designed to make the case for a particular perspective. International law theorist Martti Koskenniemi (2002: 25) states the problem thus:

30 This is noted in the fascinating "conversations" between Antonio Cassese and Bert V. Röling, the Dutch appointee to the IMFTE, which Cassese later published (with Röling 1993).

> [N]o matter how much judges may seek to proceed in good faith towards their judgments, the context of the trial cannot – unlike the history seminar – be presumed to manifest good faith on everybody's part. This is not a disinterested enquiry by a group of external observers but part of the history it seeks to interpret. Much is at stake for the protagonists – that is the nature of the trial – and no truth can remain sacred within it.

For Koskenniemi, the distinction between law and history is one of motivation. The motivation lying behind the production of historical fact and theory at law lies in each side's desire to win. This motivation thus creates an interest in outcome that categorically prevents objectivity.

There is also the question of armchair history, i.e., the history that comprises the content of mainstream discourse. For example, in his excellent study on the impact and reception of the trials following World War II, *Genocide on Trial* (2001), Donald Bloxham invites the reader to take the following challenge: name the six death camps run by the Nazis in World War II. If you think of Bergen-Belsen, Buchenwald, or Dachau (as opposed to the correct list: Auschwitz, Belzec, Chelmno, Majdanek, Sobibór, and Treblinka) that is likely because the first camps, located in Germany, were the subject of Allied prosecutions. Bergen-Belsen, Buchenwald, and Dachau were Nazi work camps: they were harsh, brutal, often deadly, but potentially survivable places. The actual death camps, all located in Poland,[31] were very different from work camps, notably in that the potential for survival was very low. Because death camps did not become the subjects of Western judicial intervention (in as much as they were located in Poland and fell under Soviet control at the end of the war), the reality of the Nazi murder system was obscured for a non-specialist audience. Bloxham shows that this historical reality has been obfuscated by Allied trials that focused on crimes against humanity visited upon Allied soldiers, in events largely occurring in Western Europe in Nazi work camps, thereby obfuscating the "true" history of the Nazi war machine, which is fundamentally a history of camps designed to permit no survivors.

Finally, the most significant element of historical obfuscation may be the charges *not* brought by the IMT. The Allies sought to avoid triggering *tu quoque* defenses, which were not admissible at the tribunal and which moreover threatened to muddy the waters of the Allied narrative. Thus crimes of which the Allied nations were also guilty were deleted from consideration. The Soviet massacre of thousands of Polish officers at Katyn in 1940, the Allied bombing of Dresden in 1944 with catastrophic civilian casualties – these were acts that the Allies did not want revisited or referenced at the IMT, and those wartime atrocities with too obvious an Allied mirror image (such as German bombing raids or Nazi aggression against Poland) were strategically omitted from indictment and prosecution (Overy 2003; Weingartner

[31] See www.jewishvirtuallibrary.org/jsource/Holocaust/cclist.html (accessed March 4, 2012).

2011). This has a direct impact on discourse concerning the waging of, and suffering occasioned by, World War II.

E The IMT and German "Reconciliation"

The IMT's final significant legacy is today's democratic Germany, a human rights leader among the most rights-conscientious nations. Germany has arguably done more than any other state to address its responsibility for the atrocities committed by its government. Beyond public gestures like reparations and memorialization, Germany tells the same story of World War II as its neighbors, a unified narrative[32] that has made projects like the European Union possible. In modern retellings, the IMT emerges as central to this narrative, a building block for shared liberal, democratic, rule-of-law values. The history of German reconciliation, however, tells a different story about the IMT's reception in Germany prior to the modern era.

The IMT is understood to function as a form of reconciliation, an institution producing a shared narrative. Thus we must briefly consider not the fable but the fact of postwar reconstruction, lustration, and trials. This history shows that the deeply remorseful Germany we know today developed first in the 1970s, encouraged by a new, querulous generation informed by a number of critical commentaries, central among them the miniseries, shown on television, *Holocaust* (Kaes 1992). The immediate postwar world was far from "reconciled." The following section considers the institutional and social elements of postwar German reconstruction to illustrate important challenges to the Nuremberg legacy.

As a first consideration, we look at war crimes trials. War crimes trials in Germany included not only the IMT, but also twelve criminal law trials at Nuremberg following the war,[33] as well as countless Allied prosecutions of war criminals. From 1946 to 1949, Allied powers held hundreds of war crimes trials in the sectors of vanquished Germany under their control, sentencing thousands of defendants to jail and hundreds to death. Extracts of several hundred cases, "selected . . . based on

[32] Borneman (2002: 282) defines reconciliation as "to render no longer opposed." Jacqueline Nießer distinguishes between reconciliations of "coexistence," "collaboration," and "taking mutual responsibility." "After Reconciliation. On the Closure of the ICTY in The Hague" December 18, 2017, available at https://erinnerung.hypotheses.org/1640. In the German context, "reconciliation" itself is a skewed and cynical category, given that the Nazi project to eliminate European Jewry was too successful, with those surviving German Jews choosing to live outside of Germany (Sa'adah 2006). *Model(ing) Justice* describes political reconciliation as a shared narrative, where singular, unified narratives have the power to unite once-opposed forces.

[33] These trials were conducted by the US alone between 1946 and 1949, and were grouped by subject: there was, for example, a doctors trial, a lawyers trial (immortalized in the film *Judgment at Nuremberg*), the IG Farben trial (considering the manufacture of Zyklon B), and the Einsatzengruppen trial (trying twenty-four heads of military groups that murdered one million Jews in Eastern Europe before the death camps were constructed). Major War Criminals (USA, France, UK, and USSR v. Hermann Goering *et al.* 1945–1946), available at http://avalon.law.yale.edu/imt/12-04-45.asp. They are typically referred to as NMTs, to distinguish them from the IMT.

the major points of municipal and international law that were raised and settled during the trials as well as the potential for the greatest legal interest," were collected in fifteen volumes by the UN War Crimes Commission immediately following the war.[34] These UNWCC extracts and reports serve as primary sources of "international law" and are referenced by contemporary ICTs. There are ongoing attempts to widen this reference base by digitizing other postwar jurisprudence.[35]

There are several issues surrounding this "baseline" of international criminal law. First, there is the technicality that such law fails to be "international" (Jain 2014). While the IMT was a multinational project applying procedure it created itself, later military trials applied the national law of the nationalities that organized them. There is a deeper and more challenging objection to this case law, however, which is that it reflects a problematically particularized perspective: it is more clearly political, in its representation of particular interests, than it is legal. The prosecutors and judges who sat in judgment of these cases were representatives of the victorious Allied nations, addressing crimes committed (in large part) against Allied soldiers. These cases were frequently retributive and the jurisprudence is marked by a palpable desire for vengeance. Chapter 2 looks at one emblematic case, *Velpke*, as an example of the justice challenge evidenced by this jurisprudence.

In addition to trials, other forms of punishment were applied to postwar Germany. The Allies oversaw an extensive "denazification" project, consisting of the "internment of Germans, who, though not guilty of any specific crimes, are considered to be dangerous to Allied purposes" (Cohen 2006b: 69). Opinions among and within Allied governments differed as to the extent that ordinary Germans should be made to feel the weight and horror of the war. The administrative reality cautioned against an extensive purge; late in 1945, General George Patton, acting governor of the province of Bavaria, was quoted as saying, "more than half the German people were Nazis and we would be in a hell of a fix if we removed all Nazi Party members from office" (Axelrod 2009). At the same time, political sentiment – echoed in the IMT's insistence that German guilt *towards Allied actors* be recognized for posterity – demanded a reckoning; Eisenhower removed Patton over his comment.

In total, in the sector under US authority, more than thirteen million Germans were reviewed regarding their wartime affiliations, and three million were charged with a variety of offenses (Beschloss 2003). While internment was conceptually designed as administrative and not punitive, harsh camp conditions, particularly during the hard winter of 1945–1946, blurred such distinctions. Moreover, Soviet work camps, for example, are estimated to have had a 33 percent mortality rate,

[34] Law Reports of Trials of War Criminals Selected and Prepared by the United Nations War Crimes Commission 1947–1949, available at www.loc.gov/rr/frd/Military_Law/law-reports-trials-war-criminals.html (accessed March 3, 2013).

[35] For example, there is an ongoing project by David Cohen and Beth van Schack at Stanford University.

making such sentences more likely to result in death than criminal sentences handed down by Allied tribunals.

As part of the "re-education" effort that was at the heart of the denazification of the Allied occupation of Germany, Germans were to be made aware of the full scope of the horrors of World War II and their collective responsibility therefor. To that end, numerous forms of re-education propaganda were created. In the immediate aftermath of the war, the US Army's "Psychological Warfare Branch" launched a campaign to familiarize the German people with the atrocities committed by Nazi Germany. Morris Janowitz, writing in the *American Journal of Sociology* about his work as an intelligence officer in the Psychological Warfare Branch, states that "the development of a sense of collective responsibility was considered a prerequisite to any long-term education of the German people" (Janowitz 1946: 141). Films such as the concentration camp documentary *Die Todesmühlen* were screened throughout Germany to acquaint Germans with the truth of concentration camps. Propaganda posters were hung showing piles of human remains with large captions reading, "Diese Schandtaten: Eure Schuld!" (These Atrocities: Your Fault!) The propaganda effort was extensive, utilizing radio and German press.

Janowitz and his colleagues measured the impact on a cross-section of one hundred Germans one month into the propaganda campaign, in June 1945. They concluded that before the end of the war there was "good evidence that the German people were . . . ignorant of the details of concentration camps in Germany," finding that psychological repression and the desire to avoid learning the unacceptable, together with the totalitarian control of information under Nazi rule, likely shielded most Germans from learning about the systematic extermination occurring in concentration camps (Janowitz 1946: 142). Thus the Allied campaign to acquaint Germans with the facts of German atrocities presented information that had not been known with precision or certitude by a majority of the German populace before the end of the war.

Janowitz found that while a majority of German respondents believed the Allied propaganda campaign – i.e., they believed the veracity of the facts presented by the Allies regarding German atrocities committed in the war – this did not result in admissions of guilt.[36] When asked who bore responsibility for atrocities, individual Germans overwhelmingly pointed to the Nazi Party or Nazi leaders. Respondents argued that the ruthlessness of the Nazi regime prevented opposition, and that individuals were powerless against it, or that Nazi atrocities were inevitable consequences of war. Although Janowitz found one "gap in the protective wall which Germans have erected to keep out all feeling of guilt about atrocities" in the question

36 Interestingly, while Janowitz's respondents largely did not resist Allied propaganda, respondents still demonstrated only a passing familiarity with facts. For example, most respondents listed the number of people killed in concentration camps in the tens of thousands, only a few spoke of one hundred thousand or more, and "one or two Social Democrats were able to conjure up the phrase "millions" (Janowitz 1946: 143).

of the treatment of Jews, a facet of Nazi rule he characterized as "a fact that even the most simple-minded of Germans could not hide from his own consciousness," (1946: 145) even here, an awareness of Jewish persecution did not lead to a sense of individual responsibility. Janowitz cites as an example the absence of German assistance in rehabilitating concentration camp victims in the aftermath of the war; those Germans living in the vicinity of concentration camps assisted victims in the camps only after having been ordered by military commanders to do so. Ultimately, Janowitz's survey found that exposure to the facts of German atrocity during the war did not increase political participation among the population.

Where perhaps Janowitz's immediate postwar data can be explained by postwar numbness, an absence of information, or even the daily obstacles to survival that might have usurped attention or energy, the 1955 survey examined by Beschloss (2003) is not subject to any similar line of explication. Beschloss argues that the survey shows an absence of guilt among Germans.[37] In the survey, Germans reported that the pre-war period was the best time in recent history. Of Hitler and the Nazi Party, the survey indicated that a majority found they had good ideas that were poorly executed (Beschloss 2003: 279). Donald Bloxham (2001: 138) similarly observed that propaganda material, such as photos from concentration camps, often caused distrust, disgust, or even angry emotional reactions, unless such materials suggested *German* suffering.

Like denazification, US "reconstruction" efforts in postwar Germany were overwhelmingly punitive. While Stimson's temperate vision had obtained as regards the IMT, Morgenthau's unforgiving plan was put in place to shepherd Germany's "transition." The Morgenthau Plan advocated the crushing of German capacity in many spheres, and guided the US occupation policy in place from 1945 to 1947.[38] Under JCS 1067, which applied only to the US zone of occupation, the US worked towards the "industrial dismantlement" (Dietrich 2013: 93) of Germany. The period was characterized by rampant food shortages, some of which were deliberate: American soldiers, for example, were told to destroy food rather than give it to German civilians, a policy that also applied to soldiers' wives (Davidson 1997: 85). Care packages and other foreign sources of food were not allowed into the country throughout at least the first year following the war.[39] Estimates place daily caloric intake for adults at between 1,000 and 1,500 calories for the years 1945–1947. Child mortality is estimated to have skyrocketed to 65 percent in some areas (Wiggers 2003: 280). Over the difficult winter of 1945–1946, with Soviet influence rising, the US viceroy charged with overseeing JCS 1067 remarked, "There is no choice between

[37] But see Gordon 1984 (who argues that difficult phrasing and inconsistent results between survey questions caution against drawing broad conclusions).

[38] Joint Chiefs of Staff directive 1067 (JCS 1067).

[39] This official US policy was supported by a not insubstantial portion of the US public: a 1945 poll found that one-sixth of Americans polled thought that even in the case of starvation, Germans should not be given food. NORC 1945: 23 (quoted in Merritt 1995).

becoming a communist on 1500 calories and a believer in democracy on 1000 calories."[40] This policy of "slow starvation" (Fossedal 1993) finally led to riots in the winter of 1947, and an eventual change of US policy, due in part to growing US recognition of the need not to lose the campaign for the "hearts and minds" of the German populace.

The emerging Cold War led to significant changes in US policy towards Germany, as the conquered enemy became a potential ally. In 1948 the punitive JCS 1067 was replaced with a more evenhanded directive, JCS 1779, which came to be known as the celebrated Marshall Plan. Under JCS 1799, more than 90 percent of the Germans originally purged under JCS 1067 were rehabilitated. Cold War concerns also led to the rearmament of West Germany in the three zones occupied by the Western Allies. In 1949, German self-rule under the Bundestag was established, and Konrad Adenauer was elected as Chancellor. Adenauer advocated a policy known as "putting the past behind us," a *Vergagenheitspolitik* (politics of the past) that recognized that "in order to avoid a renewal of German nationalism and Nazism, economic recovery and political democratization [needed to] take priority over a judicial confrontation with the crimes of the Nazi past" (Herf 1997: 209). War crimes trials continued under German self-rule but were notoriously lenient. Between 1950 and 1962, 30,000 former Nazis were investigated, nearly 13,000 were indicted, approximately 5,400 were tried, and 75 percent of these were acquitted. Of those sentenced, only 155 were convicted of murder. Legal historian Rebecca Wittmann (2005) attributes this poor conviction rate to the legal change that, in 1951, prohibited the use of Control Council Law No. 10 in German courts. The result of this was that international law was no longer available to German courts; prosecutions against war criminals proceeded under the German penal code, which under the particularities of the German murder statute made prosecutions particularly difficult. At the famous Frankfurt/ Auschwitz trials of 1963–1965, eight hundred people were investigated, twenty were indicted, and seven were found guilty of murder (Pendas 2006). At the conclusion of these trials, 57 percent of the public surveyed said further Nazi trials should not be held (Kinstler 2017).

Furthermore, at the beginning of the 1950s, "both politicians and the public intervened sweepingly – and as if doing so were a self-evident thing – for war criminals and Nazis condemned by the Allies," demanding their release from prison and rehabilitation (Frei 2002: xiv). This popular push resulted in the early release from prison of nearly all those defendants who had been jailed under Allied war crimes trials by the mid-to-late 1950s (Cohen 2006b); Nazi soldiers also had their pensions reinstated (Kinstler 2017). Frei (2002) estimates that eight hundred thousand people benefited from amnesty laws passed during this time. Indeed, the

40 General Lucious Clay, quoted in "Marshall & Time's Man of the Year," available at www.marshall foundation.org/blog/marshall-times-man-year/

Eichmann trial in Israel a decade later provided a shocking window into the quiet, undisturbed lives some former Nazis were living, even (and especially) in Germany (Arendt 1963/2010).

It was during the 1960s and 1970s that the Western narrative of German responsibility began to develop in Germany (Power 2002; Herf 1997). Levy and Sznaider (2005: 64) argue that selective memory was necessary to construct myths that would serve the budding democracy. Germans opposed the Allied project of "postwar judicial reckoning or frank public memory" (Herf 1997) and the response to the IMT and related trials following the war was negative. Due to the political problem of "victor's justice," it was not possible for the Allied initiatives to be perceived as impartial. As one observer noted, "The trials were characterized by an intermingling of military, political and purely criminal events in a manner which rendered it virtually impossible for an unprejudiced observer to obtain the facts needed to unravel the tangle of evidence" (Rückerl 1979).[41]

Ian Baruma (1994) locates the turning point in German acceptance of guilt as the broadcast of the American miniseries *Holocaust* in 1979. By the time Daniel Goldhagen produced his 1996 book *Hitler's Willing Executioners: Ordinary Germans and the Holocaust*, the German collective memory was well established: the book, arguing that German anti-Semitism was the driving rationale behind the Holocaust, and that only Germans could have perpetrated the Holocaust, was a bestseller in Germany. Setting his argument against Christopher Browning's (1992), *Ordinary Men: Reserve Police Battalion 101 and the Final Solution in Poland* (in which Browning explores peer pressure and the human need to belong in a group as explanations for Einsatzgruppen atrocities), and not engaging with other prominent Holocaust scholars, such as Raul Hilberg (1985) (who set out a structuralist explanation of the Holocaust as a product of bureaucratic inertia) or Zygmunt Bauman (2001) (who argued that the Holocaust is a prime realization of Weberian bureaucratic rationality), Goldhagen argues that Nazi actors faced neither threat of death nor promise of promotion as regards their murderous work, and that only a hatred specific to Jews – which hatred is itself singular to Germans – explains their actions.

In addition to its problematic tautological aspects, Goldhagen's work is challenged in its own terms by scholarship such as Jan Gross's *Neighbors* (2001), which discusses the fate of Jews in a Polish village in an attempt to demonstrate the depth of Polish anti-Semitism. From a public policy perspective, Goldhagen's work is troubling: arguing that the German people, collectively, are singularly, rabidly inhuman looks too much like the ideology underlying the Nazi project itself.[42] Yet perhaps what is most striking about Goldhagen's work is the popular reception it enjoyed in Germany. The German public's hunger for Goldhagen's theory indicates the scale at which a unified narrative obtains in Germany. Such a reception indicates the

[41] Quoted in Wittmann 2005: 25.

[42] In fact, Goldhagen's work even explicitly goes this far, urging readers not to mistake Germans for "us . . . normal American youth" (Goldhagen 1996: 27).

success of German re-engagement with the West, a project that sets the model for other transitional justice projects.

The above history, well documented by area scholars and historians, has seemingly made few inroads into the popular collective memory of the period, at least not for an English-speaking audience. The Nuremberg legacy thus represents an incomplete popular history, whereby the Marshall Plan of 1948 is well known but the US postwar policy JCS 1067, under which Germans were systematically and deliberately starved, is not; the US trial against Einsatzgruppen criminals (who shot hundreds of thousands of Jews and political prisoners in Eastern Europe) is known, but US agreement to release nearly all the convicted within a few years is not; and the massive postwar push to denazify Germany is known, but the quiet, successful German pushback to pardon and reinstate even very high-ranking Nazis is not.

II THE IGNORED ICT OF THE IMT ERA: THE TOKYO TRIBUNAL

At the same time that the Allies put Nazis on trial, a similar trial was convened in Tokyo. Unlike the IMT at Nuremberg, which has served as a template for the development of international criminal law, the IMTFE (or Tokyo Trial) has been largely discarded as a source of international law and as a jurisprudential model. The IMTFE's clumsy mixture of politics and law (from the decision not to try Emperor Hirohito to the US determination not to raise issues of Japanese germ warfare), the moral gray zone of a war crimes trial that would not touch the US decision to use atomic bombs on a civilian population, and the several concurrent and dissenting opinions among the international panel of judges serving at the tribunal have all added to the IMTFE's decades-long shadow position in history. There have been tepid attempts to "rehabilitate" the IMTFE in recent times,[43] owing in part to larger projects designed to unearth sources of international criminal law for modern consideration and possible application. Referenced only very sparingly in international criminal law decisions and legal guidelines, the IMTFE is an ugly stepsister in the family of international criminal law institutions.

Unlike the IMT Nuremberg, a tribunal comprised of four justices from the four victorious nations, the IMTFE was a substantially international tribunal. Eleven justices served on the tribunal, all from different nations. US General Douglas MacArthur, Supreme Commander of the Allied Forces and head of the Allied administration of postwar Japan, appointed the American Judge John P. Higgins,

[43] Totani (2008: 4) asserts that the IMTFE today provides "useful precedents" and that "the very trial that has been thoroughly discredited in the eyes of the Japanese public ... is gaining international recognition as an important precursor of international prosecutorial efforts today." The other excellent aspects of Totani's monograph notwithstanding, I believe the meager and unenthusiastic references to the IMTFE in contemporary international criminal jurisprudence do not bear this assertion out.

along with the chief prosecutor, the American Joseph Keenan.[44] MacArthur also issued the declaration establishing the IMTFE, as well as its rules of procedure.[45]

The Trial began May 3, 1946 and lasted two and a half years. The IMTFE recognized "categories" of war criminals, and concerned itself only with what it called "Category A" defendants, those who stood accused of "crimes against peace" (i.e., the waging of aggressive war). Those defendants charged with crimes against peace were also eligible to stand trial for war crimes and crimes against humanity at the IMTFE. Category "B" and "C" offenders not charged with crimes against peace could not stand trial before the IMTFE. There were 80 "Category A" accused jailed by the Allies.

Of the twenty-eight defendants appearing before the IMTFE, seven received death sentences, sixteen life sentences (thirteen of whom were released between 1954 and 1956),[46] two served jail terms, two died during trial, and one was found unfit for trial. Unlike the IMT Nuremberg, the final verdict was not unanimous. Eight justices joined the majority (with Justices Webb and Jaranilla writing separate opinions) and three contested the judgment through written dissents (Justices Pal, Bernard, and Röling).

Of the three dissents, Pal's is the most significant from a transitional justice point of view. Fellow IMTFE Judge Röling (with Cassese 1993) reports that Pal arrived at the IMTFE determined to dissent from a majority guilty verdict, and that this position made it impossible for the judges to produce a unanimous judgment. In an opinion numbering more than 1,200 pages, Pal argued for the acquittal of all defendants.[47] He did not entirely whitewash Japanese war crimes, but instead generally resisted Western categorizations of Japan as the evil actor. Pal, an Indian national, vehemently opposed Western colonialism, and used his dissent to advance an "Asia for Asians" narrative, arguing that pre-war Japan had only done what Western powers had typically done in Asia – which was to colonize, sometimes brutally – but that Japan, unlike Western nations, had more of a claim to moral right for such colonialization, since they were Asian, like their subjects.

1 *The IMTFE as Norm Maker, Historian, and Reconciler*

There is no Nuremberg-like 'legacy' for the IMTFE, no narrative wherein this tribunal pronounced progressive law, established a credible historical record, and reconciled bitter foes. Rather, the IMTFE's fate in popular discourse seemed sealed

44 Ten associate prosecutors were provided by the assisting nations as well.

45 Bassiouni (1995: 587) argues that this distinction – that the IMTFE was created by military order whereas the IMT at Nuremberg was created by treaty – helps explain the IMT's greater salience as an instrument of international criminal law.

46 In this respect, the IMTFE followed the IMT Nuremberg successor trials.

47 Röling also reports that Pal stopped attending court sessions, and missed more than one-third of the courtroom proceedings (which of course would have been necessary in order to write a 1,200-page dissent in the time available) (Röling and Cassese 1993).

by Richard Minear's *Victor's Justice: The Tokyo War Crimes Trial* (1971). As the title suggests, Minear's condemnation of the institution is complete, writing, "We have found its foundation in international law to be shaky. We have seen that its process was seriously flawed. We have examined the verdict's inadequacy as history" (1971: 180). We can add to this a failure to assist in reconciliation, the third pillar of the international criminal justice template. For example, there has been ongoing political strife regarding Japanese depictions – particularly in textbooks – of Japanese acts at Nanking in China (the "rape of Nanking"), and of the Japanese system of sexual slavery ("comfort women").[48] In 1993, in response to emerging victims' narratives and demands for a response regarding the comfort women system and Japan's role in these atrocities, the Japanese government issued an apology known as the "Kono" statement.[49] In 2006, however, Japan's Prime Minister Abe seemingly rescinded the state's apology, demanding an "objective" look at the comfort women issue.[50] In March 2007, Abe stated that "the material discovered by the government contained no documentation that directly indicated the so-called coercive recruitment by the military or the authorities."[51] By way of comparison, it would be difficult to imagine an equivalent expression regarding World War II atrocity made by a German leader.

Pal's written dissent was actually outlawed for distribution during the US occupation, but in 1952 his dissent was brought out in publication. Pal remained a hero in Japan for the remainder of his life; there is a monument dedicated to him at the Yasakuni Shrine in Tokyo.[52] Moreover, the ideas he expressed continue to enjoy a place in Japanese political life. So while Japan is also a successful modern democracy, it does not enjoy the same singularity of narrative regarding World War II that Germans and other Western nations do. Disjointed narratives – surrounding both history and territory – continue to plague Sino-Japanese relations.

The IMTFE was distinct from the IMT at Nuremberg in many ways, and did not produce a unanimous verdict. Yet it was nevertheless an ICT designed to shepherd a democratic transition, and its flaws, regarded through the lens of the international criminal justice template, are plain to see, so much so that it has been all but dismissed as international legal precedent, and is generally understood to be fatally flawed as a rule-of-law institution.

48 The Japanese government had a policy of "recruiting" women to provide sexual services to Japanese soldiers. This government practice was widespread and impacted populations throughout the Far East. Estimates of how many women were imprisoned in the comfort women system are contentious and entirely theoretical; figures ranging from 30,000 to 410,000 are cited.

49 August 4, 1993, "Statement by the Chief Cabinet Secretary Yohei Kono on the Result of the Study on the Issue of 'Comfort Women'," available at www.mofa.go.jp/policy/women/fund/state9308.html.

50 "Abe urges 'objective' look at sex slave apology, draws flak," *The Japan Times*, October 27, 2006.

51 These remarks drew strong international criticism, and the international response included a US congressional resolution recognizing Japan's responsibility for the comfort women system. H. Res. 121 July 30, 2007. In the House of Representatives, US, 110th Congress.

52 Photo available at www.flickr.com/photos/dgunn/3224087403/

III THE LONG SHADOW CAST BY THE IMT: CREATING THE ICTY

The Cold War stopped the progression of international criminal law; the Nuremberg Principles served as an intellectual basis for theoretical work towards an international criminal court, but the practicalities of the project were tabled. The human rights component of international humanitarian law, however, flourished. In addition to the Geneva Conventions of 1949, treaties signed by nearly every country on the planet and reaching the status of *jus cogens* law, a peremptory norm from which no derogation is permissible (Brownlie 1998), additional Protocols to the Geneva Conventions were negotiated, drafted, and entered into force. The Helsinki Committee, Amnesty International, and other human rights NGOs were established and prospered. The Council of Europe established a court in Strasbourg to implement its decisions, and from a handful of cases in the 1960s the European Court of Human Rights grew to a juggernaut handling hundreds of thousands of cases today. Joseph Weiler (1999) situates the inclusion of human rights notions and ideologies in cases in the 1970s before the European Court of Justice (the judicial arm of the European free trade treaties that eventually became the European Union) as foundational to the emergence of the modern European Union. The surging power of human rights discourse and institutions implementing and advancing it fed into a climate where, at the end of the Cold War, liberalism was synonymous with rule of law and human rights (Keating & Kaczmarska 2017).

International criminal law draws on the Kantian project of "cosmopolitan justice," and universalizes the possibility of a singular human rights standard. In the 1960s and 1970s, lawyers and activists "rediscovered" law's humanitarian capacity. In works like *A Theory of Justice* (Rawls 1971) and in the creation of organizations like Amnesty International and Helsinki Watch, law was set at the center of the discourse of fairness and political legitimacy. These supporters of law as insurer of human rights placed stock in law vesting at the level of the individual. This can be contrasted against realists, rationalists, and liberals who had always viewed international law and actions as a purview of the state far removed from individual rights constructions.

When war broke out in the former Yugoslavia in 1991, and reports of concentration camps and atrocities directed against civilians in Bosnia made news headlines in 1992, the decision to set up a tribunal to hear these cases, and to do so under the United Nations' peace and security mandate (Article 7), was nonetheless novel, non-obvious, and historic. At the passage of resolution 808, which established the ICTY, US Ambassador to the UN Madeleine Albright proclaimed the following:

> There is an echo in this Chamber today. The Nuremberg Principles have been reaffirmed. We have preserved the long-neglected compact made by the community of civilized nations 48 years ago in San Francisco to create the United Nations and enforce the Nuremberg Principles. The lesson that we are all accountable to international law may have finally taken hold in our collective memory. This will be no victor's tribunal. The only victor that will prevail in this endeavor is the truth.

> Unlike the world of the 1940s, international humanitarian law today is impressively codified, well understood, agreed upon and enforceable. The debates over the state of international law that so encumbered the Nuremberg Trials will not burden the Tribunal.[53]

Like the IMT before it, the ICTY was institutionally designed to operationalize norms into law, producing jurisprudence from ideology. The ICTY statute was only ten pages long in its first iteration, and famously "very thin" with respect to the guidance it gave judges and practitioners regarding legal content (Schabas 2011: 206). Additionally, the value of the ICTY was implicitly understood in terms of its impact as a historian and reconciler through its role in establishing an "official version" of events; this is the "truth" that Albright references in her remarks.[54]

A *Establishing the ICTY*

On September 25, 1991, responding to growing tensions in Yugoslavia, the United Nations Security Council passed resolution 713, affirming its "full support for the collective efforts for peace and dialogue in Yugoslavia." In July and August of 1992, the Security Council passed further resolutions condemning the conflict.[55] In October 1992, with resolution 780, the Security Council established a commission of experts to report to the Security Council regarding possible "grave breaches" of the Geneva Conventions.

To support the commission's work, the Security Council passed resolution 787 in November 1992, calling on the commission to "pursue actively its investigations [of] grave breaches ... and other violations of international humanitarian law." The commission included M. Cherif Bassiouni, a proponent of human rights who approached his role with an activist's zeal. Working outside of UN resources, Bassiouni raised $1.4 million from private organizations, and the commission accumulated 65,000 pages of documents and 300 hours of video tape describing 900 prison camps, 90 paramilitary groups, 1,500 rapes, and 150 mass graves in the former Yugoslavia (Bass 2000: 211). This material substantiated the ICTY's first indictments.

On February 9, 1993 the commission submitted its interim report to the Security Council, finding that grave breaches of the Geneva Conventions, perhaps amounting to genocide, were taking place in the former Yugoslavia, and recommending that an ad hoc tribunal be constituted (expert report paragraph 74). On February 22, 1993 the Security Council passed resolution

53 Madeleine Albright, Provisional Verbatim Record of the Three Thousand One Hundred and Seventy-Fifth Meeting, NYC, February 22, 1993, S/PV. 3175, February 22, 1993.

54 The ICTY, unlike its sister tribunal for Rwanda, established in 1994, does not explicitly mention "reconciliation" in its statute, however.

55 Security Council resolution 764 S/Res/764 (July 13, 1992) and Security Council resolution 771 S/Res/771 (August 13, 1993) respectively.

808.[56] The resolution "express[ed] once again [the Security Council's] grave alarm at continuing reports of widespread violations of international humanitarian law occurring within the territory of the former Yugoslavia," including reports of mass killings and the continuance of the practice of "ethnic cleansing" and found "that this situation constitutes a threat to international peace and security." Thus, "convinced that in the particular circumstances of the former Yugoslavia the establishment of an international tribunal would enable [persons to be brought to justice] and would contribute to the restoration and maintenance of peace," the Security Council recommended the establishment of "an international tribunal ... for the prosecution of persons responsible for serious violations of international humanitarian law committed in the territory of the former Yugoslavia since 1991" (resolution 808 point 1). In furtherance of this goal, resolution 808 requested that the Secretary-General submit, within sixty days, "a report on all the aspects of this matter, including specific proposals and where appropriate options for the effective and expeditious implementation of the decision [above]" (Id. Point 2). No further guidance was offered by the resolution.

While the public deliberations at the UN celebrated the nascent tribunal in ecstatic terms, the UN resolution calling for the ICTY left the details unconfirmed. The Secretary-General's (SG) requested report was prepared by the Office of Legal Affairs in New York.[57] The SG report considered the possibility of establishing such a tribunal based on treaty, which would have the advantage of the full participation of the states in question, but the heavy disadvantage of being debilitatingly time-consuming, with the further risk that the countries directly implicated – the emerging republics of the former Yugoslavia – would not ratify such a treaty. The SG report then considered the possibility of drafting or reviewing a statute for an international tribunal before the General Assembly, but again concluded that such action "would not be reconcilable with the urgency expressed by the Security Council in resolution 808."[58] Finally the SG report argued that under Article VII of the UN Charter, the Security Council *itself* had the capacity to establish mechanisms "aimed at restoring and maintaining international peace and security."[59] Since the tribunal was based on the Security Council's

56 Security Council resolution 808 S/Res/808 (February 22, 1993).

57 Report of the Secretary-General Pursuant to Paragraph 2 of Security Council resolution 808 (1993) S/25704, May 3, 1993 ("SG report"). The committee was headed by Carl-August Fleischhauer (Germany), who was assisted by Ralph Zacklin (UK), Larry Johnson (US), Virginia Morris (US), Daphna Shraga (Israel), and William Taubman (Libya). The names and citizenships of the Office of Legal Affairs committee are remarkable first in terms of the strong common-law tendency in the ICTY's initial procedure and second in terms of later scholarship on the subject. Zacklin, in particular, evoked public ire from both Bassiouni and ICTY Prosecutor Richard Goldstone for being "an obstructionist force." Following his appointment he published scholarship critical of the tribunal (Zacklin 2004).

58 SG report, para 21.

59 SG report, para 27.

peacekeeping authority, "the life span of the international tribunal would be linked to the restoration and maintenance of international peace and security in the territory of the former Yugoslavia."[60]

Several Security Council members expressed reservations. Russia enjoyed a traditional affinity with Serbia. Moreover, the development of any international precedent for prosecuting war crimes posed a potential general threat to Russia, in light of Russian activities in Chechnya and elsewhere. China adopted the SG report with the reservation that: "the International Tribunal established in the current manner can only be an ad hoc arrangement suited only to the special circumstances of the former Yugoslavia and shall not constitute any precedent."[61] France and Britain both had troops on the ground in Bosnia as part of the UN Protection Force, and thus feared that an aggressive or effective tribunal might jeopardize a settlement in Bosnia, by indicting leaders, or that their support of such a tribunal might put their troops at greater risk for retaliation on the ground.[62] Even strong proponents of the tribunal such as the US's UN Ambassador Madeleine Albright expressed doubt that the tribunal would ever arrest anyone, in a statement arguing that the tribunal would be effective "whether or not suspects can be taken into custody."[63] Nonetheless, on May 25, 1993 the SG report was unanimously adopted, without modification, by the Security Council.

The SG report contained, as an appendix, the ICTY Statute, a tidy document of just over ten pages, comprising thirty-four articles. The tribunal was granted competence over "persons responsible for serious violations of international humanitarian law committed in the territory of the former Yugoslavia since 1991."[64] It proposed to apply "rules of international humanitarian law which are beyond any doubt part of customary law"[65] or more specifically, the Geneva Conventions of 1949, The Hague Convention Respecting the Laws and Customs of War on Land (1907), the Genocide Convention (1948), and the Charter of the International Military Tribunal (1945).[66] These included specifically, "Grave breaches of the Geneva Conventions of 1949;"[67] "Violations of the Laws and

60 SG report, para 28.

61 UN Security Council, May 25, 1993 9 p.m., S/PV.3217.

62 Michael Scharf, who participated in the establishment of the ICTY at the US State Department, identified several members of the Security Council with reservations, who specifically regarded the ICTY as an "impediment to a negotiated peace settlement." Michael Scharf, "Indicted for War Crimes, Then What?" *The Washington Post*, October 3, 1999.

63 UN Security Council, May 25, 1993 9 p.m., S/PV.3217.

64 ICTY Statute, Article 1.

65 ICTY Statute para 3.4.

66 ICTY Statute para 3.5.

67 (Article 2) These include the following: willful killing; torture or inhuman treatment; biological experiments; willfully causing great suffering; causing serious injury to body or health; extensive destruction and appropriation of property, not justified by military necessity and carried out unlawfully and wantonly; compelling a prisoner of war or a protected civilian to serve in the armed forces of the hostile power; willfully depriving a prisoner of war or a protected person of the rights or fair and

Customs of War;"[68] "Genocide;"[69] and "Crimes against Humanity."[70] The crime of waging aggressive war, central at the IMT, was omitted. Where the IMT at Nuremberg had jurisdiction over natural persons that included organizations, the ICTY Statute refused to consider the criminality of organizations.[71]

Article 12 of the statute set forth the selection of judges; states could nominate up to two candidates, and the Security Council would select a list of between 22 and 33 names from such nominations to pass on to the General Assembly for election for a renewable period of four years. Judges would further elect a president from among themselves. The president would then select which judges should be assigned to trial and appellate chambers, and preside over appellate proceedings (in addition to being a member of the appellate chamber herself).[72] The prosecutor, who "shall act independently as a separate organ of the International Tribunal [and] not seek or receive instructions from any Government of from any other source" was to be appointed by the Security Council on nomination by the Secretary-General.[73] No institutional resources were set aside for the defense.

Selection of judges was relatively quick, and by November 1993 eleven judges were installed in temporary quarters in The Hague, led by the ICTY's first president, the prominent Italian jurist and human rights proponent Antonio Cassese. Cassese began working on securing permanent headquarters for the ICTY, including setting up a courtroom and a jail.

The selection of the first ICTY prosecutor, without whom indictments were not possible, was a complicated affair that took eighteen months. Here the varied interests of the international community in the *kind* of tribunal they were creating – an empty figurehead or an institution capable of making an impact – were most clearly on display. Cherif Bassiouni, the energetic member of the commission who had successfully pushed the project of the ICTY, lobbied hard for the post, but was ultimately rejected by Britain as too likely to be aggressive (read: to disrupt the peace process) (Bass 2000). Bassiouni's Muslim identity also posed a problem, as it was feared this might be read as less than objective among the warring Muslim, Serb, and Croat factions (Hagan 2003). Ultimately, Richard Goldstone, a South African judge of Jewish descent, was selected for the post and appointed in August 1994.

regular trial prescribed in the Conventions; unlawful deportation or transfer; unlawful confinement of a protected person; and the taking of hostages.

68 ICTY Statute Article 3.

69 ICTY Statute Article 4. The central piece of the legal definition of genocide is "the intent to destroy, in whole or in part, a national, ethnical, racial or religious group, as such."

70 ICTY Statute Article 5. These include the following: murder; extermination; enslavement; deportation; imprisonment; torture; rape; persecutions on political, racial and religious grounds; and other inhumane acts. See, e.g., Rachel Taylor "Tribunal Law Made Simple," available at www.globalpolicy.org/component/content/article/163/29333.html (summarizing ICTY foundation documents and jurisdiction).

71 ICTY Statute para 51.

72 ICTY Statute Article 14.

73 ICTY Statute Article 16.

Article 15 of the statute called on the judges of the ICTY to "adopt rules of procedure and evidence for the conduct of the pre-trial phase of the proceedings, trials and appeals, the admission of evidence, the protection of victims and witnesses and other appropriate matters." Suggestions regarding the content of such rules flowed in from many quarters.[74] Morris and Scharf (1995) note that, given the tight turnaround, anyone who was able to produce a finalized document got a hearing. The first rules of procedure and evidence were confirmed February 11, 1994. Rule 6 provides for their amendment by a plenary of ten permanent judges.[75] At the time of its closure, the ICTY Rules of Procedure and Evidence had been revised fifty times;[76] amendments were historically generated by the prosecutor's office, tribunal decisions, and UN expert groups.

Although many diverse actors were wrangled into supporting the nascent tribunal, Gary Bass wryly notes that structural hurdles to be crossed in setting up the ICTY were sufficient "to cripple the tribunal without attracting the kind of embarrassing headlines that would come from open opposition to it" (Bass 2000: 216). Drafting the statute, selecting judges, and appointing a prosecutor all stood between the conceptualized tribunal and its prescribed functions. Physical obstacles such as the lack of functioning courtrooms and staff offices, a detention center, and adequate finances also threatened the fledgling institution. The ICTY's budget in 1993 was US$276,000, and staffers reported difficulty collecting their pay (Bass 2000).

B *Monopolizing Judicial Power*

As an ad hoc tribunal, the ICTY was limited in time, scope, and jurisdiction. During the period where it issued indictments (1994–2004), the ICTY enjoyed juridical primacy over war crimes committed on the terrain of the former Yugoslavia from 1990 to 1999.[77] In postwar Bosnia, an international protectorate governed by the Dayton Accords, where the international community played a primary role through the Office of the High Representative, all war crimes cases were to be seconded to the tribunal for review before being tried domestically.[78] Only those cases the ICTY did not want to try, but which the ICTY held to merit trial (i.e., where the ICTY

74 Morris and Scharf have collected some central examples in volume 2 of *An Insider's Guide to the International Criminal Tribunal for the Former Yugoslavia: A Documentary History and Analysis* (Brill, 1995).

75 With the expansion of ICTY staff, ad litem judges were added to permanent staff.

76 The final draft is dated July 8, 2015.

77 ICTY Statute Article 9 (2). The ICTY issued its last indictment in 2004, and will complete the last of its processes (finishing ongoing trials and appeals) through the Residual Mechanism, which replaced the ICTY in July 2013.

78 This procedure was known as the "Rules of the Road." The rules were derived from two separate agreements, the Rome Agreement (Sect. 5, second paragraph) and "Procedures and Guidelines for Parties for the Submission of Cases to the International Criminal Tribunal for the Former Yugoslavia under the Agreed Measures of February 18, 1996 ('The Rules of the Road')." The Rules of the Road held that cases involving war crimes could only be domestically prosecuted after the ICTY had

found a *prima facie* case), could be tried domestically after being passed over by the ICTY.[79] Furthermore, judges and prosecutors in Bosnia were required to cooperate with the ICTY.[80]

In Croatia and Serbia, ICTY juridical supremacy was not assumed, and cooperation with the court has been dictated by national legal mandate. Cooperation with the ICTY could not be directly compelled in either Serbia or Croatia, although pressures to cooperate, largely in the form of promised EU membership and International Monetary Fund funding, were brought to bear.[81] Croatian cooperation with the ICTY, promised by Tuđman even as the war still raged, dwindled significantly with the first indictments against ethnic Croats in 1995. Ultimately, however, both countries passed laws regarding cooperation with the ICTY and have extradited indictees to the tribunal. Such extraditions were often long in coming and demonstrated a deep resistance to the tribunal, however.[82]

Finally, the ICTY's scope was limited to crimes committed within the territory of the former Yugoslavia. This does not include, based on a somewhat infamous determination of the ICTY itself,[83] any purported war crimes committed by NATO in its 1999 campaign in Serbia and Kosovo, though it does include Serb and Albanian-Serb war crimes committed in the same conflict.

determined (1) that there was a *prima facie* case and (2) that the ICTY itself was not interested in trying the case.

79 Twelve cases were transferred by the ICTY to Bosnia, http://un.org/icty/cases-e/factsheets/procfact-e.htm. See Appendix A.

80 ICTY Statute Article 29 (2b–2c).

81 Created and overseen by the UN Security Council, the ICTY exists within this ambit. Opinions differ as to the advantages and disadvantages of this situation, particularly when, as now, it is possible to compare the UN Security Council-mandated ICTY with the product of international treaty making, the International Criminal Court. An attorney working at the ICTY opined that the ICTY, as a child of the Security Council, enjoys a clout that the ICC does not. For instance, when the ICTY issues a subpoena, citizens must respond; the ICC, in contrast, has yet to clarify its subpoena process (author interviews, The Hague, November 2012).

82 Moreover, both Croatia and Serbia have independently pursued war crimes domestically. In Serbia, such pursuit has come only well after the cessation of the war, spurred on by the assassination of Serbia's president Zoran Đinić in 2003: since then, international monies and assistance have constructed a new court to deal with war crimes and organized crime in Belgrade, and the focus is largely on organized crime. In Croatia, the only former Yugoslav country evincing interest in bringing war crimes cases in the years following the war, thousands of cases were brought and tried, all of them against Croatian Serbs, usually in absentia, often with groups of defendants numbering up to one hundred at a time and disposed of within minutes; these universally criticized trials served largely to discourage departed ethnic Serbs from returning, for fear of being placed directly in jail. Thus in both Croatia and Serbia, while there has been some movement on the front of war crimes recognition, such movement has either been predicated by external necessity or has represented a further shoring up of what are perceived to be national (as in ethnic majority) interests. This will be discussed in greater detail in Chapters 5 and 6.

83 "Final Report to the Prosecutor by the Committee Established to Review the NATO Bombing Campaign Against the Federal Republic of Yugoslavia," www.un.org/icty/pressreal/p510-e.htm, June 6, 2000.

The ICTY was a product of timorous *Realpolitik*: violent conflict erupted in a remote corner of Europe, and international actors were reluctant to risk the lives of their citizens in an effort to snuff it out. A tribunal in The Hague was in all respects the most attractive form of international action for an international community unwilling to forcefully intervene but uncomfortable doing nothing; it enjoyed the moral legitimacy of a court as well as a fashionable Dutch address several hundred miles away from Bosnian battles. If the story had ended there, it might be possible to view the ICTY only in terms of what it was not; that is to say, to see it only as an ineffectual tool against regional violence and a weak attempt by the international community to protest its own impotence. The story did not end there, however. Had the ICTY been no more than an international straw man, it should have dissolved at the cessation of the Yugoslav conflict, its UN Article VII "peace and security" mandated purpose served. The end of the war, however, only saw a dramatic upsurge in the ICTY's activity and efficacy. Even as the international community retained a large and expensive physical presence in Bosnia, it continued to fund and support the ICTY. The international community's commitment to the costly ICTY in the company of other effective military measures indicates that a force beyond *Realpolitik* was at work in the decision to back the tribunal.

CONCLUSION

This chapter has articulated a particularized, tripartite legacy of the IMT that forms the basis for the received capacity of ICTs. This is the international transitional justice template. The chapter has shown how the legacy of the IMT at Nuremberg does not map onto the facts that should constitute the foundation for that legacy: the IMT is challenged as a rule-of-law institution, as a historian, and as a reconciler. While this story is known, the IMT has regardless enjoyed great notoriety, the "Teflon" tribunal, particularly when contrasted against the IMTFE, which lies nearly discarded on the dustbin of history. Finally, the chapter has traced how the IMT's legacy of rule of law, history, and reconciliation fueled the construction of the ICTY.

The next chapter considers, at a theoretical level, why ICTs, beginning with the IMT and extending to other World War II-era tribunals and beyond, are challenged in their task to produce progressive law, the first-order function for ICTs identified by the international criminal justice template.

2

Non-Derogation and International Criminal Law

Situating the ICTY

What socially constitutive work can international criminal justice institutions do, and how are they supposed to be able to do it? This chapter addresses these questions through consideration of the paradox at the heart of the *international criminal justice template*. This paradox arises from two different legitimations of international criminal law (ICL) practice. The first legitimation is ICL's forward-looking "progressive" mandate, which allows ICL institutions to ignore a central rights-oriented practice (the principle of legality/*nullum crimen sine lege*) for a rights-oriented reason (forward-looking establishment of progressive norms). The second legitimation is ICL's reliance on criminological ideologies and rationales regarding the social value and impact of punishment. These two rationales are in conflict and create what *Model(ing) Justice* labels "the problem of non-derogation."

As discussed in Chapter 1, ICL, in the name of progress, recognizes no justification for violations of international humanitarian law (IHL). In other words, IHL is "non-derogable": there is no contextualization of a violation of IHL that mitigates, justifies, or defends it. International humanitarian law, the law of war, consists of a series of binaries, where acts either violate or do not violate its tenets.[1] Once an act slips over the binary from "permissible under" to "in violation of" IHL, ICL applies non-derogable norms to the persons charged with that violation. Another way to express this idea is to say that ICL, by virtue of being non-derogable, applies an "absolute" or "strict" liability standard to the crimes it considers.

Strict liability is a legal doctrine that awards absolute legal responsibility to an individual for an injury regardless of that individual's intent or knowledge; so long as an injury is proven, there is no defense.[2] Strict/absolute liability is generally disfavored under domestic criminal law regimes, as it runs contrary to the sociological, normative purpose of criminal law, which is principally communicative (Ashworth

[1] For example, a civilian death in a war zone may or may not be recognized as a violation of IHL, because IHL contemplates legitimate/legal civilian death.

[2] *Black's Law Dictionary* defines it as "[w]hen a plaintiff makes a motion to prove harm has occurred without having to show how or why to collect damages." Available at http://thelawdictionary.org/strict-liability/#ixzz2YoQMxCQW.

2009; Duff 2009). From Beccaria onward, theories of criminal law have focused on the power of punishment to control behavior. Where an individual lacks the intent or knowledge that they are violating a norm, punishment is only punitive (and not deterrent or rehabilitative); there is no behavioral value in punishing them. In domestic regimes, strict liability crimes are heavily curtailed; the separation of *mens rea* from punishment is understood to risk violating constitutional norms (Prendergast 2011).

The following chapter explores the problem of non-derogation in ICL in three parts. The first part lays out the theory behind ICL's communicative power; this imagined capacity, the chapter argues, borrows heavily from theories regarding law's socially constitutive power, specifically transitional justice, criminal justice, and the sociology of law. The second part examines one International Military Tribunal (IMT)-era case in order to illustrate the degree to which criminal sanctions applied in the name of progress can be illiberal. The third part briefly annotates the twenty-year practice of the ICTY, to illustrate how the construction and work of the ICTY is demonstrative of the structural dilemmas extant in ICL. Through theory and example, the chapter shows how non-derogation presents a challenge for ICL, because it is simultaneously the legitimizing force for ICL as well as an obstacle to ICL's effective communication with its target audiences.

I TRANSITIONAL JUSTICE: THE POTENTIAL FOR INTERNATIONAL CRIMINAL LAW TO BE SOCIALLY CONSTITUTIVE

Early in the ICTY's existence, Payam Akhavan (1998: 737), then working in the ICTY prosecutor's office, published an article in which he argued that the value of the ICTY lay in its "internalization of expectations of individual accountability." He predicted the ICTY would herald an "emergence of habitual conformity with elementary humanitarian principles" and argued that this paradigmatic shift would impact the former Yugoslavia as well as the global community. Akhavan's article, a staple in transitional justice circles, functioned simultaneously as proof and definition of the ICTY's capacity as a mechanism of transitional justice. If the peoples of the former Yugoslavia could recognize their shared humanity, went the argument, this could trump their divergent ethnic affiliations and resolve the socio-political conflict that fed the brutality of the 1991–1995 wars.

The ICTY itself professes similar expectations. The ICTY's website describes its own work in the following terms:

> The Tribunal has laid the foundations for what is now the accepted norm for conflict resolution and post-conflict development across the globe; specifically, that leaders suspected of mass crimes will face justice. The Tribunal has proved that efficient and transparent international justice is possible.

> The Tribunal has contributed to an indisputable historical record, combating denial and helping communities come to terms with their recent history. Crimes across the region can no longer be denied. For example, it has been proven beyond reasonable doubt that the mass murder at Srebrenica was genocide.[3]

After twenty-five years of practice, the ICTY's record as a transitional justice mechanism receives a mixed reception within the former Yugoslavia as well as among its international observers. Although the former Yugoslavia is no longer at war, pervasive nationalist politics continue to threaten its constitutive countries; the "elementary humanitarian principles" Akhavan cited have not suppressed identity politics throughout the region.[4] Perhaps more surprisingly, later ICTY judgments have themselves mitigated the force of the "humanitarian principles" the ICTY articulated in early judgments; where low-level offenders in early cases faced harsh penalties, higher level offenders in more recent cases are being acquitted. Even Akhavan himself has half-repudiated the idealism of his 1998 article, arguing in 2013 (527) for the need to "adjust expectations" as regards international criminal justice.

Criminal processes have emerged as central transitional justice mechanisms based on their dual mandate of social control and punishment. International criminal law criminalizes violations of internationally recognized human rights, situating itself between international law and criminal justice (Fletcher 2002; Cassese 2003; Ratner & Abrams 2009). Lacking its own penology, ICL builds instead on the rationales used for applying criminal sanctions at the domestic level (Cassese 1998b, 2003; Bassiouni 2008; Damaška 2009; Drumbl 2009), borrowing the retribution, deterrence, and to some degree rehabilitation/restoration rubrics that underwrite criminal law in domestic jurisdictions.[5]

3 From the ICTY website: About the ICTY, www.icty.org/sections/AbouttheICTY

4 This is discussed in Chapter 5.

5 See, e.g., *Prosecutor* v. *Blagoje Simić, Miroslav Tadić and Simo Zarić, Appeals Chamber Judgment*, Case No. IT-95–9 (Int'l Crim. Trib. for the former Yugoslavia, October 17, 2003) para 1059. "It is universally accepted and reflected in judgments [of ICTY and the International Criminal Tribunal for Rwanda] that deterrence and retribution are general factors to be taken into account when imposing sentences"; *Prosecutor* v. *Milorad Krnojelac, Trial Chamber Judgment*, Case No. IT-97–25 (Int'l Crim. Trib. for the former Yugoslavia, March 15, 2002) para 508; *Prosecutor* v. *Anto Furundžija, Trial Chamber Judgment*, Case No. IT-95–17/1 (Int'l Crim. Trib. for the former Yugoslavia, December 10, 1998) para 288. *Prosecutor* v. *Dragoljub Kunarac, Radomir Kovač, and Zoran Vuković*, Case No. IT-96–23 and 23/1 (Int'l Crim. Trib. for the former Yugoslavia, June 12, 2002) (rejecting alleged trend away from retribution in international law). *Prosecutor* v. *Zejnil Delalić, Hazim Delić, Zdravko Mucić, Esad Landžo*, Case No. IT-96–21 (Int'l Crim. Trib. for the former Yugoslavia, November 16, 1998) para 1234 (deterrence "probably is the most important factor in the assessment of appropriate sentences"). Deterrence is usually characterized as general, not specific, since the tribunal has recognized "the likelihood of persons convicted here ever again being faced with an opportunity to commit war crimes, crimes against humanity, genocide or grave breaches is so remote as to render its consideration in this way unreasonable and unfair." *Prosecutor* v. *Dragoljub Kunarac, Radomir Kovač, and Zoran Vuković*, Case No. IT-96–23 and 23/1, (Int'l Crim. Trib. for the former Yugoslavia, February 22, 2001) para 840. But see *Prosecutor* v. *Mrđa, Sentencing Judgment*, Case No. IT- 02–59 (Int'l Crim. Trib. for the former Yugoslavia, March 31, 2004) para 16 (noting that the main deterrent effect is to turn perpetrators away from future wrongdoing).

International criminal legal practice differs from domestic criminal legal practice in myriad ways, any of which could impair its capacity to deter future crime or shape social expectations. For example, domestic criminal law is designed to punish all crime of a certain category, while ICL is selective, example-setting, and to some degree random, punishing only those very few actors who find themselves before ICTs. From a structural perspective, domestic criminal law exacts the will of the sovereign (Shapiro 1986), while international legal institutions are not governed by any obvious sovereign (Klabbers 2015). And from a socio-psychological vantage point, domestic criminal law punishes social deviance but ICL punishes actions that are (at the time they are committed) often in social conformity (Drumbl 2007).

Beyond the divisions listed above, ICL universally applies its form of strict liability, contravening a much lighter application of strict liability in domestic criminal law. At ICL, violations of IHL are always criminal, regardless of context: this element is central to the "progress" imagined for ICL, and a key element legitimizing ICL practice. Contrast ICL's practice with that of international human rights legal practice, which specifically recognizes a "margin of appreciation." The "margin of appreciation" imagines the possibility of different standards for different acts in different contexts. Another way to state this is that international human rights legal practice inserts flexibility for political interest (read, diversity and/or disagreement) into its practice. International criminal law explicitly forbids such recognition. The catch is that, in order to legitimize itself, ICL forbids such recognition *in the name of universally recognized human rights*. In this way, human rights (though not its doctrinal tradition, specifically its recognition of context) are put in service to IHL.

Criminal justice finds its roots in the eighteenth-century writing of Beccaria (1764; Bellamy 1995), distinguishing "punishment" from "justice" and finding social value only in the latter. Modern theorists of criminal justice (Ashworth 2009; Duff 2001; Lacey 2009, 2011) focus on the moral authority of criminal law as located in its communicative capacity. Punishment can be effectuated by any powerful body by any means for any reason; one recalls Foucault's gruesome opening to *Discipline and Punish* (1979/1995). International criminal law claims to mete out justice, however, and through this claim it places itself in a liberal, Kantian tradition (Clark 2009; Roth 2011). H. L. A. Hart's classic *Punishment and Responsibility* (1968) defined the normative justifications of "morally tolerable" punishment within the confines of the liberal state (Lacey 2009: 948). In the liberal state, constructed upon a "social contract" between governing powers and the governed, the central purpose of punishment is to communicate censure to offenders; punishment must recognize and reaffirm the citizen's personhood as within the community (Duff 2001, 2013).

Showcasing punishment, however, is insufficient in the modern liberal state. As Foucault (1995: 38) notes, the aim of the modern state is to internalize norms, so that wrongdoers judge and condemn themselves. The literature considering the value of "political trials" to instill the "right kind" of ideals and political goals for the targeted nations (Shklar 1964/1986) is applied in regard to ICTs (Osiel 1997). This is reminiscent of Akhavan's (1998: 737) "gradual internalization of expectations of individual accountability and the emergence of habitual conformity with elementary humanitarian principles," discussed at the beginning of this section.

A *Transitional Justice and the Sociology of Law*

The term "transitional justice" emerged out of social and political rebuilding in South America following decades of repressive dictatorships (Nino 1991; Orentlicher 1991; Zalaquett 1990; Teitel 2003).[6] The field developed as a set of political, moral, and legal norms regarding how best to respond to mass atrocities or unjust governance (Sharp 2018). While social rebuilding can take many forms, including truth commissions (which typically offer perpetrators amnesty in exchange for their confession of wrongdoing) and lustration (which collectively removes all state representatives from office for a certain amount of time following transition), the principal institutional mechanisms that have emerged to perform transitional justice purposes are hybrid or international courts (Alvarez 1999; Wilson 2001; Elster 2004; Douglas 2005; Luban 2010; Leebaw 2011; Gow & Kerr 2014; Hafetz 2018).

The International Military Tribunal (IMT) at Nuremberg predated the field of transitional justice by fifty years. The IMT must nonetheless be understood as a seminal transitional justice mechanism. When a Polish filmmaker speaks of expecting "a Nuremberg for Communism"[7] after the fall of the Iron Curtain, or a law professor refers to a case as "the Nuremberg trial for Cambodia,"[8] or a retired jurist characterizes Nuremberg as "the triumph of good over evil,"[9] they are in effect referencing the IMT's transitional justice capacity.

Trials, it is argued, may play a complex role that exceeds their immediate impact on punishment or retribution, "a performance that would ultimately enable the state itself to function as a moral agent" (Borneman 1997: 23). Others have similarly argued that the type of lesson being taught (i.e., political liberalism) can justify the methods used to impart the lesson, even if those methods do not meet the neutral or impartial standards typically assigned to courts (Osiel 1997; Bass 2000).

Courts are perceived as uniquely effective transitional justice mechanisms for a number of reasons, including their (perceived) capacity to perform the following

6 The field of transitional justice has branched into something of a free-for-all in the past three decades, capable of providing all things to all comers. There is an emerging literature considering this boundlessness (Israël and Mouralis 2012; Daly 2017; Gissel 2016; Sharp 2018).

7 David Scheffer, Northwestern University professor and UN Special Expert on Khmer Rouge Trials, radio address WBEZ April 2013, quoted in Florent Zwiers, "The Story of Khmer Rouge Crimes" (unpublished), on file with author.

8 Remarks of Norbert Ehrenfreund, Robert H. Jackson Center, June 13, 2005, available at www.roberthjackson.org/the-man/speeches-articles/speeches/speeches-related-to-robert-h-jackson/reflections-on-nuremberg-trial/; see also Ehrenfreund 2007.

9 Nicolas Kulish, "Poland Leads Wave of Communist-Era Reckoning," *New York Times*, February 29, 2012.

acts: punish offenders; recognize victims; set social standards regarding what is criminal or not; and locate guilt in individuals, thereby avoiding "collective guilt," which is believed by some to encourage future violence (Akhavan 2001). Antonio Cassese (1998: 229), a central figure in ICL, scholar, and former ICTY judge, makes the following case for ICTs as transitional justice mechanisms:

> Trials establish individual responsibility over collective assignation of guilt, i.e., they establish that not all Germans were responsible for the Holocaust, nor all Turks for the Armenian genocide, nor all Serbs, Muslims, Croats or Hutus but individual perpetrators – although, of course, there may be a great number of perpetrators; justice dissipates the call for revenge, because when the Court metes out to the perpetrator his just desserts, then the victims' calls for retribution are met; by dint of dispensation of justice, victims are prepared to be reconciled with their erstwhile tormentors, because they know that the latter have now paid for their crimes; a fully reliable record is established of atrocities so that future generations can remember and be made fully cognizant of what happened.[10]

International courts are seen as more effective than national courts at producing post-conflict justice because national courts are aligned with regimes that commissioned or permitted crimes. International institutions are thus seen as capable of making the "clean break" necessary in a post-conflict situation. Teitel (2000: 56) argues that "individuating wrongdoing lifts collective responsibility from the prior regime and re-legitimates state authority." Prosecution "clearly separates a newly democratic government from the abuses of its predecessor" (Hesse & Post 1999: 15). International criminal tribunals are also presented as a healthy antidote to collective guilt, where "to prevent lingering assignments of collective guilt, blame and punishment must be restricted to specific individuals and based on specific proof, itself tested through the adversary process" (Minow 1999: 40).[11]

In "criminalizing" violations of international human rights law, the IMT built on rationales used for applying criminal sanctions at the domestic level, including the communicative power of criminal law. The IMT at Nuremberg established the principle that ICTs can perform a didactic function by modeling, and thereby instilling, liberal values for a targeted audience. Ad hoc tribunals are neither able nor interested in bringing the same *kind* of justice as a national court system, the justice that comes from objectively applying the laws of a given province equally across every situation. Ad hoc courts are rather "message" courts, or "teaching

10 Cassese argued that a truth commission would be a less ideal mechanism for transitional justice in the former Yugoslavia because: "(a) they have been the scene of appalling atrocities which are beyond amnesty, (b) they are still riven by the violent nationalisms or ethnic hatred over which the wars were fought, and (c) they are not yet willing to be reconciled" (Cassese 1998b).

11 See also *Prosecutor* v. *Momir Nikolić*, ICTY Case No. IT-02-60/1-S, *Sentencing Judgment*, December 2, 2003, para 60: "By holding *individuals* responsible for the crimes committed, it was hoped that a particular ethnic or religious group (or even political organization) would not be held responsible for such crimes by members of other ethnic or religious groups, and that the guilt of the few would not be shifted to the innocent."

courts," designed to show by example that (some) crimes will not be met with impunity (statistically speaking, *most* crimes arising from a situation an ad hoc court is addressing are in fact met by impunity). Judith Shklar's *Legalism* (1964) argued that regardless of the substantive and procedural challenges levied against the IMTs at Nuremberg and Tokyo, these trials, as well as other "political trials," provide value by instilling the "right kind" of ideals and political goals for the targeted nations. Others have similarly argued that the type of lesson being taught (i.e., political liberalism) can justify the methods used to impart the lesson, even if those methods do not meet the neutral or impartial standards typically assigned to courts (Osiel 1997; Bass 2000).

Transitional justice scholars understand the task of transition as one of harnessing consent to change, and building a desire for representative (liberal) government through the process. Transitional justice sees transition as a formative, extraordinary political moment. For example, in the field's seminal work, Teitel (2000: 6) claims that "in transition, the ordinary intuitions and predicates about law simply do not apply. In dynamic periods of political flux, legal responses generate a *sui generis* paradigm of transformative law." Another way to state this would be to say that transitional justice seeks to construct government legitimacy in order to make the consent of the population meaningful. Transitional justice thus resists a political assessment of legitimacy in consent because such an assessment might not be capable of making a distinction between unjust (former) regimes and rule-abiding (future) regimes. This, together with a focus on legal mechanisms, may explain the shift in transitional justice approaches from the individually tailored solutions of early practices to the contemporary focus on objectivity and universal application (Gissel 2016).

If "justice" has been recognized by political theorists as a political and social construct that changes with regimes (Shklar 1990; Gray 2006; Sa'adah 2006), transitional justice is undecided regarding whether justice is objective or subjective. Transitional justice and ICL are thus equally trapped in a conflict between the "progressive" legal ideology that legitimizes ICTs as transitional justice mechanisms and the necessarily political interests and choices that are represented in the practice of criminal justice (Shapiro 1986; Sa'Adah 2006).

II CHALLENGING "PROGRESS" IN INTERNATIONAL CRIMINAL LAW PRACTICE: THE *VELPKE* CASE

International criminal law focuses on doctrinal clarity: what is criminalized or criminalizable, and what is not. Domestic criminal law is subject to criminological oversight, and formulated prescriptively. Many social practices with the ability to cause harm, from drug use to gum chewing to weapons possession, are not consistently the subjects of domestic criminal law. This is because the context in which activity occurs blurs its pure, doctrinal categorization in domestic law. As argued at the beginning of this chapter, ICL suffers a justice paradox, trapped in its own problem of non-derogation, because it requires the doctrinal purity of a strict liability standard to legitimize itself. The forward-looking nature of progressive ICL seeks to justify what would often be an impermissibly retroactive legal application. This strict liability standard, however, hinders ICL's communicative capacity and handicaps its ability to perform the discursive work that transitional justice imagines for law.

Poignant examples of the problem of non-derogation abound but are often camouflaged by our contemporary sympathies for purpose or politics. We thus examine one Nuremberg-era case, *Velpke Children's Hospital*. The case was reported in the United Nations War Crimes Commission (UNWCC). Although the case is referenced by the ICTY (*Kvocka et al.*, discussed in greater detail in Chapter 4), the case is selected here for its capacity to frame the problem of non-derogation, where historical distance helps us more clearly see the flaws in legal reasoning that lead to the paradox of building "progressive" law in an illiberal manner.

The *Velpke Children's Home* case was tried before a British military court in 1946.[12] The circumstances are particularly tragic, involving a "home" set up to keep the babies of Polish and Russian women who had been forcibly removed to Velpke, Germany, to work. The babies were taken from their mothers and kept in a "corrugated iron hut" with no running water, electricity, or telephone. They were tended by a "nurse," formerly a schoolteacher, with no experience with young babies, who was sent to run the home against her will. The home operated from May to December 1944, during which time more than eighty babies perished, with the principle causes of death recorded as weakness and dysentery.

Eight people stood accused.[13] The two Nazi administrators who ran the home (the first had set it up, including choosing the location, on orders from a superior, and the second had been appointed to "administer" the home) were both sentenced to death. The schoolteacher charged with running the home (who reportedly "went away for her meals and to do shopping, and was never in the home at night, though the helpers stayed there"[14]) was sentenced to fifteen years. A local doctor who "without official instructions" visited the home "to tend sick infants" and who later "only tended such of the children as [were] brought to him, and only visited the

[12] Case No. 42, Trial of Heinrich Gerike and Seven Others (The Velpke Children's Home Case) British Military Court, Brunswick, VII Law Reports of Trials of War Criminals 76 (1948) (*Velpke Children's Home*). The preface to Volume VII of the UNWCC extracts that contains the *Velpke* case finds the case significant "because the children who were barbarously dealt with were actually born in Germany, their mothers having been deported contrary to international law from an Allied country, namely Poland, while that country was occupied by the Nazis." For our purposes, *Velpke* is more significant for its application of criminal culpability as well as its commentary regarding guilt for "causing death by criminal negligence."

[13] Seven were sentenced, as one died during the course of the trial.

[14] *Velpke Children's Home* p. 80.

home to sign death certificates" was sentenced to ten years' prison.[15] The other accused – a leading Nazi in the village, the mayor of the village, and a farmer who had sent at least two children to the home – were all found not guilty.

1 The Law of *Velpke*

The prosecutor brought charges under Article 46 of The Hague Convention of 1907, which provided for the respect of family honor, individual life, and private property, and made reference to English law and murder and criminal negligence as expounded in Archbold's *Pleading, Evidence and Practice in Criminal Cases*, thirty-first edition. Quoting extensively from that work, the prosecutor elaborated on death by criminal negligence, stating that where "the probable consequence may be and eventually is death, such killing may be murder, although no stroke was struck by himself," listing the following cases as examples of such:

> As was the case of the gaoler, who causes the death of a prisoner by imprisoning him in unwholesome air; of the unnatural son, who exposed his sick father to the air against his will, by reason whereof he died; of the harlot, who laid her child in an orchard, where a kite struck it and killed it; of the mother, who hid her child in a pig-sty, where it was devoured; and of the parish officers, who moved a child from parish to parish till it died from want of care and sustenance ... If a grown-up person chooses to undertake the charge of a human creature helpless either from infancy, simplicity, lunacy, or other infirmity, he is bound to execute that charge without wicked negligence; and if a person who has chosen to take charge of a helpless creature lets it die by gross negligence, that person is guilty of manslaughter. Mere negligence will not do; there must be negligence so great as to satisfy a jury that the prisoner was reckless and careless whether the creature died or not.[16]

Because this definition is quoted extensively in the judgment, we can assume that the tribunal relied on its rationale in arriving at its sentence.

Yet is the doctrine pronounced by Archbold good law? A critical consideration of the text suggests otherwise. The text appears to lump several potentially distinguishable crimes together under the heading of criminal negligence. The jailor and parish officers, state administrators, seem differently positioned than the son and mothers, for example, who owe different duties of care. Without greater detail, it is impossible to know who among these administrators is guilty of "wicked negligence ... [being] reckless and careless whether the creature died or not." Generally, the doctrine of *respondiat superior* applies to administrators carrying out their duties, relieving them of personal responsibility for acts that are reasonably foreseeable elements of their work.

15 *Ibid.*
16 *Velpke Children's Home* p. 81 (quoting Archbold).

Taking the son and mothers, it is not clear from the text if they sought to kill father and offspring through exposure. If so, this is homicide, not manslaughter (where the difference between the two is *mens rea*, the presence or absence of an *intent to kill*). The critique of Archbold's thirty-second edition specifically notes the problem that while *mens rea* is required for every crime, the qualification of the defense of necessity or superior orders exists and is not mentioned until much later in the Archbold text, at which point there is no "adequate discussion." These defenses significantly qualify *mens rea*, the intent of the perpetrator at the time of the commission of a crime. Thus it is not clear that the English criminal law cited and relied upon in the *Velpke* decision constituted an accurate representation of criminal negligence in England at the time *Velpke* was decided. It is of course, even less clear whether such a representation would obtain today.

Moreover, even at the time the judgment was written, there was criticism of Archbold's pronouncements as "out of touch." A review of Archbold's thirty-second edition criticizes Archbold's editing as

> prepared within the limits of the practitioner's tradition of editing, which is to note the latest cases and statutes at what appear to be the most appropriate places in the traditional text. If one is left dissatisfied with the result, it is largely because this method of editing performed thirty-one times since 1822 produces a volume that is out of touch with modern thinking about criminal law.[17]

Thus in both doctrine and rationale, the Archbold reference is flawed.

Returning to the *Velpke* judgment, as regards the schoolteacher, the prosecutor said, "Although she has said that what she did she did under order, she seems to have had very little idea of service and devotion and sacrifice to duty. If you *undertake a task of skill* then in law you are called upon to show the skill of the task that you have undertaken."[18] Perhaps the most surprising is the sentence passed on the doctor who "without official instructions" visited the children in an effort to save their lives. According to the prosecution, the doctor had, by his acts, "assumed the care of those children in place of their mothers."[19] The court did not comment specifically on the doctor's defense that, "due to his large practice, he could find no time to write any letters of protest to persons in authority, or, in the later period, to visit the babies."[20] No further explanation is made of the doctor's sentence except to note that he received ten years' prison.

The *Velpke Children's Home* case makes reference to a similar trial, *Trial of Georg Tyrolt and Others by a British Military Court* (1946), a case not included in the UNWCC reports and unavailable for review. That tribunal passed death sentences

17 GLW Review, 14 *The Modern Law Review* No. 2, p. 233 (April 1951).

18 *Velpke Children's Home* p. 80 (emphasis added).

19 *Ibid.*

20 *Velpke Children's Home* p. 82.

on a doctor "responsible for the medical care and health of the children, and on . . . a nurse in whose charge [the children] were placed." A five-year prison sentence was passed on a second nurse "who also had charge of the infants for a period."[21] The *Velpke Children's Home* tribunal does not discuss the discrepancy in sentencing in the *Tyrolt* case.

2 Legal Principles in the *Velpke* Case

The *Velpke* judgment is very short, a mere six pages, and nearly half of it consists in extensive quotations from doctrinal sources. The reader is thus largely left on their own to construct the legal principles leading to the judicial outcome. What is striking is the closed circuit of the legal reasoning offered in *Velpke Children's Home* (as well as the *Tyrolt* case referenced therein). It seems that the doctor in the *Velpke* case could have escaped criminal liability only by doing nothing at all. Perhaps had he limited his "participation" in the home to signing death certificates he might not have been found guilty? Likewise, it is not clear how he or the schoolteacher in charge of the home escaped the death penalty, where others seemingly similarly positioned in the *Tyrolt* case (cited in the *Velpke* judgment), did not. Furthermore, there is no explanation of why the "two doctors [who] paid rare visits to the home before September 1944"[22] were not charged in the *Velpke* case, nor as to why, of the two nurses charged in the *Tyrolt* case, one was sentenced to death and the other to five years' prison. In short, an assessment of either the *Velpke* or *Tyrolt* cases leaves a student of ICL in the dark as concerns applicable criminal standards or possible defenses. It also leaves open the social control question of what *non-criminal* actions in such a situation might look like.

The central problem in the *Velpke* case and the law it purports to follow arises from the idea of "choos[ing] to undertake" an activity or responsibility. The court report of *Velpke* informs us that the schoolteacher was sent to run the home "against her will." How then did she "choose to undertake" her role in the home? Domestic criminal law recognizes coercion as an affirmative defense to conduct otherwise punishable as criminal. This discussion is absent in the *Velpke* judgment.

As regards the doctor, his voluntary participation appears to be closer to "choos[ing] to undertake" a role in the care of the children. The circumstances surrounding his efforts, however, complicate an assessment of his "participation" in the criminal actions, distinguishing the doctor's actions from those named in the English law of criminal negligence. The doctor did not forget to feed a child when he said he would, nor leave a child exposed outside when he said he would care for it; the doctor faced a physical situation (dying children) caused by a political circumstance over which he had no control or influence. In these circumstances, is

[21] *Velpke Children's Home* p. 81.
[22] *Ibid.* p. 77.

there a meaningful distinction to be drawn between visits conducted with or without official instruction? Would such a distinction possibly alter an assessment of the doctor's intent or responsibility, and if so, which one and in which direction?

In applying the English law of criminal negligence to the doctor's actions, the *Velpke* tribunal assesses the doctor's actions as if he had *not* been acting in the confining circumstances of the desperate days of a murderous state. The *Velpke* tribunal engages the legal fiction that the doctor enjoyed the possibility of communicating his concern regarding the conditions in the home to an administrative apparatus charged with citizens' affairs, as if a death camp for infants set up by the state itself could somehow be compared to an unattended pothole in a state-operated motorway.

Velpke and *Tyrolt* demonstrate the extent to which strict liability attended the development and application of ICL in the period following World War II. How can we explain the sentences passed on individuals before these courts except by an attendant *feeling* – the horror attached to the atrocity of allowing infants to die, and the sense that those connected to such horror should pay?

For the practitioner of ICL, there is another way to ask the question: what articulable principles can be drawn from the *Velpke* or *Tyrolt* cases? In times of war, should concerned parties write letters of protest to authorities? Would the doctor's sentence have been reduced had he done so? What person, given the situation in Nazi-ruled Germany at the time, would have engaged in such an exercise, only slightly more useless than it would have been dangerous? Is such an expectation reasonable, or fair? And even in the case of the schoolteacher, tasked with "caring" for the babies brought to her in these conditions and under such orders – how are we to understand the criminal liability of her actions? She was sent to run the home "against her will" and was provided, at first, "with no staff, no medical equipment and no records except for a register of incoming children."[23] The court notes that she "made many complaints" to the home's administrator and that one witness testified that the schoolteacher, "on finding that some of the children were dying because they needed mothers' milk, sent some back to their mothers, but that [the administrator], on discovering her action, forbade such a course."[24] At the same time, evidence showed that the sick children were not separated from the others, that infants' clothing was not kept clean, that the home was infested with flies, and that the schoolteacher "went away for her meals . . . and at night."

An analysis of *Velpke* leaves open the question of what sort of conduct *would not be criminal*. This question is larger than the procedural question of what the uncharged doctors, or acquitted defendants, did to escape prosecutorial notice and judicial pardon. Domestic criminal law, particularly common law, is rife with

[23] *Ibid.* p. 76.
[24] *Ibid.* p. 77.

examples of massive disparities between individual defendants, based on their individual conduct, post-crime cooperation, or other unrelated circumstances, and while individual cases may often seem unjust, such injustice does not necessarily rise to *systemic inequality*. The unaddressed problem in *Velpke* is more a question of criminal law as a guideline for individual conduct, an outline for what the state expects of citizens' behavior. What might the schoolteacher brought in as a nurse, or the doctor who made periodic visits, have done to *not* be guilty of criminal negligence in the *Velpke* example? What conduct on their part could have fallen within societal norms (since criminal law is designed to punish the conduct that falls outside the acceptable)? This absence of guidance, together with an absence of recognition for the changed circumstances that obtain during times of social violence, is an unaddressed problem of ICL, and will be considered in greater detail in Chapter 4.

Although the *Velpke* case has enjoyed precedential value in recent years as an element of the ICTY's JCE jurisprudence, the case is not referenced here because of its juridical centrality or significance. Rather, the case is included as an example of the kinds of cases produced by Allied jurists in specialized tribunals following the war. It is included in order to provide a means of asking "what sort of jurisprudence speaks in our name?" International criminal law draws legitimacy from a foundational universalism, the belief that violations of core crimes would be considered criminal violations by anyone. This Kantian formulation has been fitted to domestic criminal justice by criminal law theorists such as H. L. A. Hart and the modern theorists who followed him: Ashworth, Duff, Lacey. These thinkers articulate justice in terms of "what a tolerably just" (Duff 2013: 175) state would punish if it could. This formulation represents liberalism in action, where law is a necessary and effective space to address (if not fully redress) social injustice or imbalance, and where international legal intervention is necessary due to the dissolution of sovereign state capacity.

To the extent that the *Velpke* and *Tyrolt* cases pronounce a legal principle, it seems to follow Justice Jackson's famous iteration of the law applied at Nuremberg: "individuals have international duties which transcend the national obligations of obedience imposed by the individual State."[25] The IMT rejected the defenses of obeying superior orders and obeying national law. Thus it seems that the IMT and the trials that followed it began from the position the trials ostensibly were assembled to prove: the illegality of the Nazi state and all actions associated with it. Under this rationale, individuals subject to the dictates of the Nazi state should have resisted such dictates as, if not illegal during the time in which the Nazis were in power, then certainly illegal on a larger plane. Following *Velpke*, as the ICTY does in its *Kvočka* decision, discussed in greater detail in Chapter 4, ICL pronounces involvement of

[25] Trial of the Major War Criminals before the International Military Tribunal, vol. I, Nuremberg, 1947 p. 223.

any sort, even involvement intended to ameliorate criminal circumstances, to be participation in the criminal activity at the base of the situation. In short, the doctor seems to have tried to make the minor improvements available to him in the face of a horrible situation. The law as interpreted by *Velpke* suggests that doing *nothing* in the face of a horrible situation is less punishable than trying to ameliorate it, however futile such actions seem in the face of greater horror.[26]

As *Velpke* demonstrates, liberal outcomes do not emerge from prefabricated processes. Allied courts may have respected procedural requirements – they may have granted defendants counsel, informed them of the charges against them, and held a public procedure – without producing a procedure recognizable as the promise of rule-of-law liberalism. International criminal law's promise is grounded in the potential of rule-of-law liberalism to increase recognition and respect for human rights. As the *Velpke* case demonstrates, however, an assertion of criminality does not make such assertion rule-of-law compliant. Rather, effective, communicative criminal law relies on its Durkheimian roots – as a crafter of community, and a means to understand deviance – to meaningfully function as justice, and not simply punishment. Because we are unable to define what the *Velpke* doctor should have done not to violate the law (he is guilty of treating the infants, and assisting the Nazis, and he is guilty of not treating the infants, when they were in need) his is a case of punishment without justice, and a failure of ICL to realize its promise.

The *Velpke* case serves as an example demonstrating the problem of non-derogation by showcasing the fallibilities of applying a criminal standard without recognizing the larger circumstances in which those individuals found themselves. In short, the "case law" emerging from this period demonstrates a bias in opposition to individuals involved in reprehensible situations without a counterbalance, i.e., a non-derogation from principles of strict or absolute liability. For example, there is an important body of mob violence cases setting standards of guilt for mobs that turned violent, resulting in the deaths of Allied solders; this retributive case law sets the standard for modern ICL applications of conspiracy. These standards, which offer very weak protections of individual rights, exist as valid international law available for use by contemporary tribunals. The advent of new bodies practicing and applying ICL has energized projects to collect war crimes trials materials in their entirety, which may only further develop these problematic standards.The problem here is not the venue (a military court) or even the applicable law (the inconsistent Archbold). Rather, the central problem is a structural disconnect between the defendants in the dock and the individuals constructing and deciding cases against them. The communicative purpose of criminal justice in the liberal state relies on rule-of-law constructions (wherein none shall be above the rule of law) and the

[26] Judge Kwon made a similar point in his dissent in *Prosecutor v. Vujadin Popović, Ljubiša Beara, Drago Nikolić, Ljubomir Borovčanin and Radivoje Miletić, Sentencing Judgment*, Case No. IT-05–88-T (June 10, 2010) (Judge Kwon dissenting).

legitimizing force of the social contract regarding the content of what is criminalized. This normative, structural loop is not present in ICL, where conquerors sit in judgment of the conquered. This disconnect is what makes it possible for prosecutors to assert, and judges to verify, the criminal liability of individuals who find themselves with no good options. This dynamic of powerful rule setters as distinct from the population upon whom the rules are enforced was not disrupted in the construction of the ICTY.

III TASKING A COURT WITH PEACE

The ICTY was founded to address the widespread violence that occasioned the dissolution of Yugoslavia. It was a novel international institution set up under the United Nations' "Peace and Security" mandate: it was thus a court tasked with peace. Questions related to military and political responsibility were murky and contested, yet villainous acts were clear, from snipers targeting children and the elderly as they ventured forth to search for wood or water in Sarajevo, to concentration camps, organized rape and, in July 1995, recognized genocide with the massacre of more than seven thousand men and boys at Srebrenica. Thus, like eastern Germany in the *Velpke* case, Croatia and Bosnia were full of monsters and injustice, and for the reasons set forth in Chapter 1, a foreign tribunal was constructed to recognize their heinous acts through criminal charges, and to convict whomever fell under its scrutiny.

Seven years after the ICTY's creation, Gary Bass (2000: 208) summarized the institutional story of the tribunal as a "largely dispiriting one."[27] This assessment was, as it turned out, premature. Nearly two decades later, as the ICTY has closed and passed remaining duties on to its Residual Mechanism, the ICTY is generally recognized as a paradigm-setting institution, with a legacy that includes trying former heads of state, overseeing the initiation of war crimes courts in Bosnia-Herzegovina and Serbia,[28] and ushering in Croatia's entry into the European

[27] Bass (2000: 207) treats the history of war crimes prosecutions as a laudatory exploration of the liberal ideology of rule of law in place of vengeance. Nevertheless, his summary assessment of the work of the ICTY held the following:

> The establishment of The Hague tribunal was an act of tokenism by the world community, which was largely unwilling to intervene in ex-Yugoslavia but did not mind creating an institution that would give the appearance of moral concern. The world would prosecute the crimes that it would not prevent. The Tribunal was built to flounder. At first, it did not disappoint. It staggered from one crisis to another: lack of funding; lack of intelligence cooperation from the great powers; lack of staff; threats of amnesties; inability to do investigations; inability to deter war criminals as the wars raged on in Bosnia; and, after the 1995 Dayton accords brought peace and sixty thousand NATO soldiers to Bosnia, a refusal by NATO to arrest the suspects indicted by the tribunal.

[28] Court of Bosnia-Herzegovina, information available at www.sudbih.gov.ba; Special Chambers for War Crimes and Organized Crimes, information available at www.tuzilastvorz.org.rs/html_trz/pocetna_cir.htm. See also the ICTY's website regarding outreach and the development of local judiciaries, www.icty.org/sid/.

Union. This represents a shift in order of magnitude for the tribunal as an institution. Recalcitrant, uncooperative Balkan powers came to heel, participating in the arrest and extradition of the ICTY's most wanted. After nearly four years on the run, the Croatian "war hero" Ante Gotovina was arrested in the Canary Islands in December 2005.[29] Serbia extradited not only its former president Slobodan Milošević (2001), but also infamous Bosnian Serb war criminals Radovan Karadžić (2008) and Ratko Mladić (2011), both of whom were hiding in Serbia under assumed identities.[30] Gone and nearly forgotten are the days when the ICTY posted flyers with pictures of its "most wanted" (one such flyer is featured on this book's cover) and rented local billboards to champion its cause. Once the question of "impunity by default"[31] loomed over the work of the tribunal, as the UN discussed closing the ICTY even as Karadžić, Mladić, Gotovina, and other fugitives remained at large. Now, however, the tribunal asserts that it has "irreversibly changed the landscape of international humanitarian law."[32] It would be difficult to argue that this is untrue.

Yet the mere establishment of the institution did not guarantee that the tribunal would serve as an institution "of truth *and* consequence" (Trueheart 2000). The story of the growing institutional impact and efficacy of the ICTY, from indictments that were mere paper, because even NATO forces could not be induced to enforce them, to the trial of a former leader and diplomatic partner Slobodan Milošević – is a story that resides largely in the work of the ICTY prosecutors. From 1994 to 1996 this was South African Supreme Court justice Richard Goldstone. Following him, from 1996 to 1999, was Canadian jurist Louise Arbour, who indicted Milošević, among other acts.[33] From 1999 to 2007, the Swiss "bulldog" Carla Del Ponte led the prosecutor's office. Del Ponte successfully tied the work of the ICTY to larger initiatives, speaking for the tribunal before European Union representatives; she also successfully delayed Croatia's ascension to the European Union based on an absence of cooperation with the tribunal. Serge Brammertz, appointed in 2007, is expected to see through the closure of all cases under the Residual Mechanism which officially replaced the ICTY in 2016.

When Goldstone arrived on the job in 1994, a deputy prosecutor, the Australian Graham Blewitt, was already in place, working on indictments developed from the information collected through Bassiouni's work on the UN commission. Goldstone was content to leave the running of the office to Blewitt; he turned his attention to

29 Gotovina was eventually acquitted by the appeals chamber, discussed in Chapter 4.

30 These indictees were extradited as soon as they were apprehended (Karadžić in July 2008 and Mladić in May 2011); both had spent more than a decade in hiding.

31 Press Release SC/8409 Security Council 5199th Meeting (AM). (ICTY President Theodore Meron addressed the tribunal, arguing for an extension of the working mandate, saying that the ICTY "would not have fulfilled its historic mission – and it would not close its doors" without Karadžić, Mladić, and Gotovina in The Hague.)

32 "About the ICTY," www.icty.org/sections/AbouttheICTY (accessed April 13, 2016).

33 William Schabas (2011) argues that these reasoned, professional prosecutors assisted the institutional emergence of the International Criminal Court by allaying concerns of power-hungry, irrational, internationally appointed prosecutors.

the political problems facing the tribunal (Bass 2000). Insignificant funding and significant political obstacles stood in the way of the ICTY performing like a "real" court, which is to say holding trials for indicted suspects. In the summer of 1994 war raged on in Croatia and Bosnia; UN "safe havens" (like Srebrenica) were under threat, the civilian population of Sarajevo was under siege, and the thousands of blue-helmeted UN troops stationed in the region to try to prevent violence served as ready pawns through which western powers could be manipulated, as they were repeatedly captured and ransomed by Bosnian Serb forces. As European powers tried to broker a peace, pressures were exerted to ensure that such a peace was not disrupted by ICTY indictments of European "peace partners."

The Office of the Prosecutor (OTP) was originally allocated 126 positions, very few of which were filled. Blewitt brought in staff to OTP through his Anglo-American network (Hagan 2003: 63). The United States contributed twenty-two staffers to the OTP. This helped create what is generally recognized as a strong common-law preference in the early OTP.[34]

The first indictments issued by the ICTY's OTP were based on the data collected by Bassiouni in his work on the commission (Hagan 2003). Commission researchers had gathered information regarding vast human rights abuses in Bosnian Serb-run detention centers around Prijedor, as well as a massacre posing a potential instance of genocide at the Vukovar hospital in eastern Croatia. Goldstone felt pressured to issue an indictment for many reasons, not least among them that without work product from the tribunal, he was likely to face difficulties in securing funding from the UN, a process that had already been fraught with difficulty (Hagan 2003). Duško Tadić, a low-level participant whose name came up frequently in commission reports regarding atrocities in the camps in the Prijedor region, had been arrested in Munich after having been recognized by camp survivors in a government registration office. Germany was willing to extradite Tadić to the ICTY and the ICTY needed a case; thus Tadić became the first indictee to stand trial at the ICTY (Scharf 1997b; Bass 2000; Hagan 2003). Goldstone also oversaw the ICTY's first guilty plea, the voluntary confession of Dražen Erdemović.

Goldstone's strategy of starting with "small fish," either to work his way up the chain of command or simply to produce tribunal work product in order to increase institutional credibility, was instantly controversial. Cherif Bassiouni, who traveled to The Hague to brief Goldstone on the criminal information unearthed in his commission report, urged that Goldstone indict Serbs in the Romanija Corps (responsible for the siege of Sarajevo), or leaders responsible for the policies of ethnic cleansing (Bass 2000; Hagan 2003).

In 1995, amid tens of indictments for lesser participants, the OTP issued indictments for the Bosnian Serb leader Radovan Karadžić and the Bosnian Serb military

34 Both Bass (2000) and Hagan (2003) discuss the common-law tradition imported into the Office of the Prosecutor in detail.

chief Ratko Mladić. Karadžić and Mladić had been the subject of intense negotiations between Goldstone and Western peace negotiators such as Richard Holbrooke. Frozen out of the Dayton Peace Process in order to make indictment by the ICTY possible, Karadžić and Mladić nonetheless freely traveled throughout Bosnia and Serbia, their whereabouts known to the UN's police force, the Stabilization Force (SFOR), which was "authorized" but not "required" to arrest wanted war criminals indicted by the ICTY. In order to increase pressure on these two actors, in the summer of 1996 Goldstone brought a Rule 61 "trial in absentia" process against the two. At "trial," only the prosecution presented evidence; the result was an ICTY decision to issue an international arrest warrant against the two figures. Each of these warrants took more than a decade to serve.

The ICTY began trying its first war criminal in 1996, the Bosnian Serb Duško Tadić.[35] Tadić was a civilian during the Bosnian war and collaborated with the Bosnian Serb army without ever enlisting or officially serving. He was accused of killing several people and raping at least one woman at the Omarska prison camp, which he visited periodically. Tadić came to the tribunal's attention in Germany, where he was living after the war (Scharf 1997b). German law permits the extradition of suspected war criminals and, on this basis, Germany handed him over to the ICTY. Tadić was the opposite of a "big fish," involved in no way in planning or executing major war crimes. He was not a member of the Bosnian Serb governing or military apparatus, or even an unofficial paramilitary group. Tadić appears to have been a random citizen with a penchant for sadism who enjoyed the disorganization of early-wartime Bosnia to pursue his own criminal impulses. Nevertheless, this first case established several important doctrinal precedents, including joint criminal enterprise, the focus of Chapter 4.

When Goldstone left office in 1996, seventy-six indictments had been issued by the OTP. Most of these indictments targeted low- or intermediate-level Bosnian Serbs. Of those indicted, only eight were in custody. At Goldstone's departure, only one trial had been completed (*Tadić*) and one confession recorded (*Erdemović*).

Sociologist John Hagan (2003), in his in-depth assessment of the politics and personalities that oversaw the institutional success story of the ICTY, credits Louise Arbour with the ICTY's institutional success. Canadian jurist Louise Arbour arrived with two main projects: to acquire custody of the indicted, and to cull the indictment list (Trueheart 2000).[36] The OTP lacked any form of police force, and was entirely dependent upon state cooperation. Croatia had formally pledged cooperation but had furnished little; such cooperation was evidently based on the principle that as a victim of Serb aggression, Croatia could only benefit from ICTY action.[37] While Croatia's president Tuđman

[35] The *Tadić* case is considered in greater detail in Chapter 4.

[36] Arbour rescinded indictments against at least seventeen individuals (Bass 2000) in an effort to refocus the tribunal.

[37] In fact, at the time of his death in 1999, Tuđman was in the process of being indicted by the ICTY.

promised support to the tribunal and was an early supporter of the tribunal, this position changed rapidly in December 1995 when, after issuing several indictments against Bosnian Serbs, the ICTY in turn issued indictments against ethnic Croats. Serbia remained uncooperative, and Bosnia was governed under international mandate, yet international troops did not make arrests, for a combination of reasons ranging from troop safety to the received inconsequence of the ICTY.[38]

In order to bring ICTY indictees into custody, Arbour pressured NATO to assist in making arrests. NATO had so far resisted such co-option. Under Goldstone, international troops had been implicated in a significant misstep. Bosnian authorities had arrested two Bosnian Serb military leaders, General Đorđe Đukić and Colonel Aleksa Krsmanović, who had inadvertently crossed into Bosnian territory. Although these individuals had not been indicted by the ICTY at the time, their apprehension and captivity was a mitzvah the ICTY could not pass up. Đukić was the logistician of the Bosnian Serb army, working directly under Mladić; Krsmanović was a colonel allegedly involved in crimes against prisoners of war in Sokolac. Goldstone elicited the cooperation of the UN police force (then known as the Implementation Force [IFOR]) in "capturing" the two captives from the complicit Bosnian Muslim army; Đukić and Krsmanović were immediately transferred to The Hague. Ultimately, both men were released from ICTY custody within weeks, after the ICTY failed to build a case against them. Đukić, terminally ill with cancer, died a short time later, providing General Mladić with a public-relations goldmine as he attended the funeral in full military regalia. No NATO or UN troops arrested the indicted Mladić during this public spectacle. After this misstep, it was agreed that no non-indicted defendants would be arrested by NATO or UN troops.

Arbour also began the (controversial) practice of "sealed" (i.e., secret) indictments. The first such indictment was against Slavko Dokmanović, the Serb mayor of Vukovar who had overseen the massacre at Vukovar hospital. Dokmanović was lured from Serbia to a meeting in Vukovar, where he was captured by IFOR and transported immediately to The Hague.[39]

I Indicting Milošević

The cessation of hostilities left Milošević and Tuđman, architects of the wars in the former Yugoslavia, in power. In the winter of 1996, in response to Milošević's party's attempted falsification of election results that had seen an upswing in opposition parties, hundreds of thousands of demonstrators took to the streets of central Belgrade for weeks. Milošević managed the upheaval by stepping down as Serbian

[38] SFOR, the international force in Bosnia, killed indicted ICTY defendant Krsto Mićić during a shootout surrounding his arrest in 1999, an incident that provoked protest and outrage throughout Republika Srpska.

[39] Dokmanović hanged himself in his jail cell at the conclusion of his trial in 1998, on the eve of receipt of the verdict.

president and taking over as president of "rump" Yugoslavia (comprised of Serbia and Montenegro).

Throughout 1998, Serbian pressure on Kosovar Albanians mounted. In January 1999, forty-five civilians, including women and children, were murdered in the Kosovar village of Račak. Louise Arbour responded by flying to Macedonia and driving to the Kosovar border, where she was refused entry. Though she recounted this incident at the time as "the bottom of the pit," the political impact of Serbia refusing admittance to an internationally appointed official responsible for researching atrocities was significant, arguably moving international consensus towards a humanitarian operation in Kosovo – the NATO bombing in the spring of 1999 – as well as furthering political will to support an indictment. Milošević was indicted in the summer of 1999, the first international indictment against a sitting head of state. He was transferred to The Hague to stand trial in June 2001 after being ousted from power through a political uprising in Serbia.[40]

Richard Goldstone came to the ICTY fresh from work on South Africa's Truth and Reconciliation project, a consummate politician of Jewish extraction. Louise Arbour came as a jurist, an appellate judge from Ontario who learned English, her second language, later in her professional career. Carla Del Ponte, in contrast, arrived as a prosecutor, the "Iron Lady" a.k.a. "Bulldog" of Switzerland, trained up in corruption scandals. It is undisputed that Del Ponte arrived primed for battle, prepared to crack heads as needed. She is on record as criticizing the ICTY detention center in Schvenigen as "cushy." Her sympathies, she repeatedly stated, lie with the victims, and while all accused are of course innocent until proven guilty, she also advocated the use of the ICTY to try "notorious and despicable criminals" like Saddam Hussein and Osama Bin Laden.[41] Serge Brammertz has attracted considerably less fanfare than his predecessors, perhaps because he arrived at the tribunal after the indictment process had closed.

Del Ponte arrived to an ICTY that had indicted Milošević but had yet to detain him; infamous wanted war criminals Karadžić, Mladić, and Željko Ražnjatović, better known as Arkan, were still very publicly at large, enjoying basically full freedom of movement in Serbia and Serb-controlled Bosnia. Del Ponte oversaw the transfer of Milošević to The Hague (a delicate process that involved pressuring Serbia's willing but politically fragile president Đinđić: Đinđić was assassinated in 2003) and the beginning of his trial. Noting the difficulty of convicting under command responsibility, and charged with bringing cases directly against the "biggest fish" without benefit of any "pyramid strategy" that could use lower-level perpetrations against leaders, her office exploded the controversial use of the theory

40 Much has been written regarding the ICTY's trial of Slobodan Milošević. Milošević died in custody before the lengthy trial against him came to an end.

41 Victor Tsilonis, "Interview with the 'Iron Lady of The Hague,'" *Intellectum*, June 14, 2004, available at www.intellectum.org/articles /topics/bg_Carla Del Ponte.

of liability termed "joint criminal enterprise," the topic of Chapter 4, to win convictions.

Beginning in the late 1990s, international concern over rising tribunal costs and moderate tribunal results brought a series of UN resolutions designed to improve the efficiency of the institution, in some cases by directing the work of the OTP. A 1999 UN expert report made dozens of specific suggestions regarding tribunal practices and rules of procedure.[42] In 2003, the UN Security Council resolution 1503 directed the OTP to focus on the "gravest" breaches of IHL.[43] The resolution specifically named three wanted actors, Karadžić, Mladić, and Gotovina (president of the Bosnian Serb republic, leader of Srebrenica, and the Croatian general heading Operation Storm, respectively), who should occupy the attention of the tribunal.[44] The ICTY was directed to produce biannual reports on its progress as part of its refunding requests.[45] Under pressure from the UN Security Council, the ICTY was given a deadline to issue all indictments, and required to show how it was working towards closing down.[46]

Del Ponte is described by colleagues as a gifted politician, and indeed she used the politics of her office to significant effect. She brought effective political pressure to bear to apprehend Croatian general Ante Gotovina, as well as, ultimately, Mladić and Karadžić. It was Del Ponte, not the official ICTY spokesperson President Meron, who addressed the EU Ascension Committee regarding the cooperation (or lack thereof) of former Yugoslav states; on her recommendation, Croatia's membership of the European Union was delayed.[47] The Milošević trial, however, has been universally criticized in terms of its organization.[48] The prosecution's unwieldy case was broken into several parts, separating Milošević's actions in Kosovo, Bosnia, and Croatia. There were thousands of exhibits and hundreds of witnesses. The prosecutor's case seemed confused and nondirected when set against Milošević, who represented himself and used the ICTY to great grandstanding advantage. That Milošević died in the midst of this trial, and thus remains unjudged, is also laid at the OTP's feet. Though this cannot be the fault of the OTP, the argument holds that a leaner, faster trial would have allowed judgment in Milošević's lifetime.

42 UN Expert Report (1999) A/54/634. This report is considered in detail in Chapter 3.

43 Up until this time, the ICTY had asserted it was engaging a "pyramid strategy" that focused on "little fish" in order to climb the hierarchy. See 2003 ICTY UN report; see also Hazan (2004: 59).

44 See Schabas 2011 regarding discussion of whether such direction violates the right to a fair trial by challenging a defendant's presumption of innocence. In this case, commentators have argued that the Security Council is not trying the defendants, so the presumption remains intact.

45 ICTY Statute Article 34, S/25704.

46 UN resolution 1534 (March 26, 2004). At this time, both Mladić and Karadžić were still at large, and ICTY President Meron went on record to opine that without their capture, the legacy of the court would be tarnished.

47 Institutionally, the president of the ICTY represents the tribunal, not the prosecutor. Del Ponte's assumption of this duty complicates the idea of prosecutorial impartiality central to civil-law culture and procedure. This is explored more fully in Chapter 3.

48 See, e.g., Boas 2007.

Empirical considerations of the ICTY's efficacy and influence are still in their infancy[49] and there is, as yet, little hard evidence to support the argument that the ICTY has generated a reconciliatory or unifying narrative in the former Yugoslavia. Indeed, in the twenty-five years following the creation of the ICTY, the leaders and peoples of nations of the former Yugoslavia have shown, if anything, a determined resistance to the "truths" the ICTY has sought to articulate. The Croatian General Ante Gotovina, for example, a non-entity in Croatia before the war, has emerged from his ICTY indictment, years in hiding, eventual arrest, and ultimate acquittal as a *bona fide* Croatian hero.[50] Serving as leader in absentia, the far-right Serbian Radical Party (SRS) of Vojislav Šešelj was only narrowly defeated in presidential elections in 2008 while he awaited trial in The Hague.[51] Šešelj's 2016 acquittal was partially reversed in April 2018, and although his conviction should, in following Serbian law, preclude his continuing to serve in parliament, as of this writing he has neither stepped down nor been forced out. Slobodan Milošević, deposed by his own people, saw a rebound in his popularity in the years he stood trial at the tribunal.[52] Meanwhile, even established truths regarding the war – the source of mortars that killed tens of civilians on multiple occasions in Sarajevo marketplaces, for example, or the massacre (genocide) of at least seven thousand men and boys at Srebrenica in 1995 – have remained contested or unacknowledged following multiple ICTY considerations. The more abstract *truths* justifying the work of the ICTY, such as the truth of ethnic nationalism and separatism as invented by power-hungry elites and lacking any foundation in larger Balkan populations,[53] are not presently discourses of interest in the former Yugoslavia. The ICTY itself is a deeply unpopular

49 See Kristen Cibelli and Tamy Guberek, "Justice Unknown, Justice Unsatisfied: Bosnian NGOs Speak about the International Criminal Tribunal for the Former Yugoslavia," (Tufts University 2000); Lara Nettelfield, *Courting Democracy in Bosnia and Herzegovina: The Hague Tribunal's Impact in a Post-war State* (Cambridge: Cambridge University Press, 2012); Carlson et al, "Justice, Accountability and Social Reconstruction: An Interview Study of Bosnian Judges and Prosecutors," *Berkeley Journal of International Law* 18 (2000): 102–164.

50 Gotovina, who led Operation Storm in 1995 (the military operation that recaptured the Krajina for Croatia) was indicted and pursued for years by the ICTY before finally falling into tribunal custody. The trial chamber sentenced him to twenty-four years in 2011, and the appellate chamber, in a contentious 3–2 decision, acquitted him in 2012. Gotovina's interaction with the ICTY as the highest-ranking Croat before the court has bestowed hero status on him; he has become the beloved subject of banners, bumper stickers, posters, billboards, and at least one comic book.

51 The result of the second round of voting was 50 percent of the vote for Tadić's Democratic Party (DS) and 47 percent for the Serbian Radical Party (SRS), represented by Tomislav Nikolić. After breaking with the SRS, Nikolić went on to win the Serbian presidency in 2012. He has recently denied that genocide was committed at Srebrenica, and has refused to visit the commemoration of the massacre, as his predecessor Tadić did. "Serbian President Denies Srebrenica Genocide," *The Guardian*, June 2, 2012.

52 In a poll taken in 2005, Milošević was the third most popular politician in Serbia, behind Nikolić and Tadić. "Opinion Poll Shows Milošević More Popular in Serbia than Premier," BBC Monitoring International Reports, April 22, 2005, available at www.slobodan-Milošević.org/news/foneto42205.htm (last accessed February 25, 2013).

53 See Akhavan 1998.

institution, and even those populations most amenable to the ICTY, such as Bosnian Muslims, accept only those tribunal decisions "in their favor."[54]

The ICTY's significant institutional story is not matched by a similarly convincing jurisprudential story. The ICTY survived, as an institution, and prospered, in a way that is unmatched by other ad hoc tribunals (the fate of the ICC is still unknown, but it is beleaguered). The ICTY is a model ICT, and has not faced challenges to its efficacy, objectivity, or practice in the ways that have been typical of other ICTs such as the International Criminal Tribunal for Rwanda, the Extraordinary Chambers in the Courts of Cambodia, or the Special Tribunal for Lebanon. Yet the doctrinal developments of the ICTY are not equal to its institutional creativity, efficacy, and success. In substance, ICTY jurisprudence remains the justice of *Velpke*, rather than the communicative criminal justice pursued by liberal regimes.

CONCLUSION

This chapter has shown how ICL tracks the uneasy coalition between law and politics. Law serves a sovereign, and is therefore necessarily, structurally, political (Shapiro 1986). International criminal law works under similar constraints, although the sovereign is less obvious, more contested, or may arguably even be contradictory, since international organizations may, in exercising agency, diverge from following the interests of their founding member states (Klabbers 2015). Yet if legal institutions are necessarily in service to political interest, they enjoy legitimacy only so long as they act as objective arbiters of pre-existing rules.

This chapter's close reading of *Velpke* showcases the problematic foundation of ICL as "progressive" using a vehicle where the structural and moral obstacles of applying "liberalism" are more visible than in prosecutions of high-level Nazis, such as was the case at the IMT. Where IMT prosecutions against leading Nazis and their sympathizers tend to obscure questions of how "progressive" that law may be due to the moral imperative of finding a legal response to Nazi atrocity ("if what they did wasn't illegal, then it should have been!"), the prosecution of more mundane elements of life under Nazi rule helps make the case. Contrasting *Velpke* against the International Military Tribunal for the Far East (IMTFE) discussed in Chapter 1 also offers a contrasting example of the use of law as a space for debate. The IMTFE made the contestations within the institution visible, and emerged a less effective and impactful transitional justice mechanism for it. Decisions such as *Velpke*, on the other hand, shroud legal rationale, offering a determination from which principle is difficult to extract. This has proved a more fertile ground in the development of ICL, demonstrated by the resurrection of these cases in modern ICL.

[54] These challenges are considered in greater detail in Chapters 5 and 6.

PART II

Applying International Criminal Law's Paradoxes to Paradigmatic International Criminal Law Doctrine: Post-Rule-of-Law Procedure, and Illiberal Theories of Culpability

In Part II, the book applies the theories developed in Chapters 1 and 2 to paradigmatic jurisprudence from the International Criminal Tribunal for the former Yugoslavia (ICTY). Chapter 3 considers the problems and paradoxes occasioned in the ICTY's greenfield development of international criminal legal procedure, and Chapter 4 does the same for one central element of ICTY substantive doctrine, the theory of liability of joint criminal enterprise (JCE). Throughout, the chapters illustrate the problems and paradoxes occasioned by the legitimizing rationale of "progress" that underwrites international criminal law, as well as the inescapable problem of non-derogable legal doctrine in international criminal law practice; these are the theoretical paradoxes of international criminal law that are described and developed in Part I.

The ICTY has officially closed and passed outstanding matters on to the International Residual Mechanism for International Tribunals, which is hearing the ICTY's final appeals. International criminal law does not officially recognize precedent. Therefore the ICTY's decisions, rationales, and pronouncements will in the future only enjoy the importance that theorists, practitioners, or law makers afford them. Jurisprudence from the ICTY may prove to be central to future international criminal law development, of course: much as the ICTY has drawn on International Military Tribunal (IMT) at Nuremberg jurisprudence to support development of its own jurisprudence, so too may future tribunals existent and not yet imagined turn to the ICTY's archives to support their own emerging doctrine. Naturally, any future tribunal relying on ICTY procedural or substantive law will do so through its own particularized constraints and in its own specific context. It might therefore not be unreasonable for a skeptical reader to ask: what can a close reading of what is quickly becoming merely historical international criminal jurisprudence offer the forward-looking student or practitioner of international criminal law or transitional justice?

The answer is that the challenges *Model(ing) Justice* identifies in international criminal law practice are generalizable across institutions. The case study of ICTY jurisprudence in the following two chapters applies the paradoxical legitimizing force of "progressiveness" in international law and the conflict occasioned by non-derogable criminal sanction. The book's focus on the evolution of procedure in a direction prized for "efficiency" (Chapter 3) and the development of a theory of liability that permits no defense at law (Chapter 4) gives substance to the theories of international criminal law structure and practice articulated in Part I. The following chapters demonstrate the challenges inherent in international criminal tribunals' central legitimizing tenet, that they develop and apply progressive international criminal law. The following paradigmatic international criminal law practices reveal and reify the illiberal construct of exercising judicial power within a singular constraint of progressiveness.

3

Post-Rule of Law

International Criminal Procedure and Its Evolution before the ICTY

Beginning with the International Military Tribunal (IMT) at Nuremberg, international criminal tribunals (ICTs) have developed and applied a hybrid criminal procedure, drawing on practices from two of the world's major legal traditions, common law and civil law. As institutions practicing international criminal law (ICL) have expanded, and as twenty years of jurisprudence from the Yugoslav and Rwanda tribunals joins a growing jurisprudence from the International Criminal Court (ICC), international criminal procedure (ICP) has emerged as a legal field. International criminal procedure is the subject of several legal treatises,[1] and is taught in some law schools.

The value of developing *hybrid* ICP is that it is arguably inclusive (representing two major legal traditions) and distinct from any domestic system, thus creating a separate, *sui generis* realm for ICL jurists to meet (Robinson 2000; Delmas-Marty 2003). Naturally, this procedure is founded in a respect for human rights and should be progressive (Zappalà 2003). Yet since its inception at Nuremberg, individual elements of hybridity have consistently caused concern among practitioners and legal theorists, largely around questions of transposition as jurists from one tradition resisted practices from the other.[2] Transposition problems remain unresolved in modern ICP and have received extensive attention in the literature.[3] The practice of hybridity itself, however – the determination to operationalize ICL through procedures drawing from different legal traditions, with specific practices drawn from singular jurisdictions – has received less critical scrutiny.[4]

This chapter addresses the practice of hybridity in ICP, drawing examples from the construction and evolution of hybrid procedure at the ICTY to argue that ICT

[1] See, e.g., Cryer 2014; Tochilovsky 2008, 2010; Shahabuddeen 2012; Whiting 2011; May & Wierda 2002; Bassiouni 2013.

[2] For example, at the IMT, the charge of conspiracy, as drawn from the common law, was resisted by those trained in the civil-law tradition (Pomorski 1990).

[3] See, for example, the rich discussion on plea bargaining before ICTs (Henham & Drumbl 2005; Harmon & Gaynor 2007; Rauxloh 2010).

[4] Much of the critical commentary examining hybridity in fact seeks practical resolutions designed to improve the "marriage" of the two systems as represented at ICP. See, e.g., Skilbeck 2010; Fairlie 2004.

operation is "post-rule of law". Rule-of-law processes underwrite liberalism and legalism and shore up the rationale for ICL. The central function of ICTs is to deliver (as courts) and model (as didactic institutions) justice (Damaška 2009; Luban 2010; Nettelfield 2010). Yet ICTs face particular pressures that distinguish them from domestic criminal courts; specifically, to achieve convictions in order to justify the public resources expended on international trials.[5] These pressures emerge from the principal–agent relationship between ICTs and the community of states they serve, a structure that excludes the interests of third parties and is common to international organizations (IOs) generally (Klabbers 2015). Unlike other IOs, however, ICTs' failures of accountability to third parties challenge their capacity to meaningfully perform their central function (because delivering and modeling "justice" turns on the legitimacy courts enjoy before third parties) (Bodansky 2012).

The chapter is divided into four parts. Part one explores civil- and common-law systems as cultural typologies. Both traditions share similar goals and rationales for criminal sanctions – both empower a state apparatus to substitute private retribution with a public process through which the guilty are punished and the innocent exonerated – yet the means applied differ significantly. Part two contrasts the specifics of criminal procedure between the two systems, demonstrating how the logic of each typology maps onto procedural elements in domestic criminal law practice. Part three moves these considerations to the international realm, examining some specifics of ICTY procedure to show how the ICTY's evolving procedure constitutes civil-law methods *harnessed* by common-law methodologies, a situation that threatens institutional legitimacy through a structural disregard for the presumption of innocence. Part four argues that the practice of hybridity at ICL has effectively placed its institutions not as bulwarks of a cosmopolitan, global rule-of-law system, but rather as institutions that have deliberately identified themselves as exempt from rule-of-law strictures; they have become, as the title evokes, "post-rule of law". The fourth part concludes with two examples of a post-rule-of-law ICL practice, sentencing and plea bargains before the ICTY.

I LEGAL TYPOLOGIES AS LEGAL CULTURES

John Merryman's ([1969] 2007) classic monograph on the civil law distinguishes legal *traditions* (civil law and common law) from particularized legal *systems* within

[5] See, for example, Report of the Secretary-General, *The rule of law and transitional justice in conflict and post-conflict societies*, UN Doc. S/2004/616 para 42 (August 23, 2004): "The two ad hoc tribunals have grown into large institutions, with more than 2,000 posts between them and a combined annual budget exceeding a quarter of a billion dollars – equivalent to more than 15 per cent of the Organization's total regular budget. Although trying complex legal cases of this nature would be expensive for any legal system and the tribunals' impact and performance cannot be measured in financial numbers alone, the stark differential between cost and number of cases processed does raise important questions."

those traditions. In some contemporary discourse, however, making distinctions between the dichotomies of the two systems has become passé. Challenges come in several forms. Some commentators insist that the extensive borrowing between legal systems makes discussions of distinct or separate legal schools obsolete (Ambos 2003). Others seek to draw distinctions between domestic and international practices that would make categories applied to domestic legal systems inapplicable at international law (Langer 2004). Moreover, there is a scholarly split between theorists of ICL and comparative law scholars (Delmas-Marty 2003; Vogler 2011; Grande 2012), and within comparative law scholarship itself, regarding the possibility and compatibility of legal transplants.[6]

Resistance from contemporary commentators notwithstanding, this first section traces the distinct ideological impulses that distinguish the two Western legal traditions of common and civil law, arguing that these ideological frameworks substantiate individual understandings of how justice and fairness are practiced. At criminal law, procedure is the framework for substantive justice to be performed. Faulty procedure, or procedure not received as legitimate, will raise justice concerns even where the outcome is desired or understandable. Put another way, procedure seen as legitimate has the potential to make even an undesired outcome "fair" to observers (Tyler 2006). Thus the question of ICP's structure has traction far beyond its practitioners, with wider ramifications for the legitimacy of ICL and its understood capacity as a mechanism for transitional justice and institutional modeling.

A *Criminal Law Processes in Common-Law and Civil-Law Traditions*

Rule-of-law practice is central to common- and civil-law traditions in the modern age. Rule-of-law practices place the transparency and even application of democratically determined laws at the center of state action (Müller 2011). The rule of law encompasses ideas of balance, fairness, and the social contract, where the legitimacy of government rests on the consent of the governed. Rule-of-law practice is particularly central to the sensitive business of turning the massive power of the state against the individual to potentially deprive them of liberty or property: i.e., the practice of criminal law. Criminal procedure is substantive criminal law operationalized per a rule-of-law standard.

Although Western criminal systems have indeed borrowed much from each other, there remain central foundational ideologies that separate the common- and civil-law traditions (Damaška 1986). Common law, also referred to as "judge-made law" developed in England and was exported to its former colonies. Common law recognizes precedent – previously decided cases – as a form of legal authority. Also known as "adversarial law," the common-law tradition subscribes to the value of

[6] Where there is a debate regarding whether practices can be "transplanted" (Watson 1974) or whether the context in which a rule exists is essential to that rule's function, so that where a rule or practice removed from its native context likely loses significant meaning (Nelken 2003; Legrand 1997).

a contest in order to determine truth. This "marketplace of ideas" approach, wherein the strongest idea should triumph, positions the court, and very specifically the trial, as the site where social and legal norms are decided or affirmed.

Common law ensures a fair trial through procedural safeguards surrounding the performance of the trial itself (such as common law's notoriously complex rules of evidence). At common law, trials represent the exposition, climax, and dénouement of the story being told. Trials are characterized by spectacle and performance (Burns 2001) (often referred to as the central "orality" of the proceedings). Because of the uncertainty of trial outcomes, both sides in the contest (the prosecution and the defense, who are adversaries) enjoy incentives to bargain or otherwise avoid trial. In the particularized common-law system of the US, for example, plea bargaining (wherein defendant and prosecution agree on the outcome of the case and thereby avoid jury trial) is estimated to dispose of up to 95 percent of criminal cases (Fisher 2000).

Civil law, also known as "codified law" or inquisitorial law, follows the principle articulated by Montesquieu that a legal code, drafted by legislators, constitutes the law that must be applied, without creativity or approximation, by judges. Civil-law systems construct procedure around an investigation carried out by several state parties that engage in, and oversee, the state's search for the truth. This is seen as the "one case" (Ambos 2003) or "unity of meaning" (Garapon & Papadopoulous 2004) approach because impartial public officials seeking the truth of a matter construct a single *dossier* containing all evidence and argument gathered. The unity of the argument means that criminal liability is assessed before trial; in the words of ICTY defense attorney Michael Karnavas (2007), "before indicting a suspect and putting him or her through the meat-grinding process of a criminal trial, the prosecutor in the civil law system will be virtually certain that the evidence gathered and available to the court will support a guilty verdict." Trials in civil-law systems serve as moments of transparency to reveal the work of the state and are unavoidable (i.e., a defendant's admission of guilt does not cancel the requirement that she face trial). Acquittals are rare, and in the event a defendant is acquitted, this decision may be appealed by the prosecutor. Finally, civil law views law and politics as antithetical; civil-law processes are designed to limit subjectivity, understood as contradiction of the uniformity and predictability that constitutes the rule of law. From the administrative nature of judicial appointments and review, to the prohibition that judges participate in political organizations, and extending to its treatment of a singular truth, the civil law is committed to engaging in a scientific, objective pursuit of justice.

B *Legal Traditions' Ideologies and Cultures*

A central ideological distinction between common-law and civil-law systems is epistemological, and concerns the question of how best to reach truth (Damaška

1997; Zappalà 2003). It is important not to overstate this difference: some commentators would make truth "seminal" to the civil law or merely "procedural" to the common law (Fairlie 2004). Both systems seek truth, because the substantive justice of imprisoning an individual resides in truth (Holtermann 2017). Rather, the epistemological divide between the two systems consists of the means of knowing. This divide has been categorized as the "two case" vs. "one case" model (Ambos 2003) or the "dispute" versus "the official investigation" model (Damaška 1986). Common-law criminal procedure is characterized by two sides (the prosecution and the defense), each an "interested party" with a stake in the outcome of the contest. The defendant, whose liberty is at issue, is obviously an interested party. But the prosecution, too, though nominally charged with pursuing justice, tends to view convictions as "wins" and acquittals as "losses" (Pizzi 1993). At common law the prosecution and the defense separately assemble their own facts, witnesses, and arguments in order to present two competing cases, which come to a head at trial. The contest between the parties consists largely in the disclosure (or withholding) of information. The judge acts as a referee in this contest, assuring that procedural rules are followed and controlling the information available to the decision-maker, the jury. As Damaška (1986) notes, the binary nature of the contest between prosecution and defense excludes the possibility of representing a third interest, that of the victim. This is in stark contrast with civil-law traditions, where the truth is discovered through the studied construction, by disinterested parties, of all the relevant facts.

The two traditions imagine a very distinct role for the judge, what Damaška calls "separate ideas of officialdom." The civil-law judge is a bureaucrat: positions are appointed by examination, and judges in civil-law systems are both more numerous, and younger, than their common-law counterparts (Bohlander 2012). The job of the civil law judge is to decide "correctly," which may be understood as uniformly; dissenting opinions are generally swallowed except in the highest courts, and judgments move up a hierarchical pyramid to be corrected as necessary (Merryman and Perez-Perdomo, 2007, 1969; Damaška 1986). The common-law judge, on the other hand, is encouraged to "individualize" justice (Damaška 1986). This is operationalized through the production of carefully reasoned judgments, including concurring and dissenting opinions. The reasoning offered by these decisions may enter wider social conversations and direct social and political narratives, or styles of argument (Shklar 1964/1986; Osiel 1997). Thus the institutionalization of legal apparatuses translates into distinct legal cultures between the two traditions. Justice as idealized within the civil-law tradition resides in the careful, measured adherence to formalities decreed by the legislature and institutionalized in judicial practice. Justice as idealized within the common-law tradition resides in the strength of the argument made within a judicial determination.[7]

[7] These are ideal types (Weber 1904/1949). Note that the actual practice of justice in both systems would recognize both of these ideal types as important: common-law lawyers would reject the suggestion that

Commitment to one's legal culture (specifically, the understandings of how justice is served imagined through one's native legal typology)[8] appears moral, even quasi-religious.[9] In the nineteenth century, Max Weber characterized the common law system as "irrational" (Morris 1958; Hunt 1978; Weber 1954), and contemporary sources suggest little has changed regarding the distrust that legal practitioners show for typologies not their own. Even those practitioners positioned at legal crossroads – practitioners working in hybrid international systems, or comparativists interested in legal systems outside their own – exhibit great difficulty overcoming a bias towards their primary understanding of how justice, fairness, and rule of law are practiced. Interviews conducted with ICTY personnel confirmed these deep-rooted biases playing out in ICL practice. One civil-law-trained employee in the ICTY's Office of the Prosecutor (OTP), considering the deep differences he noticed between how different chambers at the ICTY work, explained the following:

> Some [ICTY procedural] rules make more sense to you, so you apply them. The rest you ignore. As you're reading through the rules, you pick the ones you like, that make sense. Everybody does this. OTP, defense, judges – they all do. This is wrong – people should come to the ICTY to learn. But instead they import some things and not others.[10]

Even where lawyers trained in one tradition seek to praise practices borrowed from the other, the prejudices emerging from their native typology emerge. Consider one common-law-trained attorney in the OTP, on the "value" of civil-law procedure:

> One of the benefits of working at the ICTY is that I see how stupid many common law things are. The civil law is totally intolerant of many stupid technical arguments why evidence shouldn't be admitted. Civil law lets in everything, and the judge can decide what weight to give things. This is very good at getting at the truth. Because the role of a good defense attorney is to stop the truth from getting out. A good defense attorney just needs to throw enough obstacles in front of the prosecutor so that he hasn't proved his case, and he's won. That's not good for truth. In order to

law for them is not "measured", and civil-law lawyers would reject the notion that strength of argument should be absent from law.

8 For a thorough definition of legal culture see Klare 1998: 167: "By legal culture I mean professional sensibilities, habits of mind, and intellectual reflexes: What are the characteristic rhetorical strategies developed by participants in any given legal setting? What is their repertoire of recurring argumentative moves? What counts as a persuasive legal argument? What types of arguments, possibly valid in other contexts (e.g., in political philosophy), are deemed outside the professional discourse of lawyers? What enduring political and ethical commitments influence professional discourse? What are understandings of and assumptions about politics, social life and justice? What inarticulate premises [are] culturally and historically ingrained in the professional discourse and outlook?" (internal citations omitted).

9 "To common law ears, the strange cluster of the words 'the Appeals Chamber convicted him' sounds blasphemous." (Gordon 2006: 45).

10 Interview May 2005 ICTY The Hague OTP.

> advance reconciliation, you don't want to use technical argument to exclude evidence. You want to let the truth get out.[11]

For this OTP employee, legal practice was still very much based in an adversarial typology, and civil-law procedure had appeal because of what it might permit him "to win." Opinion remains divided even at the highest judicial echelons. Although ICTY Justice Antonio Cassese called hybridity "felicitous" in the *Erdemović* case,[12] other judges at the ICTY are less sanguine (Wald 2001; Orie 2002).

Of course, problems of transposition and translation are only magnified for practitioners without experience of other legal cultures.[13] This has ramifications regarding equality of arms, an imbalance to which common-law processes are quite sensitive.

C Is Either Tradition "Better" for International Criminal Procedure?

Both civil law and common law search for truth: does one system do it better, or is one system better positioned to function for ICTs? International criminal law is characterized by particularities that distinguish it from domestic criminal law (Warbrick 1998; Mégret & Hoffman 2003; Langer 2005; Mégret 2009; Jackson 2009). Thus, arguably, the rationales applied to strengths and weaknesses of procedure within the two traditions must be reconfigured when applied to the international realm. For example, the presumption of innocence that obtains domestically, permitting defendants to remain free pending trial, barring extenuating circumstances, is necessarily different at ICL, where ICTs do not enjoy police powers and can have great difficulty procuring defendants. Likewise, relaxing rules of evidence is sometimes argued as essential in ICL practice, where chaotic conditions make the collection of evidence in relation to a crime difficult or render it nonexistent.

The strength of the civil law is seen as its written, multiparty investigation, where police, prosecutor, and judicial official are all charged explicitly with finding the truth of a crime, a process that translates legally into finding *all* evidence, both incriminating and exculpatory (Langbein 1985). This means that the substantial resources of the state are (at least in theory) at the service of the

11 *Ibid.*

12 *Prosecutor* v. *Dražen Erdemović*, Appeals Chamber, October 7, 1997, Separate and Dissenting Opinion of Judge Antonio Cassese para 5.

13 The defense attorney in the *Kupreskić* case, for example, admitted to being entirely confused by ICTY investigation techniques: "We ... asked the investigators to come to Vitez and not to interview only one side ... It was first time that I come across the problem of 'my witnesses and your witnesses', because in the area in which we worked, we usually had witnesses of the court, a person who has to tell the truth regardless of whether he is speaking in favour of the Defense or the Prosecution. He conveys what he saw and what he heard." *Kupreskić* Trial Transcript (August 27, 1998), available at www.icty.org, Defense Attorney Radovan, 1220:11–1221:3. See also Lerner 2001 (detailing the difficulties of explaining how the "adversarialness" of US proceedings colors all forms of evidence and inquiry for a French judge and prosecutor).

defense as well as the prosecution. The one-case approach imagines that a defendant gets what is coming to him, but not what shouldn't be. The written nature of civil-law procedure also curtails the defendant's capacity to "get off on a technicality," as it permits fewer surprises. As applied to ICL, inquisitorial traditions are argued to serve ICL's ends because of a desire for ICL procedures to produce objective history (Rauxloh 2010).

The weakness of the one-case approach hinges on the capacity of the state to represent "justice" that includes a defendant's right not to stand falsely accused or convicted. Civil-law pre-trial investigations hinge on individuals who must represent the state impartially. Some (common-law-trained) academics argue it is unrealistic to imagine that the state's investigators can remain impartial (Keen 2004), finding that civil-law processes "require[] an inordinate amount of faith in the integrity of the state and its capacity to pursue truth unprompted by partisan pressures" (Brants *et al.* 1995: 46). In the case of ICL, where the scale of atrocity, human suffering, or both, is so high, where "the very seriousness of the charge means that only limited analogies may be made with domestic processes at large" (Warbrick 1998: 53), is the impartiality of investigators taxed too heavily to be believed?

More critically, the civil-law model presumes, for the purposes of justice, a certain homogeneity of understanding, where all parties to the case, from the defendant to the state representatives, share expectations regarding justice (McKillop 1997). Heterogeneous cultural expectations present challenges to criminal trials in any legal tradition (Renteln 2005), but common-law traditions at least open a space for debate about heterogeneity of meaning, from the use of a lay jury that has the capacity to "nullify" the law as dictated by the judge (Conrad 1998) to the adversarial training that teaches liberal constructions of analogy. Civil-law traditions do not possess these same spaces or tools, and are thus arguably particularly challenged when adjudicating across heterogeneous cultures, ideas, or interpretations.

The question, then, remains: would common-law processes perform better? Common-law procedures are often referred to as "friendly for the defense," because to secure acquittal (which is generally unappealable) the defense need only introduce reasonable doubt into the prosecution's case. One the one hand, common law is criticized for its sensitivity to inequality of arms issues. The "fight" that characterizes common-law processes cannot be fair when both sides are not equipped for it. In domestic systems, a central obstacle to equity at arms is financial; what sort of representation can a defendant afford? Michael Karnavas (2007), a defense attorney at the ICTY, states that inequality of resources between prosecution and defense has characterized ICTY practice. Moreover, in the international arena, resource questions extend beyond the defendant's financial capacity to hire a competent lawyer, and include international politics and evolution of ICL procedure and judging itself. William Schabas (2011) argues that the difficulties procuring evidence from uncooperative states might argue in favor of defendants being better served by an inquisitorial system. Is it possible to equip an individual defendant for a "fair fight" when the opponent is "humanity"?

Thus the critical question should be not which tradition offers greater "efficiency," but rather whether either system offers resources to subvert Lyotard's *différend* paradox, paraphrased by Koskenniemi (2002: 17) as where "to accept a method or criterion of settlement is already to have accepted the position of one's adversary." As Martin Shapiro (1986) notes, all law necessarily serves a sovereign. As Jan Klabbers (2015) observes, for international organizations, that sovereign is the body of states constructing them. International criminal law already, problematically, holds individuals accountable for actions made possible (or sometimes even mandated) by a collective (Fletcher 2004; Allot 1990; Drumbl 2005). Does either system provide meaningful tools to permit the international organization that is an ICT to escape the principle–agent model identified by Klabbers in order to meaningfully include the interest of third parties?

II CRIMINAL LAW PRACTICE

This section describes and contrasts select elements of domestic criminal pre-trial and trial procedure within civil- and common-law systems in order to tie the procedural mechanisms used in both systems to the animating epistemological logics discussed above. Even where both systems share forms, roles, rules, and goals, it is problematic to compare any element from one system against its partner in the other without considering what a rule, or practice, means within a system, and what purpose the rule or practice serves. Thus imbalances will obtain where, for example, practitioners apply the civil law's "ease of conviction" without similarly incorporating the civil law's front-loaded, state-balanced investigation procedure.

As discussed earlier, a central distinction between the two systems is evidenced by the purpose of the trial: at civil law, the trial showcases the work of the state to the public (where the defendant's guilt has been determined in the pre-trial phase); at common law, the trial is the site where guilt or innocence is determined. The forms taken by pre-trial and trial procedures fit these distinct purposes.

A *Pre-Trial*

Pre-trial investigations begin in both systems with a crime and police investigation. When the investigation is sufficiently advanced, the prosecutor is brought in. At common law, the prosecutor has discretion as to whether or not to press charges against the accused, as well as to what the content of such charges should be;[14] this is

[14] There is a vast literature on prosecutorial discretion. See, e.g., Miller 1970 and Davis 1969. Levine (2006: 697) identifies two "filters" of discretion, the first at the macro level (which relies on the understood purpose of a statute to distinguish between "real" and "technical" crimes), and the second at the micro level (which includes "office policy, resource allocation, and the multitude of decisions

the beginning of the "bargain" with the defense, which will, in the vast majority of cases, preclude the case going to trial. In most civil-law systems, such prosecutorial discretion is substantially curtailed.[15] In civil-law systems, the "grade" of the crime determines whether there will be an administrative hearing or whether an independent investigating arm of the state will be assigned to the case.

A central feature of the civil-law pre-trial investigation is the responsibility of the arms of the state investigating to seek *incriminating and exculpatory* evidence regarding subjects of inquiry. This process is overseen by other, separate state entities, also charged with investigating the truth. This might be, as in France, the *juge d'instruction* (investigating judge), the *Ermittlungsrichter* (intermediate judges) in Germany, or the *Guidici per le indagini preliminary* (judges of preliminary inquiry) in Italy.[16] In the event that a defendant is believed to be responsible for a crime, a charge is brought against her, at which time the entirety of the dossier is made available to her. The defense is entitled to the full benefit of the information contained in the dossier; civil law hews to the theory that open investigations are the best methods of ascertaining the truth of events. Finally, at civil law, the victim of a crime may join the case, not as a witness for the state (as at common law) but as an actual party to the criminal case. Such participation begins in the pre-trial stage of the proceedings.

At common law, the prosecutor receives the police investigation, and determines whether to bring a charge and if so what charge to bring. While ostensibly an arm of the state, the common-law prosecutor is an adversarial party. This plays out, in the investigation stage, in the prosecutor's requirement to *turn over* to the defense any exculpatory evidence they find during their investigation, but not to *seek out* such exculpatory evidence. After an investigation, the prosecutor brings a charge. Charge inflation is typical. Charge inflation is an effective technique to encourage a defendant to plead guilty to a lesser charge and thus to dispense with the necessity of a trial.

prosecutors must make in each case against the backdrop of discretion exercised by other criminal justice actors").

15 There is also a significant English-language literature on prosecutorial discretion, or lack thereof, in the civil law, focusing largely on Germany and France. German civil law, for example, is said to mandate prosecution through application of the Legalitätsprinzip. Other authors, however, dispute this mandatory prosecution theory, citing the German law's Opportunitätsprinzip, a principle of expediency, which permits prosecutors not to move forward on a case based on the triviality of the offense. This is still quite distinct from US-styled prosecutorial discretion, as any application of Opportunitätsprinzip must be justifiable on "rational" grounds and can be reviewed by higher courts on this ground. See Damaška 1981 (reviewing Thomas Weigend's book); see also Langbein 1974 and the exchange between Langbein, Weinrib, Goldstein, and Marcus in the *Yale Law Journal* 1977–1978. See also Bohlander 2012 (showing that only 23.4 percent of criminal charges were actually indicted using data from the German prosecution service in 2006).

16 See discussion in Salas 2006, regarding how the German and Italian models differ from the French *juge d'instruction* and are designed to prevent the concentration of power that one finds in the French model.

The central distinction between the pre-trial process in the two systems is its purpose. At civil law, pre-trial procedure is designed to determine the likely guilt of the party charged. The standard of proof is "*intime conviction*," the "inner certainty" of the trier of fact (Ricouer 1991; Bohlander 2014).[17] This standard is the same across all stages of the proceedings, from pre-trial through the trial, which is distinct from the common law, which uses a *prima facie* standard at pre-trial, before a grand jury, to determine whether or not to go forward, and a "beyond reasonable doubt" standard at the trial phase of criminal proceedings. At civil law, the resources of the system are concentrated on determining whether or not further system resources should be expended – clearly, neither the state nor the defendant benefits from prosecuting an innocent party. Defendants imagined guilty on the balance of all evidence are sent on to trial, where an official determination of guilt is virtually assured.

At common law, the guilt of the party charged is determined at trial. Trials, however, consume substantial state resources, and are largely avoided. In addition to the work of the prosecutor in preparing for trial, there is the selection and employment of a jury, counsel for indigent defendants, and the trial itself, an affair that can range in duration from less than a day to several years. These costs must all be borne by the state. Moreover, the unscripted, oral trial process before a lay jury makes outcomes uncertain and trials carry a high likelihood of acquittal. Jury trials, the nearly mythic centerpieces of common law, are thus in fact comparatively very rare occurrences; only a tiny fraction of the criminal offenses committed in common-law systems are ever adjudicated by a judge and jury. We should therefore understand that the purpose of the pre-trial process at common law is to seek to avoid trial. This avoidance, however, is not obtained by expending additional state resources, as in the civil-law tradition, to determine the defendant's guilt during an investigative phase and therefore *to try only guilty parties*. Instead, common-law systems use prosecutorial discretion and, in some systems, plea bargaining to cull criminal charges from proceeding to trial.

B Trial

As detailed previously, a central facet distinguishing the *trial* in common- and civil-law criminal procedure begins with the *pre-trial* apparatus, which sets up what kind of truth finding (ascertaining the truth, as at common law, or confirming the truth, as at civil law) the trial is designed to produce. At common law, the trial is the proving ground, where the majority of the "action" happens.[18] At civil law, the action

[17] Bohlander finds that the level of certainty for the civil-law judge is the same as the common law's "beyond a reasonable doubt" standard.

[18] In fact, if one considers pre-trial motions at common law to be arguments about how the trial will be conducted (including discovery, which determines the information that is known and included, as well as motions regarding the inclusion and exclusion of expert testimony, evidence, and witness

happens during the investigation preceding the trial, and the trial is the transparent element of the process that allows the public to observe the judicial branch in action.[19]

The different role played by trials in the two systems is furthermore demonstrated through the different demands on the participating parties through the roles they are required to play in both systems. Common-law proceedings are understood to represent a contest between two sides, in which prosecution and defense square off, with the judge as neutral arbiter. In this conception of the trial, the intervention of judges should be limited to guiding the parties regarding the tools they are allowed to bring or use in the contest. Judicial participation is limited in part by the inferior familiarity of judges with the case. At trial, the case is laid out before the judge in its specifics for the first time; the parties are the experts, and the judge is a level removed. But judicial participation is also limited for reasons of neutrality and legitimacy: any further, or more direct, intervention on the part of judges – such as questioning a witness – is understood to threaten the objectivity of the proceedings by allowing the finder of law (the judge) to potentially influence the views of the finders of fact (the jury). The jury, after hearing the cases presented by the two opposing sides, and upon being instructed on the applicable law by the judge, retires to confidentially determine the guilt of the accused. This determination must usually be unanimous.

Civil-law trials, by contrast, are generally overseen by a three-judge panel. Judges direct the process and enjoy a much more active role than their common-law counterparts, questioning witnesses directly, and demanding further evidence, investigation, or witness testimony where they deem necessary. The dossier containing all relevant facts of a case is provided to the judges before trial, allowing each judge to become an "expert" in the case beforehand. At the end of the trial, the judicial panel convenes and determines the guilt of the accused, by majority vote.

The role of the defendant is also very different in the two systems. At common law, the defendant enjoys a right to silence because of the possibility of self-incrimination. This right means that no negative inference may be drawn from the defendant's unwillingness to address the court. As a principle, the right to silence enforces the prosecution's burden to prove its case on its own, and ensures that the defendant is treated as "innocent until proven guilty." While defendants at common law are permitted to

participation), then we can say that the trial comprises not the majority of the action but the entirety of the action at common law.

19 Michael Bohlander (2012: 67) describes the German trial thus: "Although the trial is from a traditional perspective the dramatic culmination of the struggle between prosecution and defence, and in Germany it is fair to include the court in that tug-of-war, much of what happens at trial will have been predetermined to a large degree – and mostly irreversibly so at the pre-trial stage – by the investigations of the police, the prosecution, the examining pre-trial judge and sometimes also the defense."

take the stand and speak in their defense, such statements are open to cross-examination by prosecutors, all of which may be considered by the jury in making its determination. Thus structurally, defendants are encouraged to remain silent, as their silence may not be used to make the case against them, whereas their participation may.

At civil law, defendant participation may be demanded by the judge (although it is not technically mandatory) because the defendant is not permitted, as a party with an interest in the case, to act as a witness for himself. No element of the defendant's testimony may therefore be used as a factual component to strengthen the dossier. With judges checking facts and law, as well as pronouncing the sentence, a defendant's participation can usually only help their case, by shedding light on their motivation or the context of their action. While technically "innocent until proven guilty," defendants at trial in civil law in fact carry the burden of proving their innocence at the moment of trial by showing some misstep made in the investigation. The upshot is that most defendants do address the court at civil law, which serves to add legitimacy to the proceedings because when a defendant participates in the case against them this signals their consent (Shapiro 1986).

III THE ICTY's PECULIAR HYBRID

The ICTY was designed on an adversarial procedural model. Its rules of procedure were assembled by a largely American team (Tochilovsky 2010), and early ICTY practitioners hailed mostly from common-law jurisdictions (Hagan 2003). Yet as the ICTY endured, increasing in size and beginning the work of trying cases, its procedure adopted several mechanisms borrowed from civil-law systems. These practices were pronounced more "efficient," and embraced as more familiar by the growing number of practitioners at the ICTY originating from civil-law systems. The ICTY became, in the words of one defense lawyer at the court, "an adversarial court with continental flavors."[20]

It is nonetheless an error to read additions of procedural rules practiced by civil-law systems as a sign of the "inquisitorial drift" of the ICTY (Vogler 2011). The adversarial calculus of the ICTY did not change with these evolutions. Instead, reforms introducing practices culled from civil law sought to increase the ICTY's capacity to meet the challenges of securing convictions in chaotic evidentiary circumstances. Yet *securing convictions of the accused* is a prosecutorial function, with common-law and civil-law systems differing significantly regarding how an accused becomes, and remains, someone against whom a conviction must be secured. This section discusses the evolution of ICTY procedure towards a structure facilitating conviction.

20 Interview with defense counsel before ICTY, The Hague, May 2005.

A *The ICTY at Its Inception*

When the Rules of Procedure (ROP) of the ICTY were drafted in 1994 by the first ICTY judges, the particular make-up of the court staff, as well as the influence over the tribunal exerted behind the scenes by the United States, dictated that the ostensibly "hybrid" procedure of the tribunal, intended to represent a mixture of both common and civil law, leaned decidedly towards the common law and owed a clear debt to US jurisprudence in particular (Bassiouni & Manikas 1996; Tochilovsky 2010). The OTP, while situated in The Hague in the same building as the tribunal, was not subject to administrative control in the same way that a typical civil law prosecutor would be.[21] Under the 1994 ROP the OTP investigated and drew up indictments.[22] As an "independent body," the OTP brings the charges it sees fit against a defendant. Unlike in civil law systems, the OTP is not constrained by an external body that considered the validity of the case as a whole. This pre-trial work hews closely to the procedure of adversarial systems: the OTP is required to hand over, but not to seek out, exculpatory evidence (Karnavas 2007; Harmon and Karagiannakis 2001).

Once drafted by the ICTY prosecutor, an indictment is reviewed by a chamber of judges at the ICTY, who apply a relaxed standard of proof like that of the grand jury in the US. The ICTY chamber looks at the indictment only for proof that the charges brought, if true, constitute criminal offenses (Shahabuddeen 2012). As with a hearing before a grand jury in the US, suspects before the ICTY may not contest the evidence that may result in an indictment. Furthermore, during the review of the indictment itself, the reviewing judge hears not the defendant but only the prosecutor, who may present new information to the court.[23] Civil-law systems, in contrast, typically allow an indicted person to contest the evidence against them contained in the indictment.

This means that, as at common law, the first real chance a defendant before the ICTY has to prove their innocence before an objective body is at trial. The trial itself follows a strictly common-law calculus. While ICTY judges are permitted a greater role than their common-law counterparts in that they are allowed to question witnesses and even request additional witnesses, the ROP ensure that the trial remains the space at which truth would be proven in a process where judicial control is limited by judges' inferior access to information. As at common law,

[21] As was the case with the IMT, the institutional space-sharing raises concerns regarding objectivity, because the two bodies are not perceived as sufficiently independent. (Author interviews ICTY defense counsel, The Hague, May 2005.) At common law the adversarial nature of the process requires a clear separation between judges and prosecutors. At civil law, structural distinctions are not as sharp, because both the prosecutor and the judge are working towards the same goal and thus can be understood to share interests to a certain degree.

[22] The OTP closed new indictments in 2004 as part of the ICTY's winding-down strategy.

[23] Statute of ICTY, Rule 47D.

acquittals are common: of the 161 individuals indicted by the ICTY, eighteen have been acquitted.[24]

The ROP originally drafted by the ICTY (1994) took the fundamental elements of common-law procedure as described above and made two significant, civil-law-based alterations:[25] (1) majority determination of guilt by judicial panel (instead of unanimous determination of guilt by separate fact finder, as is common to most common-law systems) and (2) the possibility for the OTP to appeal acquittals.[26] These two hybrid additions would appear to increase the power of the prosecution, first by lessening the weight necessary for it to obtain conviction (majority rather than unanimity), and second by giving the OTP "a second bite at the apple" through the right to appeal.

B Adding Civil-Law Procedure "For Efficiency": The 1999 Reforms

Since the ICTY's inception, there has been much discussion of civil-law systems' benefits in terms of "efficiency,"[27] and the reforms made to ICTY procedure have, generally speaking, taken more from civil-law-generated processes than common law. In 1999, concerned with cost and inefficiency in the two ad hoc tribunals operating under United Nations mandate, the Security Council commissioned an expert group to report on the work of the ICTY and ICTR and to submit recommendations as to how this work could be strengthened. The 126-page report articulated forty-six precise recommendations. In 2000, the ICTY and ICTR responded to the expert report's recommendations, agreeing with and adopting most of them.[28]

The procedural suggestions made by the expert report mostly called for an increase in civil-law methods, on the principle that "Some civil law models can doubtless deal with criminal law cases *more expeditiously* than the common law adversarial system."[29] The expert report further justified this by observing that, "Since the accused before the Tribunals are from civil law backgrounds, it could hardly be objectionable to them."[30]

24 ICTY website www.icty.org/sid/24 (accessed April 21, 2016).

25 See Bassiouni & Manikas 1996: 955 (where it is argued that ICTY procedure "selectively incorporate[d] civil law concepts into a predominantly common law framework") quoted in Mégret 2009.

26 In addition to appealing, the OTP under Rule 99(B) is permitted to request the arrest and detention of the acquitted accused pending the appeals hearing. ICTY Rules of Procedure and Evidence adopted pursuant to Art. 15 of the Statute of Tribunal, as amended Oct. 6 1995 ("ICTY Rules of Procedure). These particular traits were singled out for criticism by Scharf 1997a.

27 Göran Sluiter, "Beyond the Written Law: Why International Criminal Tribunals Function the Way They Do." Paper delivered at the International Law and Society Conference, Berlin, July 2007; Pizzi 2006.

28 Some recommendations had already been put into effect. Others were adopted following the expert report's recommendations. Still others, objected to in the ICTY commentary, were eventually adopted. (See in this regard recommendations regarding limiting expenses to defense bar.)

29 A/54/634 page 32, emphasis added.

30 *Ibid.*

Broadly speaking, the expert report pushed three central reforms, each of them ostensibly drawing from civil-law procedural methods. First, the ICTY created the role of a "pre-trial judge," a case-manager designed to expedite cases. The central proposed reform was the institution of a "pre-trial judge" *à la* the *juge d'instruction* who serves in some civil-law systems.[31] The goal was to streamline information by encouraging parties to stipulate to uncontested facts, and to create a dossier that would assist trial judges in being better informed when the case came to trial. In its recommendation 9, the expert report suggested that pre-trial judges should enjoy a "more interventionist role, *inter alia*, including authority to act for the Trial Chamber … and making a pre-trial report to the other judges with recommendations for a pre-trial order establishing a reasonable format in which the case is to proceed."[32] While certainly unknown at common law, the ICTY's pre-trial judge is not in fact a counterpart to the civil law's *juge d'instruction*, with that position's inherent mandate to investigate exculpatory evidence. Studying the impact of the reforms, Langer found that the addition of a pre-trial judge has made little impact on ICTY efficiency, because ICTY pre-trial judges do not have the capacity enjoyed by the *juge d'instruction* to radically alter charges or impact the case (Langer 2005).

Second, the reforms gave ICTY judges more power to limit interlocutory appeals, which the report encouraged. Interlocutory appeals are a problem at the ICTY due to their high number and their capacity to delay cases (the expert report noted that there were more than five hundred pre-trial motions in 1997 and 1998). At the same time, interlocutory appeals are part of the "game" played in the adversarial process, categorized by the UN expert report as follows:

> More of a combat situation between two parties than the protection of international public order and its values under the control of the court … This, coupled with the presumption of innocence and the principles relating to self-incrimination, results in accused, as is their right [under the ICTY Statute and human rights law] being uncooperative and insisting upon proof by the Prosecutor of every element of the crime alleged. From the standpoint of an accused, this represents optimum use of defense counsel. (UN expert report [1999] para 67.)[33]

The expert report cited as evidence of efficacy that counsel for the accused was "cooperative"[34] and chambers obtained witness statements in advance of trial, and

[31] Specifically, the *juge d'instruction* is a central figure in French criminal cases that meet a certain requirement of gravity. Bohlander (2012) notes that there is no such role in German criminal law, and that even in French criminal law, the *juge d'instruction* is being phased out.

[32] UN expert report para 83.

[33] See also para 84 regarding defense counsel reluctance to accept stipulations.

[34] The characterization of defense counsel engaging in "uncooperative" methods, when exercising the practices the adversarial system requires as an element of the protection of defendants' rights, suffers a more direct assault under the expert report in its consideration of defense counsel fees. While steering away from such blunt language in the body of its report, in its recommendations section the UN expert report (1999) suggests that "In order to reduce the potential for obstructive and dilatory tactics by assigned defense counsel, the amount of legal fees allowed might properly take into account

the trial chamber "exercised considerable control over the length of courtroom testimony and the trial was completed in about three months."[35] The report does not specify the case, whether or not "cooperation" was entailed, or the outcome for the defendant.

Finally, and perhaps most significantly, the reforms permitted greater use of written witness statements at trial, a procedure designed to cut down on the lengthy, costly process of examining live witnesses. Observers agree that in civil-law systems there is a wider use of written statements than at common law (Wald 2002; McDermott 2013). Although initially stating a preference for "live testimony" in its ROP, the ICTY reforms pushed for an increased use of written witness statements.[36] The ICTY currently advocates a "no preference alternative" (Fairlie 2004; Gordon 2006). Rule 92 *bis* essentially replaced Rule 94 *ter*, which had been even more permissive with respect to admission of written statements.[37]

The OTP, in its response to the UN expert group, suggested that efficiency demands would be met by permitting "rulings during trials on matters of fact proved to the satisfaction of the chambers, or in relation to using the record of prior testimony to create rebuttable presumptions of fact that shift the evidential burden in the course of the trial."[38]

At issue in the increase of the use of written witness statements in place of live testimony is fundamentally a question of the right of the defendant to challenge accusations brought against him. The ICTY procedure now permits the trial chamber to rule on whether or not previous witness testimony (and other facts) have been sufficiently established to be brought in as written statements, and not oral testimony. This case-by-case analysis, however, does not address structural fairness issues at stake. At civil law, these fairness issues are addressed largely by permitting the defendant access to the dossier compiled against him, and by collecting the evidence in that dossier as a neutral party, i.e., where both inculpating and exculpatory evidence is collected.[39]

While each of these three amendments to ICTY procedure does, on its face, draw on civil-law procedure, none of them preserves the meaningful characteristics that

delays in pre-trial and trial proceedings deemed to have clearly been caused by such tactics." (UN expert report [1999], "Recommendations" p. 90 para 5.)

35 *Ibid.* fn 23.

36 Written witness statements Rules 73 *bis* and *ter*.

37 *Ibid.* See *Prosecutor* v. *Dario Kordić and Mario Čerkez, Appeals Chamber Judgment*, Case No. IT-95–14/2-Y (September 18, 2000) (appeals chamber decision overruling trial chamber's admission of statement of deceased witness implicating accused that was not given under oath, never subject to cross-examination, uncorroborated by other evidence, and was verbally translated by an interpreter from Croatian to English before it was written down in English by an investigator whose native language was Dutch).

38 Response to UN expert report (1999) para 43.

39 It should be noted, however, that even civil law systems are instituting increased oral procedures regarding witness testimony, in part in response to the human rights dictates of the International Covenant on Civil and Political Rights.

these processes possess at civil law, features that serve to balance the state's interest in deterrence, punishment, and social control and the defendant's interest in due process.

C ICL and the Presumption of Innocence

The presumption of innocence is at the heart of both the civil- and the common-law systems' capacity to deliver justice: it is a fundament of rule of law, because it requires the state to affirmatively prove the guilt of an individual (rather than casting a charge at an individual, and requiring that she disprove the charge). The presumption of innocence is often the element of a legal tradition that practitioners schooled in that tradition cite as the central benefit, where the assumed critique is that the other system is less able to recognize and/or protect the presumption.[40]

The ICTY recognizes the presumption of innocence of defendants before it,[41] and like other common-law systems, links the presumption of innocence to acquittals.[42] As noted, over 10 percent of all indictments at the ICTY have resulted in acquittal, most of which "have come about in cases in which the evidence presented by the Prosecution was either insufficient to establish that specific crimes occurred, or insufficient to demonstrate that the accused bore criminal responsibility for the commission of the crime."[43] In the case of guilt by finding of the majority, this follows a civil-law model whereby a panel of judges sits in judgment of both law and facts. Where civil-law systems generally use "lay judges" to constitute two-thirds of the judicial panel, the ICTY in contrast employs only professional judges. Thus the ICTY judicial mechanism is entirely devoid of a "community" element, the peerage that civil-law systems achieve by employing lay judges and common-law systems through the use of a jury. Furthermore, as the ICTY jurisprudence has developed, there have been an increasing number of majority decisions. This means that situations obtain that one cannot find at civil law. In the event of a majority decision at

40 See Merryman and Perez-Perdomo 2007 (discussing common law lawyers' belief that civil law traditions do not include a presumption of innocence); Damaška 1973: 546 ("That continental criminal law has discarded guilt-presumptive devices while common law courts frequently operate with them is by now a cliché of comparative law"); Bohlander 2012 (arguing that the presumption of innocence "is stronger under German law than under English law and models based on the English understanding, because it attaches until the conviction has become final, that is until the last avenue of appeal has been exhausted").

41 Article 21(3) of the 1993 ICTY Statute.

42 www.icty.org/sid/9984 30 (accessed April 16, 2015).

43 *Ibid.* Recall that within the common-law tradition where the trial is a contest, acquittal can function as a demonstration of the presumption of innocence (i.e., acquittals are to be expected, and a system not returning acquittals would be suspect). Within the civil-law tradition, where trial should check the work of the state, acquittal demonstrates anomalies (which are then considered for correction by a higher court).

civil law, one judge has not been convinced to the level of *intime conviction*. What the presence of majority findings of guilt should be understood to mean for the standard "beyond a reasonable doubt" is an open question. It would seem that any doubt that can be held by a professional judge faced with all the evidence would be able, legally speaking, to constitute the sort of "reasonable doubt" that would give pause to their colleagues.

In summary, the procedural history of the ICTY permits a snapshot of the problem of hybridity in an international legal institution. Drawing procedure from two divergent cultural systems has permitted the legitimization of certain procedural applications because they *originate* in an acknowledged, rule-of-law-serving system, instead of addressing a more fundamental question, which is what function such procedure serves in the *actual* hybrid system where it is practiced. The final section observes the response of the ICTY when its practices are challenged to complete the argument that ICTs are so beyond rule of law constraints as to earn the label post-rule of law.

IV POST-RULE OF LAW: HYBRIDITY AND THE OPERATIONALIZATION OF ICL

The preceding sections: reviewed the significance of cultural and theoretical impulses underlying criminal practices in the common- and civil-law traditions (Part I); have traced these impulses through examples of their interpretation in domestic criminal procedure (Part II); and applied these to the hybrid procedure of the ICTY (Part III). This final section concludes the chapter's argument that the practice of hybridity as currently operationalized by ICTs is "post-rule of law".

The argument that ICP is *post*-rule of law is not designed as a critique of individual procedures as violating rule of law practices. The ICTY's rules were hastily assembled, in marked contrast to the deliberate construction of hybridity at the ICC, for example (Tochilovsky 2010: 160). International criminal law is a young discipline and its institutions face steep learning curves; some room for experimentation, for trial and necessary error, must be permitted. Rather, the argument that ICL as operationalized by ICP is "post-rule of law" is based in an analysis of hybridity itself – as practiced by ICTs – as *deliberately* operating outside of rule-of-law constraints. International criminal tribunals as post-rule-of-law institutions articulate the value of the rule of law, operate in its shadow, are legitimized by it, and deliberately resist rule-of-law constraints as intolerably inflexible to the task set for them.

As previous sections have detailed, criminal processes rest within and represent operationalizations of ideologies regarding the application of criminal sanctions in service to a state. Comparative law scholars have long cautioned that borrowing a practice outside of the contextualization of that practice risks losing meaning, fairness, or both. Yet these cautions, long iterated in comparative law scholarship, have been slow in coming to ICL. At ICL, the synthesis of procedure is "pragmatic" rather than "balanced or fused" (Findlay 2001). This "pragmatism" results in what John Jackson (2009: 23) calls "procedures that maximize the volume of relevant evidence and provide opportunities for testing its probative value" which are preferred because they "are likely to achieve higher levels of accuracy than procedures which limit the flow of relevant information and do not provide opportunities for testing it." Put another way: *"The rights of the accused are protected as much as they should be."*[44]

A *One Example of Post-Rule-of-Law Practice: Sentencing at ICTs*

It is widely recognized that sentencing at ICL is theoretically underdeveloped and empirically understudied (Meernik and King 2001; Drumbl 2005; Henham 2007; D'Ascoli 2011). As the International Criminal Law Services' manual titled "Sentencing" notes, "Sentencing is essentially a discretionary responsibility of the judges at the international tribunals. There are no guidelines or scales for the various crimes, as there might be in domestic jurisdictions."[45] International Criminal Tribunal for the former Yugoslavia case law emphasizes this approach as well, with myriad judicial findings emphasizing the complete discretion of the chambers in imposing the appropriate sentence.[46]

Sentences at ICL are perhaps best characterized as "predictably irrational" (Ewald 2010). The "confusing, disparate, inconsistent, and erratic" sentencing policy of the ICTY (Drumbl 2007: 11), in particular, has been characterized as a form of "Russian roulette" (Olusanya 2005). In addition to problems regarding uniformity and predictability, the content of sentences has been criticized. Some commentators critique sentencing as too aggressive because it comes at the end of the liability phase and is not reserved for its own procedure (Wald 2002). Others criticize ICTY sentences as too lenient, particularly given the gruesome nature of the crimes in question (Ohlin 2011).

44 ICTY attorney (author interview May 2005).

45 International Criminal Law & Practice Training Materials: Sentencing wcjp.unicri.it/deliverables/docs/Module_13_Sentencing_and_penalties.pdf (accessed April 27, 2015) pp. 1–76.

46 Discretion in sentencing is established in ICTY jurisprudence. See *Stakić* Trial Chamber para 884; *Delalić* Appeals Chamber para 758 (which states that a pattern of sentences does not exist yet). See also *Prosecutor* v. *Miroslav Deronjić*, Case No. IT-02-61, March 30, 2004 (where Judge Schomburg recommended a twenty-year sentence in his dissenting opinion; the majority awarded a ten-year sentence). This includes discretion in determining concurrent or cumulative sentences. *Delalić* Appeals Chamber para 771; *Prosecutor* v. *Tihomir Blaškić*, Case No. IT-95-14 (July 29, 2004), available at www.icty.org ("*Blaškić* Appeals Chamber") para 721–722 (which describes types of convictions that are impermissibly cumulative).

There are few guidelines as to sentencing stated in the ICTY Statute[47] or ROP.[48] Instead, guidelines for sentencing, such as they exist, have been articulated through ICTY case law. For example, in its cases, the ICTY has established that it has discretion to consider other potentially mitigating factors,[49] which it has defined as voluntary surrender,[50] guilty plea,[51] expression of remorse,[52] good character with no prior criminal convictions,[53] and the post-conflict conduct of the accused. And although the sole reference to Yugoslav law made by the ICTY Statute regards the practice of sentencing in the former Yugoslavia, ICTY chambers have treated this statutory reference as more of a suggestion than a rule.[54] Moreover, in making reference to Yugoslav sentencing practice, chambers have also made quite free with the *substance* of the practice. Thus, the chamber in *Babić*, without citation to Yugoslav law, held the following:

47 As regards sentencing guidelines, the ICTY Statute states, in full, the following:

1. The penalty imposed by the Trial Chamber shall be limited to imprisonment. In determining the terms of imprisonment, the Trial Chambers shall have recourse to the general practice regarding prison sentences in the courts of the former Yugoslavia.
2. In imposing the sentences, the Trial Chambers should take into account such factors as the gravity of the offence and the individual circumstances of the convicted person.
3. In addition to imprisonment, the Trial Chambers may order the return of any property and proceeds acquired by criminal conduct, including by means of duress, to their rightful owners.

Article 24 Penalties.

48 The ROP add little to the statute's bare skeleton, except to note that mitigating and aggravating circumstances shall also be considered. The rules address only one mitigating circumstance: "substantial" cooperation with the prosecutor. ICTY Rules of Procedure Rule 101(B)(ii).

49 *Prosecutor* v. *Radislav Krstić*, Case No. IT-98-33, (August 2, 2001) ("*Krstić* Trial Chamber") para 713.

50 See, e.g., *Kupreskić* Trial Chamber paras 853, 860, 863; *Prosecutor* v. *Drago Josipović, Vladimir Šantić, Zoran Kupreskić, Mirjan Kupreskić, Vlatko Kupreskić and Dragan Papić*, Case No. IT-95-16-A, (October 23, 2001), available at www.icty.org, para 430; *Kunarac* Trial Chamber para 868; *Prosecutor* v. *Biljana Plavšić*, IT-00-39&40/1-S, (February 27, 2003) paras 82–84.

51 See, e.g., *Kupreskić* Appeals Chamber para 464; *Prosecutor* v. *Goran Jelisić, Appeals Judgment*, Case No. IT-95-10, (July 5, 2001) para 122; *Prosecutor* v. *Duško Sikirica, Damir Došen and Dragan Koludžija*, Case No. IT-95-8 (November 13, 2001) paras 148–151, 192–193, 228; *Prosecutor* v. *Stevan Todorović*, Case No. IT-95-9/1, paras 75–82; *Erdemović* Sentencing Judgment II para 16(ii); *Plavšić* Sentencing Judgment paras 66–81.

52 See, e.g., *Sikirica* Sentencing Judgment paras 152, 194, 230; *Todorović* Sentencing Judgment paras 89–92; *Erdemović* Sentencing Judgment II para 16(iii); *Plavšić* Sentencing Judgment paras 66–81.

53 See, e.g., *Krnojelac* Trial Judgment para 519; *Kupreskić* Trial Chamber para 478; *Kupreskić* Appeals Chamber para 459; *Prosecutor* v. *Zlatko Aleksovski, Trial Chamber Judgment*, Case No. IT-95-14/1 (June 25, 1999) para 236; *Erdemović* Sentencing Judgment II, para 16(i).

54 *See Prosecutor* v. *Dragoljub Kunarac, Radomir Kovač and Zoran Vuković*, Case No. IT-96-23 (February 22, 2001) ("Kunarac Trial Chamber") para 349, 377; *Prosecutor* v. *Zejnil Delalić, Hazim Delić, Zdravko Mucić and Esad Landžo*, IT-96-21 (February 20, 2001) ("*Delalić* Appeals Chamber") para 818; *Prosecutor* v. *Milomir Stakić*, Case No. IT-97-24, (July 31, 2003), available at www.icty.org, ("Stakić Trial Chamber") para 887 (national sentencing "will … be considered, although in itself is not binding"); *Prosecutor* v. *Darko Mrđa, Sentencing Judgment*, Case No. IT- 02-59, (March 31, 2004) paras 121, 122, 129 (holding that national sentencing practices are "merely indicative").

> The Trial Chamber has found that Babic [sic] participated in a JCE whose objective – the forcible and permanent removal of non-Serb populations from the SAO Krajina – was carried out through persecutory acts of murders, deportations or forcible transfers, imprisonment, and destruction of property . . . The commission of this crime would have attracted the harshest sentence in the former Yugoslavia.[55]

The law of the former Yugoslavia provides for either criminal sentences of up to twenty years, or the death penalty. The death penalty, however, is not utilized by international tribunals, and thus it was suggested that life imprisonment should replace the Yugoslav death penalty tradition in sentencing before the ICTY.[56]

Academics and commentators have made various propositions regarding a hierarchy of crimes or other sentencing guidelines that would increase uniformity and predictability in international criminal law sentencing (Danner 2001). So far, the ICTY has categorically rejected such suggestions.[57] Some commentators have supported this approach. Uwe Ewald, for example, argues that there is legal significance (i.e., precedent) to the scattered World War II jurisprudence regarding sentences and their fulfillment, arguing that "the patterns of sentence at the Nuremberg and Tokyo trials as well as the so called 12 succession Trials in Germany already show that diversity in international sentencing is an obvious feature from the outset." In essence, Ewald (2010: 373) argues that there is "precedent" to find unpredictability (euphemistically referred to as "diversity") in international sentencing. Ewald's 2010 article, grounded in seven years' practice in the ICTY OTP, sets a dangerous course for ICTs. For Ewald, sentencing irregularity is not an error to be addressed or corrected, but rather a deliberate practice to be sheltered as part of the identity of ICTs. Ewald references the notion of proportionality in sentencing but dismisses such a theoretical underpinning for ICL as naught but "humble legal principles" that cannot "provide a sufficient ground for conceptualizing and operationalizing the complexity of factors "behind" international sentencing decision-making." In essence, Ewald would claim a space outside of rule-of-law constraints for ICTs.

What makes sentencing at ICL an example of post-rule-of-law practice is not that there is measurable discrepancy in sentencing between ICTs, or even within ICTs; discrepancy can be the mark of growing pains, lack of unifying processes, etc. Measurable discrepancy could be accident or error at ICL, which ICTs could address and reform. Rather, sentencing at ICTs is demonstrably post-rule of law because ICTs have not embraced error as a moment for reform, but have rather determined that rule-of-law concerns do not apply to them.

55 *Babić* Sentencing Judgment para 50.

56 Some opponents, most notably Bassiouni, argue that this violates the principle of *nullum crimen nulla poena*. See Schabas 1997.

57 *Prosecutor* v. *Radislav Krstić*, Case No. IT-98-33 (April 19, 2004) ("*Krstić* Appeals Chamber") para 242 (the appeals chamber rejected as inappropriate the setting-down of a definitive list of sentencing guidelines).

B A Second Example: Plea Bargains before the ICTY

What to do with those war criminals who admit their guilt? The problem of self-incrimination arose, unexpectedly, remarkably early in the ICTY's jurisprudence, when a young Bosnian Croat soldier who had fought for the Bosnian Serbs at Srebrenica came forward to tell his story. Dražen Erdemović, through his own admission of guilt, became the ICTY's first conviction, in 1996.

Regardless of its strong common law logic, in the initial rules of procedure, plea agreements were not provided for. The practice of plea bargaining, which is not without controversy in those jurisdictions where it is practiced, is particularly foreign to continental jurists. For those trained in civil-law jurisdictions, the self-interested, case-by-case trade between adversarial parties which is at the center of plea bargaining is counterfactual to justice itself, because law must be predictable and disinterested in order to qualify as justice.

Erdemović was a Bosnian Croat who had served in the Bosnian Muslim and Croatian armies before coming to serve in the Bosnian Serb army, where in 1995 he participated in the massacre (genocide) of more than seven thousand Bosnian Muslim men and boys at Srebrenica. By his own testimony, on July 16, 1995 Erdemović executed more than seventy civilian prisoners as a foot soldier in a firing squad (Cryer 1997). In early 1996, Erdemović and a friend, both by then living in Milošević's Serbia, gave an interview to a foreign journalist regarding atrocities they had witnessed and committed during the war. The tape of the interview was confiscated at the airport in Belgrade, and Erdemović and his friend, after giving another interview to a journalist at *Le Figaro* on the same topic, were arrested by Serbian police, indicted for war crimes, and scheduled to stand trial in a Serbian court. With international pressure and a public campaign initiated by ICTY Prosecutor Goldstone "to save [Erdemović's] life" (Hagan 2003: 76), Erdemović was transferred to the ICTY. In The Hague, Erdemović cooperated extensively with the tribunal, providing evidence and testimony against other indictees. When the OTP indicted Erdemović on war crimes charges for his role in the massacre, he pleaded guilty.

In cooperating with the ICTY, Erdemović provided critical confirmation of the events at Srebrenica, events that were powerfully contested at the time. Information regarding the location of massacres, when used in conjunction with satellite imagery, gave ICTY investigators valuable clues they used to eventually build a jurisprudence around the genocide at Srebrenica, most critically the command structure surrounding the event; the fruit of the seeds planted by Erdemović is the currently ongoing case against Ratko Mladić,[58] the general who ordered and oversaw the massacre. Moreover, Erdemović became the ICTY's "star witness" (Civikov

[58] *Prosecutor* v. *Ratko Mladić*, Case No. IT-09-92 TC (Int'l Crim. Trib. for the Former Yugoslavia November 22, 2017; the conviction by the trial chamber for genocide and other crimes, which resulted in a life sentence for the 75-year-old Mladić, is currently on appeal before the residual mechanism at the time of writing.

2009) not only for the material facts he substantiated, but also for his expressed contrition. By cooperating with the ICTY, Erdemović provided an exemplar of the transitional justice ideology underwriting the construction of a *court* to address large-scale social and political violence. The Erdemović sentencing chamber found that Erdemović's plea of guilty contributed to the discovery of truth, which it then linked directly to reconciliation, arguing, "Discovering the truth is a cornerstone of the rule of law and a fundamental step on the way to reconciliation." (*Erdemović Sentencing Judgment II* para 21.)

Thus the appearance of Dražen Erdemović, in the person of a contrite, cooperative witness, and in the situation of participant in genocide (the crime of crimes that could justify the necessity of a tribunal such as the ICTY) was – to put it crudely – a fantastic stroke of luck for the fledgling institution. Yet when Erdemović cooperated with the ICTY, there was no procedure under the ICTY's rules that permitted a judicially meaningful admission of guilt. At common law, it is possible for a defendant to save the court the trouble of a trial to determine his guilt by admitting his guilt himself (this is the value the defendant can use to "bargain" regarding the charges and sentence imposed on him). In many civil-law jurisdictions, however, this is not the case; at German law, for example, a trial is required regardless of a defendant's confession (Bohlander 2000).

i Developing Plea Bargaining at the ICTY: The Practice Instituted by *Erdemović*

Erdemović came into ICTY custody in March 1996, and in May 1996 he was indicted under two counts: (1) murder as a crime against humanity and, alternately, (2) murder as a violation of the laws and customs of war. On May 31, 1996 Erdemović made his initial appearance before the ICTY trial chamber and pleaded guilty to murder as a crime against humanity.

One can hear the unfamiliarity of this procedure leaping off the page in the transcript of Erdemović's May 31, 1996 appearance, where the civil-law-trained Justice Claude Jorda explains the following to Erdemović:

> If you plead not guilty, you are entitled to a trial . . . If you plead guilty, the trial will continue but completely differently, which I am sure you understand but which I have to explain to you. At that point you will have the opportunity during another hearing at a date which we will set at that point in agreement with everybody, you will plead guilty but you will plead under other circumstances, that is, that there were attenuating circumstances, mitigating circumstances, or aggravating circumstances. Then there will be a discussion between your attorney and the Prosecution which will not be same [sic]. Having explained this to you, the Tribunal must now ask you whether you are prepared to plead and do you plead guilty or not guilty? (Tr. Pg. 24: 6–22)

This official English version is in fact an imprecise translation of the original French, in which the hearing was conducted. I include it because it represents the material available and relied on by English speakers, including OTP Mark Harmon and the ICTY appeals chamber. The original French is clearer regarding the "other circumstances" of pleading. Specifically, the original French makes clear the distinction between what Erdemović will be invited to clarify in a later hearing (mitigating circumstances), what the prosecutor will be invited to clarify (aggravating or mitigating circumstances), and that this will signify a different sort of discussion between defense and prosecutor:

> Si vous plaidez coupable, le procès continuera, mais d'une manière tout à fait différente – ce que je crois vous devez bien saisir – mais que je dois vous expliquer, c'est-à-dire à ce moment-là vous aurez l'occasion dans une autre audience que nous fixerons, à ce moment-là évidemment en accord avec tout le monde, et vous plaiderez d'une manière différente, c'est-à-dire que vous aurez plaidé coupable, mais vous plaiderez sur d'autres circonstances, qu'elles soient des circonstances atténuantes; le Procureur plaidera éventuellement sur des circonstances éventuellement aggravantes ou atténuantes. Il y aura donc un dialogue entre votre défenseur, vous et le Procureur qui sera d'une nature différente. (French Tr. Pg. 25: 24–26: 4) [*If you plead guilty, the trial will continue, but in a totally different way – which I think you understand but which I should explain to you, which is to say at that point in the future you will have the chance in another hearing which date we will decide, at that point, obviously with everyone's agreement, you will plead in a different manner, that is to say, you will have pleaded guilty, but you will plead regarding other circumstances, most likely mitigating circumstances; the prosecutor will likely plead regarding aggravating or mitigating circumstances. Thus there will be a conversation between your defense attorney, you, and the prosecutor which will be of a different nature.*]

By clearly breaking apart who will perform what role (and taking note of the essential adversarial element of the process, where Erdemović will argue something that is potentially distinct from what the prosecutor will argue) the original French makes less of a muddle of the process than the ICTY's official English translation. Yet, as my English translation demonstrates, this is still not very clear or easy to follow. Unfortunately, the Serbo-Croatian transcript of the hearing is publicly unavailable, so it is not possible to examine what the defendant actually heard. Regardless, Justice Jorda's brief explanation of what a guilty plea means in terms of trial, even in its slightly crisper French version, raises as many questions as it answers, most specifically in terms of the stature of the defendant.

The November 1996 trial chamber judgment against Erdemović discusses his guilty plea in terms of a "defense strategy." While a guilty plea can indeed be part of a resourceful defense strategy at common law, there is nothing in Justice Jorda's description to indicate how Erdemović, in giving up his right to trial, was gaining any strategic advantage. In short, the "trade" element of a guilty plea as understood at US law is entirely absent from this description.

The question of how the process of pleading guilty works at the ICTY was not the only element of the process where there was imprecision. A central problem in the hearing, around which a divided appeals chamber later reversed the trial chamber judgment, was the question of what crime Erdemović pleaded guilty to. The indictment charged Erdemović with a crime against humanity *or alternatively* a violation of the laws and customs of war. Erdemović pleaded guilty to the former, and the OTP, in response, dropped the latter at the trial chamber's suggestion (May 31, 1996 Tr. Pg. 35: 19). The appeals chamber would go on to find Erdemović's plea uninformed because he pleaded guilty to the more serious of the two charges however. Already at Erdemović's plea appearance, it was clear that the content of the charge itself posed a problem to Erdemović's capacity to plead guilty. Again, one feels Judge Jorda's hesitancy as he essentially asks the defendant to perform the definitional work that would normally (at either civil law or common law) rest with the prosecutor and/or the court:

> The text of our Statute obliges me to ask you whether you are pleading guilty on one of the charges, that is, there are acts, they were read to you, the Tribunal understands that you accept these facts and that they have been classified a certain way legally. This is part of international law. It is a bit difficult for you, but I will try to explain it to you in a more simple fashion, that is, there are acts and these are the acts which you have just recognised that, yes, you were at Srebrenica at such and such a moment. I think that the Prosecutor will make things very clear for us. The Prosecutor classifies them, which means that it determines a certain number of conditions from which a criminal violation has been charged. At the stage that we are now in these proceedings, which is at the beginning, the proceedings against you, Mr. Erdemović, given the facts as they are today, that is, the fact that you have recognised what happened, that you were present, the various acts could either be classified as a crime against humanity or what we call violations of the laws or customs of war. Having said this, if there had been a trial, after the Tribunal would decide what, in fact, you were guilty of or not guilty of. In this case, since you have just said that you are pleading guilty, I must ask you if you are pleading guilty to the crime against humanity, that is, the version of the facts which for the Prosecutor would be a crime against humanity, or if it is a violation of the laws or customs of war. I suppose that you have spoken about this with your attorney? Mr. Erdemović, could you answer us on that point which is an important one?[59]

Justice Jorda's hopeful question regarding whether Erdemović has spoken about the content of the charges to which he is pleading guilty with his attorney does not disguise the problem, where the defendant is asked to work against his own interest by substantiating the charge against him. Note the inconsistency as Judge Jorda first states, regarding the content of the crimes charged, that "the Prosecutor will make

[59] Here the French is not substantially different (May 31, 1996 French Tr. Pg. 27: 9–18).

things clear for us" and "the Prosecutor classifies" before noting that the crimes "either be classified as a crime against humanity or what we call violations of the laws or customs of war" and concluding that "if there had been a trial, after the Tribunal would decide what, in fact, you were guilty of or not guilty of" but that in this case, the defendant himself must "classify" his acts. In its November 29, 1996 judgment (para 83), the trial chamber "reaffirm[ed] that there is no valid reason for discussing the charge of crime against humanity since Dražen Erdemović pleaded guilty to this count." The trial chamber sentenced Erdemović to ten years, and he appealed.

On appeal, the central concern articulated by the trial chamber during Erdemović's initial appearance – the validity of the plea – turned out to be a danger the trial chamber could not insulate itself against. The appeals chamber, acting *proprio motu*,[60] found that Erdemović's plea was *not* informed, and ordered a new trial. This occurred even in the face of the trial chamber's determined efforts, where the validity of the plea constituted the central focus of the audience.

The distinctions between how civil law and common law accept self-incrimination are not skin deep, but are rather built on motivating impulses within the systems themselves. At common law, the truth of a defendant's guilt should emerge through the adversarial clash of competing narratives: where a defendant admits their guilt, there is no resulting narrative clash, and thus no need for a trial, which is (at common law) the public forum permitting the clash to take place. At civil law, the truth of a defendant's guilt is determined in the investigation preceding the trial. This truth represents the diligent work of the state. At civil law, the defendant's representation of their guilt is not unlike their representation of their innocence: it is but one piece of evidence, to be considered alongside the rest by the judge (Bohlander 2000). Importantly, the defendant's representation of their guilt cannot replace the work of the state in demonstrating the defendant's guilt. Thus while guilty pleas are accepted at civil law, they do not undo the need for a trial, which is the transparent window where the work of the state is put on display for the public.

CONCLUSION

The chapter has shown that the operationalization of ICL through ICTs challenges the project of ICL, when understood as a training ground for liberal, democratic governance, or rule-of-law modeling. As Klabbers argues, accountability to third parties is a structural problem of all international organizations. International organizations practicing criminal justice, however, face double structural

60 *Propio motu* is "under its own power," which is to say, the question of whether Erdemović's appeal was informed was one that the appeals chamber raised itself. At common law, legal processes are party-driven and the court acts largely as a neutral referee, making it rare for the court to act outside of arguments raised by the parties. At civil law, the court is permitted a more active role as it is backing up the initial work of the state performed by the prosecutor.

challenges as regards accountability, as failures of "objectivity" through service to particularized interests threaten the legitimacy of the systems themselves. One ICTY defense attorney put it as follows:

> The hallmark of a good system is uniformity, courtroom to courtroom. You walk in and they all seem the same. You need certainty, predictability, uniformity. But here, the makeup of each individual trial chamber changes things, between civil law, common law, and the occasional oddball set on blazing new trails.[61]

For the defense attorney, procedural irregularities challenged the legitimacy of the processes and thus the institution.

The chapter has argued that proclaiming "hybridity" and instituting procedures, regardless of their legitimacy in their systems of origin, is insufficient to guarantee objectivity, and thus legitimacy, for ICTs. International criminal law practitioners and theorists must begin a more serious consideration of the methods and costs associated with hybrid procedures. The following chapter explores a similar problem, but with a focus on the doctrinal content, rather than the judicial procedure, of ICL as developed by the ICTY.

61 ICTY defense attorney (author interview May 2005).

4

When Non-Derogable Principles Meet Criminal Liability

The Justice Problem of Joint Criminal Enterprise

In late May 1992, as Bosnia slid into war, a Bosnian Serb policeman named Miroslav Kvočka was ordered to collect police reservists and report to a local iron ore strip mine. These events set the infamous Omarska prison camp in motion. From May to August 1992, thousands of Bosnian Muslims and other "enemies of the state" were held in warehouses on the mining site, where they endured physical, mental, and sexual violence, and organized killings were "recreational and sadistic" (Silber & Little 1997: 251). This violence was perpetuated by civilian visitors randomly arriving on site as well as guards stationed at the camp. Scenes of deprivation from the Omarska camp publicized in August 1992 brought the war in Bosnia into the global spotlight, and atrocities committed in Omarska were highlighted in the 1994 Bassiouni report to the UN[1] that informed the first indictments of the fledgling International Criminal Tribunal for the former Yugoslavia (ICTY).

In 2001, the ICTY sentenced Miroslav Kvočka to seven years' prison for his role in Omarska's horrors.[2] In its judgment, the trial chamber determined that Kvočka: worked a total of seventeen days at the camp; never threatened, harmed, or ordered harm against any detainee; repeatedly reported violence or evidence of violence to his superiors; personally protected prisoners from violence, including once by putting his body between a shooting gunman and a group of prisoners; exerted a "restraining influence" because violence in the camp decreased when he was there; bore no animus towards Bosnian Muslims and was married to one; suffered a nervous breakdown while at the camp and took one week's leave; and was ultimately dismissed from the camp because he was too sympathetic to Muslims. Nevertheless, applying World War II-era jurisprudence[3] regarding liability for those who assist in criminal systems, the trial chamber found Kvočka's awareness of violence in the camp to be legally commensurate with committing this violence himself.

[1] "Final Report of the Commission of Experts Established Pursuant to Security Council Resolution 780 (1992)" S/1994/674 May 24, 1994.

[2] *Judgment, Prosecutor* v. *Miroslav Kvočka, Mlađo Radić, Zoran Žigić and Dragoljub Prcać*, IT-98–30/1-T (November 2, 2001) ("*Kvočka et al.* Trial Chamber").

[3] *Kvočka et al.* Trial Chamber paras 265–306; this includes the *Velpke* case, examined in Chapter 2.

What is "justice" for actors like Kvočka? Although violent social dissolution can give free rein to criminal behavior and pathological actors, it also ensnares law-abiding citizens in terrible situations as the logic of moral compliance and social deviance is turned on its head (Koskenniemi 2002a; Drumbl 2007). Miroslav Kvočka was, like most defendants at the ICTY, convicted under the ICTY's most (in)famous contribution to international criminal law (ICL): joint criminal enterprise (JCE) liability. Critiqued for its possibility to "weaken" ICL (Danner & Martinez 2005) or imperil ICL's coherence (Osiel 2009), JCE nonetheless has enjoyed great *institutional* success before the ICTY. Following its first iteration in the *Tadić* appeals judgment (July 15, 1999), JCE has functioned as a standard-bearing theory of liability, forming the basis of the majority of the ICTY's post-*Tadić* indictments.[4] A string of recent high-level acquittals leaves the future of JCE in doubt, however.

This chapter contrasts early JCE jurisprudence against later JCE jurisprudence. Bold in scope and formation when it was first articulated in *Tadić*, JCE became a catch-all theory of liability, a jack-of-all-trades (van der Wilt 2007: 92) that provided a "useful" tool for the prosecution (Del Ponte and Sudetic 2009). Joint criminal enterprise has developed into a seemingly indefensible charge wherein the judicial chamber and the Office of the Prosecutor (OTP) work together. As one ICTY attorney put it, "At the Tribunal, Joint Criminal Enterprise is referred to, privately, as 'Just Convict Everybody.'"[5] More problematically, the unstable standards and conceptual contradictions inherent in JCE in the *Tadić* judgment have become only more (and not less) problematic as the jurisprudence has developed. This leads today to a protracted and problematic jurisprudence, recycling, as one observer of the *Tadić* trial noted, a situation where "there are no absolute, objective, or predetermined parameters that define illegal violence external to the proceedings themselves" (Philipose 2002: 170).

Joint criminal enterprise represents the flashpoint between international human rights law's non-derogable standard (which is essentially a form of strict liability) against domestic criminal law theory (which rejects strict liability in most cases). The chapter demonstrates that the developing substance of the JCE doctrine is a prime example of the imbalance that can accrue when legal content is developed outside of political balance or accountability.

I THE DEVELOPMENT OF JOINT CRIMINAL ENTERPRISE

"Joint criminal enterprise," the hardest-working theory in the ICTY's lexicon, is not mentioned anywhere in the ICTY statute, nor was it, before its development at the

4 Danner and Martinez (2005: 108) estimate that 64 percent of indictments between 2001 and 2004 (when indictments ceased) relied on JCE and "if all indictments that include charges that the defendant acted 'in concert' with others are viewed as implicitly employing a JCE theory, then thirty-four of the forty-three indictments confirmed between June 25, 2001 and January 1, 2004 (81% of the total), incorporate JCE."

5 Lawyer working at ICTY (author interview, The Hague, May 2005).

ICTY, any meaningful criterion of ICL practice. Joint criminal enterprise is a theory of liability based in the ICTY's "commission" jurisdiction; it is, in other words, a theory of how the ICTY recognizes defendants "do" (commit) a crime. The first element of Article 7 (Individual Criminal Responsibility) of the ICTY Statute reads: "1. A person who planned, instigated, ordered, committed or otherwise aided and abetted in the planning, preparation or execution of a crime referred to in articles 2 to 5 of the present Statute, shall be individually responsible for the crime." It is from this aspect of "commission" that JCE emerged.

A *JCE's First Articulation: The* Tadić *case*

Duško Tadić was from a prominent Bosnian Serb family in the largely Muslim town of Kozarac, and owned a café in the center of that town (Scharf 1997). A minor volunteer in the Bosnian Serb nationalist party, after the Bosnian Serb takeover of the region in April 1992 Tadić served as a checkpoint guard in a private capacity. He fled Republika Srpska for Germany when he was drafted into the army in 1993.

Tadić came to the attention of German authorities by other Bosnian refugees, who identified him as a torturer, and he was arrested in February 1994 on charges of committing crimes against humanity at the Omarska prison camp outside of Prijedor, Bosnia-Herzegovina. Coming less than a year after the inception of the ICTY, the arrest of "the butcher of Omarska"[6] constituted an important opportunity for the fledgling court[7] by providing it with a live body. In April 1995 Tadić was transferred from Germany to The Hague, and in May 1996 his trial commenced.

The ICTY Office of the Prosecutor (OTP) charged Tadić with killings, torture, rape, castration, starvation, beatings, and other abuses at the Omarska camp, as well as attacking and killing civilians during Bosnian Serb seizures of the towns of Kozarac (May 1992) and Jaskići and Sivci (June 1992), of being a political leader in the emerging Bosnian Serb state, and playing a pivotal role in the ethnic cleansing in the region.

Omarska was a prison camp constructed to house non-Serb men collected from the Prijedor region, specifically from the largely Muslim enclaves of Kozarac[8] and inner Prijedor, both of which had resisted the Bosnian Serb military takeover effected April 30, 1992. On the site of a mine complex, the warehouse-type buildings at Omarska were insufficient to contain the up to 3,000 prisoners eventually interned there. With inadequate food, water, or sanitary facilities, the Omarksa camp was described by the *Tadić* trial chamber as "the most notorious of the camps, where the most horrific conditions existed."[9] By the time of Omarska's inception, local political and military organization had effectively disarmed all non-Serbs and

6 For a detailed, dramatic discussion of the Tadić trial and the politics surrounding it, see Scharf 1997b.

7 See Chapter 2 regarding the difficulties faced obtaining custody over defendants.

8 *Tadić* Trial Chamber para 146.

9 *Tadić* Trial Chamber para 155.

FIGURE 1
Rainer Lesniewski/Getty

redistributed the weapons to Serbs; moreover, the political situation had placed all Serb men of age into some form of military service, either as police, checkpoint guards or members of the armed forces.

Although Tadić claimed that he had never visited Omarska, several witnesses placed him there on June 18, and during a few days in July 1992. The trial chamber found that while not formally involved with the administration or policing of the camp, Tadić had been present and participated in the beatings and deaths of several detainees. The trial chamber did not, however, find him guilty of the murder of those detainees presumed to be dead (a presumption made on the basis of the fact that they had been removed from common holding cells, beaten, and then never seen again), even where Tadić was found to have participated in the beatings. While the court noted that in the chaotic circumstances of war "it is inappropriate to apply rules of some national systems that require the production of a body as proof of death" it nevertheless found that "there must be evidence to link injuries received to a resulting death."[10]

In addition to Tadić's participation in crimes in prison camps, the judgment considered several deaths in villages. For those that occurred in the town of Kozarac, Tadić was indicted for the death of five Muslim men who were allegedly selected from a column of civilian deportees, lined up against a kiosk on the side of the road, and shot. Based on witness evidence, the trial chamber found it beyond a reasonable doubt that Tadić was in Kozarac that day and that he had participated in calling people out of the moving column of civilian deportees; inconsistencies in testimony prevented the trial chamber, however, from finding either that Tadić participated in the shootings as alleged or in fact that such shootings took place at all.[11]

In Jaskići and Sivci, where many Muslim refugees from Kozarac had fled, Tadić was charged with crimes committed on June 14, 1992. On that day, armed Bosnian Serb men went through the villages door to door, issuing threats and removing all men aged 15–65. In Sivci this process was relatively calm. One witness placed Tadić in Sivci that day. In Jaskići, by contrast, the process was accompanied by beatings, the firing of shots, and death threats. By the time the armed men had left the village, the remaining villagers had discovered five dead bodies, four of whom had been shot in the head. Based on witness testimony, the trial chamber found Tadić was an active member of the party that beat and removed the men from the village of Jaskići. It stopped short, however, of finding that Tadić took part in the killing of the five men.[12]

Finally, the trial chamber found that Tadić participated, by assisting in the military effort, in the ethnic cleansing of Kozarac, and was present, in a more limited role, in the Keraterm and Trnopolje prison camps. Based on Tadić's political activities and nationalist statements, the court found that Tadić was aware of a discriminatory policy and that he sought to persecute non-Serbs on religious and political grounds.[13] It held the following:

> Based on the presence of the accused at the Trnopolje camp when surviving prisoners were being deported, as well as his support *both for the concept and the creation* of a Greater Serbia, necessarily entailing, as discussed in the preliminary findings, the deportation of non-Serbs from the designated territory and the establishment of the camps as a means towards this end, the Trial Chamber is satisfied beyond reasonable doubt that the accused participated in the seizure, selection, and transfer of non-Serbs to various camps and did so within the context of an armed conflict and that while doing so, he was aware that the majority of surviving prisoners would be deported from Bosnia-Herzegovina.[14]

10 *Tadić* Trial Chamber para 240.
11 *Tadić* Trial Chamber para 341.
12 *Tadić* Trial Chamber para 375.
13 *Tadić* Trial Chamber para 477.
14 *Tadić* Trial Chamber para 461 (emphasis added).

This finding, particularly as regards Tadić's political leanings, is a central element in the trial chamber's development of a jurisprudence that would eventually be called "JCE." Similarly, it offers an important contrast against the later JCE cases explored in Part II.

i The Law of *Tadić*

To determine liability for participation in a common criminal design, the *Tadić* court reviewed World War II case law as exemplary of customary international law. The trial chamber's analysis centered on *intent* and *participation*. The court defined *intent* as "awareness of the act of participation coupled with a conscious decision to participate by planning, instigating, ordering, committing, or otherwise aiding and abetting," maintaining in addition that this must be a deliberate act that directly aids the commission of the crime itself. The deliberateness and relation to the crime should be *inferred* from the circumstances. As support for this argument, the court cited the post-World War II case *Mauthausen*,[15] in which sixty-one defendants working in a concentration camp were found guilty of murder because they must have known about the gas chambers.

In its May 1997 judgment, the trial chamber found Tadić guilty of participating in an attack on the town of Kozarac, the collection and transfer of non-Serb civilians to detention camps, and atrocities at Omarska that included beating Muslim prisoners and killing two Muslim policemen. The trial chamber found that Tadić committed these acts of persecution with the aim of establishing a "Greater Serbia" in the area through the ethnic cleansing of all non-Serbs. As regards charges of cruel treatment and inhumane acts, the trial chamber found that Tadić was both a perpetrator and an assister. The trial chamber found likewise with regard to the severe beating suffered by a Muslim prisoner at the Omarska prison camp; while the court found no direct evidence that Tadić was present when the prisoner was beaten, it found Tadić individually responsible for aiding and abetting the beating. The court cited the testimony of a witness who heard Tadić say, as he was returning the prisoner Sivac to his holding place, "You will remember, Sivac, that you cannot touch a Serb or say anything to a Serb." Based on this, the court concluded, "Even though there is no direct evidence that [Tadić] physically participated in the beating of Sivac, by these acts, [Tadić] intentionally assisted directly and substantially in the common purpose of the group to inflict severe physical suffering upon Sivac."[16]

The court acquitted Tadić of cruel treatment in the beating of one prisoner in front of a house. In this instance, the court found the prosecution witness's testimony that he had seen Tadić following the beaten prisoner insufficient to find Tadić guilty of participating in the beating within the meaning of Article 7(1)[17] The court also

[15] US Military Tribunal, Volume XI *Law Reports* 15.

[16] *Tadić* Trial Chamber para 735.

[17] *Tadić* Trial Chamber para 747.

acquitted Tadić for the five deaths in the village of Jaskići, on the grounds that while the court found Tadić had been in the village that day, it could not connect him directly to the deaths.

While the actual JCE standard was first articulated by the appeals chamber,[18] the trial chamber established several significant standards in its judgment that have framed JCE indelibly. First and most importantly, it defined a culpability standard below co-perpetration. Second, it relied on (select) World War II-era case law to assert that it was consolidating and articulating principles that constitute customary international law. Finally, the trial chamber articulated an undeniably aggressive standard regarding *commission*, where Tadić was found guilty of aiding and abetting a beating based on an unrelated, although assuredly aggressive, *statement*. The *Tadić* trial chamber stopped short, however, of finding Tadić liable for any form of commission of murder based solely on corpses found on site. The appeals chamber proceeded to undo these latter limitations.

ii The *Tadić* Appeals Chamber

The appeals chamber articulated the present JCE standard in considering the problem of the five murdered villagers in Jaskići. The trial chamber had found Tadić not guilty beyond a reasonable doubt because it reasoned that the Jaskići deaths might be attributable to members of the large Bosnian Serb force operating in Sivci on the same day. The appeals chamber held that the trial chamber had erred, and that the only reasonable factual conclusion was that those five men had been killed by the armed group that included Tadić.[19] The appeals chamber then set out to explain how "under international law, [Tadić] can be held criminally responsible for the killing of the five men from Jaskići even though there is no evidence that he personally killed any of them."[20]

Based on an analysis of Article 7(1) (commission), as well as the collective nature of crimes committed in wartime situations, the appeals chamber found that, "whoever contributes to the commission of crimes by the group of persons of some members of the group, in execution of a *common criminal purpose*, may be held to be criminally liable, subject to certain conditions."[21] The tribunal found that in a group where some members physically perpetrate a crime, the participation or contribution of other group members can facilitate the crime, and "the moral gravity of such participation is often no less – or

18 The appeals chamber used various terms to describe JCE, including "common criminal plan," "common criminal purpose," "common design or purpose," "common criminal design," "common purpose," "common design," "common concerted design," "criminal enterprise," "common enterprise," and "joint criminal enterprise."

19 *Tadić* Appeals Chamber paras 179–184.

20 *Tadić* Appeals Chamber para 185.

21 *Tadić* Appeals Chamber para 190 (emphasis added).

indeed no different – from that of those actually carrying out the acts in question."[22]

The trial chamber concluded that the ICTY Statute permitted the notion of a transfer of culpability within members engaged in a common plan. The statute was silent, however, regarding the objective and subjective elements (*actus reus* and *mens rea*) of this sort of collective criminal responsibility. Relying on World War II case law, international legislation, and other sources of customary law, the appeals chamber articulated the applicable standard in what is now the foundation of the JCE doctrine. The appeals chamber divided JCE into three categories distinguished by *mens rea*. The *actus reus* remains the same, requiring a group, a common plan/purpose, and the participation of the accused. The doctrine holds the following:

> First, in cases of co-perpetration, where all participants in the common design *possess the same criminal intent to commit a crime* (and one or more of them actually perpetrate the crimes, with intent) (JCE I).
>
> Secondly, in the so-called "concentration camp" cases, where the requisite *mens rea* comprises *knowledge* of the nature of the system of ill-treatment and *intent* to further the common design of ill-treatment. Such intent may be proved either directly or as a matter of inference from the nature of the accused's authority within the camp or organizational hierarchy (JCE II).
>
> With regard to the third category of cases, it is appropriate to apply the notion of "common purpose" only where the following requirements concerning *mens rea* are fulfilled: (i) the *intention* to take part in a JCE and to further – individually and jointly – the criminal purposes of that enterprise and (ii) the *foreseeability* of the possible commission by other members of the group of offences that do not constitute the object of the criminal purpose ... It should be noted that more than negligence is required. What is required is a state of mind in which a person, although he did not intend to bring about a certain result, was aware that the actions of the group were most likely to lead to that result but nevertheless *willingly took that risk*[23] (JCE III).

In short, JCE I concerns co-perpetration, cases where all actors, in pursuit of a common plan, possess the same criminal intention.[24] JCE II, termed a variant of JCE I, applies this common plan to concentration camp cases. Citing the *Belsen*

[22] *Tadić* Appeals Chamber para 191.

[23] *Tadić* Appeals Chamber para 220 (emphasis added).

[24] *Tadić* Appeals Chamber para 196. It bears noting that while it is the least controversial of JCE, this category is not without controversy, because there are problems with criminalizing collective guilt from a rule-of-law standpoint. Some commentators have noted the different approaches to collective crimes in common- and civil-law jurisdictions, specifically the doctrines of conspiracy versus co-perpetration, respectively. See, e.g., Hamdorf 2007. Others have disputed using terminology originating from the civil law (co-perpetration) to describe a jurisprudence that clearly borrows much from the common law. See van Sliedregt 2007; see also Cassese 2007.

case of 1945,[25] the appeals chamber noted that the elements necessary for establishing guilt in such a case are as follows:[26]

> (i) The existence of an organized system to ill-treat the detainees and commit the various crimes alleged, (ii) the accused's awareness of the nature of the system, and (iii) the fact that the accused in some way actively participated in enforcing the system, i.e., encouraged, aided and abetted or in any case participated in the realization of the common criminal design.

Finally, while there is evidence that the co-perpetration standard of JCE I finds support in varied domestic jurisdictions (although its application is still problematic, particularly as regards its second variant regarding concentration camp cases), there is less support for the final JCE category, the so-called "extended" JCE (Piacente 2004), which is the most controversial of the three. There, the chamber found culpability for a perpetrator committing an act that, while outside of the common design, led to a crime that was a *natural and foreseeable* consequence of the common design, and where the perpetrator was either *reckless or indifferent* to the risk. Applying this category, the appeals chamber found Tadić criminally responsible for the deaths of the five Jaskići villagers. The chamber reasoned (i) that Tadić had the intention to further the criminal purpose of ethnically cleansing the Prijedor region; (ii) that the deaths of non-Serbs in pursuit of this aim were foreseeable; and (iii) that although he knew that his armed group might in fact lead to killings, Tadić regardless willingly took the risk.[27]

B Kvočka *and the Evolution of Joint Criminal Enterprise*

In 2001, two years after the final *Tadić* judgment, and arising from the same Omarska prison camp where Tadić participated in violent crimes, the ICTY trial chamber ruled on the case of Miroslav Kvočka and four others.[28] Unlike Tadić, Kvočka was a moderate Bosnian Serb, not a supporter of the nationalist party, and was married to a Bosnian Muslim, as was his sister. A professional police officer in Prijedor since 1980, Kvočka responded to a call ordering him to report to the Omarska mine complex the night of May 28/29, 1992. When Kvočka arrived, he saw two police officers in an official vehicle and ten buses parked inside the complex, some containing detainees and some empty. Kvočka was ordered to collect the reserve

25 *Trial of Josef Kramer and 44 others*, British Military Court, Luneberg, September 17–November 17, 1945, UNWCC, Volume II, Page 1.

26 While the appeals chamber termed JCE II a variant of JCE I, some commentators have argued that it comes closer to JCE III, as it is possible to imagine a camp setting where a defendant would not be aware of individual crimes committed. Problems associated with applying this standard are discussed in Part II below.

27 *Tadić* Appeals Chamber para 232.

28 Kvočka had four co-defendants, all with connections to the Omarska prison camp. See Appendix A. The distinctions between them impacted the rationale the court used in sentencing them, but are unimportant in terms of its application of a collective theory of liability.

police force (a group of twenty-five basically untrained recruits) and the police station commander, and to report back to duty at the complex.[29]

The conditions at the hastily assembled prison camp of Omarska were terrible. Food rations were not equal to the detainees streaming into the camp, nor were sanitary facilities adequate, and these conditions only deteriorated with the arrival of more detainees and the increasing summer heat. Borders were porous and anyone claiming a connection to an authority was admitted. As demonstrated by the even occasional presence of thugs such as Tadić, this in itself led to many atrocities. The *Kvočka* court noted several instances in which drunken, armed men and criminals who were "totally out of control"[30] randomly appeared at the camp and engaged in violence. Police recruits, undertrained and sometimes with criminal backgrounds themselves, were permitted to carry their personal weapons in the camp.[31] Kvočka testified that while it was the job of the military police officers at the camp's entrance to determine who might enter or not, he intervened in some instances because, as he testified, "sometimes to protect people you have to bypass the usual procedure."[32]

Following orders from his superiors, Kvočka helped organize the internal security of the camp.[33] As one of a handful of professional policemen on site, it seems that Kvočka brought a small amount of order and a suggestion of professionalism to an otherwise staggeringly random and brutal operation. Indeed, several witnesses testified that "the atmosphere in the camp was generally 'better' when Kvočka was present."[34] On the other hand, Kvočka's personal position was insecure; with extensive family connections to the Muslim community, living and working in a political environment where political leaders regularly espoused, on television and radio, the policy that the population of non-Serbs in the region should be brought down to no more than 2 percent and that this should be done by any means necessary,[35] Kvočka testified that his "loyalties" were constantly questioned. Pressure could only have increased when he intervened to remove his brothers-in-law, brought in on the second day of operation, from the camp. Indeed, this action led to his eventual dismissal less than one month later, and his reassignment to another police station.[36]

Aside from this personal intervention, Kvočka seems to have challenged authority, as recorded by the trial chamber, only in a few of the "gravest" cases. On the second day of the camp's operation, a drunk man drove up beside detainee buses and started

[29] *Kvočka* Trial Chamber para 345.

[30] *Kvočka* Trial Chamber para 377.

[31] *Kvočka* Trial Chamber para 376. The *Tadić* trial chamber detailed how Serb authorities had effectively disarmed the non-Serb population in the months preceding the Serb takeover, redistributing the weapons to Serb citizens.

[32] *Kvočka* Trial Chamber paras 111; 378.

[33] *Kvočka* Trial Chamber para 346.

[34] *Kvočka* Trial Chamber para 371.

[35] This was detailed in the exposition in the *Tadić* judgment. *Tadić* Trial Chamber.

[36] Kvočka was also required, as a parting act, to bring his brothers-in-law back to the camp.

shooting, causing several deaths and injuries. Kvočka physically restrained the shooter, saving many lives in the process.[37] He also intervened in the beating of one prisoner, asserting he had been wrongly detained (the actual target was the man's sister, with a very similar name, who was a prominent local judge); Kvočka convinced the guards to release the man. Generally, however, Kvočka's response to the brutalities of the camp was to consistently and repeatedly inform his superior, the commander of the Prijedor police station, of the criminal activities he observed. For example, Kvočka cordoned off dead bodies he found next to the first arriving buses, preserving the scene for later investigation, and informed his superior; there was no later investigation. Following standard Prijedor police procedure, Kvočka made reports to his superior of all the following: reports of beatings, wrongful arrests, porous camp borders, and the murder of detainees by other guards.[38]

i Findings of the Trial Chamber

The trial chamber found that Kvočka served at Omarska for seventeen days over a one-month period. He was not found to have personally committed any of the extensive acts of violence that occurred at Omarska, nor was he found to have ordered such acts, or even participated in them by, for example, selecting certain detainees for "interrogation." Instead, he was found to be a co-perpetrator of crimes against humanity, including torture, persecution, and murder, on a theory of JCE based on his work within the JCE, the prison camp of Omarska.[39]

The trial chamber applied a two-pronged test to determine Kvočka's criminal responsibility. First, it examined the evidence before it to determine whether the time Kvočka spent at Omarska was sufficient to find that he participated in the JCE of the camp. Second, the court reviewed the evidence to determine whether his level of participation made him a co-perpetrator ("sharing the intent of the camp's evil goals") or an aider or abettor, characterized by the court as performing only his discrete job, alleviating detainee suffering when he could, and committing no violations of his own. While the court acknowledged that such a line was finely drawn, it stated that this was the standard emerging from World War II case law.

Upon examining the evidence, the trial chamber found that Kvočka was aware of the horrible conditions for detainees in the camp, of beatings, deaths, lack of food, and miserable conditions. Kvočka's *awareness* (knowledge) of the terrible conditions in the camp are the legal equivalent of intent, the trial chamber determined, based on its review of World War II case law.[40] While the trial chamber found that Kvočka

37 *Kvočka* Trial Chamber para 387.

38 *Kvočka* Trial Chamber paras 393–394.

39 The trial chamber found Omarska to be a JCE because of the serious crimes committed intentionally in order to persecute and subjugate the non-Serb detainees. *Kvočka* Trial Chamber paras 319–320.

40 "The concentration camp cases seemingly establish a rebuttable presumption that holding an executive, administrative, or protective role in a camp constitutes general participation in the crimes

himself did not physically perpetrate any of the crimes committed at Omarska, it found that he

> could have done far more to mitigate the terrible conditions in the camp . . . [by] tak[ing] steps within his designated authority to more actively prevent unauthorized outsiders from entering the camp and abusing detainees . . . ensur[ing] more detainees received medical treatment . . . prevent[ing] guards and other subordinates from beating or otherwise abusing detainees on arrival, in the dining room, or en route to the toilets.[41]

As regards Kvočka's co-defendants, the trial chamber ultimately found a spectrum of *commission*, from defendants who actively participated in violence, to those who watched detainee abuse passively, to those who pretended that things were normal when evidence clearly showed otherwise, concluding, "All three attitudes deserve to be punished."[42]

The trial chamber rejected Kvočka's contention that he lacked the authority to prevent abuses in the camp, in part relying on Kvočka's own testimony of intervention in "grave" circumstances to show that he did in fact have such authority. The trial chamber found witness testimony that Kvočka's presence improved conditions to be additionally indicative of authority. The trial chamber further found that the Prijedor police department had sufficiently increased in size that it could be viewed on par with a station, putting Kvočka in a "*de facto* position of authority and influence in the Omarska police station . . . parallel[ing] the function of a deputy commander or assistant commander."[43] Thus, according to the trial chamber, Kvočka occupied an authority position based on (1) the terrible conditions and violent crime that occurred within the camp, and (2) the trial court's finding that Kvočka was in a position to prevent crimes and alleviate suffering, and *yet did not*.[44]

Finally, the trial chamber concluded that Kvočka's participation in Omarska was not only knowing, but also willing.[45] The trial chamber accepted Kvočka's citation of the individual detainees he saved or helped as proof that Kvočka harbored no personal animus towards Muslims. This did not impact Kvočka's liability for participation in a JCE, however, because the critical intent question the trial chamber addressed was not whether Kvočka *intended* to hurt Muslims, but rather whether he *knowingly* facilitated the JCE, which was the operation of the Omarska camp. The trial chamber found that Kvočka's knowing and continued participation both

committed therein. An intent to further the efforts of the JCE so as to rise to the level of co-perpetration may also be inferred from knowledge of the crimes being perpetrated in the camp and continued participation which enables the camp's functioning." *Kvočka* Trial Chamber para 278, footnote omitted.

41 *Kvočka* Trial Chamber para 395.

42 *Kvočka* Trial Chamber para 709.

43 *Kvočka* Trial Chamber para 344.

44 The appeals chamber stressed that naturally Kvočka was not being condemned for things he did not do; given the trial chamber's language and rationale, however, this seems inaccurate.

45 *Kvočka* Trial Chamber para 404.

enabled the camp to continue its abusive practices and sent a message of approval to others in the camp – specifically guards the trial chamber found subordinate to him – condoning the abuses and deplorable conditions there.[46] For his role in the crimes at Omarska prison camp, Kvočka was sentenced to seven years, a sentence that was upheld on appeal.

ii *Kvočka* Appeals Chamber

The appeals chamber upheld the trial chamber's finding that Kvočka knowingly participated in a JCE, thereby becoming a co-perpetrator of the JCE. It also upheld the trial chamber's finding that Kvočka was only responsible for those crimes against humanity that occurred during the period he was working at Omarska, and on the basis of this, overturned two murder findings of the trial chamber, based on an inability to place those murders during Kvočka's term.[47]

Before the appeals chamber, Kvočka submitted that he was a policeman performing his duty, which due to circumstances far outside his control became a job of providing internal security at a holding center, albeit a particularly odious and dangerous one. The appeals chamber dismissed this argument, noting the following:

> Incidentally, it does not appear that maintaining a camp which seeks to subjugate and persecute detainees based on their ethnicity, nationality or political persuasion and in which living conditions are intolerable and the most serious beatings are regularly meted out can possibly be considered as performing "duties in accordance with the police requirements."[48]

In *Kvočka et al.*, the ICTY held that Kvočka's knowledge of the violence committed at Omarska was the judicial equivalent of his intent to commit such violence. Knowledge as the legal equivalent of intention is not novel at criminal law. Doctrinal contortions arise rather in the question of how to formulate *what Kvočka knew*: the *Kvočka* appellate chamber argues that because Kvočka knew of violence – saw the dead bodies (he wrote reports signaling them to his supervisors), the random shootings and beatings, and the conditions in which prisoners were kept – he therefore knew that the entire enterprise of the Omarska prison camp was illegitimate and illegal. The chamber accomplishes this by finding Kvočka engaged in "criminal participation," which, relying on several World War II-era cases for support, it defines as follows:

46 *Kvočka* Trial Chamber para 404.

47 Another point raised by defendants on appeal was the problematic lack of care taken by the trial chamber, where defendants in the case were never entirely sure of whom they were accused of/found guilty of persecuting, beating, or killing and on what day. The appeals chamber found that the trial chamber erred in its information representation approach on this score, thereby violating a principle of fair trial. The appeals chamber nonetheless found that this error did not invalidate the judgment. *Kvočka* Appeals Chamber para 74.

48 *Kvočka* Appeals Chamber para 242.

> when a detention facility is operated in a manner which makes the discriminatory and persecutory intent of the operation patently clear, anyone who knowingly participates in any significant way in the operation of the facility or assists or facilitates its activity, incurs individual criminal responsibility for participation (para 306).

The appeals chamber's rationale is that Kvočka should have been able to recognize the criminal nature of the enterprise he was engaged in, and that once he had recognized it, any further participation suggested co-perpetration.

C *Challenging the Standard in* Tadić *and* Kvočka

Both cases showcase definitional issues regarding the reach and content of JCE. While the *Tadić* court held that liability under JCE does not require physical presence on the scene of the crime, or indeed knowledge that the crime has been committed, the court did not find Tadić culpable for crimes against humanity except those with which he had a direct physical tie (albeit as tenuous as having been present either in a place on a day where crimes were committed). In a sense, the reasoning of *Tadić* does not match the holding of *Tadić* – why shouldn't Tadić be culpable for all the deaths in the Prijedor region resulting from the policy of ethnic cleansing that he physically and politically worked towards? Even the later *Kvočka* judgment acknowledged these problems, finding in 2005 that the "precise threshold of participation in JCE has not been settled."[49] Yet the *Kvočka* judgment suffers from the same issues, where, for example, Miroslav Kvočka was not charged with sexual violence at the camp, although the sexual violence was reportedly so pronounced that Kvočka would have been as aware of sexual violence as he was of other forms of violence.

Second, *Kvočka* suffers from serious procedural problems. Although the *Tadić* judgment of two years before had established JCE as a theory of liability for the commission of crimes, the prosecution in the *Kvočka* case never pleaded JCE as a theory of liability in its indictment. Instead, the prosecution's reliance on collective responsibility emerged first in its pre-trial brief, submitted two weeks before the trial. In response to Kvočka's contestation in his appellate brief, the appeals chamber allowed that the indictment was in this area "vague and . . . therefore defective."[50] The appeals chamber further noted that such failure to plead with specificity disadvantaged both the defense as well as the trial chamber. It nonetheless determined, after "a careful review of the trial record," that

> the Prosecution gave timely, clear, and consistent information to [defendants], which detailed the factual basis of the charges against them and thereby

[49] *Kvočka* Appeals Chamber para 289.

[50] *Kvočka* Appeals Chamber para 41.

> compensated for the Indictment's failure to give proper notice of the Prosecution's intent to rely on joint criminal enterprise responsibility.[51]

In this rationale, the appeals chamber echoed the trial chamber, which responded in its judgment to defendants' protests about the lack of specificity in pleading by arguing the following:

> The charges in the Amended Indictment that the accused "instigated, committed or otherwise aided and abetted" crimes may include responsibility for participating in a joint criminal enterprise designed to accomplish such crimes . . . [It is within the trial chamber's] discretion to characterize the form of participation of the accused, if any, according to the theory of responsibility it deems most appropriate, within the limits of the Amended Indictment and insofar as the evidence permits.[52]

Although the ICTY Statute precludes guilt by association or culpability based on membership in a criminal group,[53] it appears that it is precisely Kvočka's position in the Omarska camp that serves as the basis for his culpability; this is the appeals chamber's reading of World War II case law as regards JCE II.

Upon determining that the camp itself is a JCE, the tribunal employed World War II case law regarding participation in such criminal enterprises, much of which contains a very low standard for participation (and thus co-perpetration); in essence, anyone helping such a camp function becomes a co-perpetrator.

In line with this reasoning, the tribunal should have found Kvočka liable for all crimes against humanity committed while he held his position in the Prijedor police force (particularly given the tribunal's focus on finding him a *de facto* deputy as well as an early constructor of the camp). The tribunal did not so find, however, refusing to hold Kvočka liable for crimes committed in his absence from the camp (specifically for atrocities committed during the two sick leaves Kvočka took following incidents of violence he personally witnessed).[54]

The final thematic problem that arises from *Kvočka* has to do with drawing the line between co-perpetration in a JCE and aiding and abetting (a mode of commission that was explicitly recognized in the ICTY Statute, unlike JCE). In *Kvočka* we see that Kvočka's *intent* to persecute non-Serbs was determined based on his *knowledge* of the conditions that existed at the camp. Yet these same questions of *intent* and *knowledge* underlie the courts' distinctions between aiding and abetting and co-perpetration, as well as shoring up liability under JCE I, II, and III. Attempts made

51 *Kvočka* Appeals Chamber para 43.

52 *Kvočka* Trial Chamber paras 247–248.

53 Report of the Secretary-General pursuant to paragraph 2 of Security Council Resolution 808 (1993), 3 May 1993 (S/25704), §§ 50, 51. This was reaffirmed in *Prosecutor* v. *Milomir Stakić*, Case No. IT-97-24, (March 22, 2006), available at www.icty.org ("*Stakić* Appeals Chamber").

54 The appeals chamber characterizes this as a *factual* finding on the part of the trial chamber. *Kvočka* Appeals Chamber para 114. The standard for overturning a finding of fact by a lower court is more onerous than overturning an articulation of law by a lower court.

by the *Kvočka* judgments and others to elucidate and standardize these distinctions have tended only to muddle them (Ohlin 2009).

Defenders of the ICTY's developing JCE jurisprudence have argued that the court has aptly applied and updated principles arising from the Nuremberg tribunals (Ohlin 2009), and note that ICL is a "rudimentary" tool lacking the qualifiers one finds in more "mature" legal systems, such as a distinction between murder and manslaughter (Cassese 2007a). Yet the question *Kvočka* leaves unanswered is the question raised by one of his co-defendants, and the charge specifically articulated by General Gotovina's lawyers, which is explored later: JCE as a theory of strict liability. While the *Kvočka* trial chamber stressed that not everyone working in an abusive detention camp would automatically become liable as a participant in a JCE because participation must be *significant*,[55] the appeals chamber rejected this same "significance" language.[56] Thus we are left unable to say how we might distinguish culpability of those working in a concentration camp. This is perhaps not surprising, as it is in fact a holding gleaned from much of the World War II case law.

II RECENT JOINT CRIMINAL ENTERPRISE JURISPRUDENCE: *GOTOVINA, STANIŠIĆ AND SIMATOVIĆ*, AND *ŠEŠELJ*

Ante Gotovina is the Croatian general who headed the southern wing of Operation "Storm," the military operation that retook Croatian territory from Croatian Serb control in August 1995. Operation Storm, which benefited from US support,[57] was a startlingly rapid military success, retaking in a matter of days land that had been held for four years, as Croatian troops rushed through the sparsely populated remote region that the Croatian Serbs had held. Croatian Serb defenses crumpled like a house of cards, and the ethnic Serb population made a hasty exodus by cart, tractor, and car; only those too old or frail to make the journey stayed behind. It is estimated that two hundred thousand people fled. Following Croatian troops came policemen and finally displaced Croats, who had been living as refugees for years on the coast. When the dust from Operation Storm settled, approximately 150 people were found dead.[58] Massive numbers of houses had been burned or destroyed, and many of the

55 *Kvočka* Trial Chamber para 309.

56 *Kvočka* Appeals Chamber para 97.

57 See, i.e., Daković "How Operation Storm Destabilized the Balkans" August 27, 2001, www.antiwar.com/article.php?articleid=1483. (According to the former head of Croatian counterintelligence, Markica Redić, "the Pentagon undertook complete supervision during the Storm action." Moreover, Miro Tuđman, son of the late Croatian president and head of Croatia's equivalent of the CIA, has argued that during Operation Storm "all our (electronic) intelligence in Croatia went online in real time to the National Security Agency in Washington" and "we had a de facto partnership."

58 *The Prosecutor* v. *Ante Gotovina, Ivan Čermak and Mladen Markač, Amended Joinder Indictment* Case No. IT-06-90-PT (March 12, 2008) ("*Gotovina* Joinder Indictment"); the numbers are disputed.

dead – who were mostly elderly and infirm – exhibited wounds consistent with war crimes (gun shots to the back of the head; slit throats).

For his role in the military action, Gotovina was indicted on charges of persecutions, plunder, murder, inhumane acts, and cruel treatment, all committed under the JCE theory of liability. Given a head start by Croatian authorities, Gotovina fled, and remained successfully underground for four years, which made him into somewhat of a *cause célèbre* both within Croatia (where he came to symbolize patriotism and stoicism in the face of injustice, being referred to simply as "hero"[59]) and before the ICTY, where, after the death of Tuđman, he came to symbolize the tribunal's balance, demanding "leaders" from Serbia and Croatia alike.[60] Gotovina's continued absence from The Hague became a point of confrontation between Croatia, the ICTY, and the EU, ultimately stalling Croatian EU entry negotiations based on a negative report from the ICTY prosecutor. Gotovina was ultimately apprehended in the Canary Islands in 2005; the arrest was made with the assistance of the Croatian authorities, which was ironic in light of the fact that Gotovina was traveling on a Croatian-issued passport (under a pseudonym meaning "Christian Croat").

GOTOVINA TRIAL CHAMBER. On April 15, 2011, the ICTY announced its verdict in the Gotovina case, sentencing Gotovina to twenty-four years in prison.[61] Gotovina was convicted for his participation in

> a JCE whose common purpose was the permanent removal of Serb civilians from the Krajina by force or threat of force, involving the crimes of deportation/forcible transfer and persecution (deportation, forcible transfer, unlawful attacks against civilians and civilian objects, and discriminatory and restrictive measures).[62]

In its 1,300-page judgment, the trial chamber articulated four categories of action that "corroborated" its finding that there was a JCE and that Gotovina "meaningfully

59 In Croatia in 2004–2005, which coincided with the period directly preceding Gotovina's capture and during which time his absence from The Hague was delaying Croatia's accession process with the EU, Gotovina was frequently publicly commemorated, in posters, plaques, decorative frescoes, and bumper stickers displayed in towns throughout Croatia as "heroj ne zločinac": "hero, not criminal." (Field notes, on file with author.)

60 Gotovina was specifically named by the UN Security Council in resolution 1503 (August 28, 2003) when the Security Council called on states to increase cooperation with the ICTY to "bring Radovan Karadžić and Ratko Mladić, as well as Ante Gotovina and all other indictees" to the ICTY. S/Res/1503 (2003) ICTY President Meron in his statement to the Security Council said "the Tribunal will not have fulfilled its historic mission – and it will not close its doors – until Karadžić, Mladić, and Gotovina have been arrested, brought to The Hague, and tried before the Tribunal in accordance with the full procedural protections recognized by our jurisprudence." Statement by Judge Theodor Meron, President, International Criminal Tribunal for the former Yugoslavia, to the Security Council June 13, 2005, available at www.icty.org/sid/8581 (accessed June 24, 2013).

61 His co-defendants Mladen Markač and Ivan Čermak received sentences of eighteen years and an acquittal, respectively. See Appendix A.

62 *Gotovina* Appeals Chamber para 85 (summarizing *Gotovina* Trial Chamber findings, relying on *Gotovina* Trial Chamber paras 2314, 2368–2375, 2578–2587).

participated in it."[63] First, the trial chamber analyzed (over the course of approximately two hundred pages) the transcript of a meeting on the island of Brioni (just off the Croatian coast) on July 31, 1995. Present at this meeting were many of the highest-ranking officials of the Croatian government, including President Tuđman, Minister of Defense Šušak, and Chief of the Croatian Army Main Staff Červenko. Gotovina was also present at this meeting, at which Tuđman articulated his design of using military force to take back the Krajina, ensuring "that not only the Serb Krajina army, but also the Serb civilian population, would leave the Krajina."[64] Based significantly on its analysis of the Brioni meeting, the trial chamber determined there was a JCE that included Tuđman and many of his top associates, and that Gotovina's participation amounted to a "significant contribution" to this JCE. At this meeting, responding to a statement by Tuđman, Gotovina said: "A large number of civilians are already evacuating Knin and heading towards Banja Luka and Belgrade. That means that if we continue this pressure, probably for some time to come, there won't be so many civilians, just those who have to stay, who have no possibility of leaving" and, "if there is an order to strike at Knin, we will destroy it in its entirety in a few hours."[65] These statements were construed by the trial chamber as demonstrative of Gotovina's meaningful participation in a JCE, the object of which was the permanent removal of Serbs from the Krajina region.

In making its JCE determination, the trial chamber considered artillery attacks against civilians on August 4 and 5 that preceded the exodus of Serbs from the Krajina region. For example, there was an August 2, 1995 order instructing units to

> [organize] along the main attack axes, focus on providing artillery support to the main forces in the offensive operation through powerful strikes against the enemy's front line, command posts, communications centres, artillery firing positions and by putting the towns of [] Knin, Benkovac, Obravac and Gračac under fire.[66]

Additionally, the trial chamber analyzed shell markings to determine whether shelling was targeted or indiscriminate. It heard expert witness testimony, much of it conflicting, regarding the level of accuracy (based on conditions, equipment, and training) that could have been expected of the weaponry. In response to this testimony, the trial chamber developed a "200 meter" standard; shells falling within two hundred meters of a legitimate military target would be considered lawful, and shells falling outside two hundred meters of a legitimate military target would constitute "indiscriminate" shelling, which is a violation of IHL.

Finally, the trial chamber considered the crimes committed by armed units in the period directly following the military operation (the months of August and

63 This useful analysis and structure is borrowed from Judge Pocar's dissenting opinion in the *Gotovina* Appeals Chamber, discussed further later.

64 Case information sheet, Gotovina & Markač, available at www.icty.org (accessed March 4, 2013).

65 Brioni Transcript, p. 10; *Gotovina* Trial Chamber.

66 *Gotovina* Trial Chamber para 1893.

September 1995) as well as the discriminatory policy of the Croatian government towards its Serbian minority, including discriminatory property laws, in its determination that there was a JCE to illegally remove the Serbian population from Krajina.

GOTOVINA APPEALS CHAMBER. In a stunning reversal of JCE policy and development, Gotovina was acquitted, together with his co-defendant Mladen Markač, on November 20, 2012 in a 3–2 appellate chamber judgment. The majority found not only that Gotovina had not participated meaningfully in a JCE, but that there was no JCE at all, a finding one dissenting judge called "grotesque" and "contradict[ing] any sense of justice."[67] Four separate opinions were written in addition to the majority judgment, although only two addressed JCE, in a holding that gives little guidance regarding the developing substantive law of JCE, or the institutional cohesion of the ICTY.

The heart of the majority opinion was the problem of the 200-meter standard articulated by the trial chamber. The majority contested the basis and use of this standard, and when the standard fell, the majority held that the JCE finding fell with it, because according to the majority's reading of the trial chamber's judgment, only *unlawful* artillery attacks could constitute deportation.[68] Once the standard to determine lawfulness was challenged, and the artillery attacks ceased to be demonstrably unlawful (as construed by the court, recollecting that the OTP has the burden of proving that something is unlawful), by this rationale, there was no crime of deportation.

The majority characterized the trial chamber's judgment as "not explicitly consider[ing] evidence drawn from the Brioni Meeting to support its finding that unlawful artillery attacks took place"[69] but rather "consider[ing] inferences drawn from the Brioni Meeting alongside its finding that unlawful artillery attacks took place in order to establish the existence and parameters of a JCE."[70]

The majority's finding removed not only Gotovina's liability via his "meaningful participation" in a JCE, but it undid the trial chamber's finding of a JCE to illegally remove the Serb residents of the Krajina region as well. While the trial chamber had arguably dangerously overreached in naming – not merely implicating but asserting the guilt of – individuals not before the tribunal in its finding of JCE (finding Tuđman and others to be participants in the JCE), the appellate chamber also overreached in undoing the entirety of the trial chamber's findings without

67 Pocar dissenting opinion, *Gotovina* Appeals Chamber paras 26, 39.

68 "The Trial Chamber held that Serb civilians' departures from settlements at the same time as or in the immediate aftermath of artillery attacks only constituted deportation where these artillery attacks were found to have been unlawful." *Gotovina* Appeals Chamber para 87, citing *Gotovina* Trial Chamber para 1755. Judge Pocar contests both this interpretation and the holding directly in his dissent, paras 23–24.

69 *Gotovina* Appeals Chamber para 81, referencing *Gotovina* Trial Chamber paras 1893–1945.

70 *Gotovina* Appeals Chamber para 81, referencing *Gotovina* Trial Chamber para 2310.

articulating under what basis of review it did so.[71] As Pocar and Aguis each note in their acerbic dissents, for the appellate chamber to overrule 1,300 pages describing in careful detail, through the consideration of individual witnesses, documents, events, and allegations, a far-reaching plan to permanently remove the Krajina Serbs, it should give some real consideration to the substance of the trial chamber's findings. The appellate chamber's reversal of the trial chamber's epic judgment was a mere sixteen pages long.[72]

If the trial chamber's 2011 analysis of statements made at a meeting on Brioni Island seemed a thin basis for finding evidence of a common plan and convicting Gotovina to twenty-four years in prison, its judgment did at least comport with JCE jurisprudence to date: put on notice that he was working for politicians with illegal intent, Gotovina's willingness to assist them in the realization of their plan would be the sort of "risk-taking" that was criminalized in *Kvočka*. The majority opinion in *Gotovina*, however, challenges the JCE doctrine developed by the ICTY.

A *Halting "Ideological Creep"*: Perišić

A decade after the final *Kvočka et al.* judgment and two years after the final *Gotovina* ruling, the ICTY appeals chamber acquitted the Serbian General Perišić of "aiding and abetting" the Bosnian Serb army.[73] The *Perišić* case is not a JCE case, but rather a (novel) formulation of the ICTY's aiding and abetting jurisprudence (Aksenova 2015). Regardless, it is interesting for our purposes because like *Kvočka et al., Perišić* addresses the question of individual culpability within the confines of institutional legitimacy. In *Perišić*, however, the ICTY reached a very different conclusion regarding individual culpability when framed within possibly criminal state behavior.

The *Perišić* case addressed Perišić's culpability for aid provided by the Serbian army to the Bosnian Serbs. Violence in Bosnia owed a great deal to Serbian aid: ethnic Serbs were overrepresented in the Yugoslav army, particularly in the leadership, and as the country dissolved, these factions helped funnel Yugoslav resources into ethnic Serb hands in Bosnia and Croatia (Silber & Little 1997). In Bosnia, Serbian paramilitary groups aided Bosnian Serb military campaigns, and Yugoslav army supplies and personnel also crossed the border. The Serbian General Perišić was at the top of the supply train, providing materials to the Bosnian army as it ethnically cleansed and murdered Bosnian Muslims and Croats in an attempt to

[71] See Pocar's dissent paras 4–10, in which he critiques the absence of the appropriate rationale for rejecting the trial chamber's findings of fact and/or interpretations of law, both of which are subject to different standards of review.

[72] ICTY judgments routinely number in the hundreds of pages: the *Gotovina* appeals judgment is by contrast shockingly short. The attached separate and dissenting opinions outnumber the majority holding.

[73] *Prosecutor* v. *Momčilo Perišić, Judgment*, Case No. IT-04–81 (September 6, 2011); *Prosecutor* v. *Momčilo Perišić, Appeals Chamber Judgment*, Case No. IT-04–81 (February 28, 2013).

expand the territory under Bosnian Serb control. The *Perišić* trial chamber found that Perišić could approve or deny requests (para 948), and concluded that without assistance from the Serbian army, the Bosnian Serb army "would have been hampered in conducting its operations in Sarajevo and Srebrenica" (para 1622). Recall that such "operations" consisted of the brutal siege of a civilian city for more than three years (and included two large marketplace bombings and a policy of snipers targeting civilians) and the genocidal murder of eight thousand men and boys, respectively. The *Perišić* trial chamber sentenced Perišić to twenty-seven years in prison.

In acquitting Perišić in 2013, the appeals chamber, in a 3–2 decision, engaged in the precise intellectual distinction that the *Kvočka et al.* chambers had rejected. Although the appeals chamber accepted the trial chamber's findings of fact regarding the aid supplied, through Perišić as gatekeeper, from the Serbian army to the Bosnian Serb army, the appeals chamber distinguished the Bosnian Serb army from certain illegitimate elements of its practice, and then required a showing that Perišić's aid had specifically assisted the criminal, illegitimate aims of the Bosnian Serb army. As regards intent in the form of awareness – the doctrinal articulation that affirmed Kvočka's culpability for violations of international humanitarian law – three of the five judges in the Perišić appeals chamber determined that knowledge of crimes is insufficient to meet the doctrinal requirements of aiding and abetting as those three judges construed them in the case.

If the *Gotovina* acquittal shocked the ICL world,[74] the *Perišić* acquittal infuriated it. In the wake of the *Perišić* judgment, *The New York Times* reported "rifts" between the judges at the ICTY, "who claimed in private that the [recent acquittals, including *Gotovina*] had abruptly rewritten legal standards that had been applied in earlier cases."[75] These rifts came to a head when the Danish appointee to the ICTY, Judge Frederik Harhoff, circulated an email to fifty-six friends in which he specifically accused ICTY President Theodor Meron of applying "tenacious pressure" on judges to change the standards required to convict military leaders under JCE.[76] Harhoff wrote that before the ICTY today, even Hitler might not be convicted. The email, which quickly became public,[77] resulted in Harhoff's dismissal, further delaying the *Šešelj* case on which he had been serving.[78]

74 I happened to be at the ICTY on the day Gotovina was acquitted, with a group of students on a yearly excursion; our usually voluble hosts from the prosecutor's office were quiet and retiring; the mood was funereal. Interviews, The Hague, November 2011, notes on file with author.

75 Marlise Simons, "Judge at War Crimes Tribunal Faults Acquittals of Serb and Croat Commanders" *New York Times* June 14, 2013.

76 See ICTY Judge Frederik Harhoff's Email to 56 Contacts June 6, 2013, available at www.bt.dk/sites/default/files-dk/node-files/511/6/6511917-letter-english.pdf.

77 Morten Frich, "Bekymret dansk FN-dommer: Jugoslavien-generalerne går fri" ("Worried Danish ICTY Judge: The Yugoslav Generals Are Being Freed") *Berlinske*, June 12, 2013.

78 Harhoff submits that the *Šešelj* bench on which he was serving was "only a couple of months" from rendering a judgment when he was dismissed, and suggests that such eventual judgment would not have been acquittal. Frederik Harhoff, "Mystery Lane: A Note on Independence and Impartiality in

B *The Messy Present:* Stanišić and Simatović, *and* Šešelj

The *Perišić* and *Kvočka* cases are doctrinally apples and oranges: Kvočka was charged with co-perpetration and Perišić with aiding and abetting, and these disparate charges have amassed their own jurisprudence, which confounds a straight doctrinal comparison. Around the same time Perišić was acquitted, however, the ICTY acquitted two other senior Serb leaders indicted under JCE charges in the case of *Prosecutor* v. *Jovica Stanišić and Franko Simatović*.[79] The trial chamber considered the actions of those two Serb generals, whom it found directed, supplied, and organized troops who were active in violence in Croatia and throughout Bosnia, through an "inference of intent . . . to share common criminal purpose" paradigm. The trial chamber, in a 2–1 decision, found evidence insufficient to support this *mens rea* standard, which is much more lenient than the "knowledge" standard applied in *Kvočka et al.*

On December 15, 2015, the ICTY appeals chamber issued its judgment, ordering a retrial in the case. As regards the JCE portion of the 2013 judgment, the appeals chamber determined that "the absence of a thorough analysis and prior findings on the existence and scope of a common criminal purpose shared by a plurality of persons as well as on Stanišić's and Simatović's contribution to it," meant that "the trial chamber could not have properly adjudicated Stanišić's and Simatović's *mens rea*." The Stanišić and Simatović trial lasted several years, and involved nearly five thousand exhibits and more than one hundred witnesses. The appeals chamber judgment sending the case to retrial means, effectively, that we are again years away from seeing how an international tribunal applies juridical constructions of "intent" to facts it establishes.

Starker still, on March 31, 2016, the ICTY's ten-year prosecution of Serbian paramilitary warlord Vojislav Šešelj ended in acquittal.[80] Relevant portions of the more than two thousand pages that constitute the judgment, concurrence, and dissent (from the three-judge panel hearing the case, each judge in effect writing their own opinion) iterate factual and legal findings, particularly regarding the structure and application of JCE, which are violently at odds with most previous ICTY jurisprudence (finding, for example, that there were no crimes against humanity in Bosnia because the element of widespread or systematic attack on a civilian population was not met).[81] The *Šešelj* judgment thus joined several other failed cases against those alleged to be most

International Criminal Trials," FICHL Policy Brief Series No. 47 (2016), available at www.fichl.org/fileadmin/user_upload/160407_PBS_No._47__2016_.pdf.

79 *Prosecutor* v. *Jovica Stanišić and Franko Simatović*, Case No. IT-03–69 (Int'l Crim. Trib. for the former Yugoslavia May 30, 2013).

80 *Prosecutor* v. *Vojislav Šešelj*, Case No. IT-03–67 (Int'l Crim. Trib. for the former Yugoslavia March 31, 2016). The Office of the Prosecutor has announced that it will appeal the acquittal, so we are still years away from a final judgment.

81 See analysis by Marko Milanovic in EJIL Talk! Blog, April 6, 2016, available at www.ejiltalk.org/the-sorry-acquittal-of-vojislav-seselj/

responsible for the war.[82] In March 2018, the appeals chamber pronounced its judgment, leaving the trial chamber's JCE analysis intact but reversing one element of its acquittal to find Šešelj guilty for statements he made in 1992 encouraging ethnic cleansing. The appeals chamber's ten-year sentence amounted to time served, and indeed, Šešelj did not even return to The Hague to hear the sentence. Šešelj was temporarily released from custody in The Hague to undergo cancer treatment in Serbia in 2014 and has since returned to parliament as the leader of the Serbian Radical Party. Under Serbian law, individuals sentenced to more than six months' prison may not serve in parliament, but as of this writing, Šešelj has refused to vacate his seat.[83]

The *Stanišić and Simatović* case is being retried before the MICT, so while these recent judgments seriously challenge the JCE jurisprudence articulated by *Tadić* and *Kvočka et al.*, it is not clear what the final word regarding JCE liability as a controlling idea in ICL, at least as articulated by the ICTY, will be.

CONCLUSION

Joint criminal enterprise liability is a novel and contentious formulation of ICL that has attracted volumes of scholarly attention.[84] It is a creative judicial construction of the ICTY statute's language of "commission," which enabled an extraordinarily broad establishment of culpability (Danner and Martinez 2005; van Sliedregt 2012; van der Wilt 2007) and resolved evidentiary problems plaguing crimes committed in times of widespread social violence. Joint criminal enterprise facilitates the work of ICTY prosecutors by removing the necessity of definitively tying an individual to a particular crime. Proponents of JCE argue that the chaotic and collective nature of war crimes both justifies and necessitates this deviation from a fundamental element of criminal law jurisprudence. Yet the outcry that the emergence and evolution of JCE has occasioned even within communities most sympathetic to the aims of the court (and including ICTY judges themselves, at times),[85] as well as the reticence

82 See, e.g., *Prosecutor* v. *Ante Gotovina, Ivan Čermak and Mladen Markač*, Case No. IT-06–90-PT (Int'l Crim. Trib. for the former Yugoslavia November 16, 2012); *Prosecutor* v. *Ante Gotovina, Ivan Čermak and Mladen Markač*, Case No. IT-06–90-PT (Int'l Crim. Trib. for the former Yugoslavia April 15, 2011); *Prosecutor* v. *Perišić*, Case No. IT-03–69 (Int'l Crim. Trib. for the former Yugoslavia February 28, 2013); *Prosecutor v. Jovica Stanišić and Franko Simatović*, Case No. IT-03–69 (Int'l Crim. Trib. for the former Yugoslavia May 30, 2013); *Prosecutor* v. *Vojislav Šešelj*, Case No. IT-03–67 (Int'l Crim. Trib. for the former Yugoslavia March 31, 2016) and *Prosecutor v. Slobodan Milošević*, Case No IT-02–54 (case uncompleted due to *Milošević's* death).

83 Gordana Knezevic, "Serbia, and its Parliament, Grapple with Fate of War Criminal Vojislav Seselj," available at www.rferl.org/a/serbia-and-its-parliament-grapple-with-seselj-s-fate/29170982.html.

84 See, for example, special issue of the *Journal of International Criminal Law* 2004 devoted to the topic.

85 *See Prosecutor* v. *Blagoje Simić, Miroslav Tadić and Simo Zarić, Appeals Chamber Judgment*, IT-95–9 (November 28, 2006) (a decision that threw the JCE charges out because they were not properly pleaded).

that international courts following the ICTY have shown in adopting the JCE standard, is one indication of the deeply problematic nature of using the JCE theory of liability to address the vexing question of how to hold individuals responsible for criminal acts committed by, and in the name of, a collective.

If the particularly sadistic elements of the *Tadić* case helped smooth the way for a doctrinal formulation that connected bad acts to defined violations of international humanitarian law, *Kvočka et al.* laid bare the doctrinal gymnastics necessary to apply JCE. Through its "discriminatory and persecutory" language, the *Kvočka* appeals chamber accomplished a doctrinal stunt: it conflated knowledge of violence in the camp (which is uncontested) with knowledge that Omarska itself was a criminal organization. The *Kvočka* appeals chamber asserts that the criminal nature of the Omarska enterprise, so clear to it, must have been clear to the professional policeman Miroslav Kvočka, too.

In this way, the *Kvočka* decision demonstrates a strict liability standard, where to work in the camp is to be guilty of the crimes committed there. This point has not been lost on the local and international publics addressed by the ICTY. In 2004, at the height of ICTY pressure for Croatia to produce indicted General Ante Gotovina, news shows buzzed with the number "500," which was evidently the number of Croatian politicians and functionaries who might be culpable under JCE for crimes committed during the liberation of Croatian territory. More significantly, as the chapter has described, in anticipation of closure and allegedly under pressure from the tribunal's leadership, ICTY judgments have been "walking back" the sweeping moral insistences of the type evidenced in *Kvočka et al.* A decade after the final *Kvočka* judgment, the ICTY appeals chamber acquitted the Serbian General Perišić of "aiding and abetting" the Bosnian Serb army. Regardless, it is interesting for our purposes because like *Kvočka, Perišić* addresses the question of individual culpability within the confines of institutional legitimacy. In *Perišić*, however, the ICTY reached a very different conclusion regarding individual culpability when framed within what Brad Roth (2011) calls the "ruthless" (potentially immoral, but not clearly illegal) behavior of states.

This chapter has continued the examination of the ICTY as progenitor of ICL, which is a necessary function of international criminal tribunals (ICTs). Where Chapter 3 considered the question of the law of procedure, this chapter examined one element of ICL substance developed by the ICTY: the theory of liability JCE. While the *international criminal law template* finds a value in allowing courts to articulate ICL based on the conviction that such articulation and development will be *progressive* (based on a moral argument for the value of ICL and ICTs), this chapter shows that, like the World War II-era case law, the ICTY's legal pronouncements arguably fail to meet – or even to pursue – any Kantian notion of justice.

With an eye to the particular challenges that exist in prosecuting war crimes, this chapter has examined the evolving uncertainty and instability of the ICTY's JCE jurisprudence. Joint criminal enterprise challenges a central tenet upon which legal systems build their legitimacy: predictability. Although the process of crafting JCE as a theory of liability has been underway for more than a decade, defendants before the tribunal today are ever more uncertain of what constitutes the relevant degree of participation, knowledge, or intent in order that JCE apply. As matters currently stand, there is no way for a defendant to combat the charge: JCE has become a form of strict liability because there is no way to mount a defense against it (although, as the *Gotovina* case has shown, it may from time to time be possible to surmount the charge). These procedural legal problems underline more pressing institutional issues for the ICTY, one being that of its legitimacy (and therefore its potential to impact discourse in the former Yugoslavia) and another being the heritage it leaves to other ICTs, most notably the International Criminal Court.

The development of JCE, which is an example of the development of the substance of ICL, illustrates a major structural deficit of the ICTY. This chapter has examined the development of JCE and explored the present acute crisis of the doctrine. Whereas ICL, based on the principle of non-derogability, rejects the context of a crime in order to achieve a collective benefit, criminal law, developed in balance between individual rights and social deviance, necessarily includes context. The problematic development of the ICTY's JCE jurisprudence lays bare this conflict.

PART III

Narrative and Discourse Emerging from International Criminal Justice Mechanisms

Can international institutions work at a socially constitutive level, as effective (read: legitimate) domestic institutions do? The legitimacy and communicative capacity of international institutions, a central assumption permeating the use of international criminal tribunals (ICTs) to effect social reconstruction, is essentially untested.

The national narratives present across Bosnia, Serbia, and Croatia confirm a steady distrust of the International Criminal Tribunal for the former Yugoslavia (ICTY) and its processes. These narratives – concerning the underlying causes for the dissolution of Yugoslavia, the source of the aggression that began the wars in Yugoslavia, or the events that are most representative of the tragedy and criminality of the conduct of the war – are distinct among "ethnic"[1] groups and unified across national lines *by ethnicity*. Thus there are distinct Croat, Serb, and Bosniak narratives that obtain across the nation-state boundaries of Croatia, Serbia, and Bosnia, and are distinct between ethnic groups, even ethnic groups living in the same state. These "imagined communities" (Anderson 2006) do not map onto the nation-states boundaries that exist post Yugoslav dissolution, and represent a site of ongoing, unresolved tension. More significantly, none of these narratives take as their starting place the transitional justice (read: rule-of-law liberal) ideology underlying the ICTY, which is the belief in the power of rule-of-law processes to elucidate facts and foster social reconciliation through the articulation of "what really happened" as produced by an "objective" international body (Akhavan 1998; Forsythe 2006). The three distinct "ethnic" narratives reference ICTY findings only to the extent that such findings confirm "their side"; an ICTY-associated, liberal-humanist mode of assessing history, criminality, or governance has not taken broad narrative root throughout the former Yugoslavia even after more than two decades of practice.

[1] The distinctions between those who identify as Bosniak (Bosnian Muslims and Serb Muslims in the Sandžak region of Serbia) Serb, and Croat, respectively, are religious, cultural, and political; the term "ethnic" is used as an imperfect shorthand.

The following two chapters examine the social impact of the ICTY. The international criminal justice template imagines that ICTs provide an objective, "official" history, rooted in liberal humanism, which has the power to reconfigure and unify once-opposed socio-political actors. In the wake of nationalist responses to the Karadžić and Mladić verdicts, or convicted war criminal Vojislav Šešelj's successful return to elected office in Serbia, it is now passé to decry the absence of Balkan unity or reconciliation. The following two chapters theorize why this is to be expected, and how ICTs might work differently to produce different social outcomes.

5

History, Trials, and Collective Memory

Constructing "Truth"

This chapter considers the varied content of historical and political "truth" regarding the violence in the former Yugoslavia. A central tenet of the Nuremberg legacy is that the International Military Tribunal (IMT) at Nuremberg helped construct the *singular* story that Germans tell regarding the violence of World War II. The legacy of the IMT is that "truth" emerged from trials that individualized guilt. This liberal, individualist-humanist narrative supplanted the collective guilt accompanying the virulent nationalism that fueled Nazi atrocities. This singular story of the violence of World War II (with German causality at its center, and Nazi atrocity as its core) is central to "reconciled" Europe. The International Criminal Tribunal for the former Yugoslavia (ICTY), by objectively determining fact and establishing individual guilt, was imagined to combat collective nationalism in the former Yugoslavia in the same way. To date, this project has been resoundingly unsuccessful.

This chapter compares the expectations of the international criminal justice template, which are that a tribunal will assist in manufacturing a unified and unifying narrative, against contemporary narratives of the wars' causes and impacts across Croatia, Serbia, and Bosnia. The first section describes the work that a tribunal is imagined to be able to do by modeling norms based in liberal humanism, rather than ethno-nationalism. The second section examines the contemporary narratives that obtain across the former Yugoslavia. The chapter shows how the ICTY, rather than setting or changing the narrative across the former Yugoslavia, has been successfully instrumentalized by proponents of ethno-nationalist politics, furthering populist, not liberal, discourse.

I CONSTRUCTING LIBERAL-HUMANIST NARRATIVES

A central prescribed element of the ICTY's value is its role in revealing the complicated, oft-disputed violence of the Balkan wars. Like advocates of the IMT at Nuremberg before it, advocates of the ICTY point to the investigatory, research-oriented, archival aspects of the ICTY's work as central elements of its value. The ICTY is imagined to add value by producing an "official version" of the wars that tore Yugoslavia apart.[1] The strength of the evidence presented, as well as the objectivity and integrity of the institution, should overcome the nationalist narratives still pervasive throughout the former Yugoslavia.

Proponents of international criminal law (ICL) often make the case for international tribunals (ICTs) as "epistemic engines" (Holtermann 2017). In the words of Regina Rauxloh (2010: 744),

> Establishing a historical record through trial does not only help to find out what happened but moreover it provides for a mechanism to validate these findings. The limits of evidential and procedural rules confer legitimacy and credibility to the outcome. An independent court establishes facts through a public trial where each element needs to be proven beyond reasonable doubt. Thus not only will the criminal investigation uncover the truth but the test of that criminal trial will also validate it. The thorough investigation of high profile offenders, the strict rules of evidence and the rule of law that allows both sides to be heard make the international criminal trial a most appropriate forum for building an accurate historical record of the atrocities.

Thus, as a general rule, to find critiques of ICTs as historians, one must read the critical legal theorists: Koskenniemi (2002: 11), for example, rather cynically suggests that perhaps proponents of the ICTY have settled on the value of its history-telling elements because neither its deterrence nor community-building rationales are persuasive.

Koskenniemi (2002) takes these observations even further by asserting that judgments aiming at telling an official history may obstruct rather than enhance that process. He locates this problem in the individual nature of judgment, which risks "exonerating from responsibility those larger (political, economic, even legal) structures within which the conditions for individual criminality have been created – within which the social normality of a criminal society emerges" (Koskenniemi 2002: 15). The problem of situating individual responsibility as a response to collective action and as an antidote to collective guilt is a recurring criticism in considerations of international criminal justice (Fletcher 1977; Allott 1990).

A recent high-profile departure from the ranks of the ICTY-faithful made news in transitional justice circles. Following the Perišić acquittal, Refik Hodžić, a peace activist, former director of the International Center of Transitional Justice in

[1] "What the ICTY does is to produce facts, truth. The ICTY produces facts that are proven. When societies are ready to confront their past, with an open mind, objectively, then those societies, thanks to the ICTY, will have a wealth of material to look at. There are photos, videos, forensic evidence, witness statements. The OTP has something like 4.5 million pages of documents, twelve thousand hours of video and audio, hundreds of maps. However, that said, there are limits to what we, the court, can do to make them, the former Yugoslavia, face the past." ICTY personnel, author interview, The Hague, May 2005.

New York, and former ICTY spokesman, wrote an editorial dismissing the ICTY as "not our Court." Hodžić stated the following:

> This is not an exception but a rule: the Tribunal's judges have been and will always be more interested in what international law journals have to say about their judgments than the people to whose lasting peace they are supposed to be contributing ... We simply aren't, and possibly never have been, [the ICTY's] primary constituents."[2]

What makes Hodžić's change of heart so staggering for proponents of ICL is that unlike most Yugoslav criticism of the ICTY, articulating an ethno-nationalistic vision of sovereign right, Hodžić had been a key local proponent of the rule-of-law secularism that underwrites the international criminal justice template.

A decade earlier, Hodžić codirected the documentary *Blind Justice* (*Slijepa pravda*). The film investigates Bosnian responses to two of the first complete ICTY cases (trials and appeals completed). These cases involved the prison camps in Konjic and Prijedor. The camp in Konjic housed a few hundred Bosnian Serb men and women during its existence in the summer of 1992; in 2001 the ICTY appeals chamber affirmed the convictions of three defendants for killing eight people and raping two women in the camp, and sentenced them to nine, eighteen, and fifteen years, respectively (with a fourth defendant acquitted).[3] The camp in Prijedor, by contrast, imprisoned thousands of Bosnian Muslims, and was the sight of hundreds of deaths. Although sixteen cases would go on to address events related to the camp before the ICTY, the documentary addressed the first finalized case, which ended in 2001. There, three defendants initially charged with crimes against humanity up to and including genocide saw the charges reduced to "persecutions" in exchange for their pleas of guilt, and were sentenced to fifteen, five, and three years, respectively.[4]

In *Blind Justice* the filmmakers interview victims and local civilians in Konjic and Prijedor regarding the crimes committed, what they lived through, and the value of ICTY trials. The filmmakers carefully omit all context that would identify the ethnicity of the victims interviewed, however. This conscious editorial decision was central to the film, where the directors' explicit goal was to create a commonality among victims.

In the summer of 2005, the directors screened their documentary at the 8th International Conference on Democracy, which was held in Konjic, Bosnia, the site of the small prison camp featured in the film. As a "response" to the film, a local amateur filmmaker showed a brief video he had taken in Konjic during the war,

[2] Refik Hodžić, "Accepting a Difficult Truth: ICTY is Not Our Court" *Balkan Insight* March 6, 2013, www.balkaninsight.com/en/article/accepting-a-difficult-truth-icty-is-not-our-court.

[3] *Delalić* Trial Chamber.

[4] *Sikirica* Sentencing Judgment. There have been several cases related to the first Prijedor case before the ICTY: sixteen geographically related, and seven dealing with events in the camp specifically. See Appendix A.

illustrating the destruction wrought by Bosnian Serb attacks. Describing the images, the videographer decried the injustice of the Konjic judgment, saying that the ICTY prosecution "hurts Konjic because they were the first ones shown, they came first before the ICTY, those who did lesser crimes got smaller sentences."[5] Other audience members voiced similar frustrations with *Blind Justice*, pointing to the potential for the film to distort the scale of brutalities committed in the Bosnian war and demanding to know why the directors hadn't taken on Srebrenica as a subject, or if they would consider showing the "Scorpion video" in conjunction with their film in future.[6] In summary, audience response objected to the film as historical narrative; no one contested the accuracy of the events portrayed, but frustration regarding the omission of context characterized the audience response.

The directors, who are themselves a mixed Serb and Bosniak team,[7] were steadfast in their insistence that theirs was the correct approach. As one of the directors argued, they didn't want people to hear the story of a sixty-year-old woman raped three times and say "Oh, she's a Serb, I don't care."[8] More fundamentally, the directors rejected any centrality of context:

> War crimes aren't things you compare. There is no difference between the eighteen in Čelebići [the Konjic camp] and the thousands in Prijedor. It is the suffering of people that matters. In Čelebići, people's legs were burned, lots of bad stuff happened. They used hot tweezers to brand tongues. They must all be punished. Crimes against victims must be seen as such.[9]

In this rendition, war crimes are context free. This is the social and historical companion to ICL's ideology of non-derogation. *Blind Justice*'s construction, built around the universal, individual possession of human rights, mirrors the narrative promulgated by the ICTY. The ICTY's application of universal human rights principles insists that crimes are crimes, and that the appropriate question before the court is the criminality of the case before it.

The *Sikirica* sentencing judgment was one of two judgments considered by the documentary *Blind Justice*. Duško Sikirica, the named defendant and the commander of the camp, who was initially charged with genocide, admitted with his guilty plea to killing one detainee by shooting him in the head, and further admitted that there were murders, beatings, rape, sexual assault, harassment, humiliation and abuse of detainees in the camp. He denied being present during the single most

5 Audience member comment, Democracy Conference, Konjic, Bosnia, July 2005, notes on file with author. See Chapter 3 regarding non-uniformity of ICTY sentencing.

6 The "Scorpion video" shows the execution of five Bosnian men by a Serb paramilitary unit. Provided to the ICTY by Nataša Kandić of Belgrade's Humanitarian Law Center in 2005, the video proved irrefutable evidence of Serb involvement in atrocities that changed the nature of public discourse in Belgrade. Following the release of the film, Serbian leaders sought to contain the indictment by disassociating the paramilitary executioners from regular Serb forces.

7 Aldin Arnautović and Refik Hodžić.

8 Panel presentation, Konjic conference, July 2005, notes on file with author.

9 Oral statement by film director Aldin Arnautović, Konjic, Bosnia July 2005, notes on file with author.

violent incident in the camp, where at least 120 men were murdered during the course of one night: this is known as the "massacre in Room 3."

Sikirica was sentenced to fifteen years and served ten before being released. Damir Došen, a shift leader at the camp, and Dragan Kolundžija, a shift commander, were sentenced to five and three years respectively, and both were released early.[10] As part of their plea agreements, all three defendants addressed the court, offering statements of remorse. The defendants' statements of remorse are remarkable, and may partially explain the relative leniency of their sentences.

As a fact finder, however, there is a significant problem with the *Sikirica* sentencing judgment, and this is in regard to the "massacre in Room 3." Although each of the defendants was at the camp that night, all professed ignorance of the facts surrounding the massacre, and denied participation in it. Plea agreements, which are considered in closer detail in the next chapter, represent a challenging element of ICT practice, as they are not common to civil-law jurisdictions, and are recognized as highly problematic in the US, where the system relies on them to resolve cases. One benefit of plea agreements is their alleged capacity to bring facts to light and offer the resolution of material questions. One such question would concern the "massacre in Room 3"; details regarding responsibility for the incident remained unresolved even after all three defendants cooperated with the ICTY and pleaded guilty. The *Sikirica* sentencing judgment is an example of how procedural mechanisms can fail to achieve their potential, and a reminder of the incomplete history that is part and parcel of juridical determinations.

B Writing Balkan History through ICTY Judgments

Through the introduction of the rule of law in the place of lawlessness, ICTs contain a Weberian promise of order, underwritten by a Kantian argument in the universality of rights. This law-specific, rights-based narrative, centered on the universality of victimhood and the attributability of criminality, forms the centerpiece of the ICTY's narrative for the ex-Yugoslavia. This is the narrative that has failed to take root. Consider Srebrenica, and the competing narratives surrounding it. Or consider the "concentration camps" run by Bosnian Serbs: ICTY judgments have focused on the camps in Prijedor (with sixteen cases touching at least peripherally on the subject, and several focusing on crimes committed at the Keraterm camp) and yet even today "there is still no truthful discourse."[11]

From the very first ICTY cases, historians were brought before the tribunal, and accepted as "expert witnesses" in order to create context, educate the tribunal, and, in the case of genocide charges, to add material to the special intent necessary for

[10] *Sikirica* Sentencing Judgment.

[11] Alma Mašić, Youth Initiative for Human Rights (interview Sarajevo, Bosnia, March 2013, notes on file with author).

a finding of genocide. This practice changed with the Perišić case however, where the trial chamber altered settled court practice and admitted historian testimony only following oral argument and by majority opinion; the presiding judge issued a separate opinion objecting to the "lack of objective and systematic criteria in selecting documents."[12] Wilson (2011: 138) is perhaps unjustly generous when he calls the unsettled nature of the admissibility of historians as expert witnesses seventeen years into tribunal practice "remarkable."

The "template" established by the IMT, the ICTY founding documents, and tribunal representatives all contribute to the assertion that holding trials helps the "truth" of the Balkan wars emerge.[13] Such "truth" should in turn facilitate reconciliation because it is argued that credibly established history has the power to unify through its very singularity (Akhavan 1998). This is the received wisdom of the IMT and postwar Germany. Courts assist in establishing this unified, and thus unifying, narrative through their iteration of an official story based on officially sanctioned proofs.

This perspective is echoed in the foundational debates surrounding the ICTY,[14] and in ICTY judgments.[15] Richard Wilson's excellent book considering the history generated by international criminal tribunals recognizes the structural obstacles impeding legal mechanisms' work as historians (noting, at one point, that "a number of prosecutors and defense lawyers have come to realize [that] the complexity of history in the Balkans ... is such that it can lend itself to virtually any legal argument" [2011: 70]) yet nevertheless defends the historical narratives produced by and in pursuit of ICL judgments.

In its practice, the ICTY has privileged certain aspects of Yugoslavia's brutal conflict for its own consideration. Bosnian Serb-run prison camps (considered below) and the massacre at Srebrenica constitute two main areas of factual focus. Yet it is here that data suggest that the "official version" articulated by the ICTY is failing to take root among a Balkan audience. An October 2011 survey by the Organization for Security and Co-operation in Europe (OSCE) in Serbia reported the following responses to the statement "In Srebrenica, in July 1995, a few thousand Muslims/Bosniaks were executed in a few days": 72 percent of respondents had heard of the event, 40 percent believed it to have happened, and 33 percent believed it to be a war crime.[16] It is instructive to contrast these responses with responses to the

[12] *Prosecutor* v. *Momčilo Perišić*, Case IT-04–81, Decision on Admissibility of Expert Report of Patrick Treanor, Separate Opinion of Judge Moloto, November 27, 2008, para 1.

[13] "Through public proceedings, the truth about the possible commission of war crimes, crimes against humanity and genocide was to be determined, thereby established an accurate, accessible record." *Nikolić* Sentencing Judgment para 60.

[14] "It is only the truth that can cleanse the ethnic and religious hatreds and begin the healing process." Madeleine Albright, May 25, 1993 UN SCORE, 48th Session, 3217th meeting UN Doc. S/PV3217.

[15] *Nikolić* Sentencing Judgment para 60: "such a historical record would prevent a cycle of revenge killings and future acts of aggression."

[16] OSCE 2011 Survey.

question "Were Bosnian Serb women raped at the Čelebići camp in Konjic, Bosnia?" (This is the small camp referenced at the beginning of the chapter where a handful of crimes occurred; it is discussed further below.) Here 56 percent of respondents had heard of the incident, 50 percent believed it to be true, and 48 percent believed it was a war crime.[17]

The ICTY may be making some information available, but its unified, unifying official version of the Yugoslav wars for domestic consumption is not mirrored by the data on the ground. Consider the problem of the ICTY's treatment of the Markale massacre in Sarajevo. The first Markale incident, which occurred on February 5, 1994, was a single explosion in a crowded downtown Sarajevo marketplace that resulted in sixty-eight dead and more than a hundred wounded. While the event is generally attributed to a Bosnian Serb shell, there was speculation that the explosion was instead caused by a bomb planted on the site. Conspiracy theories arose instantly: these theories intimated that Bosnian Muslims were themselves responsible for the explosion because they sought to turn international public opinion against Bosnian Serbs.[18] Such theories were fueled by observations that no characteristic whistle was heard before the explosion,[19] that help arrived on the scene "too quickly," that the bomb crater was not consistent with a shell, and that injuries, which were almost universally below the waistline, were inconsistent with a shell from above.[20]

The ICTY trial of Bosnian Serb Stanislav Galić considered this first Markale explosion, with two judges (the majority) concluding that the attack was caused by a Bosnian Serb shell.[21] A third judge, however, dissented, citing among other evidence a UN official's testimony that the origin of the shell could not be determined. The *Galić* trial chamber sentenced the defendant to twenty years in jail, which was increased to life imprisonment by the appeals chamber.[22] The *Galić* trial chamber's majority decision regarding the source of the deadly shell, however, did not quiet speculation regarding the veracity of the "official version."

17 *Ibid.* One should note that responses among Bosnians to the same query would likely have been very different.

18 These theories were fueled by similar claims regarding the August 1992 "Breadline massacre," in which seventeen people were killed and dozens injured in an explosion: this explosion, also attributed to Bosnian Serbs, was similarly suspected to be the work of Bosnian Muslim forces. Leonard Doyle, "Muslims Slaughter Their Own People" *Independent* August 22, 1992.

19 Attributed to journalist Eve-Anne Prentice.

20 Karadžić addressed the Markale massacre as "staged" in his trial; see transcript from May 11, 2010, where Karadžić sought to enter two videos into evidence, the first showing a "dummy leg" at the scene before the bombing (this video was not accepted) and the second showing David Owen ascribing the Markale massacre to the Bosnian Muslims (this clip was accepted into evidence as exhibit D180).

21 *Prosecutor* v. *Stanislav Galić, Trial Chamber Judgment*, Case No. IT-98–29 (December 2, 2003) (twenty years); *Prosecutor* v. *Stanislav Galić, Appeals Chamber Judgment*, Case No. IT-98–29 (November 30, 2006) (life sentence).

22 Life imprisonment, the most severe sentence available at the ICTY, has been awarded in few cases; see Appendix A.

A second Markale explosion, in August 1995, was at issue in the ICTY case against Bosnian Serb Dragomir Milošević, Galić's chief of staff.[23] Although the Office of the Prosecutor (OTP) had requested transfer of the case against Milošević to local courts, arguing that the *Galić* trial reduced the historical importance of the *Dragomir Milošević* case, the trial chamber rejected this position and tried Milošević in The Hague. During this trial, the question of whether Bosnian Muslims "bombed their own people" again arose,[24] including references to speculation regarding earlier incidents. Dragomir Milošević's case was unanimously decided, but harm to the "official version" remains.

Consider another example: in April 2005, the ICTY expanded the joint criminal enterprise portion of the indictment against three Croatian generals (including Gotovina) to potentially include almost all members of the Croatian national and local governments between 1991 and 1995.[25] Did these statesmen, governing under a leader with clearly articulated ethnic-cleansing goals,[26] participate in a "common plan" with an illegal purpose? If ethnic cleansing was not the purpose of Croatia's "Homeland War," was it a "reasonably foreseeable" outcome?[27] Gotovina's acquittal determined him not legally responsible for the civilian murders committed during Operation Storm and the massive ethnic cleansing that was its result. What can and should such a legal finding mean regarding Gotovina's place in history, given that the ICTY's "official version" has acquitted him (by a 3–2 "victory") of wrongdoing?

Similarly, a wave of judgments in recent years has challenged established narratives of Serbian complicity in Bosnian crimes. In March 2013, General Momčilo Perišić, a Serbian general, was acquitted of charges of command responsibility for atrocities committed in Bosnia, thus delivering a serious blow to an "official version" of the wars in Yugoslavia that would view Bosnian Serb violence as the result of a Serbian "Greater Serbia" master plan. In March 2016, Bosnian Serb ex-president Radovan Karadžić, who implemented ethnic cleansing throughout Bosnia, while convicted of nine counts including genocide at Srebrenica, was acquitted for genocide in Bosnia more generally; the same held true for Ratko Mladić, who oversaw the genocide at Srebrenica. While Mladić was convicted of genocide in relation to Srebrenica in November 2017 and sentenced to life, he was not found guilty of genocide throughout Bosnia. These findings echo those of the International Court of Justice,[28] which did not find Serbia liable for genocide across Bosnia.

[23] *Prosecutor* v. *Dragomir Milošević*, Case No IT-98–29/1, (December 12, 2007), available at www.icty.org.

[24] See Reporting from Radio Netherlands Worldwide, International Justice Tribunal, "ICTY sifts through the Markale massacre," February 7, 2007.

[25] See "Joining of Gotovina Cermak Markac" (IWPR 474); *Globus* 2005.

[26] Tuđman allegedly aimed to bring the ethnic Serb population in Croatia down to 5 percent, from an estimated 12 percent. Tihomir Loza, "Tudjman's Dismal Legacy" *Transitions Online* December 13, 1999, available at www.tol.org/client/article/8203-tudjmans-dismal-legacy.html?print.

[27] This is the standard of the third variant of joint criminal enterprise. See Chapter 4.

[28] *Bosnia and Herzegovina* v. *Serbia and Montenegro* (February 26, 2007).

In March 2016, Serbian paramilitary leader Vojislav Šešelj was acquitted.[29] How should these acquittals be understood in terms of historical narrative?

The question of genocide across Bosnia was the topic of Republika Srpska Prime Minister Dodik's April 2013 testimony in the *Karadžić* case. There, Dodik characterized violence against Muslims in Republika Srpska as based on the activities of local warlords, "who tried to interpret the situation in their way and find their own responses to it."[30]

Dodik's testimony, in which he refused to "refute" his own early testimony in the *Brđanin* case, nonetheless starkly contrasted with his statements to the ICTY and may be read to show the difference a decade can make. In 2003, before the *Brđanin* court,[31] Dodik described a situation of fear and terror perpetuated by the Bosnian Serb war machine with Karadžić at the helm. In his 2013 *Karadžić* testimony, in contrast, Dodik attributed responsibility for crimes to the chaos and terror of war,[32] and used the pulpit of the ICTY to advance nationalist discourse such as the Bosniak "plan" to institute Sharia law,[33] a plan of "perseverance"[34] that is perpetually lying in wait until Bosniaks achieve a majority. In its March 2016 acquittal of Karadžić for genocide in Bosnia, the ICTY trial chamber lends credence to Dodik's submissions.

There are serious challenges facing the ICTY as a historian in terms of its epistemology, its still-developing "base-line" for what constitutes valid evidence, and even valid law. There is one final problem with the ICTY as historian that bears mention, and this is the problem of the availability of its materials. Gathered in the course of prosecutions, many ICTY materials are confidential and unavailable for scrutiny. Even the use of these materials by other courts, such as the transfer of materials from the ICTY to the War Crimes Chamber in Bosnia and other regional courts under the 11*bis* procedure, has been fraught with problems and protest. Materials that are unavailable to other courts, with their (hopefully) clear standards of confidentiality and protection, are unlikely to be available for any form of public scrutiny. Thus the argument that the ICTY will provide a valuable archive is, while

29 See Chapter 4 for a discussion of the appeals judgment's partial reversal.

30 Dodik's explanation in full reads as follows:

> Unfortunately, in Bosnia-Herzegovina, there were many local warlords who tried to interpret the situation in their way and find their own responses to it. And such – it was the same on all sides. As for your question, in my municipality, there has been a small Muslim community, and nobody bothered them. They didn't have any problems, especially not at the beginning of the war. When their crucial problem was the issue of weapons, whether those communities were armed and ready to enter into conflict with the Serbian people [*sic*]. However, that was not the case, the Muslim settlements were not bothered. Karadžić Transcript 4852:11–19 April 10, 2013.

31 *Prosecutor* v. *Radoslav Brđanin*, Case No. IT-99-36 (September 1, 2004) ("*Brđanin* Trial Chamber").

32 *Karadžić* Transcript 4852: 7–10.

33 *Karadžić* Transcript 4834: 23–4835: 2 "Wherever the Muslims established the authorities, they had to organise an Islamic state and that as long as they were a minority, they should stay calm, be integrated in the society, but once they became the majority they should strive towards this goal without any doubt." See also Id. At 4846; 4848–4849.

34 Karadžić Transcript 4848:14.

not baseless, nevertheless seriously challenged by confidentiality issues unlikely to be resolved in the immediate future.

II NON-UNIFIED BALKAN NARRATIVES

What is the accurate story of the destruction of the country called Yugoslavia? Susan Woodward (1995) explains the violence that tore Yugoslavia apart by examining economic pressures exerted by Western countries. Robert Kaplan (1992) finds the reason for the country's demise in "ancient ethnic hatreds," a thesis that while thoroughly debunked by area scholars nonetheless had a devastating impact on mainstream discussion regarding the former Yugoslavia. Robert Hayden (1999) lays the blame on the unworkable 1974 constitution. Sabrina Ramet (2006) suggests that unrepentant Serbian nationalism played a starring role.

Of course, we have no way to test the thesis of whether Yugoslavia's failure as a state was inevitable, or the product of particular circumstance. On the eve of World War II, journalist Rebecca West recorded her travels through the Balkans in her majestic *Black Lamb, Grey Falcon*. West's account is replete with scenes chillingly familiar to any contemporary student of the region: Croatian underdog frustration, Serb delusions of grandeur, and everywhere, whispers of violent nationalist politics. And even though West's travels predated the terrible violence of World War II that fuels contemporary Balkan nationalist discourse – Croatian fascist-run concentration camps, Serb monarchist violence, and communist reprisals – West's account provides what feels like an eerie premonition of future violence because so many of the political constructions feel the same. After reading West's stunning 900-page masterpiece, one might conclude, as historian Andrew Wachtel (1998) did, that Yugoslavia's collapse, while tragic, was inevitable. Such a conclusion is supported by contemporary research on violence in complex systems, which suggests that violence across the former Yugoslavia was predictable based on population structures (Sapolsky 2017).

On the other hand, the most popular politician throughout the former Yugoslavia on the eve of war in 1990 was the communist Ante Markovic (Hayden 1999). He was defeated only by a series of local, not national, elections that brought local nationalists to power, a process wherein the same nationalist politicians who would lead their followers to slaughter cooperated to assume power (Silber & Little 1997). If only elections had been national, not regional, in 1990, one wonders, might the entire war have been avoided? And then there is the contemporary evidence presented by an unlikely source: Eurovision. In this annual song contest, declaredly eternal enemies forget blood enmity to vote for their fellow "Yugoslavs" across ethnic lines (Baker 2015).

War narratives, which differ substantially across the Balkans, each follow a recognizable pattern with identifiable signposts that instantly locate the narrator in a particular "ethnic" position. Croats are defensive regarding their statehood;

their struggle for independence from Yugoslavia is known as "The Homeland War" ("Domovinski rat") and questions regarding the means used to fight that war are often construed as threats to the legitimacy of the war, and thereby the nation itself. Serbs see themselves in terms of a self-sacrificing victimhood, a narrative that begins with the loss of the Serbian kingdom in 1389 to the Ottoman Turks,[35] continues through World War II and includes the dissolution of Yugoslavia in 1991. In this narrative, Serbia is the unrecognized hero, saving European Christianity from Islam (by creating a buffer zone), from Hitler (the morass of war in mountainous Yugoslavia used up Nazi energies and permitted Allied victory), and from destructive elements within Yugoslavia. For Croats, the 1991–1995 wars represent Croatia's "1,000-year yearning for a state." For Serbs, these wars represent a contemporary example of self-sacrifice, in this instance on the altar of Yugoslav unity.[36]

The question of war narrative in Bosnia-Herzegovina is more complex. Structurally divided (after 1995) into two entities, culturally divided between three ethnicities (Croat, Serb, and Muslim/Bosniak) the Bosnian version of the wars varies almost entirely by ethnic group of the teller of the narrative (with some variation according to geography) (Carlson *et al.* 2000). Two things are nevertheless clear. First, there is no unified (and consequently unifying) narrative across Bosnia's three ethnicities, a fact that partly explains the perennial statehood problem in Bosnia, still unresolved more than twenty years after the cessation of hostilities. All three ethnic groups, for example, understood themselves to be fighting a defensive war (Ford 2012: 414). Second, thus far the work of the ICTY has fueled, and not consolidated, the three dominant, ethnically structured narratives present in Bosnia.

By trying and sentencing war criminals, the tribunal asserts that it is contesting "collective guilt," the idea that all people in the Balkans bear the responsibility for the atrocities committed throughout the 1990s, and instead individualizing guilt by locating and punishing the few responsible parties. Yet reactions to the ICTY's judgments among local populations show an increase in collective identity in the reception of both heroes and enemies, and a use of the tribunal to strengthen certain facets of national identity. Popular responses to the ICTY within Croatia, Serbia, and Bosnia demonstrate that these populations correctly understand that it is not only the individual fortunes of those few defendants appearing before the ICTY that are at stake, but also (and more critically) the historical record of the recent Balkan wars and the ethnic groups involved in them, and the narratives that will emerge from the wars.

35 The Serbs view this loss as the trading of their earthly kingdom for a kingdom in heaven.

36 Another way to phrase this distinction is to say that the Croats fought an international war and the Serbs fought an internal struggle. In the *Tadić* case, the first case considered by the tribunal, the ICTY addressed this question and determined that the 1991–1995 wars were international in nature, thus privileging the right of self-determination for the constituent republics of Yugoslavia (*Tadić* Trial Chamber). This question came before the court because the determination is an important element in the application of international law.

The following sections discuss the narratives told in Croatia and Serbia, and present some elements of the multiple narratives in Bosnia. If reconciliation as a function for ICTs consists of achieving a unified and therefore unifying narrative, the ICTY has failed to pronounce or promote such a narrative for the peoples of the former Yugoslavia. In Croatia, Serbia, and within divided Bosnia, narratives diverge sharply from the facts determined, crimes articulated, and responsibility assigned by the ICTY. Narratives show that the story of the causes and impacts of the wars across the former Yugoslavia are neither unified nor following the liberal-humanist model that is the purpose and purported capacity of the ICTY.

Croatia's "Homeland War"

"Croatian nationalism is hating Serbs more than what is normal."[37]

In 1995 Croatia emerged victorious from war. Its territory (the equivalent to its administrative borders within Yugoslavia) intact after four years of partial occupation, its own nation for the second time in history, Croatia looked expectantly towards Europe and a bright future in the first world. In the reshufflings that followed the war, Croatia suffered many disappointments, including the sullying, both domestically and abroad, of the reputation and accomplishments of its founding father, nationalist leader Franjo Tuđman, indictments of Croatian "heroes" by the ICTY, and the repeated delay of EU accession talks.[38]

The Croatian narrative of the war is first and foremost a narrative of statehood. Tuđman's focus on separating Croatia from other former Yugoslav states and shoring up the indisputability of Croatian nationhood set the parameters for the national question in Croatia. Tuđman successfully galvanized Croatian public opinion around an ideal of "European-ness," the idea that (1) Croatia and Croatians belong in Europe (as opposed to the Balkans), (2) experiments with Balkan-ness (such as the twentieth-century Croatian ideological commitment to and political participation in Yugoslavia) were the results of misconceived ideals, and (3) independent Croatia was at last realizing its "1,000-year-old dream" of statehood and entering Europe as a European state. This narrative dates the beginning of Croatia's subjugation to other states and peoples to 1102 and the pact between Croatia and Hungary, a subjugation that continued until 1991, and Croatia's secession (or independence) from Yugoslavia. This history saw only one short break: the years 1941–1945, when the Croatian Ustaša regime, a puppet state of the Nazis, founded the Independent State of Croatia (Nezavisna Država Hrvatska, or NDH). This lamentable period of Croatian history is nonetheless popularly mythologized in contemporary Croatian discourse and politics, where a focus on the legitimacy of Croatian self-determination ignores the rights abuses that characterized the NDH government.

[37] Popular Croatian joke (author interviews Zagreb, Croatia 2004–2005).
[38] Croatia entered the European Union on July 1, 2013.

Symbols associated with the NDH government, such as its flag[39] and currency,[40] were revived in Croatia's 1991 declaration of independence. One by-product of this discourse is the continued presence (and acceptance), even in otherwise mainstream political events and demonstrations, of fascist symbols and paraphernalia.[41]

Tuđman built his narrative on tensions regarding Croatia's statehood and identity that preceded the Yugoslav era and were not assuaged by several decades of participation in the Yugoslav state. Whereas a "Serb nation" has flourished for centuries, with or without a state to call its own, Croatian national identity has been more fluid and fragile, given that both its territorial and linguistic identities are somewhat fluid, with Catholicism as a unifying element. As recently as one hundred years ago, average Croatian peasants, if approached and asked about identity, might have answered "Catholic." In response to the question of what language they spoke, they would have answered "ours."[42] It is only over the course of the twentieth century, through two incarnations of Yugoslavia, that territorial understandings of Croatia have come to underlie the current Croatian state.[43]

Statehood requires the balance of identity against the elimination of threats to the state (Skocpol 1979). Tuđman's nationalist discourse targeted the Serb minority as a threat to Croatian independence, and became a somewhat self-fulfilling prophecy, as Croatian Serbs responded to announced restrictions on their minority rights through the "log revolution," setting up a separate state and carving out nearly one-third of Croatian territory for themselves.

Croatia's "Homeland War" sought to defend the territory allotted to Croatia within the state of Yugoslavia and to expand the state through acquisitions of territory

39 The modern Croatian flag is dominated by a colorful checkerboard at its center, which was also the symbol of the NDH (and was historically a Croatian pattern, seen for example on roof tiles). There is a subtle distinction between the contemporary and the historical symbol: the checkerboard of the NDH began with a white square; modern Croatia's checkerboard begins with a red square.

40 This is the "kuna," which refers to a large rodent, similar to a ferret, indigenous to Croatia. Again, as with the checkerboard, the symbol enjoys a history predating the NDH; in medieval times, taxes to Rome were paid in valuable fur pelts.

41 For example, while doing fieldwork in Croatia in 2005, I attended a parade to commemorate the anniversary of the slaughter of Ustaša forces by Tito's partisans in Bleiberg, Austria. Free buses transported spectators from the main cathedral in Zagreb to the site in Austria. The crowd, which numbered in the thousands, was a mix of ages. The buses were filled mostly with older people, who had come to commemorate the participation of a father, grandfather, or uncle in the battle itself. Groups of young people, teenagers and those in their twenties, were also on site, many of them dressed in mock Ustaša uniforms. More startling, however, was the fact that an Ustaša-dressed brigade headed the formal parade, appearing directly behind the state representative, a higher-up in the ruling party (which, while formally nationalist, is in fact moderate and democratic). I awaited the shocking image of Croatia's second-ranked politician flanked by "Ustaša" to appear in the paper the next day; it did not.

42 The phrase "naš jezik" or simply "naš" ("our language" or "ours") is often used by Bosnian-Croatian-Serbian speakers seeking to avoid "politicizing" the name of the language they are speaking, particularly when in conversation with speakers of other ethnicities.

43 Regarding the development and interchange between linguistic and political identity in the nineteenth and twentieth centuries, see Alexander 2013.

in Bosnia-Herzegovina, whose southwestern portion, "Herzegovina," is predominantly Catholic and in which many people identify as Croats. Dry, craggy, and relatively poor, the region was a feeding ground for the Croatian Ustaša during World War II. Just as Serbia eyed a "Greater Serbia" and included vast portions of Bosnia (in the east and north) in its territorial claim, elements within Croatia spoke of a "Greater Croatia" that would include Herzegovina. Tapes have surfaced of the "secret" meetings between Tuđman and Milošević during the war, where the two discussed how they would "divide Bosnia" between their two states.[44] Croatian soldiers and support helped fuel the vicious battles in Herzegovina, most famously those within the divided city of Mostar. More significantly, Croatian intransigence on the question of "Greater Croatia" proved a massive obstacle to reconstruction efforts in Mostar and throughout Herzegovina following the war.[45]

I ICTY TRIALS AND THE HOMELAND WAR. Tuđman was the first Balkan leader to acknowledge the ICTY, signing a cooperation agreement and agreeing to the aims and work of the tribunal. This early embrace quickly turned to resistance, however, when the tribunal began to investigate crimes committed *by* Croats and not simply against them.

In December 1999, Franjo Tuđman, revered by Croats as the father of the nation, lost his battle with cancer and died.[46] Under Tuđman, Croatia had faced growing international pressure and disapproval. Non-transparent state institutions, discrimination against the decimated remaining Serb minority, and non-cooperation with an increasingly demanding tribunal all brought criticism against the nascent state. At the same time, compared to other former Yugoslav actors (divided Bosnia with its separate institutions and uncooperative populations, and Milošević's Serbia, fresh from invoking the ire of NATO for its actions in Kosovo), Croatia was a stable state with the outlines of democratic institutions and processes. In many cases, these institutions were more democratic in concept than in practice (as was the case with Croatia's troubled courts, particularly the Supreme Court) (Uzelac 1998) and in many cases even only falteringly democratic in concept.

In the elections following Tuđman's death, a liberal coalition was voted into power. Until 1999, there had been very little positional difference between the Croatian Democratic Union (*Hrvatska demokratska zajednica*, HDZ) and opposition parties, particularly as regards resistance to ICTY investigations of Croatian involvement in war crimes and denial of ICTY jurisdiction over the Croatian military initiatives Oluja and Blijesak ("Storm" and "Flash") of August 1995 that

44 The transcript has been reprinted in a two-volume set, *Stijene o podjelene Bosne* (2003).

45 See *Nach Saison* (a film documenting the attempt of a German diplomat who was posted to Mostar in 1994–1996 to reunite the city) (Pepe Danquart, director).

46 Tuđman's role in Croatian politics was a long one: he was associated with the "Croatian spring" movement in the early 1970s, seeking greater independence for the Republic, and briefly jailed. He was also a historian, and his academic writings articulated many of his beliefs regarding the history of the Croatian nation.

retook Croatian territory held by Croatian Serbs. A public opinion poll in 1999, however, listed the government as the source of bad relations with the ICTY, and this appeared to prompt the opposition parties to change their position (Erozdan 2002). In the months following Tuđman's death, the new government concluded a status agreement with the ICTY,[47] extradited an ICTY indictee whom the Tuđman government had argued was too ill to be moved, and finally and most importantly, officially recognized the ICTY's jurisdiction over the Croatian military actions Storm and Flash (Erozdan 2002). This last issue had been a particular sticking point with Tuđman, who refused to concede that war crimes could be committed in actions of national liberation because such campaigns were "police actions" to restore areas under rebel control and thus outside ICTY jurisdiction. While Tuđman categorically refused to admit that any war crime could have been committed by soldiers fighting for the restoration of Croatia's borders, there was also an idea that in the scale of wrongs done to Croatia, any small accompanying wrongs enacted in restorative/reprisal-type actions did not (and could not) matter.

Following Tuđman's death, Stipe Mesić was elected president, and Ivica Račan became the prime minister of a liberal government coalition. A former Communist, Mesić was in fact the last president of Croatia within Yugoslavia, and had been filling the rolling presidency of Yugoslavia when the country disbanded in 1990. When Yugoslav and Montenegrin troops attacked the World Heritage Site city of Dubrovnik in 1991 (a well-covered though relatively bloodless moment of fighting in Yugoslavia, notable mostly for the threat posed to the exquisitely beautiful 700-year-old walled city), Mesić sailed into the harbor with several civilian boats, seeking to stop the attack.

Where Tuđman was an unapologetic firebrand with violently expressed racist opinions on Serbs and Jews, Mesić was a calm, cosmopolitan, eminently fair and reasonable figure beloved among Croats. Where Tuđman urged the celebration of Croatia's fascist government of World War II (more as representative of an independent Croatia than for its fascist character), Mesić treaded more carefully, always condemning fascist actions and beliefs. Mesić is a figure who brought balance to the Croatian political landscape.

Unlike many other Balkan politicians, Mesić was pro-ICTY, even testifying at The Hague several times. This was not without political cost: in 2001 Mesić's confidential testimony was published, most likely by political opponents seeking to capitalize on the ICTY's unpopularity with mainstream Croats.[48] In another example of strong leadership, in September 2000, twelve generals joined the nationalist HDZ party leaders in signing letters saying the government was undermining

[47] This allowed ICTY personnel freedom of movement throughout Croatia, mandated that the government would assist in ICTY investigations, and permitted a permanent ICTY presence in the form of liaison offices in Zagreb.

[48] Copies of this confidential testimony surfaced again in the 2005 presidential election, outside of the opposition party's offices.

the legitimacy of the Homeland War and Mesić retired the seven generals who were still serving. These actions distinguish Mesić from most other leaders in the Balkans, and have helped frame Croatia as cooperative, modern, and cosmopolitan, especially as compared to Serbia and Bosnia.

II TIHOMIR BLAŠKIĆ: IMPLICATING THE CROATIAN STATE IN BOSNIAN VIOLENCE. Very early in its practice, in 1996, the ICTY indicted a Bosnian Croat general, Tihomir Blaškić, for crimes against humanity committed by military and paramilitary groups under his command in the Lašva valley in central Bosnia, specifically in the village of Ahmići.[49] There, British troops discovered the bodies of at least 118 civilians, most of them women, children, and the elderly, some of whom had been burned alive in their houses. They accused the Croatian Defense Council (*Hrvatsko vijeće obrane*, HVO), the Bosnian Croat army, of perpetrating the massacre. Blaškić was the HVO commander; his headquarters were located only four kilometers away from Ahmići.

Although Blaškić initially resisted turning himself over to the ICTY, he eventually surrendered under pressure from his military superiors, and the trial began in 1997. In neighboring Croatia, Franjo Tuđman showed his resistance to Blaškić's indictment by naming him Inspector General of the Croatian Army. Tuđman refused to assist the ICTY, arguing that the information requested constituted Croatian national security secrets, and insisting that the military operations Flash and Storm were "police actions" rather than armed conflict under the ICTY jurisdiction. For his part, Blaškić argued that he had neither ordered the massacre nor been aware of it when it happened. He further argued that his attempts to investigate the massacre had been prevented by those above him in the command hierarchy.

In March 2000 the trial chamber found Blaškić guilty of ordering crimes against humanity and war crimes against Bosnian Muslim civilians (Article 7[1] of the ICTY Statute) as well as of failing, as commander, to prevent the crimes or otherwise punish the perpetrators (Article 7[3]).[50] He was sentenced to forty-five years in prison, the longest sentence the tribunal had awarded at that time. The sentence was particularly contentious as it was significantly longer than the twenty-year maximum prescribed by Yugoslav criminal law.

Upon assuming the presidency in 2001, Stipe Mesić and his office began producing documents related to the Ahmići massacre. Blaškić utilized this material in his appeal, submitting eight thousand new pages of documentation. Blaškić argued that an alternate chain of command via the Croatian state – and not the HVO military, which was the military of the Bosnian Croats – was in command in the Lašva valley, and that he did not have effective control over his troops.[51] In October 2001, a report

49 Blaškić indictment, Case No. IT-95–14, available at www.icty.org.

50 *Prosecutor* v. *Tihomir Blaškić*, Case No. IT-95–14 (March 3, 2000), available at www.icty.org ("*Blaškić* Trial Chamber").

51 *See Blaškić* Appeals Chamber.

on the Ahmići massacre originating in Tuđman's office was leaked to the press. This report, signed by Tuđman, detailed the massacre and named five men responsible for it.[52] Later leaks and documents, as well as a review of the transcripts of Tuđman's recorded meetings, revealed that the Ahmići massacre comprised part of a larger plan of "ethnic engineering" designed to goad Croats in central Bosnia to move to Herzegovina in order to give more weight to the idea of Greater Croatia. The massacre in Ahmići was intended to trigger Muslim retaliation that would encourage a Bosnian Croat exodus.

The appellate chamber ruled in 2004, reversing most of the factual determinations of the trial chamber based on new evidence and new witnesses.[53] The appellate chamber also applied a much narrower reading of the applicable law and statutes, which strengthened Blaškić's appeal.[54] When the appellate chamber pronounced its sentence, it became clear that it was essentially acquitting Blaškić; although the defendant was still found guilty of a few counts against him (ordering crimes in detention facilities, the use of protected persons for the construction of military installations, and the use of detainees as human shields), his forty-five-year sentence was reduced to nine years, of which he had already served eight years and four months. He was released immediately, with the tribunal citing good behavior, poor health, and his young children as contributing factors.

In an article printed in the weekly Croatian news magazine *Globus*, author Brian Gallagher argued that the Blaškić appellate "acquittal" should be read as an invitation for Croatia to press the ICTY to reconsider its position vis à vis Croatia's role in the Croat-Muslim conflict in Bosnia.[55] Instead, however, the Blaškić decision is more striking for what it reveals about Croatian meddling in Bosnia, specifically about the possible role played by the Croatian secret service in obfuscating and withholding war crimes evidence.

52 In addition to revealing the Tuđman administration's awareness of and complicity in the massacre (Tuđman, his son Miroslav, and his defense minister Gojko Šušak were all implicated), the leaked records also served as a warning to the five "guilty" parties named to run; indeed, there is somewhat of a precedent for this in Croatia, where even courts have announced impending indictments for war crimes as a warning to those indicted.

53 *Blaškić* Appeals Chamber.

54 In relation to Article 7(1), the appellate chamber applied a substantial likelihood standard, replacing the negligence standard applied by the trial chamber. The appeals chamber clarified, "the knowledge of any kind of risk [of violations], however low, does not suffice for the imposition of criminal responsibility[.] Under the Trial Chamber's standard, any military commander who issues an order would be criminally responsible, because there is always a possibility that violations could occur" (para 41). In response to Article 7(3), the appeals chamber re-examined command responsibility, setting a standard that "a superior will be criminally responsible through the principles of superior responsibility only if information was available to him which would have put him on notice of offenses committed by subordinates" (para 62). The article states that a superior is not relieved of criminal responsibility if "he knew or had reason to know that the subordinate was about to commit [criminal] acts or had done so" (para 406). By leaning towards a subjective knowledge as a basis for command responsibility for those further down the chain of command, the appellate chamber was criticized as reading Article 7(3) too narrowly (Drumbl 2005).

55 Brian Gallagher, "Blaškićeva presude odbačena je zbog Jordinih grešaka" *Globus* October 15, 2004.

III ANTE GOTOVINA'S REBIRTH AS CROATIAN HERO. Ante Gotovina may represent a case of a war hero *created* by the ICTY. Indicted by the ICTY in July 2001, Ante Gotovina fled, and successfully evaded capture for nearly five years. Gotovina was a mercenary soldier, a former member of the French Foreign Legion, and was allegedly wanted for crimes committed in France in the 1980s. His 2001 indictment triggered a popular uprising against the ICTY and prompted mass protests against the criminalizing of "Croatian Heroes." In the wake of Gotovina's indictment, conservative groups threatened roadblocks, public demonstrations, and general disorder. A popular retired general, Janko Bobetko, demanded new elections. Moves of support included the publication of books, the production of a Gotovina wine, billboards around the country (sporting Gotovina's face and often the caption "today Gotovina, tomorrow YOU") and even an enormous poster, hung from the enclosing wall of the historic town of Zadar, with the caption "Hero, not criminal." In 2002, a petition signed by 555 people, including prominent, mainstream journalists, academics, artists, and sports figures, was delivered to the Račan government and reprinted in several papers; this petition asserted that Gotovina's indictment had no legal foundation and backed the general's freedom.

Gotovina was finally apprehended in the Canary Islands in 2005, an arrest that was likely brought about with the assistance of the Croatian government. In the intervening years, in addition to bringing down a liberal coalition, support for Gotovina cost Croatia dearly in terms of its accession to the EU. It was clearly official Croatian assistance (for instance, Gotovina was carrying a fake, Croatia-issued passport) that helped keep the general hidden so long. Yet for all the intervening uprising, billboards supporting Gotovina, and constant scrutiny in the press, there was very little public outrage over his final deportation to The Hague; the threatened roadblocks and public disorder failed to take place.[56]

During interviews in The Hague in 2005, several ICTY personnel suggested that Gotovina was singled out by the UN in order to "right the balance" in the Balkans, and to make sure that Croatia is "pulling its weight." One interviewee said, "Gotovina is central due to his symbolic value, like Mladić and Karadžić."[57] The interviewee further explained "Croatia has a mixed record on cooperation. Thus Gotovina is about getting them to give up someone who is important to them. The true test of cooperation is giving someone you don't want to."[58] Croatian intransigence over the Gotovina issue, even under the more cooperative governing regimes following Tuđman, eventually became a sticking point in Croatia's EU accession. With his 2013 acquittal, Gotovina represents a resounding blow to the

[56] See Vjeran Pavlaković 2010 (arguing that 2005 and the failed EU accession talks – the failure of which was due to the absence of Gotovina from the ICTY docket – represented the height of public agitation in favor of Gotovina as a symbol of Croatia).

[57] Author interview OTP personnel, The Hague, May 2005.

[58] *Ibid.*

work of the ICTY. His status as Croatian hero is confirmed; ironically, this is a status he would likely never have enjoyed had not he come to the tribunal's attention.

Serbia

"Perišić *is even more of a joke than* Gotovina."[59]

In today's Belgrade, the lively, pedestrian-only area in the heart of the old city buzzes with commerce and street cafés are full. Only a few blocks away, the Ministry of Defense offers a striking anomaly. This deserted building, lawn patchy and overgrown, is rent by a perfectly cylindrical hole driven through the center of it, and stands as a reminder of and consequent monument to the NATO bombings of 1999. A recent visit found none of the hallmarks of early-2000s mainstream culture, no postcards commemorating the NATO bombings in downtown Belgrade (one had featured the US stealth bomber downed by Serbian fire with the caption, "Sorry, we didn't know it was invisible") or celebrations of battered Serbdom, such as a drawing of Asterix cartoon characters superimposed on a map of Europe with a magnified Serbia at its center, with the caption "In a time of empire, one small European nation stands alone."[60] Yet at the same time, the destroyed Ministry of Defense remains untouched. What preserves this ruined building in the middle of a bustling city? Is it politics, finances, symbolism? Or is it something else?

In Serbia, contradictions abound. Corruption is so bedeviling that a special court has been built, using international funds, to combat organized crime. At the same time, progressive Serbian NGOs are so effective that they generate much of the material used by the prosecutor in that court. In 2000, Serbia deposed a despot by tractor;[61] in 2003, a trusted democratic leader was gunned down in the street. After a decade during which fragile, democrat-led coalitions fought internally over where to stand regarding cooperation with the ICTY, recognition of Kosovo, and entry into the European Union, Serbs elected a "recovering nationalist"[62] who wanted to do all three. In April 2013, that nationalist even apologized for Srebrenica. The founding member of and program director at B92 Radio, the "guerilla" voice of the opposition through the 1990s (Collin 2001), admitted, with chagrin, that life under the

59 ICTY representative in Belgrade, reporting observations of Serbian law students to the most recent ICTY judgments (interview notes on file with author, March 2013). The *Perišić* decision is discussed below.

60 Sociologists have studied the particular brand of Serb humor and its application to the 1990s. See, e.g., Greenberg 2010.

61 Slobodan Milošević was ousted from power in October 2000 in a revolution notable, in part, for the use of farm equipment driven from the countryside into central Belgrade.

62 This is Tomislav Nikolić, who was once the deputy of Vojislav Šešelj's Serbian Radical Party. Šešelj is a paramilitary leader and politician currently on trial at the ICTY, representing himself and combatting the tribunal even more effectively than did former president Slobodan Milošević. Nikolić broke with Šešelj a few years ago over the question of Serbia's membership in the EU.

nationalists has in fact been surprisingly better for B92 than life under the democrats for the previous decade.[63]

The Serb narrative of the war, like much else in Serbia, is a study in contradiction. For Serbs, the brutal wars of Yugoslav disintegration – wars that claimed one hundred thousand lives in Croatia and Bosnia – are held at a certain distance. No battles were fought on Serbian soil; the first wartime violence to threaten Serb lives was the NATO bombing campaign over the Kosovo question in 1999.[64] Whatever discourse might once have existed regarding a "Greater Serbia," the arrival of tens of thousands of ethnic Serb peasants from Croatia and Bosnia in the final year of the war has cooled that dream, too; the cosmopolitan Serbs of Belgrade have little desire to share limited resources with these needy "brothers."

One piece of the Serb narrative is a victim story of unrecognized suffering. For instance, Milošević's war in Bosnia resulted in a military draft in Serbia, resisted by evasion and even several uprisings;[65] wartime international sanctions and their economic repercussions resulted in crushing inflation worse than Germany's in the years directly following World War I.[66] Because Bosnian Serb leaders were unreasonable, Western powers decided to negotiate with Milošević to end the war, and this ensured his position in Serbia despite the fact of his clear unpopularity with a large percentage of the Serb population. In the winter of 1996, hundreds of thousands of Serbs demonstrated for months in Belgrade against the Milošević regime, to no avail (and to little international attention). Only after Milošević started a second war, in Kosovo, and fell from international grace, were Serbian protests effective in ousting him. Both the suffering narrated by Serbs, and the fact that it has gone largely unrecognized by outsiders, are accurate: who else discusses the staggering Serbian economy of 1996 and 1997 but the Serbs who lived it, and perhaps a few sympathetic academic voices? At the same time, the potential to exaggerate, or to misappropriate context, is ever pervasive. For example, in the summer of 2004 a theater piece at Belgrade's trendy Amelia 212, titled "War and Memory," superimposed images from the NATO bombing of Belgrade onto pictures of piles of skulls typically associated with the genocidal violence in Rwanda and Cambodia. A deeply resonating self-pity pervades Serbian politics, not only in the conservative, nationalist-party voting Serbian countryside but even in its cosmopolitan capital.

The other piece of the Serbian narrative is ennui. This is communicated in various ways, the most frequent being a grunt, the shrug that says "not my problem," or both, in response to any question concerning Serb responsibility for the brutal

63 Presentation to American University of Paris student group, March 2013, notes on file with author.

64 The accuracy of the NATO arsenal ensured a low civilian casualty rate, and the war's most deadly civilian incident was the air strike of a passenger train as it crossed a targeted bridge.

65 These occurred, for instance, in Valjevo, Kragujevac, and Topola.

66 The hyperinflation of the Weimar government has been called "the most destructive case of inflation in history." NPR, "The Economic Disaster that Germany can't Forget" September 14, 2011, available at www.npr.org/blogs/money/2011/09/14/140419140/the-economic-catastrophe-that-germany-cant-forget.

events in Bosnia and Croatia. Facts related to these events – the participation of paramilitaries trained in Serbia, the use of weapons sent from Serbia, and the issuing of political directives from Serbia – are dismissed as unsubstantiated tales. The general attitude seems to be that since the war was not fought in Serbia, it should be seen as someone else's tragedy. This ennui response accompanies the victim narrative comfortably – since Serbs have already suffered so much, they do not need any more suffering.

It is the second aspect of the Serbian narrative that works in opposition to the ICTY's message. Serbia ultimately cooperated extensively with the ICTY; Serbia delivered its ex-president,[67] several high-ranking generals, and even eventually the long-elusive Karadžić[68] and Mladić, the most-wanted Bosnian Serbs who evaded capture for more than a decade. Yet such cooperation has always been of the "necessary evil" variety and not that of a "true believer" or even "partner in peace." A case in point is that of the four retired Serbian generals wanted for crimes in Kosovo who were handed over to the ICTY, a transfer that occurred in direct response to a threat to hold up a needed International Monetary Fund loan.[69] The guards' send-off was preceded by a parade in honor of the generals, and the defendants were accompanied to The Hague by an official delegation. Even Nikolić's 2013 apology regarding events at Srebrenica falls into the category of "necessary evil." In an unexpected admission, Nikolić, who had evoked ire by denying genocide in Srebrenica upon taking up the presidency in June 2012, said in an interview for Bosnian television in April 2013, "I am on my knees because of that, here I'm on my knees and begging for a pardon for Serbia because of the crime committed in Srebrenica. I apologize for all crimes committed by any individual in the name of our state and our people."[70] He had, however, preceded this statement by saying, "Everything that happened during the 1990s was some form of genocide."[71] In a later interview, he confirmed his unwillingness to classify Srebrenica as "genocide," saying that "genocide must be

67 Opposition leader Zoran Đinđić, Serbian prime minister following Milošević's ouster from 2001 until his assassination in 2003, may have paid for this with his life, since the organized criminals found responsible for his assassination acted in part over the transfer of Slobodan Milošević to the ICTY to stand trial.

68 Concealed in a thick, bushy beard, white-haired, and resembling an Orthodox priest, Karadžić had evidently lived in the capital for several years as a New Age healer under the identity of a man killed in Bosnia. Clearly assisted by state organs, his arrest is credited to the new governing coalition led by Boris Tadić's liberal democrats.

69 Davor Konjikusić, "Lack of Co-operation Has Economic Consequences for Serbia" *Southeastern European Times*, February 21, 2005, available at http://setimes.com/cocoon/setimes/xhtml/en_GB/features/setimes/features/2005/02/21/feature-02.

70 "Analysts say Nikolic's Srebrenica apology is significant," *Southeastern European Times*, April 29, 2013, available at www.setimes.com/cocoon/setimes/xhtml/en_GB/features/setimes/features/2013/04/29/feature-01.

71 "Serbian President Apologises for War Crimes" BIRN April 25, 2013, available at www.balkaninsight.com/en/article/serbia-s-nikolic-apologised-for-srebrenica-war-crime. This echoes Bosnian Serb responses recorded in the 1999 UC Berkeley survey of Bosnian judges and prosecutors: those

proven."[72] Nikolić's statement is of course significant: given his party affiliation and past connection to Šešelj, an unrepentant nationalist, such an admission is unexpected. Yet when seen in context, Nikolić's statement is less a sea-change than a tact-change. One could see it as simply another element in the "victim narrative": since Serbs have been making necessary sacrifices for nearly two decades now, Nikolić's statement could perhaps be read as just one more in the sequence.

The Srebrenica discourse is striking and important because Srebrenica is in some ways the center of the ICTY narrative regarding the dissolution of Yugoslavia. No mainstream narrative discredits the fact that thousands of Bosnian Muslim men and boys were killed in the woods around Srebrenica in July 1995.[73] The divergence in narratives generally concerns the numbers and the nature of the killings, and most particularly the charge of genocide. Early estimates of the numbers killed were widely exaggerated, in both directions, but work by local NGOs and international organizations applying reliable technology, specifically the International Commission for Missing Persons, has helped settle the debate. The official number now accepted is between seven thousand and eight thousand. The charge of "genocide" has proved more problematic. The ICTY has found that genocide occurred at Srebrenica and has so far found several defendants guilty.[74] In 2012 the Bosnian Serb leader Milorad Dodik admitted, for the first time, that the murders at Srebrenica constituted genocide. Boris Tadić, the progressive leader of Serbia for the decade preceding Nikolić, had already made a public apology for the massacre several years ago, but stopped short of calling the massacre "genocide."

While the ICTY is a central news topic in Serbia, the substance of ICTY indictments is not. Prosecution of these war participants is central to Serbian advancement towards economic prosperity and any potential membership in the European Union, and is mostly treated by the media as such.[75] Missing from these domestic conversations is the narrative of the underlying crimes that have made such prosecutions necessary. In the Serbian press, Mladić is often pictured in his wartime fatigues

Bosnian Serb respondents who were willing to answer the question about whether there was genocide in Bosnia responded that there was, but that it was against everyone. See Appendix A to UC Berkeley 1999 study. While Nikolić's surprising admission was widely reported in English-language news outlets, other elements of his interview, including his assertion that there was genocide against Serbs in Kosovo, in Croatia, and in Krajina, as well as his direct criticism of the forms of justice dispensed by the ICTY, were not mentioned. See "Nikolić se izvinio zbog Srebrenice" April 25, 2013, available at www.rts.rs/page/stories/sr/story/9/Politika/1312408/Nikolić+se+izvinio+zbog+Srebrenice.html ("Nikolić je ustvrdio da je i nad Srbima počinjen genocid na Kosovu, odakle su proterani, kao i genocid u Krajini u Hrvatskoj, odakle je, kako je naveo, proterano 300.000 ljudi. Kritikovao je rad Haškog suda, ocenivši da taj sud radi "po svojim pravilima i zakonima").

72 Daria Sito-Sucić, "Serb president seeks pardon 'on my knees' for Srebrenica" April 25, 2013, available at http://uk.reuters.com/article/2013/04/25/uk-serbia-president-srebrenica-idUKBRE93O0SZ20130425 (accessed May 10, 2013).

73 See *ICJ judgment, Bosnia* v. *Serbia* (2007).

74 See Appendix A.

75 Organization for Security and Co-operation in Europe (OSCE) survey 2011.

engaged in directorial activities, talking on the phone or with other generals, and Karadžić is pictured in a suit in governmental chambers.[76] Following Mladić's 2017 conviction for genocide at Srebrenica, images abounded of his visage on soccer jerseys and billboards.[77] The connection between these figures and the war crimes and genocide committed in Bosnia and Croatia is not part of Serbian discussions of postwar reality. Indictments of generals who were active in Kosovo preceding and following the NATO bombardment of Serbia are presented in the press as indictments for participating in Milošević's unjust regime, and not for particular actions committed in Kosovo.

In March 2013 the ICTY appellate chamber reversed the trial chamber and acquitted Serbian general Momčilo Perišić of aiding and abetting the Bosnian Serb military campaign in Bosnia and Croatia. Perišić, an officer in the (former) Yugoslav National Army (JNA), who had been charged with providing weapons to the Bosnian Serb and Croatian Serb military forces, had been found guilty of crimes against humanity and war crimes by the trial chamber, and sentenced to twenty-seven years' imprisonment.[78] The acquittal was a blow to the ICTY's construction of Serbian responsibility for arming Bosnian and Croatian Serbs during the war,[79] and might have been seen as a victory for the Serb narrative holding that the wars in Bosnia and Croatia were the tragedies of other peoples, and not of the Serbs. According to researchers at Belgrade's Humanitarian Law Center, however, the *Perišić* case has not generated this response in Serbia.[80] Perišić is seen as "an American guy"[81] whose release was due to the maneuvering of Theodor Meron, the US-appointed judge at the ICTY and long-time president of the tribunal. Serbian public opinion has been following the *Karadžić* and *Mladić* cases, two of the last cases the tribunal will hear as it moves towards shutting down (completing the cases under the Residual Mechanism) and both Karadžić and Mladić are popular figures in contemporary Serbia.[82]

76 The Humanitarian Law Center, a prominent human rights NGO led by Serbia's most recognized progressive intellectuals, noted that Karadžić and Mladić were the center of Serbian popular attention as their cases moved forward at the ICTY (author interview, March 2013). This focus on Bosnian actors belies the prevalent attitude of "not my country, not my problem" that has been frequently observed regarding questions of Serb responsibility for crimes inflicted upon Bosnians.

77 See, for example, http://balkanspost.com/article/393/celebrating-mass-murder-outrageous-reactions-icty-verdict-mladic-serbia.

78 *Perišić* Trial Chamber.

79 This is historical fact: there is no doubt that the JNA did in fact arm Bosnian Serb and Croatian Serb military forces (Silber & Little 1997).

80 In the October 2011 OSCE survey regarding attitudes towards the ICTY in Serbia, 72 percent of respondents did not know what Perišić was on trial for. OSCE survey 2011 p. 42. Regardless, 42 percent stated that they did not believe he was guilty of what he was charged with, and 49 percent did not agree with his sentence. OSCE survey 2011 pp. 43, 44.

81 In other words, Perišić is perceived as a US agent. Author interview ICTY Outreach Office, Belgrade, Serbia, March 2013.

82 See OSCE survey 2011.

Unlike within Croatia, there is evidence to suggest that Serbian political opposition to Western-oriented parties is more deeply rooted, and less transient or easily reoriented, than Croatian opposition to the same. Whereas in Croatia popular, pro-Western voices, such as that of Stipe Mesić, create a tie between Croatia's communist past and the integrated, EU member-state future, no such unifying figure exists in Serbia. Zoran Đinđić, who came the closest to such a stance, was assassinated in 2003, just as Serbia was moving out of the grip of Milošević's legacy (and the destructive Western sanctions that accompanied it). Under Boris Tadić, the pro-Western, pro-ICTY president who led several fragile coalitions in the past decade before losing to Tomislav Nikolić in 2012, other democratically oriented parties (such as that of Vojislav Koštunica) have been more skeptical of full cooperation with the West. Moreover, Tadić's and Koštunica's parties were always in near dead-heats with a conservative (nationalist) movement that continues to be strong and significant, even while the leader of one popular nationalist party, Vojislav Šešelj, was on trial in The Hague. Šešelj's criminal status and physical distance did little to decrease his popularity,[83] and his defiance of the ICTY, together with his eventual acquittal in 2016 after more than a decade of prosecution, served to turn the tribunal into a stage and megaphone for Šešelj's politics and persona. Thus while in Croatia the shadow of Tuđman has generally waned and with it, serious, rooted, politically measurable opposition to the ICTY, the same cannot be said for Serbia. Whether this is based in a strong nationalist sentiment that is more deeply rooted and less opportunistic and malleable than Croatia's, or whether nationalist parties offer something in addition to the nationalist rhetoric that echoes most strongly in their statements to external audiences, is a point disputed by Balkan scholars (Ramet 2006; Caspersen 2010). Perhaps the resiliency of nationalism owes something to that famous bad Serbian luck: at exactly the moment when the country was challenged to adapt liberal democracy in order to move "west," the question of Kosovo, the demographically impossible and emotionally charged Serb "heartland,"[84] came to a head. Whatever the reason, in the years since the war, the tool of nationalism, tamed and domesticated for easier international consumption within the Croatian

83 Šešelj's numbers were hurt, however, by his party's splintering into two. Tomislav Nikolić broke with Šešelj in 2008 over the question of Serbian accession to the EU: Nikolić is pro-EU while Šešelj is not. As noted in Chapter 4, Šešelj has returned to politics after twelve years in detention and on trial in The Hague. His 2018 sentence to ten years' prison from the ICTY appeals chamber, which will not be enforced against him due to the time he spent in detention, should disqualify him from serving in the Serbian parliament. As of this writing, Šešelj still holds elected office.

84 Kosovo is traditionally understood as the "birthplace" of the Serbian nation, the site of some of the oldest Serbian churches, and the locus of the famous 1389 battle against the Turks that resulted in five hundred years of Ottoman occupation. For the past century, however, demographics have been working against the Serbs in Kosovo. In Yugoslavia, Kosovo was the poorest region, and the second half of the twentieth century saw a significant Serbian "brain drain." Additionally, Serbian birth rates are lower than those of Kosovar Albanians. According to the last census before the 1999 conflict, Kosovo was 90 percent Kosovar Albanian; following the mass exodus of Serbs after the war, that ratio will now be even more weighted in the Albanians' favor.

context, has not seen the same transformation in Serbia. This is in spite of the fact that Serbian opposition parties and organizations are strong, deeply rooted, and very active (which must also be seen in contrast to Croatia, where opposition is smaller and more often externally based, with a few notable examples).

Bosnia

I would say this of conflict [in Syria]: I hope there are clear winners and losers. That is what is important for reconciliation. Look at the Balkans. Croatia won, and it's fine. Serbia lost – really lost, even lost Kosovo – and it's fine, too. But Bosnia, where everyone avoided having a conversation of who won and who lost? Bosnia is really not OK.[85]

The signature of the Dayton Accords in December 1995 marked the end of nearly four years of war in Bosnia and heralded the beginning of international efforts to assist in reconstructing the country. The four-year war devastated Bosnia, leaving nearly one hundred thousand dead and estimates of up to 2.5 million displaced.

Dayton's compromise divided Bosnia-Herzegovina, the most ethnically diverse of the six constituent republics of the former Yugoslavia,[86] into two entities: Republika Srpska (RS), comprising 49 percent of the territory of Bosnia and rendered fairly homogenous (Bosnian Serbs) after the successful ethnic cleansing campaigns of the war, and the Federation (Federacija), comprising 51 percent of Bosnia. The Federation, comprised largely of Muslim (Bosniak) and Bosnian Croat citizens, was in turn divided into twelve cantons.[87] While the Federation was the home of Bosniaks and Bosnian Croats, this mixture tended to be village by village, ghettoized villages side by side to form interspersed regions. Mostar, a divided Croat/Muslim city, was the most notorious example of this division: currently the city has alternate government structures, including transportation, education, and police, on either side of the river that divides the town, the Neretva.[88]

85 Dennis Gratz, President of "Naša Stranka," presentation at the American University of Paris, April 27, 2013, notes on file with author.

86 Bosnia is made up of a mixture of Bosniaks (the current term for Muslims in Bosnia and adjacent regions of Serbia) and Christians (Bosnian Serbs, Orthodox, and Bosnian Croats, Catholic). While Bosniaks constitute a plurality, no group has traditionally enjoyed an absolute majority. Bosnia held its first census since 1991 in the fall of 2013. Because Bosnia's governance structure is based on quotas derived from pre-war statistics, the census had the possibility of impacting every center of power, and was highly contentious. See Amy Dean's presentation at the American University of Paris April 27, 2013, paper on file with author. In 2016, three years after the census, the results were finally released: they show that Bosnian Muslims now hold a slim (50.11 percent) absolute majority. Bosnian Serb leaders dispute these figures. *Balkan Insight* June 30, 2016, "Census Reveals Bosnia's Changed Demography," available at www.balkaninsight.com/en/article/new-demographic-picture-of-bosnia-finally-revealed-06-30-2016

87 The RS does not share the Federation's cantonal structure, only one of several asymmetric aspects across Bosnia's two entities.

88 The destruction of Mostar's 600-year-old bridge "Stari Most" in 1993 by Bosnian Croat mortar fire symbolized for many the tragedy of Bosnia's destruction; in the wake of the war, temporary walking bridges set up between the Croat and Muslim halves of Mostar were themselves the target of vandals

In the mixed Bosniak/Croat Federation, programs like the OSCE-backed "Two Schools, One Roof" have made it possible for entirely different education systems – curricula, teachers, administrators – to operate in the same building, thus reifying the divide between Bosniak and Croat students. In some cases, Bosniaks attend in the morning and Croats in the afternoon; in other cases, the buildings themselves are divided, with different entrances for the different nationalities.[89]

The RS, meanwhile, has continued to support a policy of succession. In the immediate aftermath of the war, with nationalists still in power, the succession position meant that the RS did not fly the Bosnian flag.[90] Writing for the Bosnia Report, Refik Hodžić discussed responses to the *Karadžić* ruling as demonstrating "the stark limitations of international courts to act as catalysts for genuine social change in societies ravaged by ethnic violence."[91]

Dayton has been called a successful compromise because it pleased no one. Indeed, the structures of the Dayton Accords are often precisely those that need to be overcome in order to effectively accomplish the nation-building that is the international community's objective in Bosnia.[92] Formally separated from the rest of Bosnia under Dayton, the RS developed its own structures outside of cooperation with the Federation. Since the achievement of a Serb state was one of the goals propounded by Bosnian Serb nationalists, the RS government resisted (and continues to resist) efforts to encourage cooperation with its co-nationals in the Federation. For this reason, critics of Dayton have argued that the Accords legitimized, sanctioned and ultimately officiated the terrible ethnic cleansing that caused the majority of the non-Serb population to flee the RS during the war.

and destruction, as certain members of the separated populations worked to keep the separation permanent.

89 "Students share the bell," one frustrated NGO leader who works with youth told me. Author interview Sarajevo, Bosnia, March 2013.

90 "Flag politics" constitute an everyday reality throughout the Balkans, where pockets of territory show their resistance to the dominant state, and the colors of their ethnic make-up, by flying the flag of the state where their ethnicity is a majority. Thus in the Herzegovina region in Croatia, Croatian flags fly all over, including over state buildings; the most southernly town in Montenegro sports the Albanian flag (favored by proponents of Kosovo), etc.

91 *The International Center for Transitional Justice*, 8 October 2014, www.ictj.org/news/karadzic%E2%80%99s-trial-ends-his-legacy-lives

92 As Dennis Gratz, president of the progressive, multi-ethnic party "Naša Stranka" notes, there are 180 ministries in Bosnia: simply providing cars and staff for these ministries "blows up" the Bosnian budget. (Presentation at The American University of Paris, April 26, 2013, notes on file with author.) The Dayton Accords effectively make Bosnia ungovernable. An additional problem has arisen for the Dayton Accords in the form of a successful lawsuit by Bosnian citizens including the named plaintiff, Jakob Finci, against Bosnia-Herzegovina before the European Court of Human Rights. The Dayton Accords distribute power based on membership of ethnic groups, but only recognize the three dominant groups. Finci, a member of the Bosnian Jewish community, is excluded from holding office under Dayton. The court held that this is a violation of Article 14 of the European Convention of Human Rights. *Case of Sejdić and Finci* v. *Bosnia and Herzegovina* (Applications nos. 27996/06 and 34836/06) December 22, 2009.

While day-to-day life in Bosnia is peaceful, the divisions introduced by Dayton have created a two-state structure internally with few overlaps or little agreement, where even basic communication between the two entities is hard-won. For some, future violence seems probable.[93] Kosovo's successful bid for independence, for example, has proved a useful precedent for leaders in RS, who echo the language of self-determination in pushing the argument that the RS should leave Bosnia. The question of the RS's place in Bosnia remains contested and uncertain. Milorad Dodik, president of the RS, testified in April 2013 before the ICTY *on behalf of* Radovan Karadžić. In his testimony Dodik maintained that there was no plan to create a Greater Serbia, that Karadžić never ordered any crimes, that Bosnian Muslims were responsible for the dissolution of Yugoslavia by organizing Bosnia's secession in 1992, and that "where they were not armed, where they did not support military activities of the Muslims, Muslims were not touched, and there were no elements of conflict or crimes against them."[94] Reminded by the prosecutor of previous statements he had made before the RS parliament, such as his claim that "it should be openly said that the crimes were orchestrated under the leadership of the Serbian Democratic Party" (Karadžić's party) and that the perpetrators "must answer for them before The Hague Tribunal," Dodik replied that he made these statements for political reasons and they were not true.[95] It bears recollection that Milorad Dodik was the "progressive" politician called to speak on behalf of Biljana Plavšić's "remorse" at her sentencing hearing in 2003, a case further discussed in the next chapter.

CONCLUSION

This chapter has considered the problem of the use of ICTs to produce narratives or serve as historians. While history and law share a commitment to facts (and each has developed scientific procedures to produce and verify facts), law's "interested" relationship to facts, particularly at common law, shapes the way each fact is expressed before a court. Facts alone, of course, do only one part of the work in establishing collective memory. As Tuomas Forsberg (2003: 73) notes,

> Even if factual truth is established, facts do not speak for themselves. In political life, it is the interpretation that the facts are given that is most important; and if the different interpretative frameworks do not converge, facts alone will not help to form a shared past.

93 Goran Šimić, professor and BiH government consultant on transitional justice, predicts a return to violence. Lecture at American University BiH March 10, 2013 (notes on file with author).

94 Karadžić Transcript 4864: 19–21 (April 10, 2013). See also "Karadžić Was Innocent, Dodik Tells Hague Tribunal" BIRN April 10, 2013, www.balkaninsight.com/en/article/accusations-of-crimes-political-speech-claims-dodik.

95 Dodik stated, "You can consider this as political discourse which need not necessarily be based on facts." Karadžić Transcript 4904: 3–4 (April 10, 2013).

Yet as this chapter has shown, the ICTY suffers from more than a lacking reception of the facts it establishes: there are problems with the facts themselves.

This chapter has challenged the international criminal justice template's prediction regarding the power of a tribunal to apolitically produce a singular historical narrative. While the chapter has discussed examples from the ICTY that demonstrate these difficulties, the wider argument is that all tribunals would face similar difficulties. *Model(ing) Justice* does not contend that the ICTY *could have been* a better historian. Rather, the chapter showcases the particular social and political elements that challenge the ICTY's capacity to produce a unifying narrative of the causes and impact of the wars across the former Yugoslavia.

6

Failures in Reconciliation

The Lost Opportunity of Milan Babić, "Reformed Nationalist"

In 2002, Biljana Plavšić, former Bosnian Serb president, held her nose and pleaded guilty to "persecutions" of tens of thousands of Bosnian Muslims before the International Criminal Tribunal for the former Yugoslavia (ICTY).[1] International luminaries including Madeleine Albright and Elie Wiesel testified at her sentencing hearing on the importance of her gesture for "the victims" and "for humanity"[2] as well as its significance for reconciliation and peace.[3] The *Plavšić* indictment described more than one hundred criminal incidents, which claimed more than fifty thousand lives and destroyed at least 830 villages;[4] Plavšić's address to the tribunal, however, contained no specific acknowledgment of the scale of this suffering or her role in perpetrating it, and instead reiterated the sorts of nationalist arguments that underwrote the violence her plea acknowledged.[5] Regardless, the tribunal noted the "courage" that Plavšić's acknowledgment of violence represented,[6] accepted her statement as "an expression of remorse"[7] with the possibility to "promote reconciliation in Bosnia and Herzegovina and the region as a whole"[8] and sentenced her to eleven years' imprisonment.[9]

One year later, Milan Babić, former president of the Serb "break-away" republic that controlled vast tracts of Croatian territory between 1991 and 1995, pleaded guilty

1 *Prosecutor* v. *Plavšić*, Case No. IT-00–39&40/1-S, Amended and Consolidated Indictment (Int'l Crim. Trib. for the former Yugoslavia March 7, 2002) [hereinafter Plavšić Indictment]; see also *Prosecutor* v. *Plavšić*, Case No. IT-00–39&40/1-S Sentencing Judgment (Int'l Crim. Trib. for the former Yugoslavia February 27, 2003) [hereinafter Plavšić Judgment].

2 Plavšić December 17 Hearing Transcript 458–461.

3 *Ibid.*

4 Plavšić Indictment.

5 Plavšić December 17 Hearing Transcript 609:4–612:21. Notwithstanding its content, her intervention and plea of guilty was globally received as a sincere expression of remorse.

6 Plavšić Judgment para 73.

7 *Ibid.* para 78, quoting the language of prosecution witness Mirsad Tokača.

8 *Ibid.* para 80.

9 This sentence is significantly lower than the 15–25 years recommended by the OTP, especially when considered in light of how long she actually served (six years, because convicted defendants come up for early release after serving two-thirds of their sentences in European jails).

to persecutions that claimed the lives of 230 people.[10] Although not under investigation by the ICTY, Babić surrendered himself to the tribunal when he learned his name had been mentioned within the Milošević indictment.[11] Securing no immunity,[12] Babić cooperated "extensively" with the Office of the Prosecutor (OTP)[13] "at great danger to his family and his own personal safety";[14] the material he provided would later form the basis of his own indictment and conviction. Yet the *Babić* sentencing chamber, unique among all plea bargain cases, issued a sentence *in excess* of that requested by the OTP (in Babić's case, thirteen years instead of the less than eleven recommended by the OTP); in its judgment, the tribunal chastised Babić for "his lack of moral strength [which] prevented him from standing against injustice" and for insufficiently acknowledging "the full significance of the role he played in Croatia in that period."[15]

How to reconcile these two judgments? At one level, they are perhaps relatively congruent, as they concern two senior (although politically marginalized[16]) ethnic Serb leaders, both pleading guilty, both receiving similar sentences. The facts of the cases, the profiles of the two defendants, and the tribunal's construction of these

10 *Prosecutor* v. *Babić*, Case No. IT-03–72, Joint Motion for Consideration of a Plea Agreement between Milan Babić and the Office of the Prosecutor (Int'l Crim. Trib. for the former Yugoslavia January 22, 2004); Babić January 27 Plea Hearing Transcript at 54–55; *Prosecutor* v. *Babić*, Case No. IT-03–72, Sentencing Judgment (Int'l Crim. Trib. for the former Yugoslavia June 29, 2004) [hereinafter Babić Sentencing Judgment].

11 Babić Sentencing Judgment para 2.

12 Other defendants have secured significant immunity at the tribunal. For example, Miroslav Deronjić worked extensively with the OTP in exchange for a limited indictment that only referenced his participation in the destruction of one village in eastern Bosnia, and omitted other instances of participation, including in the planning and perpetration of the massacre at Srebrenica. Judge Schomburg wrote a blistering dissent vigorously protesting against promises in this regard made by the prosecutor. *Prosecutor* v. *Deronjić*, Case No. IT-02–61, Dissenting Opinion of Judge Wolfgang Schomburg (Int'l Crim. Trib. for the former Yugoslavia March 30, 2004) paras 6–16.

13 Babić Sentencing Judgment para 74.

14 *Ibid.* (quoting the Prosecution Sentencing Brief).

15 *Ibid.* para 98.

16 Although both Plavšić and Babić were public figures occupying leadership positions, both of them were largely figureheads. Plavšić endorsed and encouraged the brutal nationalist measures of her government, but the actual planning and architecture of Bosnian violence were carried out by other leaders, centrally Plavšić's co-president Radovan Karadzić, implementing policies generated by a circle of leaders in Belgrade. See Marko Attila Hoare "Vindication or Travesty? Operation Storm's Ante Gotovina and Mladen Markac Acquitted" November 19, 2012, https://greatersurbiton.wordpress.com/2012/11/19/vindication-or-travesty-operation-storms-ante-gotovina-and-mladen-markac-acquitted/ (arguing that there is a flawed construction of responsibility by ICTY prosecutions, which insufficiently addressed how Bosnian violence was a Serbian brainchild). Babić was *de jure* commander of Krajina's armed forces, but it is undisputed that actual control of armed forces (some of whom went on to commit serious crimes against civilian populations) remained throughout this time with Milan Martić and others. Martić was convicted of war crimes in connection with the shelling of Zagreb and events in Krajina and sentenced to thirty-five years in prison, which was upheld on appeal. *Prosecutor* v. *Martić*, Case No. IT-95–11, Judgment (Int'l Crim. Trib. for the former Yugoslavia, June 12, 2007); *Prosecutor* v. *Martić*, Case No. IT-95–11 Appeals Chamber Judgment (Int'l Crim. Trib. for the former Yugoslavia October 8, 2008).

profiles in juridical terms, however, reveal deep inconsistencies between the two cases. Biljana Plavšić, ardent and unrepentant nationalist, pleaded guilty to the destruction wrought by the politics she advocated while vigorously reasserting nationalist rationales for such policies. Unsurprisingly, she did not cooperate in any way with the OTP following her sentencing, and she eventually recanted her admissions.[17] Milan Babić, on the other hand, broke with Milošević early in the war *because of* the latter's use of violence. While war still raged he attempted, albeit unsuccessfully, to work towards a political solution for Serbs in Croatia. Following the war, he refused requests from nationalists to speak about his experiences (which would have contributed to and supported nationalist discourse).[18] In public testimony and unreservedly before the ICTY prosecutor, Babić repented his support for the politics of nationalism which so disastrously impacted his country. He cooperated extensively in five other cases before the ICTY before committing suicide in his cell in 2005, the image of a man consumed by guilt.

These individual distinctions might be little more than colorful personal histories but for the tribunal's divergent treatment of the cases *precisely as regards their potential as reconciliatory instruments*. In the tribunal's treatment, Plavšić's case epitomizes "the most important sentencing hearing that is likely to be conducted or has ever been conducted"[19] because of the significance of her admission in terms of "peace" and "reconciliation" in the former Yugoslavia.[20] For the *Plavšić* chamber, no recitation of fact proved capable of refuting the narrative of Plavšić as an exemplary convert to liberalism, and the ICTY continued to treat Plavšić as if she were performing this role even after she very publicly stopped.[21] Babić's actual transformation from nationalist to committed liberal, meanwhile, is discounted by a chamber focused on his personal flaws (specifically, the "ethno-nationalism" and "vanity" which Babić explained kept him in office even after he realized that the politics of nationalism would harm

[17] Biljana Plavšić, *Svedočim [I Testify]*, 2005 (Plavšić's memoirs); Margaretha Nordgren, *Meeting with Biljana Plavsic*, VI January 9, 2009 (Swedish newspaper), http://vitidningen.episerverhotell.net/templates/PrintPage.aspx?id=10784 (accessed September 1, 2015): "Jag offrade mig själv. Jag har inte gjort något fel, men min advokat rådde mig att erkänna punkten brott mot mänskligheten för att kunna kohandla om de andra åtalspunkterna. Annars hade rättegången pågått i tre, tre och ett halvt år. Det var för lång tid med tanke på hur gammal jag är!" ("I sacrificed myself. I did nothing wrong, but my attorney advised me to recognize a crime against humanity to avoid the other charges. Otherwise the trial might have taken three, three and a half years. That was too long, given how old I am").

[18] Transcript at 188, *Prosecutor* v. *Babić*, Case No. IT-03–72 (Int'l Crim. Trib. for the former Yugoslavia April 2, 2004) [hereafter Babić April 2 Hearing Transcript] (answering Judge Orie's question regarding why he waited until 2001 to come forward, and not directly following the war, Babić explained that he had been in too tenuous a situation as a refugee in Serbia to make public statements, citing an example of declining to speak publicly in favor of a Serbian nationalist cause).

[19] Plavšić December 18 Hearing Transcript 639:23–24 (Mr. Pavich, counsel for the defense).

[20] *Ibid.* at 369–378 (Mrs. Del Ponte, Office of the Prosecutor).

[21] Decision of the President on the Application for Pardon or Commutation of Sentence of Mrs. Biljana Plavšić, Case No. IT-OO-39 & 40/l-ES (September 14, 2009) [hereafter Plavšić Early Release Decision] (describing Plavšić's rehabilitation).

civilians).[22] For the *Babić* chamber, no contextual explanation or action taken on Babić's part can inhibit the tribunal from punishing him. In other words, Plavšić's case is construed as *political* by the tribunal, whereas Babić's case remains personal. Yet the content of Plavšić and Babić's two statements, as well as their interactions with the tribunal, suggest precisely the opposite: Plavšić's remorse is always, obviously, only personally motivated, whereas Babić actively seeks a larger, politically meaningful role for his interventions.

In the following sections, the chapter argues that the *Plavšić* and *Babić* judgments represent conflicting, and unresolved, sources of legitimation for international criminal law (ICL). In *Plavšić*, an international community eager to assert its own singular rule-making capacity used the willingness of one (albeit non-ideal) defendant to shore up the entire ICL process as a means of communicating "liberal" values. Thus the *Plavšić* case follows Shklar's calculus regarding the value of political trials as didactic actors. This didactic capacity is evidenced in the transitional justice-based insistence on the value of Plavšić's plea "for reconciliation" in the former Yugoslavia. Although Plavšić never abandons her nationalist beliefs, she does abandon nationalist politics in favor of solutions championed by Western powers; this "path," which is synonymous with moral rectitude and reminiscent of the self-congratulatory rhetoric associated with the foundation of the International Military Tribunal discussed earlier, is thus presented as the reconciliatory path she must model for her countrymen.

In contrast, while Milan Babić actually makes a personal journey from nationalist to liberal beliefs, this journey is undertaken outside the confines of Western institutions or policymakers and therefore is without the capacity to demonstrate the morality of Western paradigms and practices. Thus it is not received or recognized by the tribunal, which instead assesses Babić's criminal liability through a criminal justice calculus. Under a criminal justice rubric, neither the content of the crimes before the tribunal nor the legitimacy of the tribunal itself is in question or at stake. Discounted as a didactic example, the only service Babić can render the tribunal is as an object of punishment.[23] Taken together, this incongruent jurisprudence reveals the unresolved legitimation crisis at the heart of ICL.

I PLEADING GUILTY TO ATROCITY: CONTRASTING THE *PLAVŠIĆ* AND *BABIĆ* PROCESSES

As discussed in Chapter 3, when the Rules of Procedure of the ICTY[24] were drafted in 1994 by the first ICTY judges, the particular make-up of the court staff, as well as

[22] Babić Judgment.

[23] Punishment under a criminal justice rubric can be said to serve a "didactic" purpose only to the extent it teaches its objects to recognize the power of the state over their bodies and minds (Foucault 1995; Garland 1993). This is distinct from the didacticism imagined by advocates of transitional justice, who imagine that institutions can model behavior. This is a dichotomy between preach (convince) versus punish (subjugate).

[24] The rules have now been revised forty-nine times; the latest revision dates from May 2013. See www.icty.org/sid/136.

the influence over the tribunal exerted behind the scenes by the United States, dictated that the "hybrid" procedure of the tribunal, which had been intended to represent a mixture of the dominant global legal systems of common and civil law, leaned decidedly towards an adversarial (common law) procedure. The adversarial legal tradition practiced in the United States imagines that court judgments are spaces of debate (Kagan 2009). This marketplace-of-ideas model explains not only the use of adversarial processes to advance legal argumentation, but also the form that judgments take, where decisions include both the reasoned opinion in favor of the judicial determination and, where relevant, dissenting opinions.

Regardless of the strong US influence, plea bargaining, a central element of US criminal-law practice, was not initially permitted by the ICTY rules. The self-interested barter at the center of plea bargaining is in many ways an affront to jurists trained in a civil-law tradition, and was further considered possibly inappropriate given the gravity of crimes the ICTY was construed to try. It was only after Dražen Erdemović[25] came forward to admit responsibility for dozens of murders in conjunction with the Srebrenica massacre of July 1995 that the ICTY initiated plea bargains.

A *Introducing Plea Bargaining to International Criminal Law*

As practiced at US law, plea bargaining can consist of "charge bargaining" and/or "sentence bargaining," wherein a mitigation of charges and/or sentence length is traded with the defendant in exchange for their admission of guilt. Following the *Erdemović* case, the ICTY has engaged in variations of both forms. Under a charge-bargaining rubric, the OTP revises the indictment against the accused, dropping certain charges in exchange for the accused's plea of guilt.[26] Sentence bargaining, on the other hand, is more complex and much less assured. In exchange for a plea of guilty, the OTP will recommend a shortened sentence for the accused, sometimes joining with defendant's counsel to agree on a proposed sentence length. International Criminal Tribunal for the former Yugoslavia chambers are not bound by this suggestion (Combs 2006). International Criminal Tribunal for the former Yugoslavia case law has found the defendant's guilty plea and/or statement of remorse as a mitigating factor to be considered in sentencing, ostensibly resulting in shortened sentences (Dixon & Demirdjan 2005). The bottom line, however, is that after confirming the OTP's charges,[27] the trial chamber is free to pronounce the

[25] *Prosecutor* v. *Erdemović, Sentencing Judgment*, Case No. IT-96–22 (Int'l Crim. Trib. for the former Yugoslavia November 29, 1996); *Prosecutor* v. *Erdemović, Appeals Judgment*, Case No. IT-96–22 (Int'l Crim. Trib. for the former Yugoslavia October 7, 1997) (hereafter Erdemović Appeals Judgment); *Prosecutor* v. *Erdemović, Sentencing Judgment*, Case No. IT-96–22 (Int'l Crim. Trib. for the former Yugoslavia March 5, 1998).

[26] Amended indictments must be submitted to the trial chamber for approval, but thus far, no indictment has been refused amendment for the purpose of securing a guilty plea.

[27] The trial chamber is permitted to enquire into the terms of the plea agreement, and has discretion regarding acceptance of a guilty plea. See *Prosecutor* v. *Momir Nikolić, Sentencing Judgment*, Case

sentence it deems fit regardless of what the OTP, defense, or previously decided cases might suggest.

As discussed in Chapter 3, the *Erdemović* case coincided with pressure from the UN to increase ICTY efficiency as well as the concern that the ICTY violated defendants' rights through the length of its proceedings. Instituting a practice of plea bargaining carried the promise of addressing both institutional challenges. Hybridizing plea bargains by maintaining the complete judicial independence of the trial chamber regarding sentence length assuaged concerns, most often iterated by civil law jurists, related to justice. And insistence that plea bargains and statements of remorse increased tribunal legitimacy and social reconstruction (borrowing heavily from the *Erdemović* experience) seemed to address concerns that plea bargains might threaten ICTY legitimacy, not bolster it.

Following *Erdemović* there have been nineteen guilty pleas before the ICTY. These pleas comprise one-third of all convictions before the tribunal and have been cited repeatedly as important reconciliatory mechanisms by expert witnesses appearing before the tribunal, and in tribunal judgments themselves.[28] Guilty pleas are argued to advance the cause of reconciliation in a variety of ways, among them access to information in the possession of

No. IT-02–60/1-S (Int'l Crim. Trib. for the former Yugoslavia December 2, 2003) para 54 (hereafter Nikolić Sentencing Judgment).

28 Although "reconciliation" is not formally part of the ICTY's mandate, reconciliation among the former warring peoples in the Balkans is an oft-cited goal of the ICTY. Chief Judge Antonio Cassese named reconciliation as central to the tribunal's work in his 1994 report to the UN (UN doc. IT/68 [28 July 1994], para 16). See Sikirica para 149; see also "The Trial Chamber accepts that acknowledgement and full disclosure of serious crimes are very important when establishing the truth in relation to such crimes. This, together with acceptance of responsibility for the committed wrongs, will promote reconciliation." *Prosecutor* v. *Biljana Plavšić, Sentencing Judgment*, IT-00–39&40/1-S, 27 February 2003 (para 80). See, e.g., *Prosecutor* v. *Nikolić*, Case No. IT-02–60/1-S, 2 December 2003 (para 145) (identifying the tribunal's mandate as restoring peace and promoting reconciliation). See also Clark 2009. "Truth is the cornerstone of the rule of law, and it will point towards individuals, not people, as perpetrators of war crimes. And it is only the truth that can cleanse the ethnic and religious hatreds and begin the healing process." Provisional Verbatim Record of the 3217th Meeting of the Security Council, May 25 1993, Statement by the Representative of the United States, cited in *Prosecutor* v. *Nikoc*, para 60 fn 106. See also Akhavan, 1998 (arguing that the truth of the Balkan wars is principally a truth of elite politicians fomenting nationalism to serve their own power interests and that by prosecuting those most responsible for the wars of the former Yugoslavia and individualizing their guilt, the ICTY could free citizens of the former Yugoslavia from the weight of collective responsibility and recast nationalist arguments in the light of political realism).

On the other hand, reconciliation is absent from the ICTY founding documents, in contrast to its sister court, the International Criminal Tribunal for Rwanda. Moreover, proponents of the tribunal's work often bristle at the suggestion that the ICTY should be judged against a standard as wide and undefined as "reconciliation." One senior ICTY employee exploded when I asked a question about reconciliation in a semi-structured interview in 2005: "Where do you get this idea about reconciliation! There is no mandate for reconciliation! Look in the Security Council documents, the court documents, it's not there. This idea of reconciliation has been projected onto the ICTY by diplomats. But it's ridiculous to charge the court with reconciliation!" Interview, The Hague, May 2005, notes on file with author.

the accused,[29] bringing relief to victims,[30] as well as increasing tribunal legitimacy through the specter of defendant cooperation. Centrally, nearly all guilty pleas are accompanied by a statement of remorse from the defendant at the sentencing hearing. Such tidy soundbites, articulated in Bosnian/Croatian/Serbian, are highlighted by the ICTY as important reconciliatory mechanisms for the peoples of the former Yugoslavia.

The two plea bargains considered herein were the eighth and seventeenth, respectively, to be entered before the ICTY. Coming only one year apart, they both occurred as the ICTY was experiencing its political ascent. The challenges of the tribunal's early years, with a tiny budget and no international cooperation on the ground to make arrests, had been triumphantly overcome: on the eve of Plavšić's trial, when she changed her plea to guilty, the ICTY had Slobodan Milošević in custody, the first sitting head of state to face indictment and trial before an international court. This is not to say that the tribunal didn't still face significant challenges, most notably the intransigence of nationalist politics in the Balkans bent on defying the tribunal, and the accompanying threat to peace and security represented by such politics.[31] The *Plavšić* and *Babić* cases, concluded in 2003 and 2004, should therefore be read against these two backdrops: the institutional ascent of the tribunal, which had an annual budget of more than $200 million at this time, as well as the ongoing success of hardline nationalist politicians in Bosnia, Croatia, and Serbia.

B *Plavšić and Babić before the ICTY*

Biljana Plavšić was a biologist on the faculty of the University of Sarajevo before entering politics and rising to a leadership position in the Bosnian Serb nationalist party. As Bosnia descended into war, and throughout the war's most brutal episodes, she served as one member of the tripartite Bosnian Serb presidency. In the push to "cleanse" territory to create a Greater Serbia, the war in Bosnia claimed one hundred thousand lives and created an estimated 2.7 million refugees.[32] Plavšić became infamous for her inflammatory, nationalist rhetoric. In 1992, following a massacre by Serb paramilitaries in Bijelina, a photograph circulated showing her stepping over the body of a dead civilian to kiss the notorious paramilitary leader "Arkan," whom she called "a real Serb hero."[33] She is reported to have claimed

[29] "[A] guilty plea contributes directly to one of the fundamental objectives of the international tribunal: namely, its truth-finding function." *Prosecutor* v. *Sikirica et al.* Case No. IT-95–8, 13 November, 2001 (para 149); "[A] guilty plea is always important for the purpose of establishing the truth in relation to a crime" *Prosecutor* v. *Todorović, Sentencing Judgment*, Case No. IT-95–9/1-S, 31 July 2001 (para 81). "Discovering the truth is a cornerstone of the rule of law and a fundamental step on the way to reconciliation." *Prosecutor* v. *Erdemović Sentencing Judgment* Case No. IT-96–22, 5 March 1998 (para 21).

[30] Nikolić Sentencing Judgment.

[31] For example, Serbian pro-democracy president Zoran Đinđić was assassinated in March 2003.

[32] See http://balkansnet.org/refugees.html (accessed August 26, 2015).

[33] See, e.g., Slavenka Drakulic, "The False Repentance of Biljana Plavšić" Eurozine October 23, 2009.

"There are 12 million Serbs and even if six million perish on the field of battle, there will still be six million to reap the fruits of the struggle."[34] Touring scenes of destruction in eastern Bosnia in 1992, she remarked "I'd like to see Eastern Bosnia completely cleansed of Muslims," whom she referred to as "genetically deformed material" (Giovani 2003). In her 2005 memoirs, she continued to advocate the benefits of an ethnically cleansed Bosnia, "One next to another, but not together, so that we can save our lives and they can save their souls." Serbian Radical Party President Vojislav Šešelj, himself "a declared Serb nationalist"[35] categorized her as "insufferably extremist."[36]

In 1995 the Dayton Accords ended the war and split Bosnia into two entities: the Federation (51 percent of the territory, comprised of Bosnian Muslims and Bosnian Croats) and Republika Srpska (RS) (49 percent of the territory, and nearly entirely ethnically cleansed of non-ethnic Serbs). Plavšić's wartime co-president Radovan Karadžić, the most powerful member of the RS tripartite presidency and a central architect of the murder and terror that characterized the war in Bosnia, was banned from public office. Karadžić nominated Plavšić to run for president of RS and she won the 1996 election. Plavšić eventually broke with Karadzic and the other hardline nationalists over implementation of the unpopular Dayton Accords. With the international community's assistance and even, on one occasion, military intervention,[37] Plavšić remained in power to serve her two-year mandate. In exchange, she oversaw a program more moderate than that advocated by her former colleagues. By the end of 1997 Plavšić had begun to cooperate with international actors, removing Ratko Mladić as Commander of Bosnian Serb forces, for example.[38] In 1998, she lost her bid for re-election and quit the political scene.

After leaving power, Plavšić was indicted by the ICTY on charges that included genocide.[39] She did not defy the tribunal as some of her countrymen had done, and was thus able to negotiate significant concessions regarding her physical presence in The Hague.[40] Still, she rejected the charges against her until the last minute, when on the eve of her trial and facing a possible life sentence, Plavšić pleaded guilty to "persecutions."[41] In exchange the OTP dropped all other charges against her and

34 "Biljana Plavšić: Serbian iron lady'" BBC News, February 27, 2003.

35 Milošević Hearing transcript August 30, 2005 p. 43373:1–2.

36 *Ibid*. 43371:25–43373:1.

37 Transcript Plavšić Sentencing Hearing.

38 After more than a decade on the run, Mladić was apprehended by the ICTY. He is now standing trial for charges that include genocide in relation to the massacre of more than 7,000 Bosnian Muslims at Srebrenica.

39 The Prosecutor of the Tribunal Against Momcilo Krajisnik and Biljana Plavšić, Amended Consolidated Indictment, Case No. IT-00–39 & 40-PT, 7 March 2002.

40 Plavšić received very special handling by the OTP from the beginning of her case: she negotiated her arrival in The Hague to follow Orthodox Christmas, and was released provisionally before her trial date. Provisional release is almost never awarded by the tribunal.

41 *Prosecutor* v. *Plavšić, Plea Agreement of Biljana Plavšić*, Case No. IT-00–39&40/1-S, (Int'l Crim. Trib. for the former Yugoslavia September 30, 2002) (hereafter Plavšić Plea Agreement).

recommended a fifteen- to twenty-five-year sentence;[42] Plavšić eventually received eleven years.

It was while serving her sentence in a comfortable Swedish prison[43] that Plavšić first recanted her statement of remorse; she affirmed this position in other interviews and in her memoirs. Although the OTP had entered the plea agreement "without prejudice,"[44] which would allow the revisitation of the dropped charges in the event of changed events, the ICTY trial chamber did not permit this.[45] Plavšić came up for parole six years into her eleven-year sentence,[46] and she was released in 2009, without mention of the fact that she had retracted the admissions underlying her sentence.[47] At the time of writing she lives comfortably in Belgrade.

Like Biljana Plavšić, Milan Babić was a part-time politician rocketed to power during, and by, events connected with the dissolution of the former Yugoslavia. A dentist by training, Babić became a central figure in the Serbian nationalist party in Croatia in February 1990.[48] Following Croatia's secession from Yugoslavia in February 1991, Babić's party advocated the creation of an independent Serb state in the territory known as Krajina,[49] and realized this through the so-called log revolution, where Croatian Serbs barred access to the Krajina territory by blockading all major thoroughfares with logs. In April 1991, Babić became president of this territory. In the following months, Croatian Serbs ethnically cleansed Krajina of non-Serbs through force and violence: 230 people were killed in this campaign and tens of thousands fled the violence. Although Milan Babić was the *de jure* leader of this entity, Milan Martić, operating a shadow government taking its instructions from Belgrade, organized and enacted the violence. In early 1992, Babić broke with Milošević over the question of targeting civilians (Glenny 1996; Silber & Little 1997).[50] Babić spent the remainder of the war politically sidelined, although still

42 Amended Consolidated Indictment, Schedules A, B, C, and D; see also Plavšić Sentencing Judgment paras 41–43.

43 European countries cooperate with the ICTY by jailing convicted defendants. Not all European jails are created equal, however, and Scandinavian prisons are generally the most comfortable. Plavšić's placement in a Swedish prison likely reflects another aspect of her negotiation with the tribunal. Plavšić's Swedish prison offered horseback riding as a prisoner activity. Because Plavšić was of retirement age, she was not required to work in prison, and the prison report stated that she passed her time knitting and baking.

44 Plavšić Plea Agreement.

45 Plavšić Early Release Decision.

46 Parole guidelines are determined by the states housing ICTY convicts; serving in Sweden, Plavšić was subject to Swedish regulations about the timing and criteria for parole, which she met.

47 Plavšić Early Release Decision. The tribunal stopped at the phrase, "sufficient reconciliation," and did not explicate further.

48 Babić Sentencing Judgment.

49 Krajina, which means "the end," is a territory settled by Serbs in the seventeenth and eighteenth centuries, and designed as a buffer zone between the Ottoman and Austro-Hungarian empires. The territory is located in the "elbow" of Croatia, on the Bosnian border.

50 In the relevant literature there is a mixed assessment of Babić's role in the war, his relationship with Milošević, and his character. The so-called log revolution in Knin represents the commencement of violence in the dissolution of Yugoslavia, and Babić played a central role in this event. Journalist

officially occupying minor political positions, and fled Krajina in the path of Operation Storm[51] in 1995 along with two hundred thousand ethnic Serbs in one of the war's most massive ethnic cleansing incidents.[52]

Babić's story intersected with that of the ICTY in October 2001, after Babić learned that he had been named as member of a joint criminal enterprise in the Milošević indictment. From his home in Belgrade, Babić reported to representatives of the ICTY and made himself available for questioning. By the prosecutor's own admission, Babić's availability was "extensive"[53] and he cooperated with the OTP over a period of several months. In interviews with Babić, the OTP amassed a documentary trove of more than 1,200 interview transcript pages containing descriptions of the events, players, and actions surrounding the Croatian Serb takeover of the Krajina territory in Croatia, as well as specific information as to the ways in which such a takeover was effectuated, including details about the support of both Milošević and the Yugoslav army.[54] Babić made such statements while fully admitting his own role and his own guilt, and without bartering for any form of immunity. In 2003, Babić was indicted based on information he provided.[55] Although the OTP called for a sentence of "less than 11 years," Babić received thirteen. He committed suicide in The Hague, while testifying for the OTP in the *Martić* case,[56] in 2005. At the time of his death, Babić had testified against Milošević,[57] Krajišnik,[58] and

Misha Glenny (1996) thus puts Babić's "badness" on par with Milošević's. Journalists Silber and Little (1997) are more agnostic on the subject of Babić's character and motivation, and present him as manipulated, bullied, and finally discarded, by his patron Milošević. The ICTY's sentencing judgment of Babić does not shed light on how to interpret Babić's actions, although non-contested evidence was offered demonstrating that Babić worked towards a political solution in Krajina because he was opposed to violence and its cost for civilians.

51 The Krajina question was eventually resolved militarily. "Operation Storm," which retook Krajina, has itself become the subject of ICTY prosecution. *Prosecutor* vs. *Ante Gotovina, Ivan Čermak* and *Mladen Markač*, Case No. IT-06–90-PT (Int'l Crim. Trib. for the former Yugoslavia April 15, 2011).

52 The numbers are disputed. The BBC reports that 200,000 fled (Matt Prodger, "Evicted Serbs remember Storm" BBC News August 5, 2005). Croatia has put the number at 90,000, the United Nations at between 150 and 200,000, and Serbian sources at 250,000. Carl Bildt, the European Union Special Envoy to the former Yugoslavia, called it "the most efficient ethnic cleansing we've seen in the Balkans" (quoted in Daniel Pearl, "Few Serbs Chased from Croatia in 1995 Have Made it Back Home" *The Wall Street Journal* April 22, 1999); Marko Hoare notes that the Serbs organized the flight themselves, thus differentiating this incident from other instances of ethnic cleansing during the war.

53 *Prosecutor* v. *Milan Babić, Sentencing Hearing*, Case No. IT-03–72, (April 2, 2004) Tr. 78:20 ("Babić Sentencing Hearing").

54 Babić's testimony implicated Serbs from Serbia in the highest echelons of power for responsibility for the violence in Croatia. The ICTY has found it difficult to juridically establish the link between Serbian power brokers (in the government and the military) with war in the former Yugoslavia (see, for example, acquittal of Serbian general by ICTY *Prosecutor* v. *Perisic* 2011), although this link is widely recognized. Thus Babić's testimony was singular and critical for the prosecution.

55 Babić Indictment.

56 Martić Judgment.

57 *Prosecutor* v. *Slobodan Milošević*, Case No IT-02–54 (Int'l Crim. Trib. for the former Yugoslavia) (case uncompleted).

58 *Prosecutor* v. *Krajišnik* Case No IT-02–54 (Int'l Crim. Trib. for the former Yugoslavia).

Martić,[59] and was due to testify against Simatović,[60] Stanišić,[61] and Šešelj.[62] Martić's defense counsel described him as the trial's "most important prosecution witness."[63]

II CONSTRUCTING GUILT, CRIMINALITY, AND PUNISHMENT IN *PLAVŠIĆ* AND *BABIĆ*

When a defendant pleads guilty before the ICTY, the trial chamber must determine that the plea was "voluntary, informed, and unequivocal, and that there was a sufficient factual basis for the crime and the accused's participation in it"[64] before finding guilt. Sentencing is a separate phase, wherein evidence (largely testimony) is produced to support the parties' arguments regarding sentence length. Both Plavšić and Babić negotiated pleas of guilt with the OTP, which in both cases produced an amended indictment as well as a "factual statement" signed by each defendant accompanying the plea. Both then faced a public hearing to determine sentencing, where witnesses for the OTP and the defense (and some witnesses who were jointly submitted) testified regarding elements that the tribunal should consider when awarding the sentence.

During Plavšić's two-and-a-half-day hearing, witnesses spoke to two themes: the brutal trauma of the war experience (three witnesses) and Plavšić's central postwar role in implementing the Dayton Accords (five witnesses). The reconciliatory potential of Plavšić's plea of guilt effectively took center stage, as the prosecution and defense worked together to create a story of a leader on the path to liberalism, and an institution (the ICTY) making such a path possible. In this narrative, Plavšić's postwar conduct emerged as more important, and more noteworthy, than her wartime conduct. Babić's two-day hearing was a markedly different affair. No international names or figures spoke on his behalf. Instead, two witnesses presented information to the tribunal: Mladen Lončar, a Croatian psychiatrist speaking to the trauma of ethnic cleansing as lived by the Croatians driven out of Krajina, and Drago Kovačević, a Croatian Serb working as a social worker in Belgrade, but who had been a local politician in a multi-ethnic party in Krajina and who had worked with Babić in that capacity. The joint narrative of the prosecution and defense, while less seamlessly imagined than in the Plavšić hearing, was the story of a man overcome by events, taken in by nationalism and fear before recognizing, and then rejecting, these political outcomes.

The following discussion focuses on the three most divergent areas of the *Plavšić* and *Babić* judgments: (i) the chambers' constructions of criminality (more

59 Martić Judgment.

60 *Prosecutor* v. *Stanišić and Simatović*, Case No. IT-03–69 (Int'l Crim. Trib. for the former Yugoslavia).

61 *Ibid.*

62 *Prosecutor* v. *Šešelj*, Case No IT-03–67 (Int'l Crim. Trib. for the former Yugoslavia).

63 Janet Anderson, "Babić Suicide a Blow for Prosecutors" March 10, 2006 IWPR.

64 Plavšić Sentencing Judgment para 5.

specifically, the role and construction of "intent" in each judgment); (ii) the chambers' construction of factors to be considered for sentencing (mitigating and aggravating elements of the cases); and (iii) the narrative arcs of each case (which players impacted them, and how). Finally, the section demonstrates how these constructions support, and are supported by, two diverging rationales for ICL legitimacy, preaching (Shklar's didactic liberalism) vs. punishment (the criminal justice rubric of control).

A *Intent and Questions of Criminality in* Plavšić *and* Babić

Both Plavšić and Babić were charged with "persecutions"[65] and convicted of committing these acts under the "joint criminal enterprise" (JCE) theory of liability, discussed in detail in Chapter 4. For both Plavšić and Babić, charged with committing persecutions under the theory that they *knew of persecutions* committed by their colleagues (JCE I) or that *persecutions were reasonably foreseeable* (JCE III) based on their activities, their intent is discerned either from their actual or reasonable knowledge. In juridical terms, neither chamber needs to speak to "intent" beyond "knowledge" or "foreseeability," the elements required to substantiate JCE. In both cases, evidence was offered that spoke to both defendants' actual or reasonable knowledge. The *Plavšić* judgment, however, does not discuss Plavšić's intent qua motivation or knowledge. The judgment references "intent" only once, in relation to the gravity of the persecutions charge.[66] In this way, the *Plavšić* chamber subsumes any and all discussions of intent into the "gravity of the crime" of persecutions.[67] The *Babić* chamber, however, entitles an entire section of its judgment "Babić's intent."[68] Moreover, the silence in *Plavšić* and focus in *Babić* lead directly to jurisprudential divergences in the two cases. In *Plavšić*, ducking the question of Plavšić's intent (her evil intention) allows the chamber to focus on what it characterizes as Plavšić's *benevolent intention* following the war, i.e., her role in supporting the Dayton Accords. In *Babić*, a juridically unnecessary focus on

[65] In Plavšić's plea agreement, "persecutions" are articulated as follows:

> a. the existence of an armed conflict; b. the existence of a widespread or systematic attack directed against a civilian population; c. the accused's conduct was related to the widespread or systematic attack directed against a civilian population; d. the accused had knowledge of the wider context in which her conduct occurred; e. the accused committed acts or omissions against a victim or victim population violating a basic fundamental or human right; f. the accused intended to commit the violation; g. the accused's conduct was committed on political, racial, or religious grounds; and h. the accused's conduct was committed with an intent to discriminate.

In signing the plea agreement, Plavšić acknowledged that she understood that the prosecutor was required to show these elements in order to prove the charge against her to which she was pleading guilty. See Plavšić Plea Agreement.

[66] Plavšić Judgment para 52.

[67] Which it finds to be a "crime of utmost gravity." Plavšić Judgment para 52.

[68] Babić Judgment.

motivation allows the chamber to morally condemn Babić, thereby depriving his case of didactic, political potential.

We begin in *Plavšić*, using the judgment's characterization of Plavšić's criminality as an example. In its submissions, through its witnesses, and in its closing statement at Plavšić's hearing, the OTP described the horrific violence of the war in Bosnia. The OTP positioned Plavšić as "one of the beacons" of that violence, a politician who "imbued [others] with a mission to use criminal means to achieve her vision of an ethnically separated Bosnia," i.e., to beat, rape, and kill civilians.[69] The OTP spoke to the "efficiency and ruthlessness of the campaign of persecutions" as well as its scale.[70] The OTP also noted that Plavšić "was one of the leaders of the [ethnic cleansing] effort, and she embraced its goal and supported it in various ways."[71] This description makes it clear that Plavšić had real-time knowledge of crimes committed, and that she shared the evil intent of those who perpetrated the crimes. The OTP's indictment (to which, again, Plavšić pleaded guilty) goes farther, defining her participation as including "planning, instigating, ordering"[72] ethnic cleansing.

The *Plavšić* judgment, however, subtly but importantly rewrites Plavšić's participation. The judgment lists the grave crimes as laid out in the indictment, but tweaks Plavšić's role. After reviewing the crimes as included in the indictment, the judgment characterizes Plavšić as having "participated in the cover up of these crimes by making public statements of denial for which she had no support. When she subsequently had reason to know that these denials were in fact untrue, she did not recant or correct them."[73] The judgment culls this information from the "factual basis" filed together with Plavšić's plea agreement.[74] Unlike the indictment, which is a public document articulating legal charges, the factual basis is a confidential, *ex parte* document reciting facts, and it was first made public on the date of Plavšić's hearing.[75] The significance of these distinctions is that the indictment comprises the official record of Plavšić's crime which, once she pleads guilty, effectively becomes an official record of her condemnation (together with the tribunal's judgment). When the indictment and the factual basis cannot be reconciled, this presents a problem: first and foremost, a legal problem for the chamber, but ultimately also a historical and social problem for those who would use ICTY judgments for larger societal purposes.

69 Plavšić December 17 Sentencing Hearing Transcript p. 630.

70 *Ibid.* p. 623.

71 *Ibid.* p. 630.

72 Plavšić Indictment.

73 Plavšić Judgment para 17.

74 Factual Basis for Plea of Guilty September 30, 2002, available at www.haguejusticeportal.net/Docs/Court%20Documents/ICTY/Plavsic_Factual_Basis_Plea_guilt.pdf

75 *Ibid.*; *Prosecutor* v. *Plavšić*, Case No. IT-00–39&40/1S, Order for Release of Confidential Document (Int'l Crim. Trib. for the former Yugoslavia December 16, 2002), available at http://icr.icty.org/ (sign-in required).

This is the case in *Plavšić*, where the judgment's characterization of Plavšić's role, drawn from the factual basis, contravenes what the judgment recognizes as Plavšić's crime, which is having "planned, instigated, ordered and aided and abetted persecutions of the Bosnian Muslim, Bosnian Croat and other non-Serb populations of 37 municipalities in Bosnia and Herzegovina."[76] Note further that intent is problematically absent from the judgment's descriptions of Plavšić's role, because such descriptions call into question Plavšić's knowledge. Plavšić could hardly plan, instigate, or order without knowledge. The *Plavšić* judgment suggests that Plavšić did not have real-time knowledge of the violence: consider the quote above ("when she *subsequently had reason to know*"[77]) as well as a later description: "as a leader and *later an accused, she learned a great deal about the gravity and nature of the crimes* committed by the forces which she led and inspired during the war; and she recognizes her obligation to accept responsibility *for acts committed by others.*"[78] Here the chamber follows Plavšić's own iteration; in her statement addressing the tribunal, Plavšić states that through the indictment and with the help of her lawyers, conducting "our own investigation and evaluation" she has "*now come to the belief* and accept the fact that many thousands of innocent people were the victims of an organized, systemic effort to remove Muslims and Croats from the territory claimed by Serbs."[79] These statements place Plavšić's knowledge after the fact, which would challenge the indictment's charge of "planning, instigating, ordering" and thereby, arguably, the criminal charges themselves.

The upswing of these machinations is that in *Plavšić*, the question of intent as regards *her crimes* is recharacterized as a question of intent regarding *her plea of guilt*. This sleight-of-hand permits the *Plavšić* chamber to consider the possible power of Plavšić's *admission of guilt* under the category of intent, i.e., it allows her admission of guilt, instead of remaining only a possible mitigating factor at sentencing (discussed below), to wriggle into the construction of her criminality itself. This thus permits the *Plavšić* chamber to turn its consideration of her postwar conduct, which juridically can only exist as a mitigating circumstance, into a consideration of Plavšić's motivation (which speaks to her intent and, thereby, her criminality itself).

In its sentencing judgment, the *Plavšić* chamber devotes fifteen paragraphs to considering the value of Plavšić's remorse as a reconciliatory mechanism, and nine paragraphs to the significance of her postwar conduct. Both of these categories are properly understood as "mitigating" factors, where mitigation refers to the length of the sentence. The *Plavšić* judgment tips its hand, however, when it begins its consideration of the "substantial" mitigating circumstances in the Plavšić case by discussing "Mrs. Plavšić's … unprecedented steps *to mitigate the crime against*

76 Plavšić Judgment para 3.
77 *Ibid.* para 17 (emphasis added).
78 *Ibid.* para 19 (emphasis added).
79 Plavšić December 17 Sentencing Hearing Transcript p. 609 (emphasis added).

humanity for which she is responsible."[80] The problem here is that crimes cannot be mitigated. Mitigating *circumstances* can alter the classification of a crime: a murder charge (requiring premeditation) may be reduced to a lesser charge,[81] such as manslaughter, for example. In domestic criminal law, an affirmative defense can defeat a charge even where true (where the crime is still murder, but the justification of self-defense removes the punishment. Note that affirmative defenses are not available at ICL due to the non-derogable nature of the rights infringed by violations of international humanitarian law) (Shniderman & Smith 2015). One does not mitigate the crime: rather, one mitigates punishment for a given crime or, depending on the elements of the crime in question and the facts collected regarding it, one reassigns criminal definition, sometimes through mitigating circumstances. The *Plavšić* judgment problematically conflates the categories of criminality (intent, pertaining to crime's definition) and context (mitigation or aggravation, pertaining to eventual sentence).

By contrast, the *Babić* chamber pens an entire portion of its sentence under the heading "Babić's intent." Because Babić cooperated so extensively with the OTP, giving informational interviews as well as testifying in several other cases, questions of Babić's intent (both his motivation and his knowledge) are well documented. The *Babić* judgment notes that "Babić explained that as of August 1991 he shared the intent of others with whom he participated in planning the campaign of persecutions to forcibly resettle the Croat and non-Serb populations from the targeted areas."[82] Babić admitted he knew of the mistreatment, deportations, and destruction of property connected to the ethnic cleansing of Krajina, and that he knew there was a possibility that murders might result, though he was unaware at the time of the two hundred killings that took place during this period.[83] The *Babić* chamber had so much information regarding Babić's intent that it rejected Babić's initial plea of guilt as an aider and abettor of a JCE, expressing doubt regarding the accuracy of this legal categorization;[84] Babić revised his plea to participating as a "co-perpetrator" of a JCE, which was in turn accepted by the tribunal.

In its judgment, the *Babić* chamber resists what it characterizes as the parties' assessment that Babić's liability is "lessened by the fact that he did not intend the commission of the murders as such but was merely aware that murders were being committed as part of the JCE."[85] This reaction on the part of the *Babić* chamber is in line with JCE liability, which requires, in its most extreme form, mere "knowledge of the foreseeability" of a crime. Moreover, the chamber pushed back at attempts to allow factual elements only considerable as mitigating (in terms of sentence) to

80 Plavšić Judgment para 61 (emphasis added).

81 See, e.g., *People* v. *Morrin*, 31 Mich. App. 301, 187 N.W.2d 434 (1971) (where the mitigating circumstances of heat of passion reversed a first-degree murder charge).

82 Babić Judgment para 26.

83 *Ibid.* paras 26–27.

84 *Ibid.* paras 6–8.

85 *Ibid.* para 38.

encroach on questions of criminality themselves. Thus the *Babić* judgment applied a standard criminal justice rubric, fitting the facts of the case solidly into the doctrinal rubric established by JCE case law.

The *Babić* chamber was substantially aided by the OTP, which itself pushed back against imprecise queries with curt, doctrinal summaries. In one example, Judge Orie investigated facts from the factual statement, trying to ascertain what sort of unlawful killings occurred against civilians:

> Is this to be understood, that Mr. Babic was aware that civilians were killed as collateral damage to justified military action? Or was – I mean, you can kill – it sounds very horrible. But you can kill civilians in two different ways; either by using wrong military equipment for an attack not targeting precisely, and thus killing civilians as – not as collateral damage but more or less as a consequence of improper military action; and of course, you can also save the lives of the civilians during the attack, and then kill them afterwards.[86]

The OTP responded not to the question asked but instead placed Babić's admissions into a doctrinal framework: "Mr. Babic was very clear saying it was not legitimate military actions, but ethnic cleansing campaign in an attack that was actually illegal. And in the course of this attack, civilians were killed." Here the OTP neatly reformulated Judge Orie's factual question into a legal category, and then made this legal categorization synonymous with Babić's factual submissions, thereby making Babić the originator of the legal formulation.[87]

In summary, the two cases offer several contradictions. While the *Babić* chamber applied JCE relentlessly, it supported this application of the legal standard with a (juridically unnecessary) discussion of Babić's intent, which reads like an insistence on his bad character. Meanwhile, the *Plavšić* chamber connected Plavšić's intent to the gravity of the crime; gravity it then distanced from Plavšić by repeatedly considering her "lesser role" in the JCE. The transformation of intent in the *Plavšić* judgment from what is required under JCE (knowledge or foreseeability) into what is characterized by the judgment as Plavšić's after-the-fact realization, allowed the judgment to make Plavšić's plea of guilt itself legally commensurate with furthering the work and purpose of the ICTY.[88] This is a central piece of the juridical puzzle that transforms the *Plavšić* case into a didactic example modeling liberal values.

86 Babić April 1 Sentencing Transcript pp. 179–180.

87 *Ibid.* There is a storied history of asking defendants to provide not just facts but also law: the Erdemović chamber required Erdemović to categorize his crimes as either crimes against humanity or war crimes, explaining to him that had there been a trial the OTP would have done this, but since he was pleading guilty, he should do it himself. Transcript, *Prosecutor* v. *Erdemović*, Case No. IT-96–22 (Int'l Crim. Trib. for the former Yugoslavia May 31, 1996). The appeals chamber later reversed the trial chamber in part because Erdemović, in choosing "crimes against humanity" which was the more severe of the two charges, demonstrated he was not adequately informed. See Erdemović Appeals Judgment, and discussion in Chapter 3.

88 "[I]t may be argued that by her guilty plea, Mrs. Plavšić had already demonstrated remorse. … [T]here is a further and significant circumstance to be considered, namely the role of the guilty

B The Jurisprudence of Punishment: Distinct Formulations of "Aggravation" and "Mitigation" in Plavšić and Babić

As demonstrated above, in the *Plavšić* judgment, elements of what juridically should have been considered as contextual (going to mitigating circumstances that might impact sentence length) were blurred by considerations of Plavšić's criminality as attached to her intent. The *Babić* judgment, meanwhile, applied the facts doctrinally. This section considers important distinctions in the two chambers' constructions of context, i.e., of mitigating and aggravating factors to be considered in formulating the sentence.

Sentencing itself is only very broadly defined by the ICTY Statute,[89] and sentencing is notoriously unpredictable at the ICTY; each trial chamber is permitted to largely construct its own rationale for the sentence it awards. In cases of plea agreements, the OTP and the defense make sentencing recommendations, which may or may not correspond. Such recommendations, agreed or not, do not bind the trial chamber in any way; it remains entirely free to assign the sentence it determines. The ICTY rules note that aggravating and mitigating circumstances may be taken under consideration during sentencing. The rules themselves define only one "mitigating" circumstance: "substantial cooperation" with the prosecution.[90] ICTY practice has developed other aggravating and mitigating factors that are often reiterated in later case law, though such reiterations do not bind the ICTY as regards the specifics of sentence length.

The *Plavšić* chamber engaged in a brief (eight-paragraph) consideration of possible aggravating circumstances. This followed a lengthy summarization (twenty-five paragraphs) of details from the prosecution witnesses called at the hearing in order to conclude that the crime at issue was "of utmost gravity" and occurred with "massive scope."[91] Following other ICTY cases, the judgment necessarily noted that Plavšić's leadership position was an aggravating circumstance, which it immediately mitigated by asserting that Plavšić was not "in the very first rank of leadership."[92] The tone and language, deferential and apologetic, is in marked contrast to the *Babić* chamber's construction of his leadership as an aggravating circumstance.

The *Plavšić* chamber next turned to mitigating circumstances, where it recognized four: her guilty plea (in conjunction with what it said regarding her remorse

plea of the accused in establishing the truth in relation to the crimes and furthering reconciliation in the former Yugoslavia." Plavšić Judgment para 73.

89 Article 24 of the ICTY Statute; see discussion in Chapter 3.

90 ICTY Rules of Procedure and Evidence T/32/Rev. 48, 19 November 2012 Rules (Rule 101 (B) (ii))

91 Plavšić Judgment paras 27–52.

92 *Ibid.* para 57. The entire argument reads "The Trial Chamber accepts that the superior position of the accused is an aggravating factor in the case. The accused was not in the very first rank of the leadership: others occupied that position. She did not conceive the plan which led to this crime and had a lesser role in its execution than others. Nonetheless, Mrs. Plavšić was in the Presidency, the highest civilian body, during the campaign and encouraged and supported it by her participation in the Presidency and her pronouncements."

and what it offered in terms of reconciliation); her voluntary surrender; her post-conflict conduct (specifically her assistance in implementing the Dayton Accords) and her age.[93] The chamber attached "great weight" to Plavšić's guilty plea and post-conflict conduct, which it found to be "a formidable body of mitigation." It ignored testimony regarding Plavšić's ongoing nationalist beliefs and exhortations, and dismissed discussion of her refusal to cooperate (finding that a refusal to cooperate with the OTP could not constitute an "aggravating" circumstance, but simply that her refusal to cooperate obviated the possibility that "cooperation with the OTP" might count in mitigation towards her sentence.)[94] This is significant because either of these elements might have influenced the tribunal's consideration of Plavšić's post-conflict conduct.

The *Babić* judgment determined that Babić's crime was of "extreme gravity" and was "characterized by ruthlessness and savagery."[95] It determined his leadership role was an aggravating factor, because his participation was "substantial."[96] The judgment specified two main reasons for this finding: first, as a leader Babić "enlisted the resources" at his disposal to further the JCE and second, Babić's involvement "gained momentum over time," which "amplified its consequences."[97] The judgment thus rejected the parties' contentions that Babić's role in the JCE was limited, and that this should be considered in mitigation. The judgment accepted the parties' other submissions regarding mitigation: Babić's admission of guilt, his cooperation (for which the judgment affords "substantial mitigating weight"), show of remorse, voluntary surrender, and personal and family circumstances.[98]

Finally, and significantly, the *Babić* judgment rejected the parties' contention that Babić's postwar conduct should count as mitigating.[99] The *Babić* chamber offered the example of Plavšić's postwar conduct as a standard against which to consider Babić:[100] such conduct included support for Dayton and the removal of obstructionist officials from office. This presupposes, of course, that one is in a political position capable of performing such acts: the standard would thus fail as any kind of doctrinal gage. At the same time, the standard as articulated by the *Babić* chamber ignored the motivation for these acts which, as argued above, in Plavšić's case were as easily construed as personal self-interest (remaining in power) as ideological commitment. Finally, the *Babić* judgment's conclusion on this score ignored factual evidence presented at the sentencing hearing, which spoke to Babić's attempts to thwart violent objectives, often at grave bodily risk to himself,[101]

93 *Ibid.* para 62.
94 *Ibid.* para 110.
95 Babić Judgment para 53.
96 *Ibid.* para 57.
97 *Ibid.* para 61.
98 *Ibid.* paras 63–89.
99 *Ibid.* para 95.
100 *Ibid.* para 94.
101 Two instances of personal harm to Babić were detailed in the sentencing hearing, both of which were petulantly dismissed by Judge Orie. In a further irony, the risks that Plavšić took when she defied her hardline colleagues in favor of the international community (risks for which she received police and

as well as his work towards a political solution for Krajina within Croatia as early as 1992, and again in 1995.[102]

In summary, the two cases diverge significantly in terms of how they structure and weigh the construed aggravating and mitigating factors. In terms of aggravation, Babić's leadership position was construed as a destructive force due to its "power of inertia," while the destructive capacity of Plavšić's infamous nationalist rhetoric was unaddressed. Plavšić's leadership role was downplayed, whereas Babić's was amped up. But it is in the constructions of meaningful mitigation that the two cases most importantly diverge, where the reconciliatory capacity of Plavšić's plea of guilt, in a category invented by the tribunal, through witnesses sympathetic to the socially constitutive aims of the tribunal,[103] took on a mitigating capacity large enough to mitigate her crime itself. Babić, on the other hand, had only a tribunal functionary, the erstwhile prosecutor Ms. Uertz-Retzlaff, to speak for him regarding the importance of his cooperation.

C *Comparing and Contrasting Reconciliation Narratives in* Plavšić *and* Babić

One of the values of the ICTY is to perform liberalism in the Balkans, to offer an antidote to the dead end of nationalist politics that tore Yugoslavia apart, and continues to threaten peace in its successor states. By this account, rule-of-law processes are substituted for primordial, essentialist collectives as a means of national organization. This is one of the "truths" the tribunal is meant to pronounce, a truth that might have, in the words of the *Erdemović* sentencing judgment, the potential to "cleanse[] the ethnic and religious hatreds and begin[] the healing process." This is a role that the tribunal has often imagined for itself, and which is referenced expressly in the *Plavšić* hearing by the OTP in terms of the "linked" concepts of accountability and reconciliation served by the tribunal,[104] and noted by the *Babić* chamber, in passing, as a benefit of his statement of remorse.[105]

military protection from the international community) are described at length at the Plavšić sentencing hearing, and elicit praise for her "courage."

102 Factual Statement of US Ambassador Peter Galbraith in Milošević case, quoted in Babić Judgment para 24.

103 Madeleine Albright was the US's representative to the UN when the ICTY was created, and her views on the possibility of the tribunal acting to promote liberal values are well documented; Alex Borraine, who spoke about reconciliation at Plavšić's hearing, founded the International Center for Transitional Justice; Elie Wiesel, a Holocaust survivor, has written extensively regarding recognition and victimhood.

104 Plavšić December 17 Sentencing Hearing Transcript, p. 620: 21. See also: "The parties to this litigation share the view that it is only through the establishment of truth about what occurred in Bosnia and Herzegovina that the fragile and vital process of reconciliation can begin. Furthermore, we agree that it is only through the establishment of truth that the unhealthy shackles of revision that debilitate the former Yugoslavia and that foster suspicion, ethnic hatred, and civil unrest can be broken." Plavšić December 16 Sentencing Hearing Transcript, p. 376: 15–21.

105 Babić Judgment. The value of articulating remorse is standard fare in plea bargain judgments.

Both the *Plavšić* and *Babić* hearings and judgments speak to questions of nationalism, liberalism, and reconciliation. As noted above, the judgments turn commonsense readings on their heads in this regard, turning an unapologetic Serbian nationalist (Plavšić) into a forward-marching democratic liberal (and thereby insisting that she remain a public figure, and perform as an example), and condemning a *bona fide* repentant, reformed nationalist (Babić) into a petty attention-seeker (and thereby denying Babić a public role). In this vein, this section closes by briefly contrasting the narrative arcs – the stories told – through the *Plavšić* and *Babić* processes.

In her closing statement, Prosecutor Carla Del Ponte characterized Plavšić as on a "path" or "trajectory" towards rule-of-law liberalism.[106] Prosecutor Del Ponte made this argument in spite of what she named as a stubborn refusal on Plavšić's part to cooperate in other cases before the tribunal: Del Ponte refers to such (nonexistent) cooperation as "the last step of [Biljana Plavšić's] journey."[107] Some have speculated that Plavšić "fooled" the ICTY with her "false repentance" (Harmon and Gaynor 2007; Cook 2005; Drakulic 2009). While this may be true, the trial transcript does not support such an interpretation. Indeed, there were many instances where the *Plavšić* chamber was invited to consider Plavšić's actual beliefs and motivations beyond Plavšić's lukewarm statement of remorse (which referenced Serb victims as often as Muslim and Croat victims) and which, as noted above, in its very form reiterated the kinds of nationalist rationalizations that underwrote Bosnian brutality (largely, the "people" as a collective body capable of honorable actions, and being shamed). Rather it seems more likely that the chamber decided to accept the defense's injunction "to consider the positive effects of [Plavšić's] guilty plea as the only political leader willing to step forward and act responsibly for wrongs committed during the war."[108] The more pressing question then becomes, why wouldn't, or couldn't, the *Babić* chamber, receiving the narrative of a one-time political leader stepping forward and actually claiming responsibility, accept the narrative of liberal rehabilitation when it was presented to them?

Both the OTP and the defense presented Babić's story as that of a rehabilitated nationalist. In calling the witness Kovačević to testify regarding the political environment of fear and propaganda under which Serbs in Croatia lived and the ways in

[106] "I have followed this file step by step. Mrs. Plavšić's guilty plea did not take us by surprise, since it was nothing but a further step in her development since 1995, basically starting with the Dayton Accords. During these days we have heard testimony dating back to this period. It made it possible for us to understand that Dayton was, for her, the starting point of a new development, of a new trajectory . . . [S]ince Madam Plavšić started a new path by her guilty plea, by admitting her personal criminal responsibility, and above all by accepting to pay the price for her crimes before justice, in our submission the accused Plavšić should not only enjoy mitigating factors but she should also have a reduced sentence." Plavšić December 17 Sentencing Hearing Transcript pp. 636–637 (Carla Del Ponte, OTP).

[107] *Ibid.*

[108] Plavšić December 16 Sentencing Hearing Transcript 380:8–10.

which this made all information suspect for them, the parties were iterating that Babić:

> Only became radicalized through moves of the political leaderships both in Belgrade and Zagreb and a large-scale and sophisticated Serbian media campaign to revive peoples' old fears and insecurities, leading to separation of communities along ethnic lines and resulting in violence of the dominant ethnic group against the others.[109]

Over two days of testimony, the witness Kovačević – who was himself a former politician from Krajina, although he had worked in a multi-ethnic party – tried to provide detailed information regarding the political and cultural climate of fear and intimidation that prevailed in Krajina during the time Babić served in office. He recounted details of Babić's personal experiences of violence, including the murder of Babić's father-in-law by Croatian soldiers, who set fire to houses in the village of Vrlika in 1991 (Babić's house was burned down, and his own mother narrowly escaped);[110] he described an attempt on Babić's life by troops loyal to ethnic Serb interests. This considered and articulate testimony did not reach the bench, however.

One particular example of a determined witness and a deaf chamber is illustrative: in 1992, after Babić had broken with Milošević, he was attacked in his home by Krajina police while meeting with SDS party members, and was badly beaten and hospitalized as a result (Silber & Little 1997). Kovačević testified that the pro-Milošević attackers "shouted insults at [Babić]," and made specific mention of one particular insult, a word which was initially translated as "prefect."[111] Distracted by Kovačević's "hearsay"[112] testimony, Judge Orie shut down this line of questioning as "really entering the realm of speculation."[113] What was nearly lost in the fracas was the actual meaning of the insult shouted at Babić. The word in question was originally translated as "prefect," which an overwhelmed translator later replaced with the original Bosnian-Croatian-Serbian word, "župan," and which was finally paraphrased by defense counsel, in an aside, as "traitor." It was only the following day, when Kovačević was invited by the bench to revisit the term, that he was permitted to explain its significance. "Župan" refers to the head of an administrative territory in

109 Babić Sentencing Judgment para 90; this is significant because it is quoting the *Prosecution's* Sentencing Brief para 57 (arguing that Babić's prior character should be a mitigating factor in judgment).

110 Babić April 1 Sentencing Hearing p. 144.

111 *Ibid.*

112 Kovačević was testifying to exchanges he had not personally witnessed which are inadmissible, as hearsay, in some national jurisdictions. However, US rules of evidence do not apply at the ICTY, and hearsay is admissible, as Judge Orie noted in the very same breath: "What words were exactly used by the attackers if the witness has not been there, of course, is hearsay. I'm not saying hearsay is not admissible in the Tribunal." *Ibid.* 151: 5–7 (J. Orie).

113 *Ibid.* 148: 11.

Croatia.[114] Thus this insult, when directed at Babić, implied that Babić was a stooge, a Croatian stand-in, and a traitor to the Serb cause. Kovačević went on to testify that this term was used in pamphlets distributed criticizing Babić, and that Kovačević had personally heard it used, both during negotiations between political factions, and, incidentally, by Biljana Plavšić in public addresses.

Throughout his testimony, Kovačević tried to give accounts regarding which officials (and from which entities) were present at which meetings, to show the complexity of loyalties, and to give voice to the overwhelming atmosphere of fear and uncertainty during the period. Yet Kovačević, whose account reads as reasoned and articulate, failed to reach his audience as a witness: he was repeatedly interrupted, scolded, redirected, told to go faster or roughly instructed only to answer the immediate question either by counsel or by the presiding judge.[115] At one point, defense counsel began "cross-examining" him like a hostile witness (regarding the precision of a date he'd given) until the presiding judge asked counsel to stop.[116] Kovačević's testimony was repeatedly subjected to a rigorous evidentiary standard inappropriate to the proceedings,[117] where both witnesses were appearing for the OTP and the defense, and where facts were "stipulated," meaning they were not in contention. This also set Kovačević's testimony apart from the other witness, Dr. Lončar, who testified to "facts" outside his realm of expertise and for which, by his own admission, there was no scientific support.[118] Furthermore, there is a very stark contrast between the reception and treatment of Kovačević's testimony and testimony made by witnesses at Plavšić's sentencing

[114] "The word Zupan [*sic*], under the circumstances, meant traitor, a traitor of national interest because its meaning derives from the fact that the Republic of Croatia determined its territorial organizations by establishing counties as administrative units. And a Zupan [*sic*] or a prefect is somebody who is the head of this administrative unit in Croatia." Babić April 2 Sentencing Hearing pp. 181:24–182:4.

[115] *Ibid.* p. 152.

[116] Babić April 1 Sentencing Hearing p. 167.

[117] See, e.g., Judge Orie's discount of "speculation" regarding the attack on Babić: "I mean, this witness has testified that he heard from others, including Mr. Babic, that Mr. Babic was attacked in his apartment, and I do not think that on the basis of his knowledge, unless there is a good foundation for it, we could hear any further evidence in that respect. Please proceed." *Ibid.* p. 148 (J. Orie).

[118] Dr. Lončar, who was qualified to speak to his experience treating trauma victims in Croatia, also testified to the reception of Babić's admission of guilt:

> I've talked mostly to Serbs from urban areas, but I also had contacts with Serbs who have returned to their homes. This work was done in mixed villages, mostly in Banovina area. I went to those villages. I talked to people of Serb ethnicity there. What I can say, and let me repeat once again that no official statistics was done. There was no official record-taking or research, so this is all a result of the exchanges in these interviews, but what I can say is that I have not met any Serbs who had a negative attitude towards the admission of guilt of Mr. Babic. What I also noticed among Serbs in Croatia is that there was a certain feeling of relief among them. The admission of guilt of Mr. Babic and the message that it sent was that we should focus on universal human emotions and treat it as such. This led to the fact that the Serbs do not feel a collective guilt now but, rather, this guilt has been individualised and attributed to a person.

Ibid. p. 112.

hearing, where, for example, Elie Wiesel "testified" by video link, read a prepared statement, and took no questions.[119]

More significantly, in terms of the capacity of the process to perform a socially constitutive role, Kovačević's testimony spoke to the formulation and consequences of nationalist politics, and in this way followed the argument offered by transitional justice advocates in terms of "truths" the ICTY might promote. The *Babić* chamber was evidently interested in the social implications of Babić's admission of guilt in other contexts, and the bench peppered Dr. Lončar with questions about how Babić's "individualization of guilt" might impact other Serbs who felt guilty (or whether Babić was being "scapegoated");[120] whether taking statements from victims was actually therapeutic;[121] and what factors, external or internal, might have "changed" Babić (into someone with extreme, nationalist views).[122] Yet as regards Mr. Kovačević's testimony regarding circumstantial pressures and contexts, the trial chamber's dismissal of this line of argument was complete: it did not reference Kovačević's testimony even once in its judgment.[123]

In closing arguments, the *Babić* defense counsel specifically invited the tribunal to contrast Babić and Plavšić. Babić's defense counsel was seemingly trying to consider the nationalist motivations, and later redemptions, of both defendants, as a way of addressing the tribunal's larger, to some extent unofficial, reconciliation mandate. To this end, Babić's defense reminded the chamber to consider public statements regarding nationalist rhetoric and "the fuel [they] fed to the fire," and invited comparison with Plavšić, saying, "She said horrible, horrible things, racist things, ugly things."[124] Counsel continued, "You ask the Prosecution to provide you with the worst of what Mr. Babić said ... So that if that is a legitimate mitigating factor ... it should weigh more heavily in his favor, the nature of what was said."[125] Despite floundering through the legal categories, Babić's counsel nevertheless tried to hold the substance of the comparison:

> With respect to [Plavšić's and Babić's] role, various degrees of responsibility, in paragraph 1 of the Plastic [*sic*] judgment, the Court found that she embraced and supported the objective of ethnic cleansing. I guess Mr. Babić did, but not in exactly the same way and under the same circumstances. *And I don't know how to articulate*

119 Plavšić December 17 Sentencing Hearing Transcript pp. 455–461.

120 Babić April 1 Sentencing Hearing Transcript p. 116 (Judge El Mahdi).

121 *Ibid.* p. 118 (Judge Orie: he requested a reading list on the topic).

122 *Ibid.* pp. 121–125 (Judge Orie). This exchange is perhaps the most problematic, as the witness is asked to opine on what impacted Babić, even though the witness does not know Babić. Dr. Lončar nevertheless, albeit cautiously, opined that propaganda turned Babić into an extremist.

123 The only reference the judgment makes to Kovačević is descriptive, noting he testified "about Babić's personality and positions at the time of the commission of the crimes." Babić Sentencing Judgment para 15.

124 Babić April 2 Sentencing Hearing p. 242.

125 *Ibid.*

> *that any better, but I think that the Tribunal ought to have a sense of that at this point.*[126]

Defense counsel's plea for the tribunal to "have a sense" is precisely what was lost (a loss that is clearly felt), in these judgments.

D *Tying* Plavšić *and* Babić *to ICL's Legitimizing Discourse*

This chapter has argued that the *Plavšić* and *Babić* cases are meaningfully divergent and cannot be reconciled, particularly as regards the role the ICTY is meant to play in social reconstruction, and the significance of defendant cooperation with respect to that role. Does the chapter get it right? There are many distinctions between the *Plavšić* and *Babić* cases, any of which undoubtedly influenced the chambers' deliberations and judgments. Biljana Plavšić came first in time and was a *bona fide* public figure whose plea represented a change of heart (as regards fighting the charges) after nearly two years of defying the tribunal; Milan Babić was an unemployed refugee in Serbia who prostrated himself before the tribunal before even being indicted. The *Plavšić* sentencing hearing was an international event, attended by some of the top names and key players in the rarified world of transitional justice and public diplomacy, and this would have added glamour and historical import to the proceedings; Babić's sentencing hearing featured only two witnesses, both private individuals from the former Yugoslavia decidedly devoid of glitz. Defense counsel, and even the bench, in the *Plavšić* hearing appeared more organized, thoughtful, and attentive than their counterparts in the *Babić* chamber.[127] In the *Babić* process, Babić's strongest proponent at all times was the prosecutor, whose strongest loyalty, in turn, was to tribunal doctrine.

Realists like Jeremy Rabkin (2007) might argue that the *Plavšić* and *Babić* cases prove nothing further than the political impetus fueling ICL: Plavšić was useful to the international community as a model, Babić was not, and there is little more explanation required. Under this account, one might also note that the ICTY needed to justify itself and its practice in relation to Plavšić precisely *because* she was an infamous public figure and much was at stake. Yet if ICL (and law generally) should be read as politics (i.e., interest) by another name, this does not answer the query as to why the rationales offered through the two judgments are so divergent. Why the distinctions in terms of their criminal charges (intent), and the varied applications of

126 *Ibid.* (emphasis added).

127 For example, Plavšić's counsel seems to have succeeded, in his opening and closing addresses, in constructing the intellectual approach the bench followed in its sentencing judgment. One of Babić's lawyers, by contrast, made his closing statement extemporaneously ("Your Honour, I have not written a speech. I'm more used to working from notes and speaking rather extemporaneously, so that I cannot tell you [how long the intervention will be]. I have not timed it.") (*Ibid.* p. 189). This rambling, disjointed intervention addressed the question of "how crimes against humanity can occur" (*Ibid.* p. 234) and likely damaged Babić's case by attempting to compare him to the "sham" of remorse offered by Biljana Plavšić (*Ibid.* pp. 241–244).

aggravating and mitigating circumstances? Law's legitimacy derives from its distinction from politics: why risk muting that distinction through a muted doctrinal consideration? Realist explanations cannot adequately respond to diverging rationales, offered by careful and invested doctrinal professionals, in the *Plavšić* and *Babić* cases.

In another vein, in a recent article, Saira Mohamed (2015) tries to marry the conflicting rationales of ICL through a theory she terms "aspirational expressivism." Mohamed argues that because international criminal tribunals are sites of storytelling (the narrative value espoused by Shklar, and adopted by proponents of transitional justice), they provide ideal sites to set forth aspirations for human behavior, which is, she argues, what legitimizes criminal law. Mohamed sets out to answer the paradox that domestic criminal law addresses deviance, but that international criminal law often adjudicates acts that are not deviant, because they represent a new social norm, or because they represent responses that any normal person would have if subjected to the same circumstances. Thus for Mohamed, the diverging rationales offered in *Plavšić* and *Babić* are not irreconcilable, but rather meet as criminal justice processes are put in service to didactic aims (her "aspirational expressionism").

As with realist explanations, however, Mohamed's theory fits *Plavšić*, but cannot explain *Babić*. Babić seems to have made the journey ICL aspires to express: from nationalist mouthpiece to remorseful humanitarian, Babić's trajectory is an example of the very truths that transitional justice theory advocates as advantageous and essential. Where Plavšić's story tells none of the abstract truths "judicial romanticism" presages for international criminal tribunals (Forsythe 2006), Babić's story illustrates many of them.

Proponents of international criminal tribunals as transitional justice mechanisms argue that trying individual criminal cases can have wide social benefits. Such benefits arguably extend to teaching respect for the rule of law, reconstructing divided societies, and enabling peace. Although this school is contemporaneously referred to as "judicial romanticism" it has deep theoretical roots reaching at least as far back as the work of Hart, Raz, and Dworkin, all of whom advocated law's capacity to articulate, and construct, social and moral norms. Moreover, given the steep price tag that international criminal tribunals carry, and their fragile existence outside the power structure of any particular state, there is pressure to justify such tribunals' efficacy in sweeping terms. Here we find the *Plavšić* case, where Biljana Plavšić is a vehicle for demonstrating Western liberalism's triumph over nationalism, a didactic "preaching" in the tradition of Shklar's argument for the value of political trials. Other defenders of ICL, however, insist that ICL cannot and should not be assessed outside of its own careful application and articulation of recognized legal norms. This positivist school assesses ICL jurisprudence in terms of its own substance, and rejects any wider social measurement to evaluate ICL legitimacy. Here morality is protected through consistent, constant application of norms. Here we find Babić, a vehicle for punishment through a strict criminal justice formulation to his process.

CONCLUSION

This chapter has argued that divergences in judicial reasoning and outcome in the *Plavšić* and *Babić* cases illustrate one of the book's central arguments regarding the paradoxical clash of legitimacy in ICL between natural law and criminal justice legitimization. Yet some might query, do the divergences visited here matter? If two Balkan leaders most internationals have never heard of were incongruously handled, or sentenced, what impact does that ultimately have on the practice of ICL? The ICTY is universally unpopular among its Balkan audiences, and there is no data that indicates that Babić's heartfelt plea for tolerance in the face of nationalism mattered one whit more, or less, than Plavšić's lukewarm endorsement of Western liberal policies. The process of plea bargaining itself would appear to be confusing and foreign to a Balkan audience, which already overwhelmingly ignores material produced by the ICTY, gleaning its information regarding war crimes prosecutions largely from local media.[128]

International criminal law remains susceptible to the challenge identified by Koskenniemi (2002) in his now classic article, where he notes the thin line between punishing violations of law versus punishing what can come to be seen, retroactively, as bad political decisions. Proponents of liberalism hold rule of law as a method or a process for producing rights-respecting state institutions. In the divergences between the *Plavšić* and *Babić* judgments, we see the juxtaposition of rule-of-law processes with rule-of-law outcomes. Only the first is a meaningful category capable of delivering on law's socially constitutive potential.

[128] See, e.g., OSCE survey 2011.

Conclusion

Towards "ICL 3G"

Model(ing) Justice challenges the operationalization of international humanitarian norms through international criminal tribunals (ICTs). It develops two theories to make this challenge: the first, the *international criminal justice template*, is an ideal type designed to demonstrate the illiberal construct of international criminal-law institutions. The second, the *problem of non-derogation*, critiques ICTs from within a liberal order, as violating rule-of-law norms. In support of these theories, *Model(ing) Justice* has explored numerous examples of International Criminal Tribunal for the former Yugoslavia (ICTY) case law against the categories it articulates, as a means of assessing liberal/illiberal institutional practice. By articulating and applying the international criminal justice template and the problem of non-derogation, *Model(ing) Justice* offers theoretical tools for assessing ICTs as transitional justice mechanisms and operationalizing the core rights protected by international humanitarian law into international criminal law (ICL).

Of course, to be applied, international humanitarian law must be operationalized; that some of this development will be obtained through the work of tribunals is just as it should be. That these tribunals will err and require correction is the way of the world. And even ICTs as flawed as the ICTY confer benefits, none of which the analysis in this book would wish away. These benefits include convicting some violent, dangerous individuals who threatened the peace and well-being of their communities even after the war; setting norms regarding acceptable behavior and established rights; and bringing suffering and atrocity to world attention. One has only to consider Joshua Oppenheimer's stunning 2012 documentary *The Act of Killing* to see the potential impact of *not* challenging social violence. Oppenheimer documents a modern Indonesia run by those who perpetrated the massacres of more than one million of their countrymen in 1965. In this system, government criminality is legitimate: officials openly shake down merchants, list exploitation as a benefit of holding public office, and make a movie celebrating the violence they perpetrated. *The Act of Killing* demonstrates the argument underlying transitional justice, which is that "justice" is what the leader says it is (Teitel 2000; Sa'adah 2006) and liberal, democratic transition requires a move to new justice norms. The justice norms articulated by the post-1965 Indonesian regime are perverse by any Rawlsian or Kantian standard. International criminal tribunals, while flawed for the reasons explored in the previous chapters, still attempt to challenge the perversity of authoritarianism. The paradox of legitimizing their practice through the articulation of "progressive" law, and the problem of non-derogation, results in ICTs practicing their own sort of authoritarianism. There are nonetheless important distinctions in degree between the flawed, criminal Indonesian governance and the flawed, self-congratulatory neo-colonialism of ICTs.

Model(ing) Justice has shown how the ICTY, and other ICTs more generally, suffer a legitimacy deficit because they exact the social control of criminal law outside of the political constraint of a sovereign state. Thus legal and procedural deficits in ICTY practice are not "deviations" or anomalies, but rather indications of an underlying structural problem of ICTs. This disconnect has permitted the development of ICL in the flawed template of the IMT at Nuremberg, and results in substantive and procedural law that should best be understood as *post-rule of law*. Post-rule-of-law processes interrupt the imagined transitional justice goals afforded international criminal courts, foremost among them the construction of an "official history" as well as the modeling of political liberalism. If ICTs are perceived as more political than legal – if they remain, as they are at present, institutions to which more powerful countries subject less powerful countries, and refuse to subject themselves[1] – then the ICT movement will fail. Such a failure would imperil the human rights ideology paired with (though existing separately from) ICL, and would endanger the project of the recognition of non-derogable human rights as a whole. It is thus imperative that those interested in the advancement of Kantian justice norms through the operationalization of international humanitarian law begin work towards a third generation of ICL, "ICL 3G." ICL 3G would build on the significant achievement of articulating prevention of violations of core rights (first-generation ICL, the legacy element of the Nuremberg Principles), and respond to the pushback of second-generation ICL (the analysis offered by *Model(ing) Justice* constitutes one element of this pushback). ICL 3G should focus, as all celebrated operationalizations of rule-of-law liberalism do, on liberal processes, rather than imagined liberal outcomes.

Those evaluating ICTs generally view them either negatively (dismissing them as "political") or positively (celebrating them as moral). For international relations theorists, ICTs are often discussed as expensive, unwieldy, and ineffective mechanisms to implement political goals (Rabkin 2007). For proponents of ICL practice, ICTs represent important landmarks in liberalism's justice project, and evidence of humanity's "progress."[2] Law has a "grammar" (Koskenniemi 2002) that distinguishes

[1] One prominent example is the US refusal to join the ICC.

[2] Teitel (2012), for example, refers to ICL as "Humanity's Law."

it from other fields. Law is ultimately inseparable from politics, because it exists to serve a sovereign (Shapiro 1986).

Model(ing) Justice has examined how to properly configure the role of ICTs. What should ICTs do/achieve? What designates an ICT "a success"? And, of course, planted within such considerations are questions of audience and aim – success for whom, and doing what? These questions impact the perceived legitimacy of ICTs, and legitimacy is a crucial axis for ICTs. On the one hand, legitimacy is structurally distinct for ICTs. Where consent is represented by office and process (Shapiro 1986) at domestic law, such consent is significantly attenuated at an international level (Scheingold [1964] 2004; Klabbers 2015.) On the other hand, the legitimacy produced by legal pronouncements is one of the imagined values added through the use of courts (as opposed to truth commissions, grassroots organizing, etc.) as transitional justice mechanisms. *Model(ing) Justice* has examined the systemic, cultural distinctions between the common and the civil law that challenge even legal professionals operating across systems to understand procedure across the divide. It has further detailed the objective deficits in the hybrid procedure that has evolved before the ICTY. Finally, *Model(ing) Justice* has made the argument, based in social contract theory, that without a discursive connection between an institution, the peoples subject to its mandate, and the sovereigns that it serves, an institution is structurally imbalanced and cannot therefore avoid growing towards an unjust jurisprudence. In the case of the ICTY, such injustice is apparent in its imbalanced procedure as well as its articulation of substantive law, such as its joint criminal enterprise jurisprudence.

Model(ing) Justice begins its analysis of contemporary transitional justice with the International Military Tribunal (IMT) at Nuremberg because that is where the field of transitional justice itself locates its own foundation (Teitel 2003). The IMT at Nuremberg was many things in 1946: it was contested, innovative, massive, boring. As Chapter 1 showed, the *actual* IMT at Nuremberg differs significantly from the *mythologized* IMT at Nuremberg. In the intervening years, much of what was problematic with the IMT at Nuremberg as a rule-of-law institution has disappeared from the discussion of the IMT at Nuremberg among proponents of ICL. For such proponents, what remains is the rosy institutional fact that the Allied powers established a trial instead of erecting a scaffold (although a skeptic might replace "instead of" with "before"). Of course, for ICL, the IMT at Nuremberg is but the beginning of the movement. As Chapter 1 outlined, the IMT at Nuremberg founded a vigorous international humanitarian law campaign, with the Geneva Conventions of 1949 and the Convention on the Prevention of Genocide (1949) following it. The IMT at Nuremberg also gave rise to the modern ideology of transitional justice, and placed ICTs as central mechanisms for its realization.

Chapter 2 described the obstacle to operationalizing "progressive" ICL as the problem of non-derogation. Legitimizing its content through an ideology of rights recognition and protection and its practice through the criminological logic of social control, ICL emerges as a kind of strict liability. This doctrinal inflexibility makes it difficult for ICL to perform the second-order functions identified in the international criminal justice template, namely establishing accepted versions of events and facilitating political reconciliation.

Chapters 3 through 6, respectively, examined the work of the ICTY against each of the three categories that comprise the *international criminal justice template*. One of *Model(ing) Justice*'s basic goals is to examine structural hurdles that impede local acceptance of the narrative pronounced by international criminal courts. As discussed in Chapter 3, civil-law audiences (which comprise most of the globe, and all of the Balkans) are unaccustomed to viewing trials as spaces where guilt is discovered; rather, in civil-law systems, trials should showcase the work already conducted by the state. The Kelsonian theoretical underpinnings of the civil law restrict court capacity regarding lawmaking; at civil law, law is made by legislatures and implemented by courts.[3] Furthermore, the rights discourse prominent at common law, where courts are charged with articulating and ensuring fundamental rights, is much more muted at civil law, where courts are mostly legal implementers, not inventors.

THE FUNCTIONS OF ICTS: DOES THE INTERNATIONAL CRIMINAL JUSTICE TEMPLATE GET IT RIGHT?

What Should We Measure?

The "Nuremberg legacy" – the belief that ICTs have the capacity to institute liberal values and respect for human rights – was originally articulated by the victorious Allied powers, most particularly the United States. The "myth of Nuremberg" centered on the value of holding individuals accountable for designated international crimes (defined in the Charter for the IMT at Nuremberg as (i) crimes against peace, (ii) war crimes, (iii) crimes against humanity, and (iv) conspiracy to commit these three crimes) in order to address the destructive phenomenon of collective guilt; under this framework, the most responsible individuals would be identified and punished, and the population at large could move forward, having affirmed the guilt of certain individuals and having reaffirmed their own humanity by doing so.

In the decades following World War II, the Nuremberg myth/legacy came to be professed by the vanquished themselves. This unified narrative of World War II, wherein both victorious and vanquished peoples recount the same version of events and their significance, forms the centerpiece of political reconciliation. Political reconciliation makes it possible for once-opposed states to cooperate in the international realm, regardless of the antipathies or mistrust still felt by individuals within

[3] Shapiro's (1986) prototype correctly contests this; regardless, the theoretical prejudice against judicial "lawmaking" remains central to the civil law.

nations towards individuals of other nations.[4] Political reconciliation is the centerpiece of transitional justice ideology, in so far as such reconciliation is generally equated with peace (Crocker 2003; Villa-Vicencio 2004; Bloomfield 2006).

It is undeniable that Germany (and Japan) experienced political reconciliation as well as profound political change following World War II, as they moved from autocratic, rights-denying regimes to democratic, rights-articulating ones. It is also true that German (and Japanese) citizens were subjected to ICL prosecutions by the international occupying powers. As explored in Chapter 1, however, overwhelming evidence suggests that the actual journey from autocracy to democracy, and from a rights-denying to a rights-protecting regime, owes little to the work or example of the IMT at Nuremberg (and even less to the IMT at Tokyo). In spite of volumes of compelling evidence to the contrary, however, the "myth of Nuremberg" continues to dominate mainstream discussion of the capacity of ICTs to function as transitional justice mechanisms.

Proponents of the use of the ICTY to effect reconciliation argue that the tribunal's narrative can function as a palliative to the nationalist politics and discourse that began the war and continue in its aftermath (Akhavan 1998; Wilson 2011). This unified, and thereby unifying, narrative lies at the heart of a political definition of reconciliation. Chapter 6 has argued that both the ICTY's development and application of legal categories regarding remorse, and its instrumentalized treatment of defendants before the tribunal, interfere with its capacity to convincingly articulate for a Balkan audience its unifying version of events (not just facts, but also, and more importantly, a legal frame to understand and accept individuals' criminality).

ARE THESE THE RIGHT FUNCTIONS?

Model(ing) Justice argues that the significance of ICTs lies in their use as transitional justice mechanisms. As such, ICTs are proposed as responses to instances of mass violence, intractable conflict, or pervasive social upheaval for the numerous secondary functions they are said to perform while in the process of (and indeed through the process of) adjudicating individual cases.

Many proponents of the ICTY claim a restricted role/standard for the ICTY. Some believe the ICTY's role is simply to "work properly," a process-based argument that locates the institution's "success" in a consideration of the institution's work in its own terms. The most extreme of such arguments locate "success" in terms of mere existence (Meron 1997; Cassese 1998b; Arbour 1999a). This school of ICTY defenders recognizes that deterrence, distributive justice, punishment, respect for rule of law, and rehabilitation are all recognized tenets of (domestic) criminal law. They protest, however, that no one court or one court decision can necessarily achieve all

4 Political reconciliation, a collective recognition, should be distinguished from the individual measure of "forgiveness," although forgiveness and reconciliation are often conflated in transitional justice considerations. See Chapter 6.

these aims, but rather that courts, acting correctly, make these aims possible. Such narrow, case-by-case, procedural arguments relating to the ICTY's mandate are typically raised in response to the criticism or criticisms, that the institution has not effectuated either reconciliation, deterrence, or retribution, at least not to any significant degree.

On the face of it, of course, ICTs are charged simply with adjudicating individual cases. There is no cost–benefit analysis that could ever condone the use of ICTs simply for the purpose of adjudicating the guilt or innocence of the few individuals who have been (and who foreseeably will be) brought before them, however.[5] The IMT at Nuremberg worked for nearly a year to try two dozen individuals; the ICTY and the International Criminal Tribunal for Rwanda (ICTR) are said to have consumed up to 25 percent of the UN's annual budget,[6] and over the course of two decades have between them produced fewer than one hundred convictions; the International Criminal Court has been in operation nearly two decades and has produced a handful of verdicts, at significant expense.

Furthermore, even if ICT function is more appropriately assessed against a simple adjudicatory standard (following Arendt [1963/2010] and Fuller [1969] who argue that a court's job is to hear the case before it), ICTs retain the criminal definition problems highlighted by the inherent strict liability of the problem of non-derogation.

ARE THESE CRITIQUES BASED IN UNREASONABLE STANDARDS OR ON UNATTAINABLE IDEALS?

Some theorists have postulated that "fair enough," rather than "fairest of all," is sufficient for international criminal trials (Warbrick 1998). Frédéric Mégret (2009) advances a considered discourse arguing that international tribunals are "different" and should not be held to the same procedural standards as domestic criminal justice institutions. *Model(ing) Justice* argues the opposite: international criminal courts are more sensitive to procedural anomalies than domestic courts. This is because, in the absence of consent, legitimacy is built on office and procedure. With court legitimacy subject to them, procedural standards should be higher, not lower, than what might obtain domestically.

From the other side, is identifying the international criminal justice template the same as suggesting that ICTs be assessed against a panacea ("straw man") standard?

5 Augustine Brannigan is currently conducting research comparing the costs of large, multi-year domestic trials with international criminal trials: he is interested, among other things, in determining whether the cost–benefit losses he sees as constituting the surest proof of the dismantlement of the ICL system (Brannigan 2011) also obtain for complex domestic criminal litigation. Presentation question and answer, *Law & Society Association Annual Conference* (Hawai'i May 2012), notes on file with author.

6 This figure is cited in Brannigan 2011 and has been confirmed by ICTY officials, who nonetheless contest that it is "not the whole story" because the ICTY, for example, also receives considerable funding from outside the UN. Author interviews, The Hague, November 2012. To date, the ICTY has cost more than $3 billion.

Model(ing) Justice shows that sophisticated, recent accounts of ICL institutions (Subotić 2009; Nettelfield 2010; Wilson 2011; Clark 2014), which of course would dispute the notion that ICTs *by themselves* produce good governance, reconciliation, or accepted histories, nonetheless continue to evaluate ICT capacity in the shadow of the expectation that ICTs contribute meaningfully to these goals. As with Weber's ideal types, there is value in identifying the prototype because it continues to govern expectations even of the most sophisticated observers and because it has expectation-setting value that is not recognized by many works that consider the transitional justice or governance capacity of ICTs. *Model(ing) Justice* argues that the elements considered as essential to assessing ICT capacity continue to define our expectations for ICTs, in spite of the empirical, theoretical, and historical evidence challenging ICT capacity in these areas.

DOES MODEL(ING) JUSTICE CHERRY-PICK ITS CASES?

The cases which have been examined herein, with the goal of assessing the ICTY's work against the proposed prototype of the international criminal justice template, are discouraging, and perhaps even shocking, but they are not atypical or unrepresentative of the overall work, practice, and record of the ICTY or, indeed, other ICTs. Some of the cases examined in these pages are even the subject of ICTY celebration. For example, the ICTY website highlights *Kvočka et al.*, the case examined in Chapter 4, as an example of the ICTY's accomplishments.[7] Recall that the named defendant in *Kvočka et al.*, Miroslav Kvočka, was a Bosnian Serb police officer who received a seven-year sentence from the ICTY for his role in co-perpetrating a joint criminal enterprise, which in this case was the prison camp itself. The ICTY celebrates the case for "establish-[ing] that a 'hellish orgy of persecution' occurred in the Omarska, Keraterm and, Trnopolje camps of northwestern Bosnia."[8] *Model(ing) Justice*, in contrast, has examined *Kvočka et al.* for the problematic facts of the case and its troubling development regarding standards of criminal intent.

FINAL THOUGHTS: WHERE DO WE GO FROM HERE?

The development of human rights law constitutes one of the revolutionary advances of the last century. With the Geneva Conventions and the establishment of prominent human rights enforcement mechanisms – not only the advisory bodies of the United Nations[9] but more significantly the toothy courts of supranational (though

7 www.icty.org/sections/AbouttheICTY

8 *Ibid.*

9 See, for example, the Human Rights Council enacted in 2006 by the United Nations, which evaluates situations involving breaches of human rights and makes recommendations: www2.ohchr.org/english/bodies/hrcouncil/

still limited) jurisdiction[10] – a revolution in politics, law, and statecraft has been effected. Nation states, sovereign since the Peace of Westphalia, have acknowledged in theory a higher sovereignty in the rights of man, and have begun to put this concept into practice. Likewise, international law, which for centuries regulated only interstate conduct, has begun to manifest at the level of the individual, both by circumscribing governments' actions towards their citizens, and by holding individuals accountable for breaches of humanitarian law.

Consider the corpses of dozens of women and children smoldering in the remains of a house which had been padlocked from the outside before being set alight,[11] or the bodies of men and boys, blindfolded and manacled, who had been shot cleanly through the head at close range.[12] These are unequivocally criminal scenes. There is no context that can justify them, and no system in the world under which they would be legal. Someone (or many someones) brought these events to pass; often, someone higher up the chain of authority authorized the events, or encouraged them, or failed to discourage them when others committed similar crimes, and this, too, seems readily identifiable as a crime. International criminal law begins with one deceptively simple principle: punish the guilty who might otherwise, due to circumstances partly connected to their own violence and criminality, go free. The moral and political power of this principle – to expand the reach of justice and to combat impunity – has propelled several ad hoc ICTs in the twentieth century, beginning with the tribunals following the devastating violence of World War II (the IMT at Nuremberg and the International Military Tribunal for the Far East at Tokyo), re-engaging after a long period dominated by the Cold War with the ICTY (1993) and its sister institution for Rwanda, the ICTR (1994), and culminating in the foundation of "the court for the twenty-first century" (Ellis & Goldstone 2008), the International Criminal Court (2002).

While the twentieth century witnessed mass violence on a global scale unparalleled in history, it also heralded a burgeoning global awareness of standards of behavior grouped under the heading of human rights, and the potential power of this awareness should not be downplayed. Although it remains uncertain whether institutions promising to hold perpetrators of gross violations of international humanitarian law responsible for their actions have prevented, or will prevent, crimes from occurring, it is absolutely clear that reports of the 8,000 Muslim men killed in the remote wooded area of Bosnia in July 1995 have circled the globe, and that those reports have connected the name of what was once an inconsequential Bosnian village with the concepts of genocide and international judicial retribution. In the wake of this public, judicial response to the massacre

10 This list would include the International Court of Justice, the International Criminal Court, and regional courts such as the European Court of Justice (European Union), European Court of Human Rights (the Council of Europe), the Inter-American Court of Human Rights, and ECOWAS.

11 *Prosecutor* v. *Milan Lukić and Sredoje Lukić*, Case No. IT-98-32/1 (July 20, 2009).

12 *Prosecutor* v. *Radislav Krstić*, Case No. IT-98-33 (August 2, 2001).

at Srebrenica, it has become harder to imagine that any would-be international humanitarian law violator, no matter how remotely located, could remain unaware that their actions could be construed as a gross violation of humanitarian law, and subject to punishment as such. As the trial chamber said in the *Nikolić* sentencing judgment (2003, para 88):

> as international criminal law has moved from "law in theory" to "law in practice," the principles of international humanitarian law have taken hold to the extent that in the face of such widespread and massive crimes a person being called to participate in the criminal enterprise *might* consider the Geneva Conventions and the consequences of disregarding the principles contained therein.

While this growth in the awareness and import attached to human rights law is impossible to measure in quantitative terms, it may perhaps be inferred from the growth in number, size, and strength of institutions charged with applying universal humanitarian norms. There is no question that the ICTY, and the global ICL project it has advanced, has made a considerable impact in human rights norms and awareness. Rather, the salient contemporary question posed by *Model(ing) Justice* concerns the *way* the ICTY, and other ICTs, impact human rights.

The test case of the former Yugoslavia, the target of the most sustained ICT transitional justice project in history, animates our consideration of the possibilities and pitfalls of putting ICL practice and institutions in service to social reconstruction. At a time when ICL is faltering, where an increasing discourse challenges ICL in its own rule-of-law terms, the lessons learned regarding the illiberal growth of ICL within the ICTY's jurisprudence can be marshaled to reconsider the field and its practices. Rule-of-law practice is a process, not an outcome (Bickel 1977), and this book examines the processes developed through twenty years of ICTY jurisprudence that have led to the subpar transitional justice outcomes evidenced throughout the former Yugoslavia. But if the ICTY is not the *model* justice that rule-of-law liberalism demands, and if the justice *modeled* by the ICTY has been fundamentally illiberal, the aim of the book remains to *perfect the promise of* ICL through an engagement with process. This will entail a process that respects legality, predictability, and established rights, and is critical of how the actors within and outside of it shape its dictates.

APPENDIX A

ICTY Prosecutions as of June 2018[1]

[1] See www.icty.org for complete information on cases.

Case Number	Case "in a Nutshell"	Defendants[2]	Procedural Outcome and Sentence
IT-94–1	"Prijedor" 7(1)[3] JCE: willful killing; murder; torture	Duško Tadić (BS) – president of local board of SDS	Trial (7/14/1997): 20 years Appeal (7/15/1999): 20 years Trial II (11/11/1999) (9 additional counts): 25 years Appeal (1/26/2000): 20 years – Early release 7/2008
IT-94–2**	"Sušica Camp" persecutions; rape; murder	Dragan Nikolić (BS) – commander of Sušica camp	Sentencing judgment (12/18/2003) (plea bargain): 23 years Sentencing appeal (2/4/2005): 20 years Early release 8/2013
~~IT-94-3~~	"Prijedor"	Goran Borovnica (BS)	Proceedings terminated, accused died before transfer to ICTY
IT-94–4		Željko Mejakić Močila Gruban Dušan Knežević	Joined IT-95–8/1
IT-94–5		Radovan Karadžić Ratko Mladić	See IT-95–18 re Karadžić See IT-09–92 re Mladić

(continued)

[2] Defendants' ethnicities and/or side they fought for, where different, denoted as Croat (C); Serb (S); Bosnian Croat (BC); Bosnian Serb (BS); Bosnian Muslim (Bosniak) (B); Kosovar Albanian (KA); Macedonian (M). Other abbreviations, and color-coding, are defined at the end of this appendix.

[3] Article 7(1) of ICTY Statute regarding "commission."

(continued)

Case Number	Case "in a Nutshell"	Defendants	Procedural Outcome and Sentence
IT-95–8**	"Keraterm Camp" (Prijedor, BiH) indictment charged genocide, due to alleged massacre of over 120 men in Room 3 at the camp; reduced to "persecutions" with plea bargain	Duško Sikirica (BS) – commander of security at camp Damir Došen (BS) – shift leader at Keraterm camp June–August 1992 Dragan Kolundžija (BS) – shift commander at Keraterm camp June–July 1992 Charges withdrawn: Nikica Janjić (deceased); Dragan Kondić; Goran Lajić; Dragomir Šaponja; Neđeljko Timarac	Sentencing judgment (11/13/2001) (plea bargain all 3) – Sikirica: 15 years Early release 6/2010 – Došen: 5 years Early release 2/2003 – Kolundžija: 3 years Early release 12/2001
IT-95–8/1		Dušan Fustar Predrag Banović Dušan Knežević Nenad Banović	See IT-02–65 and IT-02–65/1

IT-95–9	"Bosanski Šamac" (prison camp) 7(1) JCE: persecutions	Blagoje Simić, MD (BS) – president of Municipal Board of SDP, Serb Crisis Staff (highest-ranking civilian in municipality) Miroslav Tadić (BS) – in TD Simo Zarić (BS) – in TD	Trial (10/17/2003) – Simić: 17 years – Tadić: 8 years Early release 11/2004 – Zarić: 6 years Early release 1/2004 Appeal (11/28/2006) – Simić: 15 years (reduced) Early release (UK) 3/2011 – Tadić and Zarić: sentence unchanged
IT-95–9/1**	"Bosanski Šamac" (prison camp) persecutions	Stevan Todorović (BS) – chief of police in Bosanski Šamac	Sentencing judgment (7/31/2001) (plea bargain): 10 years – Early release 6/2005 – Died 9/2006
IT-95–9/2**	"Bosanski Šamac" (prison camp) torture	Milan Simić (BS) – member of BS crisis staff	Sentencing judgment (10/17/2002) (plea bargain): 5 years – Early release 11/2003
IT-95–10**	"Brčko" (Luka camp) genocide; murder; plunder; inhumane acts	Goran Jelisić (BS) – acted under authority of Brčko police	Trial (12/14/1999) (plea bargain): 40 years (Trial went forward on genocide charge: acquitted‡) Appeal (7/5/2001): sentence unchanged Request for review (5/2/2002): dismissed

(continued)

(continued)

Case Number	Case "in a Nutshell"	Defendants	Procedural Outcome and Sentence
IT-95–10/1**	"Brčko" murder (admitted to killing at least 10 people); rape; humiliating and degrading treatment	Ranko Češić (BS) – member of TD; became BS Police Reserve Corps member	Sentencing judgment (3/11/2004) (plea bargain): 18 years – Early release (DK) 5/2014
IT-95–11	"Shelling of Zagreb" "RSK" 7(1) JCE: persecutions; murder	Milan Martić (CS) – president, SAO Krajina	Trial (9/27/2007): 35 years Appeal (10/8/2008): affirmed Serving sentence in Estonia
IT-95–12**	"Stupni Do" (37 villagers killed); Vareš (looting, detaining 250 Muslim men, sexual assaults) 7(1) & 7(3)[4] murder; inhumane treatment; extensive destruction	Ivica Rajić (BC) – HVO commander in Central Bosnia	Sentencing judgment (5/8/2006) (plea bargain): 12 years – Early release 8/2011
IT-95–13/1	"Vukovar Hospital" (massacre of 200 people from hospital at Ovcara)	Mile Mrkšić (S) – colonel in JNA Veselin Šljivančanin (S) – major in JNA	Trial (9/27/2007) – Mrkšić: 20 years – Radić: acquitted‡ – Šljivančanin: 5 years

4 Article 7(3) of the ICTY Statute regarding "commission."

	7(1) JCE: murder; torture; cruel treatment	Miroslav Radić (S) – captain in JNA ("Serbian Generals")	Appeal (5/5/2009) – Mrkšić: unchanged Died 8/2015 serving sentence in Portugal – Šljivančanin: 17 years (increased) Review judgment by the appeals chamber (12/8/2010) – Šljivančanin: 10 years (increased from TC; reduced from AC) – Early release 7/2011
~~IT-95-13a~~	"Vukovar Hospital" Murder; a+a	Slavko Dokmanović (S) – JNA and Serb paramilitary soldier	Captured by IFOR 6/27/1997. Committed suicide in custody (on eve of verdict) 6/1998
IT-95–14	"Lašva Valley" 7(1) JCE 7(3) CR	Tihomir Blaškić (BC) – colonel in HVO [charges withdrawn: Ivan Santić; Pero Skopljak; Zoran Martinić]	Trial (3/3/2000): 45 years. Appeal (7/29/2004): 9 years (reduced) Request for review (11/23/2006): dismissed – Early release (time served) 8/2004
IT-95–14/1	"Lašva Valley" 7(3) CR: Outrages on personal dignity; a+a	Zlatko Aleksovski (BC) – commander of prison facility at Kaonik	Trial (6/25/1999): 2.5 years; Appeal (3/24/2000): 7 years (increased) – Early release 11/2001
IT-95–14/2	"Lašva Valley" attack on Ahmići (100 civilians killed)	Dario Kordić (BC) – president of the HDZ-BiH (leading political figure)	Trial (2/26/2001) – Kordić: 25 years – Čerkez: 15 years

(continued)

(continued)

Case Number	Case "in a Nutshell"	Defendants	Procedural Outcome and Sentence
	7(1) individual criminal responsibility for common plan	Mario Čerkez (BC) – commander of Vitez Brigade of HVO	Appeal (12/17/2004) – Kordić: sentence affirmed Early release (Austria) 6/2014 – Čerkez: reduced to 6 years, released 12/2004, sentence served
IT-95–15	"Lašva Valley" murder	Zoran Marinić (BC) – military policeman for HVO	Proceedings terminated 10/2/2002, indictment withdrawn because low-level perpetrator, transferred to BiH Prosecutor, indicted 2012
IT-95–16	"Lašva Valley" attack on Ahmići (100 civilians killed) 7(1) JCE: murder; persecutions; inhumane acts	Zoran Kupreškić (BC) – member of HVO Vlatko Kupreškić (BC) – member of HVO Mirjan Kupreškić (BC) – member of HVO Vladimir Šantić (BC) – local commander of military police and "Jokers" Drago Josipović (BC) – member of HVO Šantići Dragan Papić	Trial (1/14/2000) – Josipović: 15 years – Šantić: 25 years – Z. Kupreškić: 10 years – M. Kupreškić: 8 years – V. Kupreškić: 6 years – Papić: acquitted‡ Appeal (10/23/2001) – Papić: affirmed – Josipović: 12 years (reduced) Early release 1/2006 – Šantić: 18 years (reduced)

		– member of HVO Marinko Katava [charges withdrawn]	Early release 2/2009 – Z. Kupreškić: acquitted‡ (reduced) – M. Kupreškić: acquitted‡ (reduced) – V. Kupreškić: acquitted‡ (reduced)
IT-95–17**	"Lašva Valley" murder; persecutions	Miroslav Bralo (BC) – member of "Jokers"	Sentencing judgment (12/7/2006) (plea bargain): 20 years Sentencing appeal (4/2/2007): confirmed sentence
IT-95–17/1	"Lašva Valley" torture; outrages upon personal dignity; rape	Anto Furundžija (BC) – local commander of "Jokers"	Trial (12/10/1998): 10 years Appeal (7/21/2000): affirmed – Early release 8/2004
IT-95–18*	"Srebrenica" and "Sarajevo" 7(1) JCE: genocide; crimes against humanity; violations of laws of war	Radovan Karadžić (BS) – president of RS	Trial (3/24/2016): 40 years On appeal before MICT
~~IT-96–20~~	"Sarajevo" inhumane acts (firing on civilian targets)	Đorđe Đukić (BS) – assistant commander of logistics VRS	– Released 4/1996 for ill health – Died 5/1996
IT-96–21	"Čelebići Camp" (established by Bosnian Muslim and Bosnian Croat forces; Bosnian Serbs imprisoned) 7(1) JCE: willfully causing suffering and killing	Zejnil Delalić (B) – coordinator of Bosnian Muslim and Croat forces; commander of First Tactical Group of Bosnian Army Hazim Delić (B) – deputy commander, then commander Bosnian Muslim forces	Trial (11/16/1998) – Mucić: 7 years – Delić: 20 years – Landžo: 15 years – Delalić: acquitted‡

(continued)

(continued)

Case Number	Case "in a Nutshell"	Defendants	Procedural Outcome and Sentence
	7(3) CR	Zdravko Mucić – commander Esad Landžo – guard	Appeal (2/20/2001) Mucić, Delić, Hazim, Landžo: sentencing remitted to trial chamber for possible adjustment Trial sentencing (10/9/2001) sentences adjusted: Sentencing appeal (4/8/2003) sentences unchanged: – Mucić: 9 years (increased) Early release 7/2003 – Delić: 18 years (reduced) Early release 6/2008 – Landžo: unchanged Early release 4/2006
IT-96–22**	"Pilica Farm" ("Srebrenica") murder (he personally killed approximately 70 people)	Dražen Erdemović (BC) – soldier working with VRS	Sentencing judgment (11/29/1996) (guilty plea): 10 years Appeal (10/7/1997) ruled that guilty plea not informed and new plea should be entered; Second sentencing (3/5/1998): 5 years – Early release 8/1999
IT-96–23 & IT-96–23/1	"Foča" torture, rape, enslavement	Dragoljub Kunarac (BS) – leader of VRS reconnaissance unit for local Foča Tactical Group	Trial (2/22/2001) – Kunarac: 28 years – Kovač: 20 years

		Radomir Kovač (BS) – subcommander of VRS and paramilitary Zoran Vuković (BS) – subcommander of VRS and paramilitary	– Vuković: 12 years Early release 3/2008 Appeal (6/12/2002): all sentences affirmed
IT-96–23/2**	"Foča" "Karaman's house" torture; rape	Dragan Zelenović (BS) – soldier and *de facto* military policeman in Foča	Sentencing judgment (4/4/2007) (plea bargain): 15 years Sentencing appeal (10/31/2007): affirmed
IT-96–23/2§	"Foča" "Karaman's house"§	Radovan Stanković Gojko Janković§	Case transferred to BiH court under 11 bis; Stanković convicted in 2006 and sentenced to 16 years; served sentence in Foca and escaped in 2007, re-apprehended 1/2012§
~~IT-97–24~~	"Prijedor" 7(1) JCE and 7(3) CR: genocide; extermination; murder; torture	Simo Drljaca (BS) – chief of police Prijedor Milan Kovačević (BS) – leading figure in Prijedor crisis staff	Drljaca killed during arrest 7/1997. Kovačević died 8/1998 while trial ongoing
IT-97–24	"Prijedor" (Omarska, Keraterm and Trnopolje camps) 7(1) JCE: persecutions; extermination; murder	Milomir Stakić (BS) – leading figure in Prijedor municipal government	Trial (7/31/2003): life imprisonment†; Appeal (3/22/2006): 40 years (reduced)
IT-97–25	"Foča" 266 disappearances from KP Dom	Milorad Krnojelac (BS) – commander of "KP Dom" detention camp	Trial (3/15/2002): 7.5 years Appeal (9/17/2003): 15 years (increased) – Early release 7/2009

(continued)

(continued)

Case Number	Case "in a Nutshell"	Defendants	Procedural Outcome and Sentence
IT-97–25/1§		Savo Todorović and Mitar Rašević§	Case transferred to BiH court under 11 bis; sentenced to 12.5 and 8.5 years respectively, on appeal, Rašević reduced to 7 years§
~~IT-97–27~~	"Sanski Most" murder; rape; inhumane acts	Željko Raznatović (S) – "Arkan"; leader of paramilitary group "Serbian Volunteer Guard" ["Arkan's Tigers"]	Murdered in mafia-related violence in Belgrade in 2000
IT-98–29	"Sarajevo" sniper attacks on civilians; Markale marketplace bombing 2/5/1994 (60 killed)	Stanislav Galić (BS) – commander of "Sarajevo Romanija Corps" of VRS	Trial (12/2/2003): 20 years Appeal (11/30/2006): life imprisonment†
IT-98–29/1	"Sarajevo" sniper attacks; use of modified air bombs; mortar attack on Markale marketplace 8/28/1995 (34 killed)	Dragomir Milošević (BS) – chief of staff to Galić	Trial (12/12/2007): 33 years Appeal (11/12/2009): 29 years (reduced)
IT-98–30/1	"Omarska, Keraterm and Trnopolje Camps" 7(1) JCE: persecutions; murder; torture	Miroslav Kvočka (BS) – police officer attached to Omarska camp Dragoljub Prcać (BS)	Trial (11/2/2001) – Kvočka: 7 years Early release 3/2005 – Prcać: 5 years

		– retired policeman mobilized as administrative aid to camp commander Milojica Kos (BS) – guard shift leader Mlađo Radić (BS) – police officer attached to camp as guard shift leader Zoran Žigić (BS) – taxi driver, Keraterm camp guard	Released 3/2005, served sentence in full – Kos: 6 years [final] Early release 7/2002 – Radić: 20 years – Žigić: 25 years Appeal (2/28/2005)(all but Kos) all sentences unchanged Request for review submitted by Radić and Žigić (6/6/2006): dismissed
IT-98–32	"Višegrad" 7(1) JCE; a+a: Drina river (5 dead); acquitted of Pionirska Street incident (house fire 60 dead)	Mitar Vasiljević (BS) – member of "White Eagles" paramilitary group	Trial (11/29/2002): 20 years Appeal (2/15/2004): 15 years Early release 3/2010
IT-98–32/1	"Višegrad": Pionirska Street (house fire, 60 dead); Bikavic (house fire, 70 people dead); Drina river (5 dead)	Milan Lukić (BS) – leader of "White Eagles" paramilitary group Sredoje Lukić (BS) – member of "White Eagles"	Trial (7/20/2009) – Milan Lukić: life imprisonment† – Sredoje Lukić: 30 years Appeal (12/4/2012) – M. Lukić: affirmed† Serving sentence in Estonia – S. Lukić: 27 years (reduced) Serving sentence in Norway
IT-98–33	"Srebrenica-Drina Corps" a+a: genocide; murder; persecutions;	Radislav Krstić (BS) – chief of staff/deputy commander VRS	Trial (8/2/2001): 46 years; Appeal (4/19/2004): 35 years (reduced)

(continued)

(continued)

Case Number	Case "in a Nutshell"	Defendants	Procedural Outcome and Sentence
IT-98–34	"Tuta and Štela" torture; unlawful labor; persecutions	Mladen Naletilić (BC) – founder and commander of "Convicts Battalion" Vinko Martinović (BC) – subordinate to Naletilić	Trial 3/31/2003: – Naletilić: 20 years – Martinović: 18 years Early release 12/2011 Appeal (5/3/2006): affirmed
IT-99–36	"Krajina" 7(1) JCE and 7(3) CR: genocide; persecutions; wanton destruction; a+a BS forces in killing 140 civilians in Kozarac 5/1992; 8 civilians in Jaskići 6/1992; 300 BC and B men in Biščani 7/1992	Radoslav Brđanin (BS) – leading political figure in ARK	Trial (9/1/2004): 32 years Appeal (4/3/2007): 30 years Serving sentence in Denmark
~~IT-99–36/1~~	"Krajina" 7(1) JCE: genocide; extermination; torture; wanton destruction	Momir Talić (BS) – chief of staff/deputy commander JNA in Banja Luka; VRS commander	Died 5/2003 while trial ongoing
IT-99–36/2		Stojan Župljanin	See IT-08–91
IT-99–37		Milutinović et al.	See IT-05–87
IT-00–39	"Bosnia and Herzegovina" 7(1) JCE: persecutions	Momčilo Krajisnik (BS) – member of RS presidency	Trial (9/27/2006): 27 years Appeal (3/17/2009): 20 years (reduced)

IT-00–39&40/1**	"Bosnia and Herzegovina" 7(1) JCE: persecutions	Biljana Plavšić (BS) – member of RS presidency	Trial chamber (2/27/2003) (plea bargain): 11 years – Early release 9/2009
IT-00–41§	"Lašva Valley"§	Ljubičić§	Referred to BiH under 11 bis§
IT-01–42	"Dubrovnik" attacks on civilians; wanton destruction	Pavle Strugar – JNA commander [charges withdrawn; Milan Zec]	Trial (1/31/2005): 8 years Appeal 7/17/2008): 7.5 years (reduced)
IT-01–42/1**	"Dubrovnik" a+a and 7(3) CR: murder; cruel treatment; attacks on civilians; willful damage	Miodrag Jokić – commander in Yugoslav navy	Sentencing judgment (3/18/2004): 7 years Sentencing appeal (8/30/2005): affirmed – Early release 9/2008
IT-01–42/2§		Vladimir Kovačević§	Referred to Serbia under 11 bis; Serbian court found unfit to stand trial 12/1997§
IT-01–43		Dragan Obrenović	See IT-02–60/2
IT-01–44		Dragan Jokić	See IT-02–60
IT-01–45		Ante Gotovina	See IT-06–90
IT-01–46		Rahim Ademi	See IT-04–78
IT-01–47	"Central Bosnia" cruel treatment; plunder	Enver Hadžihasanović – senior ABiH officer Amir Kubura – senior ABiH officer ~~Mehmed Alagić~~	Trial (3/15/2006) – Hadžihasanović: 5 years – Kubura: 2.5 years Appeal (4/22/2008) – Hadžihasanović: 3.5 years (reduced)

(continued)

(continued)

Case Number	Case "in a Nutshell"	Defendants	Procedural Outcome and Sentence
		~~– senior ABiH officer~~ (deceased and proceedings terminated)	– Kubura: 2 years (reduced) Early release 4/2006
IT-01–48‡	"Grabovica-Uzdol" 7(3) CR: murder	Sefer Halilović – deputy commander of staff of ABiH	Trial (11/16/2005): acquitted Appeal (10/16/2007): affirmed‡
IT-02–53		Blagojević et al.	See IT-02–60
~~IT-02–54~~	"Kosovo; Croatia; Bosnia-Herzegovina" genocide; deportation; murder; extensive destruction	Slobodan Milošević (S) – president of FY; President of Serbia	Died while trial ongoing; proceedings terminated
IT-02–55	Macedonia		Prosecutor requested deferral of cases involving Macedonian victims to ICTY; deferred 5 cases but did not defer "all future cases" (10/4/2002)
IT-02–56		Momir Nikolić	See IT-02–60/1
IT-02–57		Vujadin Popović	See IT-05–88
IT-02–58		Ljubisa Beara	See IT-05–88
IT-02–59**	"Vlašić Mountain" (massacre of 200 Muslim military-aged men in bus convoy): murder; inhumane acts	Darko Mrđa (BS) – member of special BS police unit "Intervention Squad"	Sentencing judgment (3/31/2004) (plea bargain): 17 years

IT-02–60	"Srebrenica" a+a murder and persecution	Vidoje Blagojević (BS) Dragan Jokić (BS)	Trial (1/17/2005) – Vidoje Blagojević: 18 years – Dragan Jokić: 9 years Appeal (5/9/2007) – Vidoje Blagojević: 15 years – Dragan Jokić: 9 years
IT-02–60/1**	"Srebrenica"	Momir Nikolić (BS) Assistant Commander VRS	Sentencing judgment (12/2/2003) (plea bargain): 27 years Sentencing appeal (3/8/2006): 20 years (reduced)
IT-02–60/2**	"Srebrenica" indictment: 5 counts including complicity in genocide, murder, etc. PB to Count 5, persecutions.	Dragan Obrenović (BS) – VRS officer Zvornik Brigade	Sentencing judgment (12/10/2003) (plea bargain): 17 years – Early release 9/2011
IT-02–61**	"Glogova" village of Glogova razed	Miroslav Deronjić (BS) – leader of SDS	Sentencing judgment (3/30/2004) (plea bargain): 10 years Sentencing appeal (7/20/2005): affirmed Died 2007 in prison
~~IT-02–62~~	"Medak Pocket"	Janko Bobetko (C) – chief of HV	Initial indictment 8/23/2002; died and proceedings terminated
IT-02–63	"Srebrenica"	Drago Nikolić	See IT-05–88

(continued)

(continued)

Case Number	Case "in a Nutshell"	Defendants	Procedural Outcome and Sentence
IT-02–64		Ljubomir Borovčanin	See IT-05–88
IT-02–65§	"Prijedor"§	Željko Mejakić (commander Omarska camp), Momčilo Gruban, Dusan Knežević & Dušan Fuštar§	Referred to BiH under 11 bis Mejakić: 21 years Gruban: 11 years, 7 on appeal Knežević: 31 years Fuštar: 9 years (guilty plea)§
IT-02–65/1**	"Omarska and Keraterm Camps" 7(1) crimes against humanity (persecutions)	Predrag Banović (BS) – guard at Keraterm camp	Trial chamber (10/28/2003) (plea bargain): 8 years -Early release 11/2008
IT-03–66	7(1) JCE murder Lapusnik prison camp (9 deaths)	Fatmir Limaj (KLA) – leader in KLA Isak Musliu (KLA) – leader in KLA Haradin Bala – prison guard (charges withdrawn: Agim Murtezi)	Trial (11/30/2005) – Limaj: acquitted‡ – Musliu: acquitted‡ -Bala: 13 years Appeal (9/27/2007): TC affirmed‡
IT-03–67*	"Vukovar" "Zvornik" "Sarajevo" 7(1) JCE: crimes against humanity; violations of the laws of war	Vojislav Šešelj (S)	Trial (3/31/2016): acquitted‡ Appeal (4/11/2018) ten years, Šešelj free in Serbia based on time served

IT-03–68	7(1) wanton destruction (destroyed 50 BS villages) specifically Jezestica 7(3) murder (victims murdered and beaten in Srebrenica police station September 1992–March 1993) a+a	Naser Orić (B) – senior commander Bosniak forces in eastern BiH 1992–1995	Trial (6/30/2006): 2 years Appeal (7/3/2008): acquitted‡ (reduced)
IT-03–69*	Military training throughout Krajina; directed "Scorpions" paramilitary unit 7(1) JCE: crimes against humanity; violations of laws of war	Jovica Stanišić (S) Franko Simatović (S) – defendants held senior positions in Serbian State Security Service.	Trial (5/30/2013): acquitted Appeal (12/15/2015): retrial ordered Retrial before MICT began June 2017
IT-03–70	"Srebrenica"	Vujadin Pavković	See IT-05–87 (joined)
IT-03–72**	"RSK" 7(1) JCE	Milan Babić (CS) – president of RSK	Trial chamber (6/29/2004) (plea bargain): 13 years Sentencing appeal (7/18/2005) sentence affirmed Committed suicide in ICTY cell March 2006

(continued)

(continued)

Case Number	Case "in a Nutshell"	Defendants	Procedural Outcome and Sentence
IT-03–73		Ivan Čermak Mladen Markač	See IT-06–90
IT-04–74	HVO in Herzegovina 7(1) JCE: grave breaches of GC; violations of laws of war; crimes against humanity	Jadranko Prlić (BC) Bruno Stojić (BC) Slobodan Praljak (BC) Milivoj Petković (BC) Valentin Čorić (BC) Berislav Pušić (BC) – all political & military leaders in HVO	Trial (5/29/2013); Appeal (11/29/2017) all affirmed -Prlić: 25 years -Stojić: 20 years -Praljak: 20 years Public suicide at ICTY on reading appeal (11/2017) -Petković: 20 years -Čorić: 16 years -Pušić: 10 years
~~IT-04–75~~	"Krajina" 7(1) JCE 7(3) CR	Goran Hadžić (CS) – president of RSK	– Released 4/2015 for ill health – died 7/2016
IT-04–76		Mirko Norac	See IT-04–78
IT-04–78§	"Medak Pocket"§	Rahim Ademi (C)§ Mirko Norac (C)§	Referred to Croatia under 11 bis; appeals judgment by Croatian Supreme Court November 2009 acquitting Ademi and 6-year sentence for Norac§
IT-04–79		Mićo Stanišić	See IT-08–91
IT-04–80		Zdravko Tolimir Milan Gvero Radivoje Miletić	See IT-05–88

IT-04–81	Sarajevo, Srebrenica, Zagreb 7(1) a+a: crimes against humanity; violations of laws of war 7(3) CR: crimes against humanity; violations of laws of war	Momčilo Perišić (S) – JNA officer who made weapons provisions to VRS and SVK possible	Trial (9/6/2011): 27 years Appeal (3/2013): acquitted‡
IT-04–82	Macedonia 7(1) JCE: violations of laws of war (murder) 7(3)	Ljube Boškoski (M) – minister of the interior Johan Tarčulovski (M) – police officer, presidential security unit	Trial (7/10/2008) – Boškoski: acquitted‡ – Tarčulovski: 12 years Appeal (5/19/2010) Sentences affirmed
~~IT-04–83~~	Violations of laws of war (cruel treatment)	Rasim Delić (B) – commander of ABiH	Trial (9/15/2008): 3 years Appeal (6/29/2010) (accused died on 4/16/2010 while on provisional release; appeals chamber terminated proceedings and ruled the Trial Chamber judgment should be considered final)
IT-04–84	"Kosovo"	Ramush Haradinaj (KA) – commander in KLA Idriz Balaj (KA)	Trial (4/3/2008) – Haradinaj: acquitted‡ – Balaj: acquitted‡

(continued)

(continued)

Case Number	Case "in a Nutshell"	Defendants	Procedural Outcome and Sentence
	7(1) JCE: crimes against humanity; violations of laws of war	– member of KLA Lahi Brahimaj (KA) – member of KLA General Staff	– Brahimaj: 6 years Appeal (7/21/2010) partial re-trial ordered for all Brahimaj's sentence of 6 years affirmed Retrial (11/29/2012) All three acquitted‡
IT-05–86§		Vinko Pandurević (BS) Milorad Trbić§ (BS)	Pandurević: see IT-05–88 Trbić: referred to BiH under Rule 11 bis§
IT/05/87	"Kosovo" "Šainović et al." 7(1) JCE: crimes against humanity; violations of laws of war	Milan Milutinović (S) – president of Serbia 1997–2002 Nikola Šainović (S) – deputy prime minister of Serbia 1994–2000 Dragoljub Ojdanić (S) – VJ chief of staff; minister of defense Nebojša Pavković (S) – VJ commander Vladimir Lazarević (S) – leader VJ Pristina Sreten Lukić (S) – head of Serbian internal affairs 1998–1999	Trial (2/29/2009) – Milutinović: acquitted‡ [final] – Šainović: 22 years – Ojdanić: 15 years [final] Early release 7/2013 – Pavković: 22 years – Lazarević: 15 years – Lukić: 22 years Appeal (1/23/2014) – Šainović: 18 years (reduced) Early release (Sweden) 7/2015 – Pavković: 22 years (affirmed) Serving sentence in Finland – Lazarević: 15 years (affirmed) Early release 9/2015 – Lukić: 20 years (reduced) Serving sentence in Poland
IT-05–87/1	"Kosovo"	Vlastimir Đorđević (S)	Trial (2/23/2011): 27 years

	7(1) JCE: crimes against humanity; violations of laws of war	– assistant minister of Serbian ministry of internal affairs	Appeal (1/27/2014): 18 years (reduced) Serving sentence in Germany
IT-05–88	Popović et al. "Srebrenica" 7(1) JCE: genocide; crimes against humanity; violations of the laws of war	Vujadin Popović (BS) Ljubiša Beara (BS) Drago Nikolić (BS) Ljubomir Borovčanin (BS) Radivoje Miletić (BS) Milan Gvero (BS) Vinko Pandurević (BS) – all VRS leaders	Trial (6/10/2010) – Popović: life imprisonment† Serving sentence in Germany – Beara: life imprisonment† Serving sentence in Germany – Nikolić: (plea bargain)** 35 years Died 10/2015 on provisional release in Serbia – Borovčanin: 17 years Only defendant not to appeal sentence – Miletić: 19 years – Gvero: 5 years Early release 6/2010 – Pandurević: 13 years Appeal (1/30/2015) All affirmed except – Miletić: 18 years (reduced) Serving sentence in Finland
IT-05–88/1§		Milorad Trbić§	Referred to BiH under 11 bis; 30 year sentence§
IT-05–88/2	"Srebrenica" 7(1) JCE: genocide; conspiracy to commit genocide; crimes against	Zdravko Tolimir (BS) – assistant commander of VRS, reported directly to Mladić	Trial (12/12/2012): Life imprisonment† (genocide) Appeal (4/8/2015) affirmed Died 2/2016

(continued)

(continued)

Case Number	Case "in a Nutshell"	Defendants	Procedural Outcome and Sentence
	humanity; violations of the laws of war		
IT-06–90‡	"Operation Storm" 7(1) JCE	Ante Gotovina (C) – HV commander Mladen Markač (C) – commander of special police of Croatian ministry of interior Ivan Čermak (C) – commander of Knin Garrison, Croatian assistant minister of defense 1991–1993	Trial (4/15/11) – Gotovina: 24 years – Markač: 18 years – Čermak: acquitted‡ [final] Appeal (11/16/2012) – Gotovina: acquitted‡ – Markač: acquitted‡
IT-08–91	"Bosnia & Herzegovina" 7(1) JCE: crimes against humanity; violations of laws of war	Mićo Stanišić (BS) – minister of internal affairs in RS Stojan Župljanin (BS) – chief of security services in Banja Luka	Trial (3/27/2013) – Stanišić: 22 years – Župljanin: 22 years Appeal (6/30/2016) affirmed
IT-09–92*	"Bosnia & Herzegovina"	Ratko Mladić (BS) – general in VRS, oversaw Srebrenica massacre	Trial (11/22/2017) Life imprisonment† (genocide) Appeal before MICT

Abbreviations:

a+a: Aiding and abetting
ABiH: Army of Bosnia-Herzegovina (Bosniak)
ARK: Autonomous Region of Krajina (BiH)
CR: Command responsibility
HV: Croatian Army
JCE: Joint criminal enterprise
JNA: Yugoslav National Army (*de facto* Serbian)
KLA: Kosovo Liberation Army (Kosovar Albanian)
RSK: Republic of Srpska Krajina (Bosnian Serb)
SAO Krajina: Serbian Autonomous District Krajina
SDS: Serbian Democratic Party (Bosnian Serb)
SVK: Army of Srpska Krajina (Bosnian Serb)
TD: Territorial Defense
VRS: Republika Srpska Army (Bosnian Serb)

Coding:

* = proceedings not yet finalized (as of December 2017)
** = plea bargain/guilty pleas
† = life imprisonment
‡ = acquitted
§ = referred to a national jurisdiction under 11 bis
[~~TEXT~~] = proceedings halted due to death of defendant

Of note:

161 individuals indicted
69 individuals sentenced
20 guilty pleas
18 acquittals
5 life sentences: Galić [IT-98–29] (final)*
Lukić [IT-98–32/1] (currently on appeal)*
Popović and Beara [IT-05–88] (currently on appeal)*
Tolimir [IT-05–88/2] (currently on appeal)*

Bibliography

Ainley, Kirsten. "Evaluating the Evaluators: Transitional Justice and the Contest of Values." *International Journal of Transitional Justice* 11, no. 3 (2017): 421–442.

Akhavan, Payam. "Justice in The Hague, Peace in the Former Yugoslavia? A Commentary on the United Nations War Crimes Tribunal." *Human Rights Quarterly* 20, no. 4 (1998): 737–816.

"Beyond Impunity: Can International Criminal Justice Prevent Future Atrocities?" *The American Journal of International Law* 95, no. 1 (2001): 7–31.

Reducing Genocide to Law: Definition, Meaning, and the Ultimate Crime. Cambridge University Press, 2012.

"The Rise, and Fall, and Rise, of International Criminal Justice." *Journal of International Criminal Justice* 11 (2013): 527–536.

Aksenova, Marina. "The Specific Direction Requirement in Aiding and Abetting: A Call for Revisiting Comparative Criminal Law." *Cambridge Journal of International and Comparative Law* 4, no. 1 (2015): 88–107.

Alexander, Ronelle. "Language and Identity: The Fate of Serbo-Croatian." In *Entangled Balkans*, edited by Rumen Daskalov and Tchavdar Marinov. Brill, 2013, 341–417.

Alexander, Ronelle and Ellen Elias-Bursać. *Bosnian, Croatian, Serbian: A Textbook with Exercises and Basic Grammar*. University of Wisconsin Press, 2010.

Ali, Rabia and Lawrence Lifschultz. *Why Bosnia? Writings on the Balkan War*. Pamphleteer's Press, 1993.

Allott, Philip. *Eunomia: New Order for a New World*. Oxford University Press, 1990.

"The Concept of International Law." *European Journal of International Law* 10, no. 1 (1999): 31–50.

The Health of Nations: Society and Law beyond the State. Cambridge University Press, 2002.

Alter, Karen J. and Laurence R. Helfer. "Legal Integration in the Andes: Law-Making by the Andean Tribunal of Justice." *European Law Journal* 17, no. 5 (2011): 701–715.

Alvarez, Jose E. "Rush to Closure: Lessons of the Tadić Judgment." *Michigan Law Review* 96, no. 7 (1998): 2031–2112.

"Crimes of States/Crimes of Hate: Lessons from Rwanda." *Yale Journal of International Law* 24 (1999): 365.

"Do Liberal States Behave Better? A Critique of Slaughter's Liberal Theory." *European Journal of International Law* 12, no. 2 (2001): 183–246.

Ambos, Kai. "Individual Criminal Responsibility in International Criminal Law: A Jurisprudential Analysis – From Nuremberg to the Hague." In *Substantive and*

Procedural Aspects of International Criminal Law: The Experience of International and National Courts, edited by Gabrielle Kirk-McDonald and Olivia Swaak-Goldman. Kluwer Law International, 2000, 1–31.

"International Criminal Procedure: 'Adversarial', 'Inquisitorial' or Mixed?" *Third International Criminal Law Review* 3 (2003): 1–37.

Anderson, Benedict. *Imagined Communities: Reflections on the Origin and Spread of Nationalism*. Verso, 2006.

Annan, Kofi. "Advocating for an International Criminal Court." *Fordham International Law Journal* 21, no. 2 (1997): 363–366.

Anzulovic, Branimir. *Heavenly Serbia: From Myth to Genocide*. New York University Press, 1999.

Arbour, Louise. "The Prosecution of International Crimes: Prospects and Pitfalls." *Washington University Journal of Law and Policy* 1 (1999a): 13.

"The Status of the International Criminal Tribunals for the Former Yugoslavia and Rwanda: Goals and Results." Paper presented at the Hofstra Law and Policy Symposium, 1999b.

"In Our Name and on Our Behalf." *The International and Comparative Law Quarterly* 55 (2006): 511–526.

"Economic and Social Justice for Societies in Transition." *NYU Journal of International Law and Policy* 40 (2007): 1.

Arendt, Hannah. *Eichmann in Jerusalem*. Penguin Classics, 1963/2010.

Armstrong, Elizabeth A. and Suzanna M. Cage. "Movements and Memory: The Making of the Stonewall Myth." *American Sociological Review* 71, no. 5 (2006): 724–751.

Ashworth, Andrew. *Principles of Criminal Law* (sixth edition). Oxford University Press, 2009.

Assmann, Jan. *Cultural Memory and Early Civilization: Writing, Remembrance, and Political Imagination*. Cambridge University Press, 2011.

Assmann, Jan and John Czaplicka. "Collective Memory and Cultural Identity." *New German Critique* 65 (1995): 125–133.

Axelrod, Alan. *Patton*. Palgrave Macmillan, 2009.

Babic, Jovan. "War Crimes: Moral, Legal, or Simply Political?" in *War Crimes and Collective Wrongdoing: A Reader*, edited by Aleksandar Jokić. Wiley-Blackwell, 2001, 57–71.

Badar, Mohamed Elewa. "'Just Convict Everyone!' – Joint Perpetration: From *Tadić* to *Stakić* and Back Again." *International Criminal Law Review* 6 (2006): 293–302.

Bagaric, Mirko and John Morss. "International Sentencing Law: In Search of a Justification and Coherent Framework." *International Criminal Law Review* 6 (2006): 191.

Baker, Catherine. "Gender and Geopolitics in the Eurovision Song Contest." *Contemporary Southeastern Europe* 2, no. 1 (2015): 74–93.

Banac, Ivo. *The National Question in Yugoslavia: Origins, History, Politics*. Cornell University Press, 1984.

Raspad Jugoslavije: eseji o nacionalizmu i nacionalnim sukobima. Durieux, 2001.

Baruma, Ian. *The Wages of Guilt: Memories of War in Germany and Japan*. Farrar Straus, and Giroux, 1994.

Bass, Gary Jonathan. *Stay the Hand of Vengeance: The Politics of War Crimes Tribunals*. Princeton University Press, 2000.

Bassiouni, M. Cherif. "Nuremberg Forty Years after: An Introduction." *Case Western Reserve Journal of International Law* 18 (1986): 261.

"Crimes against Humanity: The Need for a Specialized Convention." *Columbia Journal of Transnational Law* 31 (1993): 457.

"Searching for Peace and Achieving Justice: The Need for Accountability." *Law and Contemporary Problems* 59, no. 4 (1996): 9–28.

International Criminal Law: Multilateral and Bilateral Enforcement Mechanisms. Brill, 2008.

Crimes against Humanity: Historical Evolution and Contemporary Application. Cambridge University Press, 2011.

Introduction to International Criminal Law. Martinus Nijhoff Publishers/Brill Academic Publishing, 2013.

Bassiouni, M. Cherif and Peter Manikas. *The Law of the International Criminal Tribunal for the Former Yugoslavia*. Transnational Publishers, 1996.

Bauman, Zygmunt. *Modernity and the Holocaust*. Cornell University Press, 2001.

Bedford, Sybille. *The Faces of Justice: A Traveller's Report*. Simon & Schuster, 1961.

Bellamy, Richard (ed). *Beccaria: On Crimes and Punishments and Other Writings*. Cambridge University Press, 1995.

Beresford, Stuart. "Unshackling the Paper Tiger – The Sentencing Practices of the Ad Hoc International Criminal Tribunals for the Former Yugoslavia and Rwanda." *International Criminal Law Review* 1 (2001): 33.

Beschloss, Michael R. *The Conquerors: Roosevelt, Truman and the Destruction of Hitler's Germany, 1941–1945*. Simon & Schuster, 2003.

Bickel, Alexander M. *The Morality of Consent*. Yale University Press, 1977.

The Least Dangerous Branch: The Supreme Court at the Bar of Politics. Yale University Press, 1986.

Bickford, Louis. "Human Rights Archives and Research on Historical Memory: Argentina, Chile, and Uruguay." *Latin American Research Review* 35, no. 2 (2000): 160–182.

Bloomfield, David. "On Good Terms: Clarifying Reconciliation." Berghof Report No. 14 (2006).

Bloxham, Donald. *Genocide on Trial: War Crimes Trials and the Formation of Holocaust History and Memory*. Cambridge University Press, 2001.

Boas, Gideon. "Creating Laws of Evidence for International Criminal Law: The ICTY and the Principle of Flexibility." *Criminal Law Forum* 12, no. 1 (2001): 41–90.

The Milošević Trial: Lessons for the Conduct of Complex International Criminal Proceedings. Cambridge University Press, 2007.

Boas, Gideon, William A. Schabas, and Michael P. Scharf. *International Criminal Justice: Legitimacy and Coherence*. Edward Elgar, 2013.

Bodansky, Daniel. "Legitimacy in International Law and International Relations." In *Interdisciplinary Perspectives on International Law and International Relations: The State of the Art*, edited by Jeffrey Dunoff and Mark Pollack. Cambridge University Press, 2012, 321–342.

Boerma, N. Westendorp. "Collective Guilt (A Survey)." *Synthese* 8, no. 3/5 (1950): 213–221.

Bohlander, Michael. "Plea Bargaining Before the ICTY." Available at SSRN 1592902 (2000).

Principles of German Criminal Procedure. Hart Publishing, 2012.

"Language, Culture, Legal Traditions, and International Criminal Justice." *Journal of International Criminal Justice* 12, no. 3 (2014): 491.

Bolton, John R. "The Risks and Weaknesses of the International Criminal Court from America's Perspective." *Law and Contemporary Problems* 64, no. 1 (2001): 167–180.

Alexander. "Can Truth Telling Promote Reconciliation?" *The Collection of TRC Speeches* (1998): 1.

Boraine, Alexander L. "Transitional Justice: A Holistic Interpretation." *Journal of International Affairs-Columbia University* 60, no. 1 (2006): 17.

Borneman, John. *Settling Accounts: Violence, Justice, and Accountability in Postsocialist Europe*. Princeton University Press, 1997.

"Reconciliation after Ethnic Cleansing: Listening, Retribution, Affiliation." *Public Culture* 14, no. 2 (2002): 281–304.

Bose, Sumantra. *Bosnia after Dayton: Nationalist Partition and International Intervention*. Oxford University Press, 2002.

Boutros-Ghali, Boutros. "A Grotian Moment." *Fordham International Law Journal* 18 (1994): 1609.

Brannigan, Augustine. "Is the Sun Setting on Cosmopolitan Justice?" *Society* 48 (2011): 420–425.

Brants, Chrisje, Stewart Field, and Nico Jörg. "Are Adversarial and Inquisitorial Systems Converging?" In *Criminal Justice in Europe: A Comparative Study*, edited by Christopher Harding, Philip Fennel, Nico Jörg, and Bert Swart. Clarendon Press, 1995, 41–56.

Bringa, Tone. *Being Muslim the Bosnian Way: Identity and Community in a Central Bosnian Village*. Princeton University Press, 1995.

Brooks, Rosa Ehrenreich. "The New Imperialism: Violence, Norms, and the 'Rule of Law'." *Michigan Law Review* 101, no. 7 (2003): 2275–2340.

Browning, Christopher R. *Ordinary Men: Reserve Police Battalion 101 and the Final Solution in Poland*. HarperCollins Publishers, 1992.

Brownlie, Ian. *Principles of Public International Law* (fifth edition). Oxford University Press, 1998.

Burchard, Christoph. "The Nuremberg Trial and Its Impact on Germany." *Journal of International Criminal Justice* 4 (2006): 800–829.

Burg, Steven L. and Paul S. Shoup. *The War in Bosnia-Herzegovina: Ethnic Conflict and International Intervention*. M.E. Sharpe, 1999.

Burns, Peter. "An International Criminal Tribunal: The Difficult Union of Principle and Politics." *Criminal Law Forum* 5 (1994): 341.

Burns, Robert P. *A Theory of the Trial*. Princeton University Press, 2001.

Buruma, Ian. *The Wages of Guilt: Memories of War in Germany and Japan*. Farrar Straus Giroux, 1994.

Buscher, Frank M. *The US War Crimes Trial Program in Germany, 1946–1955*. Greenwood Press, 1989.

Caianiello, Michele. "Law of Evidence at the International Criminal Court: Blending Accusatorial and Inquisitorial Models." *North Carolina Journal of International Law and Commercial Regulation* 36, no. 2 (2010): 287–318.

Carlsnaes, Walter Emmanuel, Thomas Risse, and Beth A. Simmons. *Handbook of International Relations*. Sage Publications Ltd, 2012.

Carlson, Kerstin Bree. "Post Rule of Law: The Structural Problem of Hybridity in International Criminal Procedure." *The Italian Law Journal* 2, no. 1 (2016): 33–64.

"Reconciliation through a Judicial Lens: Competing Legitimation Frameworks in the ICTY's Plavšić and Babić Judgments." *Denver Journal of International & Comparative Law* 44, no. 2 (2016): 281–322.

"International Criminal Law and Its Paradoxes: Implications for Institutions and Practice" *Journal of Law & Courts* 5, no. 1 (2017): 33–53.

Carlson, Kerstin, Daska Babcock-Halaholo, Anne Mahle, Laurel Fletcher, Harvey Weinstein, and Damir Arnault. "Justice, Accountability and Social Reconstruction: An Interview Study of Bosnian Judges and Prosecutors." *Berkeley Journal of International Law* 18, no. 1 (2000): 102–164.

Casper, Jonathan D. *Criminal Courts: The Defendant's Perspective*. University of Michigan Library, 1978.

Caspersen, Nina. *Contested Nationalism: Serb Elite Rivalry in Croatia and Bosnia in the 1990s*. Berghahn Books, 2010.

Caspersen, Nina and Gareth R. V. Stansfield. *Unrecognized States in the International System*. Routledge, 2011.

Cassese, Antonio. "On the Current Trends towards Criminal Prosecution and Punishment of Breaches of International Humanitarian Law." *European Journal of International Law* 9 (1998a): 2–17.

"Reflections on International Criminal Justice." *Modern Law Review* 61 (1998b): 1.

International Criminal Law. Oxford University Press, 2003.

"The Proper Limits of Individual Responsibility under the Doctrine of Joint Criminal Enterprise." *Journal of International Criminal Justice* 5 (2007a): 133.

"On Some Problematical Aspects of the Crime of Aggression." *Leiden Journal of International Law* 20 (2007b): 841, 844.

Cibelli, Kristen and Tamy Guberek. "Justice Unknown, Justice Unsatisfied: Bosnian NGOs Speak About the International Criminal Tribunal for the Former Yugoslavia." Tufts University, 2000.

Citron, Rodger. "The Nuremberg Trials and American Jurisprudence: The Decline of Legal Realism and the Revival of Natural Law." In *The Nuremberg Trials: International Criminal Law Since 1945*, edited by Herbert Reginbogin and Christoph Safferling. De Gruyter Saur, 2006: 139–150.

Civikov, Germinal. *Srebrenica. Der Kronzeuge* (Srebrenica: The Star Witness). Promedia, (2009).

Clark, Janine Natalya. "Plea Bargaining at the ICTY: Guilty Pleas and Reconciliation." *European Journal of International Law* 20, no. 2 (2009): 415–436.

"Peace, Justice and the International Criminal Court Limitations and Possibilities." *Journal of International Criminal Justice* 9, no. 3 (2011): 521–545.

International Trials and Reconciliation: Assessing the Impact of the International Criminal Tribunal for the Former Yugoslavia. Routledge, 2014.

Clark, Roger S. "Nuremberg and the Crime against Peace." *Washington University Global Studies Law Review* 6 (2007): 527–550.

Climo, Jacob J. and Maria G. Cattell. *Social Memory and History: Anthropological Perspectives*. Altamira Press, 2002.

Cogan, Jacob. "International Criminal Courts and Fair Trials: Difficulties and Prospects." *Yale Journal of International Law* 27 (2002): 111.

Cohen, David. "Beyond Nuremberg: Individual Responsibility for War Crimes." In *Human Rights in Political Transitions: Gettysburg to Bosnia*, edited by Robert Post and Carla Hesse. Zone Books, 1999, 53–92.

Indifference and Accountability: The United Nations and the Politics of International Justice in East Timor. EastWest Institute, 2006a.

"Transitional Justice in Divided Germany 1945." In *Retribution and Reparation in the Transition to Democracy*, edited by Jon Elster. Cambridge University Press, 2006b, 59–88.

Cohen, Lenard J. *The Socialist Pyramid: Elites and Power in Yugoslavia*. Mosaic Press, 1989.

Broken Bonds: Yugoslavia's Disintegration and Balkan Politics in Transition. Westview Press Boulder, 1995.

Cohen, Lenard J. and Jasna Dragović-Soso. *State Collapse in South-Eastern Europe: New Perspectives on Yugoslavia's Disintegration*. Purdue University Press, 2008.

Collin, Matthew. *Guerrilla Radio: Rock n Roll Radio and Serbia's Underground Resistance*. Nation Books, 2001.

Combs, Nancy. "Procuring Guilty Pleas for International Crimes: The Limited Influence of Sentencing Discounts." *Vanderbilt Law Review* 59, no. 1 (2006): 69.

"Testimonial Deficiencies and Evidentiary Uncertainties in International Criminal Trials." *UCLA Journal of International Law and Foreign Affairs* 14, no. 1 (2009): 235.

Fact-Finding without Facts: The Uncertain Evidentiary Foundations of International Criminal Convictions. Cambridge University Press, 2010.

Conant, Lisa. *Justice Contained: Law and Politics in the European Union*. Cornell University Press, 2002.

Connerton, Paul. *How Societies Remember*. Cambridge University Press, 1989.

"Cultural Memory." In *Handbook of Material Culture*, edited by Chris Tilley, Webb Keane, Susanne Kuechler, Mike Rowlands, and Patricia Spyer. Sage Publications Limited, 2006, 315–324.

How Modernity Forgets. Cambridge University Press, 2009.

Conrad, Clay S. *Jury Nullification: The Evolution of a Doctrine*. Carolina Academic Press, 1998.

Cook, Julian A. "Plea Bargaining at The Hague." *Yale Journal of International Law* 30 (2005): 473–506.

Cooper, Belinda. *Modernity and the Holocaust*. Cornell University Press, 1989.

War Crimes: The Legacy of Nuremberg. TV Books Inc., 1999.

Cover, Robert M. "The Origins of Judicial Activism in the Protection of Minorities." *The Yale Law Journal* 91, no. 7 (1982): 1287–1316.

"Violence and the Word." *Yale Law Journal* 95, no. 8 (1986): 1601–1629.

Crocker, David. "Truth Commissions, Transitional Justice, and Civil Society." In *Truth v. Justice: The Morality of Truth Commissions*, edited by Robert I. Rotberg and Dennis Thompson. Princeton University Press, 2000, 309.

"Reckoning with Past Wrongs: A Normative Framework." In *Dilemmas of Reconciliation: Cases and Concepts*, edited by Carol A. Prager and Rudy Govier. Wilfrid Laurier University Press, 2003, 39–63.

Cryer, Robert. *An Introduction to International Criminal Law and Procedure*. Cambridge University Press, 2014.

"One Appeal, Two Philosophies, Four Opinions, and a Remittal: The Erdemovic Case at the ICTY Appeals Chamber." *Journal of Conflict and Security Law*, 2, no. 2, (1997): 193–208.

Daly, Tom Gerald. *The Alchemists: Questioning our Faith in Courts as Democracy-Builders*. Cambridge University Press, 2017.

Damaška, Mirjan. "Evidentiary Barriers to Conviction and Two Models of Criminal Procedure: A Comparative Study." *University of Pennsylvania Law Review* 506 (1973): 506–589.

"The Reality of Prosecutorial Discretion: Comments on a German Monograph." *American Journal of Comparative Law* 29 (1981): 119.

The Faces of Justice and State Authority: A Comparative Approach to the Legal Process. Yale University Press, 1986.

Evidence Law Adrift. Yale University Press, 1997.

"The International Criminal Court between Aspiration and Achievement." *UCLA Journal of Law and Foreign Affairs* 14 (2009): 19.

Danner, Alison. "Constructing a Hierarchy of Crimes in International Criminal Law Sentencing." *Virginia Law Review* 87, no. 3 (2001): 415–501.

"Enhancing the Legitimacy and Accountability of Prosecutorial Discretion at the International Criminal Court." *The American Journal of International Law* 97 (2003): 510–552.

Danner, Alison Marston and Jenny S. Martinez. "Guilty Associations: Joint Criminal Enterprise, Command Responsibility, and the Development of International Criminal Law." *California Law Review* 93, no. 1 (2005): 75–170.

Darrow, Mac and Louise Arbour. "The Pillar of Glass: Human Rights in the Development Operations of the United Nations." *The American Journal of International Law* 103 (2009): 446–501.

D'Ascoli, Silvia. *Sentencing in International Criminal Law: The Approach of the Two ad hoc Tribunals and Future Perspectives for the International Criminal Court*. Hart Publishing, 2011.

Davidson, Eugene. *The Death and Life of Germany: An Account of the American Occupation*. Knopf, 1959.

The Nuremberg Fallacy: Wars and War Crimes since World War II. Macmillan, 1973.

The Trial of the Germans: An Account of the Twenty-two Defendants before the International Military Tribunal at Nuremberg. University of Missouri, 1997.

Davis, Kenneth. *Discretionary Justice: A Preliminary Inquiry*. Louisiana State University Press, 1969.

Deák, István. "Misjudgment at Nuremberg." *New York Review of Books* (1993).

Deák, István, Jan T. Gross, and Tony Judt. *The Politics of Retribution in Europe*. Princeton University Press, 2000.

Delmas-Marty, Mireille, "The Contribution of Comparative Law to a Pluralist Conception of International Criminal Law." *Journal of International Criminal Justice* 1, no 1 (2003): 13–25.

Del Ponte, Carla and Chuck Sudetic. *Madame Prosecutor: Confrontations with Humanity's Worst Criminals and Culture of Impunity*. Other Press, 2009.

Dembour, Marie-Bénédicte. "What are Human Rights? Four Schools of Thought." *Human Rights Quarterly* 32, no. 1 (2010): 1–20.

De Than, Claire and Russel Heaton. *Criminal Law* (fourth edition). Oxford University Press, 2013.

Dietrich, John. *The Morgenthau Plan: Soviet Influence on American Postwar Policy*. Algora Publishing, 2013.

Dixon, Rodney and Alexis Demerdjian. "Advising Defendants about Guilty Pleas before International Courts." *Journal of International Criminal Justice* 3, no. 3 (2005): 680–694.

Dizdarević, Raif. *Put u raspad : stenogrami izlaganja Raifa Dizdarevića u raspravama iza zatvorenih vrata dr žavnog i politi čkog vrha Jugoslavije*. Institut za istoriju, 2011.

Donia, Professor Robert J. and Professor John V. A. Fine Jr. *Bosnia and Hercegovina: A Tradition Betrayed*. Columbia University Press, 1995.

Donnelly, Jack. "Cultural Relativism and Universal Human Rights." *Human Rights Quarterly* 6 (1984): 400.

Realism and International Relations. Cambridge University Press, 2000.

Universal Human Rights in Theory and Practice. Cornell University Press, 2003.

Douglas, Lawrence. *The Memory of Judgment: Making Law and History in the Trials of the Holocaust*. Yale University Press, 2005.

Drakulic, Slavenka. "The False Repentance of Biljana Plavsic." Eurozine (October 23, 2009).

Drapac, Vesna. "The End of Yugoslavia." *Contemporary European History* 10, no. 2 (2001): 317–331.

Drumbl, Mark. "Collective Violence and Individual Punishment: The Criminality of Mass Atrocity." *Northwestern University Law Review* 99, no. 2 (Winter 2005): 539–610.

Atrocity, Punishment, and International Law. Cambridge University Press, 2007.

"The Principle of Legality in International and Comparative Criminal Law (review)." *Human Rights Quarterly* 31, no. 3 (2009): 801–806.

Duff, Antony. *Punishment, Communication and Community*. Oxford University Press, 2001.

The Trial on Trial: Truth and Due Process. Hart Publishing, 2004.

"Can We Punish the Perpetrators of Atrocities?" In *The Religious in Response to Mass Atrocity: Interdisciplinary Perspectives*, edited by Thomas Brudholm and Thomas Cushman. Cambridge University Press, 2009: 79–104.

"Relational Reasons and the Criminal Law I." In *Oxford Studies in Philosophy of Law: Volume 2*, edited by Leslie Green and Brian Leiter. Oxford University Press, 2013: 175–208.

Dworkin, Ronald. *Taking Rights Seriously*. Harvard University Press, 1978.

Law's Empire. Harvard University Press, 1986.

Ehrenfreund, Norbert. *The Nuremberg Legacy: How the Nazi War Crimes Trials Changed the Course of History*. St. Martin's Press, 2007.

Eisenberg, Mel. "Private Ordering Through Negotiation: Dispute Settlement and Rulemaking." *Harvard Law Review* 89 (1976): 637.

Ellis, Mark S. and Richard Goldstone. *The International Criminal Court: Challenges to Achieving Justice and Accountability in the 21st Century*. International Debate Education Association, 2008.

Elster, Jon. *Closing the Books: Transitional Justice in Historical Perspective*. Cambridge University Press, 2004.

Ely, John. *Democracy and Distrust: A Theory of Judicial Review*. Harvard University Press, 1980.

Erceg, Heni. *Ispodvijesti o ratu u Hrvatskoj*. Feral Tribune, 1995.

Erozden, Ozan. "Croatia & the EU: A Difficult Year of Cooperation." Central European University, 2002.

Esman, Milton J. and Ronald J. Herring. *Carrots, Sticks, and Ethnic Conflict: Rethinking Development Assistance*. University of Michigan Press, 2001.

Estrin, Saul. *Self-Management: Economic Theory and Yugoslav Practice*. Cambridge University Press, 2010.

Evans, Peter B., Dietrich Rueschemeyer, and Theda Skocpol. *Bringing the State Back In*. Cambridge University Press, 1985.

Evans, Richard J. "History, Memory, and the Law: The Historian as Expert Witness." *History and Theory* 41, no. 3 (2002): 326–345.

Ewald, Uwe. "'Predictably Irrational': International Sentencing and Its Discourse against the Backdrop of Preliminary Empirical Findings on ICTY Sentencing Practices." *International Criminal Law Review* 10, no. 3 (2010): 365–402.

Ewick, Patricia and Susan S. Silbey. *The Common Place of Law: Stories from Everyday Life*. University of Chicago Press, 1998.

Fairlie, Megan. "The Marriage of Common and Continental Law at the ICTY and its Progeny, Due Process Deficit." *International Criminal Law Review* 4 (2004): 243–319.

Feeley, Malcolm. "Perspectives on Plea Bargaining." *Law & Society Review* 13, no. 2 (1979): 199–209.

The Process Is the Punishment: Handling Cases in a Lower Criminal Court. Russell Sage Foundation, 1992.

Feeley, Malcolm and Edward Rubin. *Federalism: Political Identity and Tragic Compromise*. University of Michigan Press, 2008.

Judicial Policy Making and the Modern State: How the Courts Reformed America's Prisons. Cambridge University Press, 2000.

Field, Stewart and Andrew West. "A Tale of Two Reforms: French Defense Rights and Police Powers in Transition." *Criminal Law Forum* 6, no. 3 (1995): 473–506.

Finch, George A. "The Nuremberg Trial and International Law." *The American Journal of International Law* 41, no. 1 (1947): 20–37.

Findlay, Mark. "Synthesis in Trial Procedures? The Experience of International Criminal Tribunals." *International and Comparative Legal Quarterly* 50 (2001): 26–53.

Fine Jr., John V. A. *When Ethnicity Did Not Matter in the Balkans: A Study of Identity in Pre-Nationalist Croatia, Dalmatia, and Slavonia in the Medieval and Early-Modern Periods*. University of Michigan Press, 2006.

Finkielkraut, Alain. *La mémoire vaine: du crime contre l'humanité*. Editions Gallimard, 1989.

Fisher, George. "Plea Bargaining's Triumph." *Yale Law Journal* 109 (2000): 857.

Fiss, Owen M. and Judith Resnik. *Adjudication and Its Alternatives: An Introduction to Procedure*. Foundation Press, Thomson/West, 2003.

Fletcher, George P. *Rethinking Criminal Law*. Little, Brown and Company, 1977.

"The Storrs Lectures: Liberals and Romantics at War: The Problem of Collective Guilt." *Yale Law Journal* 111, no. 7 (2002): 1499–1573.

"Collective Guilt and Collective Punishment." *Theoretical Inquiries in Law* 5, no. 1 (2004): 163–178.

Fletcher, Laurel E. and Harvey M. Weinstein. "Violence and Social Repair: Rethinking the Contribution of Justice to Reconciliation." *Human Rights Quarterly* 24, no. 3 (2002): 573–639.

Focarelli, Carlo. *International Law as Social Construct: The Struggle for Global Justice*. Oxford University Press, 2012.

Follesdal, Andreas. "The Legitimacy of International Human Rights Review: The Case of the European Court of Human Rights." *Journal of Social Philosophy* 40, no. 4 (2009): 595–607.

Ford, Stuart. "A Social Psychology Model of the Perceived Legitimacy of International Criminal Courts: Implications for the Success of Transitional Justice Mechanisms." *Vanderbilt Journal of Transnational Law* 45 (2012): 405.

Forsberg, Tuomas. "The Philosophy and Practice of Dealing with the Past: Some Conceptual and Normative Issues." In *Burying the Past: Making Peace and Doing Justice*, edited by Nigel Biggar. Georgetown University Press, 2003: 65–84.

Forsythe, David P. *Human Rights in International Relations*. Cambridge University Press, 2006.

Fossedal, Gregory A. *Our Finest Hour: Will Clayton, the Marshall Plan, and the Triumph of Democracy*. Hoover Institute Press, 1993.

Foucault, Michel. *Power/Knowledge: Selected Interviews and Other Writings, 1972–1977*. Vintage, 1980.

The Archaeology of Knowledge. Vintage, 1982.

Discipline & Punish: The Birth of the Prison. Vintage, 1995.

Franck, Thomas M. "Legitimacy in the International System." *The American Journal of International Law* 82, no. 4 (1988): 705–759.

Fairness in International Law and Institutions. Clarendon Press, 1995.

Frei, Norbert. *Adenauer's Germany and the Nazi Past: The Politics of Amnesty and Integration*. Columbia University Press, 2002.

Friedländer, Saul. *Memory, History, and the Extermination of the Jews of Europe*. Indiana University Press, 1993.
Fukuyama, Francis. *The End of History and the Last Man*. The Free Press, 1992.
Fuller, Lon L. "Positivism and Fidelity to Law: A Reply to Professor Hart." *Harvard Law Review* 71, no. 4 (1958): 630–672.
The Morality of Law: Revised Edition (The Storrs Lectures Series). Yale University Press, 1969.
Gagnon, V. P. *The Myth of Ethnic War: Serbia and Croatia in the 1990s*. Cornell University Press, 2004.
Garapon, Antoine and Ioannis Papadopoulous. *Juger en Amerique at en France: Culture juridique française et common law*. Odile Jakobs, 2004.
Garland, David. *Punishment and Modern Society: A Study in Social Theory*. University of Chicago Press, 1993.
The Culture of Control: Crime and Social Order in Contemporary Society. University of Chicago Press, 2002.
Gauthier, David P. *Morals by Agreement*. Oxford University Press, 1986.
Gibson, Catherine. "Testing the Legitimacy of the Joint Criminal Enterprise Doctrine in the ICTY: A Comparison of Individual Liability for Group Conduct in International and Domestic Law." *Duke Journal Comparative and International Law* 18, no. 521 (2008): 521–547.
Gibson, James L. "Understandings of Justice: Institutional Legitimacy, Procedural Justice, and Political Tolerance." *Law and Society Review* 23, no. 3 (1989): 469–496.
"The Contributions of Truth to Reconciliation: Lessons from South Africa." *Journal of Conflict Resolution* 50, no. 3 (2006): 409–432.
Ginsburg, Tom. *Judicial Review in New Democracies: Constitutional Courts in Asian Cases*. Cambridge University Press, 2003.
Giovani, Janine Di. *Madness Visible: A Memoir of War*. Vintage, 2003.
Gissel, Line Engbo. "Contemporary Transitional Justice: Normalising a Politics of Exception." *Global Society* (2016): 1–17.
Glasius, Marlies. "Do International Criminal Courts Require Democratic Legitimacy?" *European Journal of International Law* 23 (2012): 43–66.
Glenny, Misha. *The Fall of Yugoslavia: The Third Balkan War*. Penguin Books, 1996.
The Balkans: Nationalism, War, and the Great Powers, 1804–2011. Penguin Books, 2012.
Glueck, Sheldon. *The Nuremberg Trial and Aggressive War*. AA Knopf, 1946.
Golden, Charles. "Where Does Memory Reside, and Why Isn't It History?" *American Anthropologist* 107, no. 2 (2005): 270–274.
Goldhagen, Daniel. *Hitler's Willing Executioners: Ordinary Germans and the Holocaust*. Vintage, 1996.
Goldstein, Abraham S. and Martin Marcus. "The Myth of Judicial Supervision in Three 'Inquisitorial' Systems: France, Italy, and Germany." *Yale Law Journal* 87, no. 2 (1977): 240–283.
Goldstein, Ivo. *Croatia: A History*. McGill-Queen's University Press, 1999.
Holokaust u Zagrebu. Zidovska opcina Zagreb, 2001.
Hrvatska 1918–2008. Novi Liber, 2008.
Goldstone, Richard J. "50 Years after Nuremberg: A New International Criminal Tribunal for Human Rights Criminals." In *Contemporary Genocides: Causes, Cases, Consequences*, edited by Albert J. Jongman. PIOOM, 1996, 215.
Goodale, Mark. *Surrendering to Utopia: An Anthropology of Human Rights*. Stanford University Press, 2009.

Gordon, Gregory S. "Toward an International Criminal Procedure: Due Process Aspirations and Limitations." *Bepress Legal Series* (2006): 1695.

Gordon, Sarah S. *Hitler, Germans, and the Jewish Question*. Princeton University Press, 1984.

Gow, James and Rachel Kerr. "Introduction: Trials and Tribulations at the ICTY" in *Prosecuting War Crimes: Lessons and Legacies of the International Criminal Tribunal for the Former Yugoslavia*, edited by James Gow, Rachel Kerr, and Zoran Pajić. Routledge, 2014.

Grande, Elisabetta "Italian Criminal Justice: Borrowing and Resistance." *American Journal of Comparative Law* 48 (2000): 227.

"Comparative Criminal Justice." In *The Cambridge Companion to Comparative Law*, edited by Mauro Bussani-Ugo Mattei. 2012, 191–209.

Gray, David. "An Excuse-Centered Approach to Transitional Justice." *Fordham Law Review* 74 (2006): 2621.

Greenberg, Jessica. "'There's Nothing Anyone Can Do About It': Participation, Apathy, and 'Successful' Democratic Transition in Postsocialist Serbia." *Slavic Review* 69, no. 1 (2010): 41–64.

Grodsky, Brian. "Re-Ordering Justice: Towards A New Methodological Approach to Studying Transitional Justice." *Journal of Peace Research* 46, no. 6 (2009): 819–837.

Gross, Jan Tomasz. *Neighbors: The Destruction of the Jewish Community in Jedwabne, Poland*. Princeton University Press, 2001.

Grosser, Alfred. *Le crime et la mémoire*. Flammarion, 1991.

Grossman, Nienke. "The Normative Legitimacy of International Courts." *Temple Law Review* 86 (2013): 61–106.

Guttenplan, Don D. *The Holocaust on Trial*. WW Norton & Company, 2002.

Hafetz, Jonathan. *Punishing Atrocities through a Fair Trial: International Criminal Law from Nuremberg to the Age of Global Terrorism*. Cambridge University Press, 2018.

Hagan, John. *Justice in the Balkans: Prosecuting War Crimes in the Hague Tribunal*. University of Chicago Press, 2003.

Hagan, John and Ron Levi. "Crimes of War and the Force of Law." *Social Forces* 83 (2005): 1499–1534.

Hagan, John and Sanja Kutnjak Ivković. "War Crimes, Democracy, and the Rule of Law in Belgrade, the Former Yugoslavia, and Beyond." *The Annals of the American Academy of Political and Social Science* 605, no. 1 (2006): 129–151.

Reclaiming Justice: The International Criminal Tribunal for the Former Yugoslavia and Local Courts. Oxford University Press, 2011.

Halbwachs, Maurice. *On Collective Memory*. University of Chicago Press, 1992.

Halliday, Terence C., Lucien Karpik, and Malcolm M. Feeley. *Fighting for Political Freedom: Comparative Studies of the Legal Complex and Political Liberalism*. Hart Publishing, 2007.

Halpern, Jodi and Harvey M. Weinstein. "Rehumanizing the Other: Empathy and Reconciliation." *Human Rights Quarterly* 26 (2004): 561.

Hamdorf, Kai and "The Concept of a Joint Criminal Enterprise and Domestic Modes of Liability for Parties to a Crime: A Comparison of German and English Law." *Journal of International Criminal Justice* 5, no. 1, (2007): 208–226.

Harmon, Mark B. and Fergal Gaynor. "Ordinary Sentences for Extraordinary Crimes." *Journal of International Criminal Justice* 5, no. 3 (2007): 683–712.

Harmon, Mark B. and Magdalini Karagiannakis. "The Disclosure of Exculpatory Material by the Prosecution to the Defense under Rule 68 of the ICTY Rules." In *Essays on ICTY Procedure and Evidence in Honour of Gabrielle Kirk McDonald*, edited by Richard May. Brill, 2001: 315–328.

Hart, H.L.A. *Concept of Law*. Clarendon Press, 1963.

Punishment and Responsibility. Oxford University Press, 1968.

Hart, H.L.A. and Lon L. Fuller. *The Hart-Fuller Debate in the Twenty-First Century*, edited by Peter Cane. Hart, 2010.

Hathaway, Oona A. "Do Human Rights Treaties Make a Difference?" *Yale Law Journal* 111 (2002): 1935–2042.

"The New Empiricism in Human Rights: Insights and Implications." *Proceedings of the Annual Meeting (American Society of International Law)* 98 (2004): 206–211.

"Between Power and Principle: An Integrated Theory of International Law." *The University of Chicago Law Review* 72 (2005): 469–536.

"Why Do Countries Commit to Human Rights Treaties?" *The Journal of Conflict Resolution* 51 (2007): 588–621.

Haviv, Ron, Chuck Sudetic, and David Rieff. *Blood and Honey: A Balkan War Journal*. TV Books, 2000.

Hayden, Robert M. *Blueprints for a House Divided: The Constitutional Logic of the Yugoslav Conflicts*. University of Michigan Press, 1999.

Hayner, Priscilla B. *Unspeakable Truths: Transitional Justice and the Challenge of Truth Commissions*. Routledge, 2010.

Hazan, Pierre. *La Justice face à la guerre: De Nuremberg à La Haye*. Stock, 2000.

Justice in a Time of War: The True Story Behind the International Criminal Tribunal for the Former Yugoslavia. Texas A&M University Press, 2004.

Hazard, Geoffrey C. "Social Justice through Civil Justice." *University of Chicago Law Review* 36 (1969): 669.

Helfer, Laurence and Karen Alter. "Legitimacy and Lawmaking: A Tale of Three International Courts." *Theoretical Inquiries in Law* 14 (2013): 479.

Helfer, Laurence R., and Anne-Marie Slaughter. "Toward a Theory of Effective Supranational Adjudication." *Yale Law Journal* 107 (1997): 273.

"Why States Create International Tribunals: A Response to Professors Posner and Yoo." *California Law Review* 93, no. 3 (2005): 899–956.

Heller, Kevin Jon. *The Nuremberg Military Tribunals and the Origins of International Criminal Law*. Oxford University Press, 2011.

Henham, Ralph. "Developing Contextualized Rationales for Sentencing in International Criminal Trials: A Plea for Empirical Research." *Journal of International Criminal Justice* 5, no. 3 (2007): 757–778.

Henham, Ralph and Mark Drumbl. "Plea Bargaining at the International Criminal Tribunal for the Former Yugoslavia." *Criminal Law Forum* 16, no. 1 (2005): 49–87.

Herf, Jeffrey. *Divided Memory: The Nazi Past in the Two Germanys*. Harvard University Press, 1997.

Hesse, Carla and Robert Post. *Human Rights in Political Transitions: Gettysburg to Bosnia*. Zone Books, 1999.

Hilberg, Raul. *The Destruction of the European Jews*. New York: Holmes & Meier, 1985.

Hinton, Alexander Laban. *Transitional Justice: Global Mechanisms and Local Realities after Genocide and Mass Violence*. Rutgers University Press, 2011.

Hinton, Alexander Laban, Kevin Lewis O'Neill, and Victoria Sanford. *Genocide: Truth, Memory, and Representation*. Duke University Press, 2009.

Hirschl, Ran. "'Negative' Rights vs. 'Positive' Entitlements: A Comparative Study of Judicical Interpretations of Rights in an Emerging Neo-Liberal Economic Order." *Human Rights Quarterly* 22, no. 4 (2000): 1060–1098.

"The Judicialization of Mega-Politics and the Rise of Political Courts." *Annual Review of Political Science* 11 (2008): 93–118.

Hoare, Marko Attila. "Genocide in Bosnia and the Failure of International Justice." *Working Paper Series* 8 (2008).

Hodžić, Refik. "Living the Legacy of Mass Atrocities: Victims' Perspectives on War Crimes Trials." *Journal of International Criminal Justice* 8 (2010): 113–136.

Holtermann, Jakob v. " 'One of the Challenges that Can Plausibly Be Raised Against Them'? On the Role of Truth in Debates about the Legitimacy of International Criminal Tribunals." In *The Legitimacy of International Criminal Tribunals*, edited by Nobuo Hayashi and Cecilia M. Bailliet. Cambridge University Press, 2017: 206–227.

Horowitz, Donald L. *Ethnic Groups in Conflict*. University of California Press, 2000.

Horvat, Srećko and Igor Štiks (editors), *Welcome to the Desert of Post-Socialism. Radical Politics after Yugoslavia*. Verso Brooklyn, 2015.

Hughes, Edel, William Schabas, and Ramesh Chandra Thakur. *Atrocities and International Accountability: Beyond Transitional Justice*. United Nations University Press, 2007.

Hunt, Alan. *The Sociological Movement in Law*. Springer, 1978.

Explorations in Law and Society: Toward A Constitutive Theory of Law. Routledge, 1993.

Huyse, Luc. "Justice after Transition: On the Choices Successor Elites Make in Dealing with the Past." *Law & Social Inquiry* 20, no. 1 (1995): 51–78.

Ignatieff, Michael. *Human Rights as Politics and Idolatry*. Princeton University Press, 2001.

Israël, Liora and Guillaume Mouralis. "General Introduction." In *Dealing with Wars and Dictatorships*, edited by Liora Israël and Guillaume Mouralis. T.M.C. Asser Press, 1–20, 2012.

Jackson, John. "Finding the Best Epistemic Fit for International Criminal Tribunals: Beyond the Adversarial–Inquisitorial Dichotomy." *Journal of International Criminal Justice* 7, no. 1 (2009): 17–39.

Jain, Neha. *Perpetrators and Accessories in International Criminal Law: Individual Modes of Responsibility for Collective Crimes*. Hart Publishing, 2014.

Janowitz, Morris. "German Reactions to Nazi Atrocities." *American Journal of Sociology* 52, no. 2 (1946): 141–146.

Jansen, Stef. "If Reconciliation Is the Answer, Are We Asking the Right Questions?" *Studies in Social Justice* 7, no. 2 (2013): 229–243.

Jaspers, Karl. *The Question of German Guilt*. Fordham University Press, 2009.

Johnson, Larry D. "Closing an International Criminal Tribunal While Maintaining International Human Rights Standards and Excluding Impunity." *American Journal of International Law* 99, no. 1 (2005): 158–174.

Johnson, Scott T. "On the Road to Disaster: The Rights of the Accused and the International Criminal Tribunal for the Former Yugoslavia." *International Legal Perspectives* 10 (1998): 111.

Jokic, Alexandar. "War Crimes: Moral, Legal or Simply Political?" In *War Crimes and Collective Wrongdoing: A Reader*, edited by Alexandar Jokic. MA Blackwell, 2001.

Jones, Priscilla Dale. "Nazi Atrocities against Allied Airmen: Stalag Luft III and the End of British War Crimes Trials." *The Historical Journal* 41, no. 2 (1998): 543–565.

Jović, Dejan. *Jugoslavija, dr žava koja je odumrla : uspon, kriza i pad Kardeljeve Jugoslavije, 1974–1990*. Prometej, 2003.

Judah, Tim. *Kosovo: War and Revenge*. Yale University Press, 2002.

The Serbs: History, Myth and the Destruction of Yugoslavia. Yale University Press, 2010.

Kadijević, Veljko. *Moje viđenje raspada : vojska bez držâve*. Politika, 1993.

Kaes, Anton. *From Hitler to Heimat: The Return of History as Film*. Harvard University Press, 1992

Kagan, Robert A. *Adversarial Legalism: The American Way of Law*. Harvard University Press, 2009.

Kaminski, Marek M. and Monika Nalepa. "Judging Transitional Justice: A New Criterion for Evaluating Truth Revelation Procedures." *Journal of Conflict Resolution* 50, no. 3 (2006): 383–408.

Kant, Immanuel. "The Idea for a Universal History with a Cosmopolitan Purpose." In *Political Writings*, edited by H.S. Reiss. Cambridge University Press, 1991, 41–53.

Kaplan, Robert. *Balkan Ghosts: A Journey Through History*. Picador, 1992.

Karnavas, Michael G. "Gathering Evidence in International Criminal Trials – the View of the Defence Lawyer." In *International Criminal Justice: A Critical Analysis of Institutions and Procedures*, edited by Michael Bohlander. Cameron May Ltd., 2007, 75–152.

"The ICTY Legacy: A Defense Counsel's Perspective." *Goettingen Journal of International Law* 3 (2011): 1053–1092.

Keating, V.C. and K. Kaczmarska. "Conservative Soft Power: Liberal Soft Power Bias and the 'Hidden' Attraction of Russia." *Journal of International Relations and Development* (May 11, 2017): 1–27.

Keen, Peter Carmichael. "Tempered Adversariality: The Judicial Role and Trial Theory in the International Criminal Tribunals." *Leiden Journal of International Law* 17, no. 4 (2004): 767–814.

Kelsen, Hans. "Will the Judgment in the Nuremberg Trial Constitute a Precedent in International Law?" *The International Law Quarterly* 1, no. 2 (Summer, 1947): 153.

Kennedy, David. "The Disciplines of International Law and Policy." *Leiden Journal of International Law* 12, no. 01 (1999): 9–133.

"My Talk at the ASIL: What Is New Thinking in International Law?" *Proceedings of the Annual Meeting (American Society of International Law)* 94 (2000): 104–125.

Kerr, Rachel. *The International Criminal Tribunal for the Former Yugoslavia: An Exercise in Law, Politics, and Diplomacy*. Oxford University Press, 2004.

"Peace through Justice? The International Criminal Tribunal for the Former Yugoslavia." *Southeast European and Black Sea Studies* 7, no. 3 (2007): 373–385.

Kerr, Rachel and Eirin Mobekk. *Peace and Justice*. Polity, 2007.

King, Henry T. Jr., "Nuremberg and Crimes against Peace." *Case Western Reserve Journal International Law* 41 (2009): 281.

Kinstler, Linda. "The Last Nazi Hunters." *The Guardian*, 31 August 2017.

Kissinger, J. and Henry A. "The Pitfalls of Universal Jurisdiction." *Foreign Affairs* 80 (2001): 86–96.

Klabbers, Jan. *An Introduction to International Institutional Law* (third edition). Cambridge University Press, 2015.

Klare, Karl E. "Legal Culture and Transformative Constitutionalism," *South African Journal on Human Rights* 14, no. 1 (1998): 146–188.

Koh, Harold. "Why Do Nations Obey International Law?" *Yale Law Journal* 106 (1997): 2599.

Koller, David S. "The Faith of the International Criminal Lawyer." *NYU Journal of International Law and Policy* 40 (2007): 1019.

Koskenniemi, Martti. "Carl Schmitt, Hans Morgenthau, and the Image of Law in International Relations." In *The Role of Law in International Politics*, edited by Michael Byers. Oxford University Press, 2000.

"Between Impunity and Show Trials." *Max Planck Yearbook of United Nations Law* 6, no. 1 (2002a): 1–32.

"'The Lady Doth Protest Too Much': Kosovo, and the Turn to Ethics in International Law." *The Modern Law Review* 65, no. 2 (2002b): 159–175.

From Apology to Utopia: The Structure of International Legal Argument. Cambridge University Press, 2006.

Fragmentation of International Law: Difficulties Arising From Diversification and Expansion of International Law. Report of the Study Group of the International Law Commission. Erik Castrén Institute of International Law, 2007.

"The Fate of Public International Law: Between Technique and Politics." *The Modern Law Review* 70, no. 1 (2007): 1–30.

The Politics of International Law. Hart Publishing, 2011.

Kostić, Roland. "Transitional Justice and Reconciliation in Bosnia-Herzegovina: Whose Memories, Whose Justice?" *Sociologija LIV* 4, 2012.

Kranzbuhler, Otto. "Nuremberg Eighteen Years Afterwards." *DePaul Law Review* 14 (1964): 333.

Kritz, Neil J. *Transitional Justice: How Emerging Democracies Reckon with Former Regimes*. United States Inst of Peace Press, 1995.

"Coming to Terms with Atrocities: A Review of Accountability Mechanisms for Mass Violations of Human Rights." *Law and Contemporary Problems* 59, no. 4 (1996): 127–152.

"Policy Implications of Empirical Research on Transitional Justice." In *Assessing the Impact of Transitional Justice: Challenges for Empirical Research*, edited by Hugo Van der Merwe, Victoria Baxter, and Audrey Chapman. US Institute of Peace Press, 2009.

Kritz, Neil J. and Jakob Finci. "A Truth and Reconciliation Commission in Bosnia and Herzegovina: An Idea Whose Time Has Come." *International Law Forum du droit internationale* 3 (2001): 50–58.

Krog, Antjie. *Country of My Skull: Guilt, Sorrow, and the Limits of Forgiveness in the New South Africa*. Times Books, 1999.

Ku, Julian and Jide Nzelibe. "Do International Criminal Tribunals Deter or Exacerbate Humanitarian Atrocities." *Washington University Law Review* 84 (2006): 777.

Kubek, Anthony. "The Morgenthau Plan and the Problem of Policy Perversion." *The Journal of Historical Review* 9, no. 3 (1989): 1.

Kumm, Mattias. "The Legitimacy of International Law: A Constitutionalist Framework of Analysis." *European Journal of International Law* 15, no. 5 (2004): 907–931.

Kymlicka, Will. *Liberalism, Community, and Culture*. Oxford University Press, 1991.

Justice in Political Philosophy. Edward Elgar Publishers, 1992.

The Rights of Minority Cultures. Oxford University Press, 1995.

Contemporary Political Philosophy: An Introduction. Oxford University Press, 2001.

Kymlicka, Will and Magda Opalski. *Can Liberal Pluralism Be Exported? Western Political Theory and Ethnic Relations in Eastern Europe*. Oxford University Press, 2002.

Lacey, Nicola. "Historicising Criminalisation: Conceptual and Empirical Issues." *Modern Law Review* 72, no. 6 (2009): 936–960.

"Community, Culture and Criminalization." In *Crime, Punishment and Responsibility: The Jurisprudence of Antony Duff*, edited by Rowan Cruft, Matthew H. Kramer, and Mark R. Reiff. Oxford University Press, 2011: 292–310.

Lamont, Christopher K. *International Criminal Justice and the Politics of Compliance*. Lund Humphries Publishers, 2013.

Lampe, John R. *Yugoslavia as History: Twice There was a Country*. Cambridge University Press, 2000.

Landsman, Stephan. "Retroactive Trials and Justice." *Michigan Law Review* 96 (1998): 1456–1473.

Langbein, John H. "Controlling Prosecutorial Discretion in Germany." *University of Chicago Law Review* 41, no. 3 (1974): 439–467.

"The Criminal Trial before the Lawyers." *University of Chicago Law Review* 45 (1978): 263–316.

"The German Advantage in Civil Procedure." *University of Chicago Law Review* 52 (1985): 823–866.

Langbein, John H. and Lloyd L. Weinreb. "Continental Criminal Procedure: 'Myth' and Reality." *The Yale Law Journal* 87, no. 8 (1978): 1549–1569.

Langer, Maximo. "The Rise of Managerial Judging in International Criminal Law." *Bepress Legal Series* 343 (2005): 1–64.

Langer, Maximo and Joseph Doherty. "Managerial Judging Goes International but Its Promise Remains Unfulfilled: An Empirical Assessment of the ICTY Reforms." *Yale Journal of International Law* 36 (2011): 241.

Laternser, Hans. "Looking Back at the Nuremberg Trials with Special Consideration of the Processes against Military Leaders." *Whittier Law Review* 8 (1986): 557.

Leebaw, Bronwyn Anne. "The Irreconcilable Goals of Transitional Justice." *Human Rights Quarterly* 30, no. 1 (2008): 95–118.

Judging State-Sponsored Violence, Imagining Political Change. Cambridge University Press, 2011.

Legrand, Pierre. "The Impossibility of Legal Transplants." *Maastricht Journal of European and Comparative Law* 4 (1997): 111–124.

Lerner, Renée Letow. "The Intersection of Two Systems: An American on Trial for an American Murder in the French Cour d'Assises." *University of Illinois Law Review* (2001): 791–892.

Levine, Kay. "The Intimacy Discount: Prosecutorial Discretion, Privacy, and Equality in the Statutory Rape Caseload." *Emory Law Journal* 55 (2006): 691.

Levy, Daniel and Natan Sznaider. *Holocaust and Memory in the Global Age*. Temple University Press, 2005.

Human Rights and Memory. Pennsylvania State University Press, 2010.

Linz, Juan J. and Alfred Stepan. *Problems of Democratic Transition and Consolidation: Southern Europe, South America, and Post-Communist Europe*. Johns Hopkins University Press, 2011.

Lovrenović, Ivan and Predrag Lucić. *Stenogrami o podjelene Bosne*. Dani Biblioteka, 2003.

Luban, David. "Fairness to Rightness: Jurisdiction, Legality and the Legitimacy of International Criminal Law." In *The Philosophy of International Law*, edited by Samantha Besson and John Tasioulas. Oxford University Press, 2010.

MacDonald, David. *Balkan Holocausts? Serbian and Croatian Victim-Centred Propaganda and the War in Yugoslavia*. Manchester University Press, 2002.

"Living Together or Hating Each Other." In *Confronting the Yugoslav Controversies. A Scholars' Initiative*, edited by Charles Ingrao and Thomas A. Emmert. Purdue University Press, 2009: 390–424.

Mackenzie, Ruth and Philippe Sands. "International Courts and Tribunals and the Independence of the International Judge." *Harvard International Law Journal* 44 (2003): 271.

Maga, Timothy P. *America Attacks Japan: The Invasion That Never Was*. University Press of Kentucky, 2002.

Magas, Branka. *The Destruction of Yugoslavia: Tracking the Break-Up 1980–1992*. Verso, 1993.

Maguire, Peter. *Law and War: International Law and American History*. Columbia University Press, 2010.

Malcolm, Noel. "Bosnia and the West: A Study in Failure." *Quadrant* 39, no. 6 (1995): 12.
Markovits, Inga. "Selective Memory: How the Law Affects What We Remember and Forget about the Past: The Case of East Germany." *Law & Society Review* 35, no. 3 (2001): 513–563.
Marrus, Michael R. *The Holocaust in History*. Plume, 1989.
Perspectives on the Holocaust. Mecklermedia, 1989.
The Nuremberg War Crimes Trial, 1945–46: A Documentary History. Bedford/St. Martin's, 1997.
The Origins of the Holocaust. De Gruyter, 2011.
Martin, Francesco Forest. *International Human Rights and Humanitarian Law: Treaties, Cases and Analysis*. Cambridge University Press, 2006.
May, Richard and Marieke Wierda. "Trends in International Criminal Evidence: Nuremberg, Tokyo, The Hague, and Arusha." *Columbia Journal of Transnational Law* 37 (1998): 725.
International Criminal Evidence. Brill, 2002.
Mazower, Mark. *Dark Continent: Europe's Twentieth Century*. Vintage, 2000.
The Balkans: A Short History. Modern Library, 2002.
McCann, Michael W. *Rights at Work: Pay Equity Reform and the Politics of Legal Mobilization*. University Of Chicago Press, 1994.
McDermott, Yvonne. "The Admissibility and Weight of Written Witness Testimony." *Leiden Journal of International Law* 26, no. 4 (2013): 971–989.
McEvoy, Kieran. "Imperfect Justice at Nuremberg and Tokyo." *Journal of Law and Society* 34 (2007): 411–440.
McKillop, Bron. "Anatomy of a French Murder Case." *American Journal of Comparative Law* 45, no. 3 (Summer, 1997): 527–583.
McMahon, Patrice C. and David P. Forsythe. "The ICTY's Impact on Serbia: Judicial Romanticism Meets Network Politics." *Human Rights Quarterly* 30, no. 2 (2008): 412–435.
Meernik, James. "Victor's Justice or the Law? Judging and Punishing at the International Criminal Tribunal for the Former Yugoslavia." *Journal of Conflict Resolution* 47, no. 2 (2003): 140–162.
"Justice and Peace? How the International Criminal Tribunal Affects Societal Peace in Bosnia." *Journal of Peace Research* 42, no. 3 (2005): 271–289.
Meernik, James and Kimi Lynn King. "The Effectiveness of International Law and the ICTY – Preliminary Results of an Empirical Study." *International Criminal Law Review* 1 (2001): 343.
Mégret, Frédéric. "The Politics of International Criminal Justice." *European Journal of International Law* 13, no. 5 (2002): 1261–1284.
"Three Dangers for the International Criminal Court: A Critical Look at a Consensual Project." *Finnish Yearbook of International Law* 12 (2002): 195–247.
"In Search of the 'Vertical': An Exploration of What Makes International Criminal Tribunals Different (and Why)?" Working Paper Series (2008): 1–57.
"Beyond Fairness: Understanding the Determinants of International Criminal Procedure." *UCLA Journal of International Law and Foreign Affairs* 14 (2009): 37.
Mégret, Frédéric and Florian Hoffman. "The UN as a Human Rights Violator? Some Reflections on the United Nations Changing Human Rights Responsibilities." *Human Rights Quarterly* 25, no. 2 (2003): 314–342.
Meijers, Tim and Marlies Glasius "Trials as Messages of Justice: What Should be Expected of International Criminal Justice?" *Ethics & International Affairs* 30, no. 4 (2016): 429–447.

Meltzer, Bernard D. "Robert H. Jackson: Nuremberg's Architect and Advocate." *Albany Law Review* 68 (2004): 55, 57.

Mendeloff, David. "Truth-Seeking, Truth-Telling, and Postconflict Peacebuilding: Curb the Enthusiasm?" *International Studies Review* 6, no. 3 (2004): 355–380.

Meron, Theodor. "From Nuremberg to the Hague." *Military Law Review* 149 (1995): 107.

"International Criminalization of Internal Atrocities." *American Journal of International Law* 89 (1995): 554.

"Answering for War Crimes: Lessons from the Balkans." *Foreign Affairs* 76 (1997): 2–8.

"Is International Law Moving Towards Criminalization?" *European Journal of International Law* 9 (1998): 18–31.

"Reflections on the Prosecution of War Crimes by International Tribunals." *The American Journal of International Law* 100, no. 3 (2006): 551–579.

Merritt, Richard L. *Democracy Imposed: US Occupation Policy and the German Public, 1945–1949*. Yale University Press, 1995.

Merryman, John Henry and Rogelio Perez-Perdomo. *The Civil Law Tradition: An Introduction to the Legal Systems of Europe and Latin America* (third edition). Stanford University Press, 2007.

Mesić, Stipe. *Kako je srušena Jugoslavija*. Mislavpress, 1994.

Mettraux, Guénaël. "Judicial Inheritance: The Value and Significance of the Nuremberg Trial to Contemporary War Crimes Tribunals." In *Perspectives on the Nuremberg Trial*, edited by Guénaël Mettraux. Oxford University Press, 2009a, 599.

The Law of Command Responsibility. Oxford University Press, 2009b.

Milgram, Stanley. *Obedience to Authority: An Experimental View*. Harper Perennial Modern Classics, 2009.

Miller, Frank. *Prosecution: The Decision to Charge a Suspect with a Crime*. Little, Brown and Company, 1970.

Milosevic, Milan. "The Media Wars." In *Burn This House*, edited by Jasminka Udovicki and James Ridgeway. Duke University Press, 1997, 108–129.

Minear, Richard H. *Victors' Justice: The Tokyo War Crimes Trial*. Princeton University Press, 1971.

Minow, Martha. *Between Vengeance and Forgiveness: Facing History after Genocide and Mass Violence*. Beacon Press, 1999.

Breaking the Cycles of Hatred: Memory, Law, and Repair. Princeton University Press, 2003.

Moeller, Robert G. *War Stories: The Search for a Usable Past in the Federal Republic of Germany*. University of California Press, 2001.

Mohamed, Saira. "Deviance, Aspiration, and the Stories We Tell: Reconciling Mass Atrocity and the Criminal Law." *Yale Law Journal* 124, no. 5 (2015).

Moravcsik, Andrew. "Taking Preferences Seriously: A Liberal Theory of International Politics." *International Organization* 51 (1997): 513–553.

"The Origins of Human Rights Regimes: Democratic Delegation in Postwar Europe." *International Organization* 54 (2000): 217–252.

Morgenthau, Hans, Kenneth Thompson, and David Clinton. *Politics among Nations*. McGraw-Hill, 2005.

Morris, Clarence. "Law, Reason, and Sociology." *University of Pennsylvania Law Review* 107, no. 2 (1958): 147–165.

Morris, Virginia and Michael Scharf. *An Insider's Guide to the International Criminal Tribunal for the Former Yugoslavia: Documentary History and Analysis* (two volumes). Brill, 1995.

Mundis, Daryl A. "From 'Common Law' Towards 'Civil Law': The Evolution of the ICTY Rules of Procedure and Evidence." *Leiden Journal of International Law* 14, no. 2 (2001): 367–382.

"The Legal Character and Status of the Rules of Procedure and Evidence of the ad hoc International Criminal Tribunals." *International Criminal Law Review* 1 (2001): 191.

Murphy, Colleen. *The Conceptual Foundations of Transitional Justice*. Cambridge University Press, 2017.

Müller, Jan-Werner. *Contesting Democracy: Political Ideas in Twentieth-Century Europe*. Yale University Press, 2011.

Nalepa, Monika. "Reconciliation, Refugee Returns, and the Impact of International Criminal Justice: The Case of Bosnia and Herzegovina." In *Transitional Justice: NOMOS Li*, edited by Melissa Williams, Rosemary Nagy, Jon Elster. New York University Press, 2012, 316–359.

Neier, Aryeh. "What Should be Done About the Guilty?" *The New York Review of Books* 37, no. 1 (1990): 32–35.

"Rethinking Truth, Justice, and Guilt after Bosnia and Rwanda." In *Human Rights in Political Transitions: Gettysburg to Bosnia*, edited by Carla Hesse and Robert Post. Zone Books, 1999, 39–52.

Nelken, David. "Comparatists and transferability." In *Comparative Legal Studies: Traditions and Transitions*, edited by Pierre Legrand and Roderick Munday. Cambridge University Press, 2003, 437–466.

Nettelfield, Lara. "Research and Repercussions of Death Tolls: The Case of the Bosnian Book of the Dead." In *Sex, Drugs, and Body Counts: The Politics of Numbers in Global Crime and Conflict*, edited by Peter Andreas and Kelly M. Greenhill. Cornell University Press, 2010, 159–187.

Courting Democracy in Bosnia and Herzegovina. Cambridge University Press, 2012.

Neuffer, Elizabeth. *The Key to My Neighbor's House: Seeking Justice in Bosnia and Rwanda*. Picador, 2002.

Nino, Carlos. "The Duty to Punish Past Abuses of Human Rights Put into Context: The Case of Argentian." *Yale Law Journal* 100 (1991): 2619.

Nollkaemper, Andre. "The Legitimacy of International Law in the Case Law of the International Criminal Tribunal for the Former Yugoslavia." In *Ambiguity in the Rule of Law. The Interface between National and International Legal Systems*, edited by Thomas A.J.A. Vandamme and Jan-Herman Reestman. Europa Law Publishing, 2001, 13–23.

Nollkaemper, André and Harmen van der Wilt. *System Criminality in International Law*. Cambridge University Press, 2009.

Nonet, Philippe, Philip Selznick, and Robert Allen Kagan. *Law & Society in Transition: Toward Responsive Law*. Transaction Publishers, 1978.

Nora, Pierre. *Le Debat – Histoire, Politique, Societe*. Gallimard, 1980.

"Between memory and history: Les lieux de mémoire." *Representations* 26, no. 26 (1989): 7–24.

Norrie, Alan. *Crime, Reason and History*. Butterworths, 2001.

O'Donnell, Therese. "Executioners, Bystanders and Victims: Collective Guilt, the Legacy of Denazification and the Birth of Twentieth-Century Transitional Justice." *Legal Studies* 25, no. 4 (2005): 627–667.

Ohlin, Jens. "Joint Criminal Confusion." *New Criminal Law Review* 12 (2009): 406–419.

"Proportional Sentences at the ICTY." In *The Legacy of the International Criminal Tribunal for the Former Yugoslavia*, edited by Bert Swart, Göran Sluiter, and Alexander Zahar. Oxford University Press, 2011: 406–419.

Olick, Jeffrey K. "What Does it Mean to Normalize the Past? Official Memory in German Politics since 1989." *Social Science History* 22, no. 4 (1998): 547–571.

"Collective Memory: The Two Cultures." *Sociological Theory* 17, no. 3 (1999): 333–348.

The Politics of Regret: On Collective Memory and Historical Responsibility. Routledge, 2007.

"Between Chaos and Diversity: Is Social Memory Studies a Field?" *International Journal of Politics, Culture and Society* 22 (2009): 249–252.

Olick, Jeffrey K and Daniel Levy. "Collective Memory and Cultural Constraint: Holocaust Myth and Rationality in German Politics." *American Sociological Review* 62 (1997): 921–936.

Olick, Jeffrey K., Vered Vinitzky-Seroussi, and Daniel Levy. *The Collective Memory Reader*. Oxford University Press, 2011.

Olsen, Tricia D., Leigh A. Payne, and Andrew G. Reiter. "The Justice Balance: When Transitional Justice Improves Human Rights and Democracy." *Human Rights Quarterly* 32, no. 4 (2010a): 980–1007.

Transitional Justice in Balance: Comparing Processes, Weighing Efficiency. United States Institute for Peace, 2010b.

Olusanya, Olaoluwa. *Sentencing War Crimes and Crimes against Humanity under the International Criminal Tribunal for the Former Yugoslavia*. Europa Law Publishing, 2005.

Orentlicher, Diane F. "Settling Accounts: The Duty to Prosecute Human Rights Violations of a Prior Regime." *Yale Law Journal* 100 (1991): 2537–2615.

"Shrinking the Space for Denial. The Impact of the ICTY in Serbia" Open Society Justice Initiative. Available at www.opensocietyfoundations.org/sites/default/files/serbia_20080501.pdf (2008).

"That Someone Guilty Be Punished: The Impact of the ICTY in Bosnia." Open Society Justice Initiative. Available at www.opensocietyfoundations.org/sites/default/files/that-someone-guilty-20100708.pdf (2010).

"Review Essays: From Viability to Impact: Evolving Metrics for Assessing the International Criminal Tribunal for the Former Yugoslavia." *International Journal of Transitional Justice* 7 (2013): 536–546.

Orie, Alphons. "Accusatorial v. Inquisitorial Approach in International Criminal Proceedings Prior to the Establishment of the ICC and in the Proceedings before the ICC." In *The Rome Statute of the International Criminal Court: A Commentary*, edited by Antonio Cassese, Paula Gaeta, and John R.W.D. Jones. Oxford University Press, 2002, 1439–1495.

Osiel, Mark. *Mass Atrocity, Collective Memory, and the Law*. Transaction Publishers, 1997.

Making Sense of Mass Atrocity. Cambridge University Press, 2009.

Overy, Richard. "The Nuremberg Trials: International Law in the Making." In *From Nuremberg to The Hague*, edited by Phillippe Sands. Cambridge University Press, 2003, 1–29.

Pavlaković, Vjeran. "Croatia, the International Criminal Tribunal for the former Yugoslavia, and General Gotovina as a Political Symbol." *Europe-Asia Studies* 62, no. 10 (2010): 1707–1740.

Pendas, Devin O. *The Frankfurt Auschwitz Trial, 1963–1965: Genocide, History, and the Limits of the Law*. Cambridge University Press, 2006.

Perica, Vjekoslav. *Balkan Idols: Religion and Nationalism in Yugoslav States*. Oxford University Press, 2004.

Peskin, Victor. "Courting Rwanda: The Promises and Pitfalls of the ICTR Outreach Programme." *Journal of International Criminal Justice* 3, no. 4 (2005): 950–961.

International Justice in Rwanda and the Balkans: Virtual Trials and the Struggle for State Cooperation. Cambridge University Press, 2008.

Philipose, Elizabeth. "Prosecuting Violence, Performing Sovereignty: The Trial of Dusko Tadic." *International Journal for the Semiotics of Law* 15, no. 2 (2002): 159–184.

Piacente, Nicola. "Importance of the Joint Criminal Enterprise Doctrine for the ICTY Prosecutorial Policy." *Journal of International Criminal Justice* 2, no. 2 (2004): 446–454.

Pizzi, William T. "Understanding Prosecutorial Discretion in the United States: The Limits of Comparative Criminal Procedure as an Instrument of Reform." *Ohio State Law Journal* 54 (1993): 1325.

"Overcoming Logistical and Structural Barriers to Fair Trials at International Tribunals." *International Commentary on Evidence* 4, no. 1 (2006): 1051–1567.

Pomorski, Stanislaw. "Conspiracy and Criminal Organization." In *The Nuremberg Trial and International Law*, edited by George Ginsburgs and V.N. Kudriavtsev. Martinus Nijhoff Publishers, 1990, 213–229.

Popov, Nebojša and Drinka Gojković. *The Road to War in Serbia: Trauma and Catharsis*. Central European University Press, 2000.

Power, Samantha. *A Problem from Hell: America and the Age of Genocide*. Basic Books, 2002.

Prendergast, David, "The Constitutionality of Strict Liability Offences." *Dublin University Law Journal* 33 (June 24, 2011): 285. Available at SSRN https://ssrn.com/abstract=2359084

Primus, Richard. "A Brooding Omnipresence: Totalitarianism in Postwar Constitutional Thought." *Yale Law Journal* 106 (1996): 423–457.

Provost, Rene. *International Human Rights and Humanitarian Law*. Cambridge University Press, 2003.

Quinn, Joanna R. "Introduction," in *Reconciliation(s): Transitional Justice in Postconflict Societies*, edited by Joanna R. Quinn. McGill-Queen's University Press, 2009: 3–14.

Rabkin, Jeremy. "No Substitute for Sovereignty: Why International Criminal Justice Has a Bleak Future – and Deserves It." In *Atrocities and International Accountability: Beyond Transnational Justice*, edited by William A. Schabas, Ramesh Thakur, and Edel Hughes. United Nations University Press, 2007.

The Three Yugoslavias: State-Building and Legitimation, 1918–2005. Indiana University Press, 2006.

Ramet, Sabrina P. and Vjeran Pavlaković. *Serbia since 1989: Politics and Society under Milosevic and After*. University of Washington Press, 2006.

Balkan Babel: Politics, Culture, and Religion in Yugoslavia. Westview Press, 1992.

Ramet, Sabrina Petra. Balkan Babel: Thinking about Yugoslavia: Scholarly Debates about the Yugoslav Breakup and the Wars in Bosnia and Kosovo. Cambridge University Press, 2005.

Ratner, Steven R., Jason Abrams, and James Bischoff. *Accountability for Human Rights Atrocities in International Law: Beyond the Nuremberg Legacy*. Oxford University Press, 2009.

Rauxloh, Regina E. "Negotiated History: The Historical Record in International Criminal Law and Plea Bargaining." *International Criminal Law Review* 10 (2010): 739–770.

Rawls, John. *A Theory of Justice*. Belknap Press, 1971.

Political Liberalism. Columbia University Press, 1993.

The Law of Peoples. Harvard University Press, 2001.

Raz, Joseph. *The Authority of Law: Essays on Law and Morality*. Oxford University Press, 2009.

Renteln, Allison Dundes. *The Cultural Defense*. Oxford University Press, 2005.

Resnik, Judith. *Managerial Judges*. Rand, 1982.

Ricouer, Paul. "Le Juste, entre le légal et le bon." *Esprit* 174 (1991): 5–21.

Le juste, la justice et son échec. L'Herne, 2005.

Memory, History, Forgetting. University Of Chicago Press, 2006.

Rieff, David. *Slaughterhouse: Bosnia and the Failure of the West*. Touchstone, 1996.

A Bed for the Night: Humanitarianism in Crisis. Simon & Schuster, 2003.

Roberts, Geoffrey. "Ensuring Fair and Expeditious Trials at the International Criminal Tribunal for the Former Yugoslavia." European Journal of International Law 11, no. 3 (2000): 569–589.

Robinson, P.L., *Stalin's Wars: From World War to Cold War, 1939–1953*. Yale University Press, 2006.

Roht-Arriaza, Naomi. "State Responsibility to Investigate and Prosecute Grave Human Rights Violations in International Law." *California Law Review* 78, no. 2 (1990): 449–513.

Impunity and Human Rights in International Law and Practice. Oxford University Press, 1995.

The Pinochet Effect: Transnational Justice in the Age of Human Rights. University of Pennsylvania Press, 2005.

"The New Landscape of Transitional Justice." In *Transitional Justice in the Twenty-First Century: Beyond Truth Versus Justice*, edited by Naomi Roht-Arriaza and Javier Mariezcurrena. Cambridge University Press, 2006.

Röling, Bert V. "The Nuremberg and the Tokyo Trials in Retrospect." In *Perspectives on the Nuremberg Trial*, edited by Guénaël Mettraux. Oxford University Press, 2008: 455–472.

Röling, Bert V. and Antonio Cassese. *The Tokyo Trial and Beyond*. Polity Press, 1993.

Rosenberg, Gerald N. *The Hollow Hope: Can Courts Bring about Social Change*. University of Chicago, 1991.

Roth, Brad R. *Governmental Illegitimacy in International Law*. Oxford University Press, 2001.

Sovereign Equality and Moral Disagreement: Premises of a Pluralist International Legal Order. Oxford University Press, 2011.

Rothe, Dawn L. and Christopher W. Mullins. "Beyond the Juristic Orientation of International Criminal Justice: The Relevance of Criminological Insight to International Criminal Law and its Control: A Commentary." *International Criminal Law Review* 10, no. 1 (2010): 97–110.

Rousseau, Jean-Jacques, John Locke, and David Hume. *Social Contract – Essays by Locke [An Essay Concerning the True Original, Extent and End of Civil Government]; Hume [of the Original Contract]; Rousseau [The Social Contract]*, edited by Ernest Barker. Oxford University Press, 1958.

Rowen, Jamie. *Searching for Truth in the Transitional Justice Movement*. Cambridge University Press, 2017.

Rückerl, Adalbert. *The Investigation of Nazi Crimes 1945–1978: A Documentation*. Muller, 1979.

Sa'adah, Anne. *Germany's Second Chance: Trust, Justice, and Democratization*. Harvard University Press, 1998.

"Regime Change: Lessons from Germany on Justice, Institution Building, and Democracy." *The Journal of Conflict Resolution* 50 (2006): 303–323.

Sadat, Leila Nadya. *The International Criminal Court and the Transformation of International Law: Justice for the New Millennium*. Transnational Publishers Inc, 2002.

"The Nuremberg Trial, Seventy Years Later" *Washington University Global Studies Law Review* 15, no. 4 (2015): 575–592.

Sadat, Leila Nadya and S. Richard Carden. "The New International Criminal Court: An Uneasy Revolution." *Georgetown Law Journal* 88 (1999): 381.

Safferling, Christoph Johannes Maria. *Towards an International Criminal Procedure*. Oxford University Press, 2001.

Salas, Denis. "The Role of the Judge," in *European Criminal Procedures*, edited by Mireille Delmas-Marty and J.R. Spencer. Cambridge University Press, 2006, 488–541.

Sapolsky, Robert. *Behave*. Random House, 2017.

Sarat, Austin. *Imagining Legality: Where Law Meets Popular Culture*. University of Alabama Press, 2011.

Transitions: Legal Change, Legal Meanings. University of Alabama Press, 2012.

Sarat, Austin and Nasser Hussain. *When Governments Break the Law: The Rule of Law and the Prosecution of the Bush Administration*. New York University Press, 2010.

Sarat, Austin and Thomas R. Kearns. *Justice and Injustice in Law and Legal Theory*. University of Michigan Press, 1999.

Sarkin, Jeremy. "Atrocity, Punishment, and International Law." *Human Rights Quarterly* 30, no. 4 (2008): 1028–1042.

Scalia, Damien, Mina Rauschenbach, and Christian Staerklé. "Paroles d'accués sur la légitimitéde la justice pénale internationale." *Chronique de criminologie* (juillet/septembre 2012): 727–746.

Schabas, William. *Unimaginable Atrocities: Justice, Politics, and Rights at the War Crimes Tribunals*. Oxford University Press, 2012.

"Sentencing by International Tribunals: A Human Rights Approach." *Duke Journal Comparative and International Law* 7 (1997): 461–518.

"Mens Rea and the International Criminal Tribunal for the Former Yugoslavia" *New England Law Review* 37, no. 4 (2003): 1015–1036.

"State Policy as an Element of International Crimes." *The Journal of Criminal Law and Criminology* 98, no. 3 (2008): 953–982.

Genocide in International Law: The Crime of Crimes. Cambridge University Press, 2009.

An Introduction to the International Criminal Court. Cambridge University Press, 2011.

Schabas, William A. and Shane Darcy. *Truth Commissions and Courts: The Tension between Criminal Justice and the Search for Truth*. Springer, 2010.

Scharf, Michael. "A Critique of the Yugoslavia War Crimes Tribunal." *Denver Journal of International Law and Policy* 25 (1997a): 305–312.

Scharf, Michael *Balkan Justice: The Story Behind the First International War Crimes Trial since Nuremberg*. Carolina Academic Press, 1997b.

Scharf, Michael and Valerie Epps. "The International Trial of the Century: A Cross-Fire Exchange on the First Case before the Yugoslavia War Crimes Tribunal." *Cornell International Law Journal* 29 (1996): 635.

"Trading Justice for Efficiency Plea-Bargaining and International Tribunals." *Journal of International Criminal Justice* 2, no. 4 (2004): 1070–1081.

Scheffer, David J. "The Tool Box, Past and Present, of Justice and Reconciliation for Atrocities." *The American Journal of International Law* 95, no. 4 (2001): 970–977.

Scheingold, Stuart A. *The Rule of Law in European Integration: The Path of the Schuman Plan*. Greenwood Press, 1976.

The Politics of Rights: Lawyers, Public Policy, and Political Change. University of Michigan Press [1964], 2004.

Scheingold, Stuart A. and Lynne A. Gressett. "Policy, Politics, and the Criminal Courts." *Law & Social Inquiry* 12, nos. 2–3 (1987): 461–505.

Schlütter, Birgit. *Developments in Customary International Law: Theory and the Practice of the International Court of Justice and the International ad hoc Criminal Tribunals for Rwanda and Yugoslavia*. Martinus Nijhoff, 2010.

Schmitz, Hans Peter and Kathryn Sikkink. "International Human Rights." In *Handbook of International Relations*, edited by Walter Carlsnaes. Sage Publishing, 2012: 827–851.

Schomburg, Wolfgang. "Jurisprudence on JCE – Revisiting a Never Ending Story." (availabe at: http://www.cambodiatribunal.org/assets/pdf/court-filings/ctm_blog_6_1_2010.pdf) (accessed July 2018).

Schopflin, George. *Nations, Identity, Power*. New York University Press, 2000.

Schwartz, Barry. "The Social Context of Commemoration: A Study in Collective Memory." *Social Forces* 61, nos. 2 (1982): 374–402.

Schwartz, Barry, Yael Zerubavel, and Bernice Barnett. "The Recovery of Masada: A Study in Collective Memory." *The Sociologial Quarterly* 27, no. 2 (1986): 147–164.

Sell, Louis. *Slobodan Milosevic and the Destruction of Yugoslavia*. Duke University Press Books, 2002.

Sellars, Kirsten. "Imperfect Justice at Nuremberg and Tokyo." *European Journal of International Law* 21, no. 4 (2010): 1085–1102.

Shahabuddeen, Mohamed. *International Criminal Justice at the Yugoslav Tribunal: A Judge's Recollection*. Oxford University Press, 2012, 129–186.

Shandley, Robert R. *Unwilling Germans? The Goldhagen Debate*. University of Minnesota Press Minneapolis, 1998.

Shapiro, Martin. *Courts: A Comparative and Political Analysis*. University of Chicago Press, 1986.

Shapiro, Martin and Alec Stone Sweet. *On Law, Politics, and Judicialization*. Oxford University Press, 2002.

Sharp, Dustin N. *Re-Thinking Transitional Justice for the 21st Century*. Cambridge University Press, 2018.

Shaw, Rosalind, Lars Waldorf, and Pierre Hazan. *Localizing Transitional Justice: Interventions and Priorities after Mass Violence*. Stanford University Press, 2010.

Shklar, Judith N. *Legalism: Law, Morals, and Political Trials*. Harvard University Press, 1964/1986.

The Faces of Injustice. Cambridge University Press, 1990.

Shniderman, Adam B. and Charles A. Smith. "Toward Justice: Neuroscience and Affirmative Defenses at the ICC." In *Studies in Law, Politics, and Society* volume 66, edited by Austin Sarat. Emerald Group Publishing Limited, 2015, 87–113.

Sikkink, Kathryn. The Justice Cascade: How Human Rights Prosecutions Are Changing World Politics. W. W. Norton & Company, 2011.

Silber, Laura and Allan Little. *Yugoslavia: Death of a Nation*. Penguin Books, 1997.

Simic, Olivera. "Bringing 'Justice' Home? Bosnians, War Criminals and the Interaction between the Cosmopolitan and the Local." *German Law Journal* 12 (2011): 1388.

Skapska, Grazyna. "Settling Accounts with the Past, the Conceptualization of Difference and the Dilemmas of the Law-governed State." In *Central and Eastern Europe after*

Transition, edited by Alberto Febbrajo and W. Sadurski. Ashgate Publishing Group, 2010.

Skilbeck, Rupert. "Frankenstein's Monster: Creating a New International Procedure." *Journal of International Criminal Justice* 8, no. 2 (2010): 451–462.

Skocpol, Theda. *States and Social Revolutions: A Comparative Analysis of France, Russia and China*. Cambridge University Press, 1979.

Skouteris, Thomas. "Engaging History in International Law." In *New Approaches to International Law*, edited by Jose Maria Beneyto, and David Kennedy. Asser Press, 2012, 99–120.

Slaughter, Anne-Marie. "International Law in a World of Liberal States." *European Journal of International Law* 6 (1995): 503.

"A Liberal Theory of International Law." *Proceedings of the Annual Meeting (American Society of International Law)* (2000): 240.

Sluiter, Göran and Sergey Vasiliev. *International Criminal Procedure: Towards a Coherent Body of Law*. Cameron May International Law & Policy, 2009.

Smit, Dirk Van Zyl. "International Imprisonment'." *International & Comparative Law Quarterly* 54 (2005): 357, 367.

Smith, Bradley F. *Reaching Judgment at Nuremberg*. Basic books, 1977.

The Road to Nuremberg. Basic Books New York, 1981.

Snyder, Jack and Leslie Vinjamuri. "Trials and Errors: Principle and Pragmatism in Strategies of International Justice." *International Security* 28, no. 3 (2004): 5–44.

Sohn, Louis B. "The New International Law: Protection of the Rights of Individuals Rather than States." *The American University Law Review* 32 (1982): 1–64.

Steinberg, Jonny. "Liberia's Experiment with Transitional Justice." *African Affairs* 109, no. 434 (2010): 135–144.

Stensrud, Ellen Emilie. "New Dilemmas in Transitional Justice: Lessons from the Mixed Courts in Sierra Leone and Cambodia." *Journal of Peace Research* 46, no. 1 (2009): 5–15.

Stokes, Gale. "Independence and the Fate of Minorities, 1991–1992." In *Confronting the Yugoslav Controversies: A Scholars' Initiative*, edited by Thomas A. Emmert, and Charles Ingrao. Purdue University Press, 2009, 82–112.

Stover, Eric and Harvey M. Weinstein. *My Neighbor, My Enemy: Justice and Community in the Aftermath of Mass Atrocity*. Cambridge University Press, 2004.

Subotić, Jelena. *Hijacked justice: Dealing with the Past in the Balkans*. Cornell University Press, 2009.

"The Cruelty of False Remorse: Biljana Plavsic at The Hague." *Southeastern Europe* 36 (2012): 39–59.

Sudetic, Chuck. *Blood and Vengeance: One Family's Story of the War in Bosnia*. Norton, 1998.

Swart, Mia. "Judicial Lawmaking at the ad hoc Tribunals: The Creative use of the Sources of International Law and 'Adventurous Interpretation'." *Zeitschrift für ausländisches öffentliches Recht und Völkerrecht* 70 no. 3 (2010): 459–486.

Swedberg, Richard. "How to Use Max Weber's Ideal Type in Sociological Analysis." *Journal of Classical Sociology* (2017): 181–196.

Sweet, Alec Stone, Wayne Sandholtz, and Neil Fligstein. *The Institutionalization of Europe*. Oxford University Press, USA, 2001.

Tallgren, Immi. "The Sensibility and Sense of International Criminal Law." *European Journal of International Law* 13, no. 3 (2002): 561–595.

"The Durkheimian Spell of International Criminal Law." (September 20, 2012): 137–169.

Tanner, Marcus. *Croatia: A Nation Forged in War*. Yale University Press, 2001.

Taylor, Charles. *Multiculturalism: Examining the Politics of Recognition*. Princeton University Press, 1994.

Taylor, Telford "Nuremberg and Vietnam: An American Tragedy." *New York Times Books* 1970.

The Anatomy of the Nuremberg Trials: A Personal Memoir. Knopf, 2012.

Teitel, Ruti G. *Transitional Justice*. Oxford University Press, 2000.

"Transitional Justice Genealogy." *Harvard Human Rights Journal* 16 (2003): 69–94.

Humanity's Law. Oxford University Press, 2012.

Tesanovic, Jasmina. *The Diary of a Political Idiot: Normal Life in Belgrade*. Cleis Press, 2000.

Teubner, Günther. "Exogenous Self-Binding: How National and International Courts Contribute to Transnational Constitutionalization." In *Transconstitutionalism*, edited by Giancarlo Corsi, Elena Esposito, and Alberto Febbrajo. Ashgate, 2015 (available at SSRN DOI: 10.2139/ssrn.2432628).

Thaman, Stephen C. "Plea-Bargaining, Negotiating Confessions and Consensual Resolution of Criminal Cases." *Zeitschrift für die Gesamte Strafrechtswissenschaft* 486, no. 493 (2007): 1992.

Thieroff, Mark and Amley, Jr. Edward A. "Proceeding to Justice and Accountability in the Balkans: The International Criminal Tribunal for the Former Yugoslavia and Rule 61." *Yale Journal of International Law* 23 (1998): 231.

Tieger, Alan. "Non-State Actors and the Case Law of the Yugoslavia War Crimes Tribunal." *Proceedings of the Annual Meeting (American Society of International Law)* 92 (1998): 48–52.

Tochilovsky, Vladimir. "Proceedings in the International Criminal Court: Some Lessons to Learn from ICTY Experience." *European Journal of Crime, Criminal Law & Criminal Justice* 10 (2002): 268.

Jurisprudence of the International Criminal Courts and the European Court of Human Rights. Martinus Nijhoff, 2008.

"The Nature and Evolution of the Rules of Procedure and Evidence." In *Principles of Evidence in International Criminal Justice*, edited by Karim A.A. Khan, Caroline Buisman, and Christopher Gosnell. Oxford University Press, 2010, 157–184.

Todorov, Tsvetan. *The New World Disorder*. Polity Press, 1980.

"Memory as Remedy for Evil." *Journal of International Criminal Justice* 7 (2009): 447–462.

Mémoire du mal Tentation du bien: Enquête sur le siècle. Robert Laffont, 2012.

Tomuschat, Christian "The Legacy of Nuremberg." *Journal of International Criminal Justice* 4, no. 4 (September 1, 2006): 830–844.

Totani, Yuma. *The Tokyo War Crimes Trial*. Wiley Online Library, 2008.

Trbovich, Ana S. A *Legal Geography of Yugoslavia's Disintegration*. Oxford University Press, 2008.

Trueheart, Charles. "A New Kind of Justice" *The Atlantic*. (April 2000).

Tuðman, Franjo. *Bespuâca povijesne zbiljnosti: rasprava o povijesti i filozofiji zlosilja*. Nakladni zavod Matice hrvatske, 1989.

Twinning, William. "Some Scepticism about Some Scepticisms." *Journal of Law and Society* 11 (1984): 137.

Globalization and Legal Theory. Cambridge University Press, 2000.

Tyler, Tom R. *Why People Obey the Law*. Princeton University Press, 2006.

Burn This House, edited by Jasminka Udovicki, and James Ridgeway. Duke University Press, 1997.

Tyler, Tom R.Tyler, Tom and Steven Blader. *Cooperation in Groups: Procedural Justice, Social Identity, and Behavioral Engagement (Essays in Social Psychology)*. Psychology Press, 2000.

United States Institute on Peace. "Transitional Justice: Information Handbook." (2008).
Utley, Freda and Egon Heymann. *The High Cost of Vengeance*. H. Regnery Company, 1949.
Uzelac, Alan. "Role and Status of Judges in Croatia." (1998) (available at: http://www.alanuzelac.from.hr/Pdf/Radovi/en-crojud.pdf) (accessed August 2018).
van Caenegam, William. "Advantages and disadvantages of the adversarial system in criminal proceedings." 1.1. 1999 Bond University E papers.
van der Wilt, Harmen. "Joint Criminal Enterprise: Possibilities and Limitations." *Journal of International Criminal Justice* 5 (2007): 91.
Van Dyke, Ruth and Susan E. Alcock. *Archaeologies of Memory*. Wiley-Blackwell, 2008.
van Sliedregt, Elies "Pluralism in International Criminal Law." Editorial, *Leiden Journal of International Law* 25, no. 4 (2007).
International Criminal Responsibility in International Law. Oxford University Press, 2012.
van Verseweld, Annemieke. *Mistake of Law: Excusing Perpetrators of International Crimes*. Springer, 2012.
Vasielev, Sergey. "International Criminal Trials: A Normative Theory." PhD thesis, University of Amsterdam, 2014.
Veitch, Scott. *Law and the Politics of Reconciliation*. Ashgate, 2007.
Villa-Vicencio, Charles. "Reconciliation." In *Pieces of the Puzzle: Keywords on Reconciliation and Transitional Justice*, edited by Charles Villa-Vicencio and Erik Doxtader. Institute for Justice and Reconciliation, African Minds, 2004.
Vinjamuri, Leslie and Jack Snyder. "Law and Politics in Transitional Justice." *Annual Review of Political Science* 18 (2015): 303–327.
Vogler, Richard. "Making International Criminal Procedure Work: From Theory to Practice." In *Exploring the Boundaries of International Criminal Justice*. Ashgate, 2011, 105–112.
Vujačić, Veljko. "Elites, Narratives, and Nationalist Mobilization in the Former Yugoslavia." *Comparative Politics* (2007): 103–124.
Wachtel, Andrew. *Making a Nation, Breaking a Nation: Literature and Cultural Politics in Yugoslavia*. Stanford University Press, 1998.
Wald, Patricia M. "International Criminal Tribunal for the Former Yugoslavia Comes of Age: Some Observations on Day-to-Day Dilemmas of an International Court." *Washington University Journal of Law and Policy* 5 (2001): 87.
"Dealing with Witnesses in War Crime Trials: Lessons from the Yugoslav Tribunal." *Yale Human Rights Development Law Journal* 5, no 1 (2002): 217–239.
"Review: *Justice in a Time of War: The True Story behind the International Criminal Tribunal for the Former Yugoslavia* by Pierre Hazan: James Thomas Snyder." *American Journal of International Law* 99, no. 3 (2005): 720–726.
"Foreword: War Tales and War Trials." *Michigan Law Review* (2008): 901–922.
Walker, Edward. *Dissolution: Sovereignty and the Breakup of the Soviet Union*. Rowman & Littlefield Publishers, 2003.
Walzer, Michael. *Spheres of Justice: A Defense of Pluralism and Equality*. Basic Books, 1984.
Just and Unjust Wars: A Moral Argument with Historical Illustrations. Basic Books, 2006.
Warbrick, Colin. "International Criminal Courts and Fair Trial." *Journal of Conflict Security Law* 3, no. 1 (1998): 45–64.

Watson, Alan. *Legal Transplants: An Approach to Comparative Law*. University Press of Virginia, 1974.

Weber, Max. "Objectivity in Social Science and Social Policy." In *The Methodology of the Social Sciences*, edited and translated by Edward A. Shils and Henry A. Finch. Free Press, 1904/1949.

Max Weber on Law in Economy and Society, translation by Edward Shils, edited with introduction and annotations by Max Rheinstein. Harvard University Press, 1954.

Wechsler, Herbert. "The Issues of the Nuremberg Trial." In *Principles, Politics, and Fundamental Law: Selected Essays*, edited by Herbert Wechsler. Harvard University Press, 1961.

Weiler, Joseph. *The Constitution of Europe: 'Do the New Clothes Have an Emperor?' and Other Essays on European Integration*. Cambridge University Press, 1999.

Weingartner, James J. *Americans, Germans, and War Crimes Justice: Law, Memory, and "The Good War."* Prager, 2011.

Whiting, Alex. "The ICTY as a Laboratory of International Criminal Procedure." In *The Legacy of the International Criminal Tribunal for the Former Yugoslavia*, edited by Bert Swart, Alexander Zahar, and Goran Sluiter. Oxford University Press, 2011.

Wildt, M. "Des vérités qui different. Historiens et procureurs face aux crimes de Nazis." In *Le génocide des juifs entre procès et histoire, 1943–2000*, edited by Florent Brayard. Editions Complexe, 2000: 245–260.

Wiggers, Richard Dominic. "The United States and the Refusal to Feed German Civilians after World War II." In *Ethnic Cleansing in Twentieth-Century Europe*, edited by Steven Bela Vardy and T. Hunt Tooley. Columbia University Press, 2003: 274–288.

Williams, Bernard. *Truth and Truthfulness: An Essay in Genealogy*. Princeton University Press, 2010: 245 – 260.

Wilson, Richard. *The Politics of Truth and Reconciliation in South Africa: Legitimizing the Post-Apartheid State*. Cambridge University Press, 2001.

Writing History in International Criminal Tribunals. Cambridge, 2011.

Wimmer, Andreas, Richard J. Goldstone, Donald L. Horowitz, Ulrike Joras, and Conrad Schetter. *Facing Ethnic Conflicts: Toward a New Realism*. Rowman & Littlefield Publishers, 2004.

Winston, Morton. "Hannah Arendt and the Challenge of Modernity: A Phenomenology of Human Rights (review)." *Human Rights Quarterly* 31, no. 1 (2009): 278–282.

Wittmann, Rebecca. *Beyond Justice: The Auschwitz Trial*. Harvard University Press, 2005.

Woodward, Susan L. *Balkan Tragedy: Chaos and Dissolution after the Cold War*. Brookings Institution Press, 1995.

Wright, Quincy. "The Law of the Nuremberg Trial." *The American Journal of International Law* 41, no. 1 (1947): 38–72.

Zacklin, Ralph. "The Failings of Ad Hoc International Tribunals." *Journal of International Criminal Justice* 2 (2004): 541.

Zalaquett, José. "Confronting Human Rights Violations Committed by Former Governments: Applicable Principles and Political Constraints." *Hamline Law Review* 13 (1990): 623.

"Balancing Ethical Imperatives and Political Constraints: The Dilemma of New Democracies Confronting Past Human Rights Violations." *Hastings Law Journal* 43 (1992): 1425.

Zappalà, Salvatore. *Human Rights in International Criminal Proceedings*. Oxford University Press, 2003.

Zoglin, Katie. "The Future of War Crimes Prosecutions in the Former Yugoslavia: Accountability or Junk Justice?" *Human Rights Quarterly* 27, no. 1 (2005): 41–77.

Zürn, Michael. "Global Governance and Legitimacy Problems." *Government and Opposition* 39, no. 2 (2004): 260–287.

Index